Fodor's

ESSENTIAL
EGYPT

Welcome to Egypt

Egypt engages all the senses. See the sun rise on a Nile cruise or set at an ancient temple. Hear the call to prayer echo amid winding streets. Smell spices while shopping in a market. Taste Egyptian comfort food in a classic eatery. Feel warm waters on a Red Sea dive. Note that this book was updated during the pandemic. When planning, confirm that places are still open, and let us know when we need to make updates at editors@fodors.com.

TOP REASONS TO GO

★ **Archaeology:** From Giza's pyramids to the Valley of the Kings—ancient Egypt awaits.

★ **The Nile:** Cruise its surface, explore its banks, and swim in its waters.

★ **Ages-old markets:** Carpets, metalwork, perfume, and gold entice savvy bargainers.

★ **Diving:** The marine life in waters off Sharm el-Sheikh and Hurghada is legendary.

★ **Coptic churches:** Early Christian sites abound in Old Cairo and beyond.

★ **Traditional cuisine:** Egypt has its own flavorful takes on Middle Eastern dishes.

Contents

MAPS

Chapter 1

EXPERIENCE EGYPT

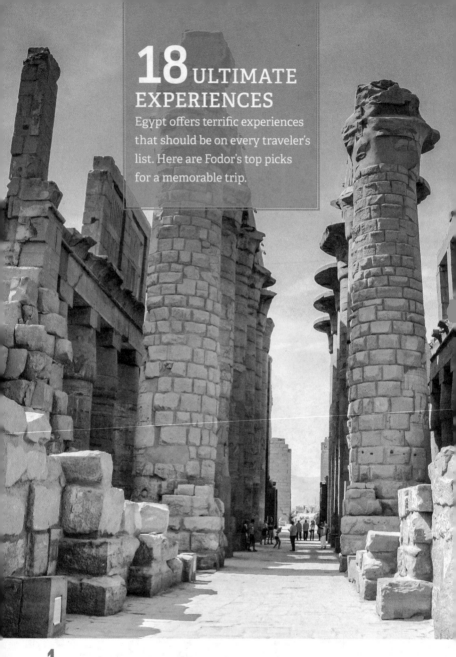

18 ULTIMATE EXPERIENCES

Egypt offers terrific experiences that should be on every traveler's list. Here are Fodor's top picks for a memorable trip.

1 Explore a Temple Complex That's Layered in History

One of the world's largest religious complexes, Karnak isn't just one temple but an amalgamation of sanctuaries, shrines, obelisks, and sacred spaces constructed by successive rulers over more than a millennia. *(Ch. 5)*

2 Pay Homage to Nefertari

The intricately painted Valley of the Kings tomb belonging to the favorite wife of ancient Egypt's great builder, Ramses II, is magnificent. *(Ch. 5)*

3 Cruise Along the Nile

One of the best ways to reach the Nile Valley's ancient sites is aboard a traditional sailing vessel or a larger Nile cruiser. *(Ch. 8)*

4 Find Royal Treasures

See Egypt's greatest artifacts in Cairo's expansive museums, including the Egyptian Museum, National Museum of Egyptian Civilization, and Grand Egyptian Museum. *(Ch. 3)*

5 Go Diving in the Red Sea

Egypt has lots of accessible coastline to explore, and the Red Sea is a vastly underrated diving destination. Up to 20% of the fish swimming in its waters are found nowhere else. *(Ch. 7)*

6 Learn About New Finds at an Ancient Site

Near the country's first capital of Memphis, Saqqara was ancient Egypt's original necropolis. Recent archaeological finds here are rewriting history in real time. *(Ch. 3)*

7 Lounge on a Beach

In Sharm el-Sheikh, at the southern tip of the Sinai Peninsula, turquoise waters lap golden-sand shores that are anchored by jagged purple-gray mountains. *(Ch. 7)*

8 Channel Agatha Christie

Aswan's Old Cataract hotel is where Agatha Christie wrote *Death on the Nile*. Overnight in her suite, or grab a drink on the terrace overlooking the river. *(Ch. 6)*

9 Study Dramatic Tomb Paintings

In the Valley of the Kings, the tomb paintings of Egypt's most intriguing pharaohs are as vivid now as when they were first created—3,500 years ago. *(Ch. 5)*

10 Be Awed by the Pyramids of Giza

The enduring icons of Egypt and the last surviving wonders of the ancient world will stop you in your tracks no matter how many pictures you've seen before you finally witness them in person. *(Ch. 3)*

11 Uncover Coptic Cairo

Egypt has one of the oldest and largest populations of Christians in the Middle East, and you can learn about their beliefs and storied history in the museums and churches of Coptic Cairo. *(Ch. 3)*

12 Discover Nubian Culture

Joy radiates from the colorful buildings and murals in the Nubian villages on Elephantine Island and Gharb Soheil near Aswan. Kick back in a café, and enjoy the Nubian hospitality. *(Ch. 6)*

13 Admire Ottoman-Era Architecture

In Cairo's Citadel, a lofty seat of power for seven centuries, the pencil-thin minarets of the Mosque of Muhammad Ali tower over an ornate interior and marble courtyard. *(Ch. 3)*

14 Take Time to Honor Isis

Set on a Nile island dotted with palm trees, the Temple of Isis has an idyllic backdrop and is likely where the last Egyptian hieroglyphs were carved. *(Ch. 6)*

15 Visit Ramses II's Lakeside Temples

Saved from rising Lake Nasser waters in the 1960s, the temples of Abu Simbel exude timeless majesty from their outpost on Egypt's southern frontier. *(Ch. 6)*

16 Get Lost While Finding Souvenirs

Lose yourself in Cairo's Khan el-Khalili, a medieval market where stalls are piled high with metal lamps, colorful scarves, and kitschy souvenirs. *(Ch. 3)*

17 Seek Ancient Knowledge

A love letter to the lost library of antiquity, the Bibliotheca Alexandrina has museums, a planetarium, and, of course, shelf space for 8 million books. *(Ch. 4)*

18 Sail on a *Felucca*

For an intimate, slow-travel Nile experience, hire a *felucca*—a traditional, non-motorized sailboat—for a short journey or an overnight adventure. *(Ch. 6)*

WHAT'S WHERE

1 Cairo. One of the largest cities in the Middle East, the capital of Egypt thrums with an energy like nowhere else in the country. The Pyramids of Giza, the only survivors of the Seven Wonders of the Ancient World, are on Cairo's western outskirts, but the city's modern culture is just as enchanting as its deep history.

2 Alexandria. Egypt's pearl on the Mediterranean is the urban antithesis of Cairo. Breezy and relaxed, Alexandria is the place to find a sea-view café, sit back with a coffee, and watch the world go by. History buffs will find the trove of Greek and Roman treasures in Alexander the Great's city plenty impressive.

3 Luxor and the Nile Valley. Billed as the world's greatest open-air museum, Luxor has an unbelievable cache of ancient temples and tombs that will astound even the most jaded traveler. Explore the rest of the region's historic sites on a cruise on the legendary Nile River, a bucket-list-worthy experience.

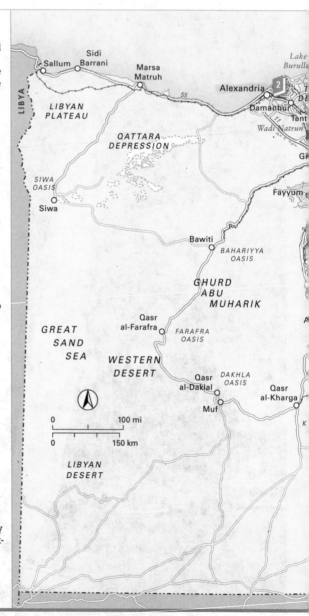

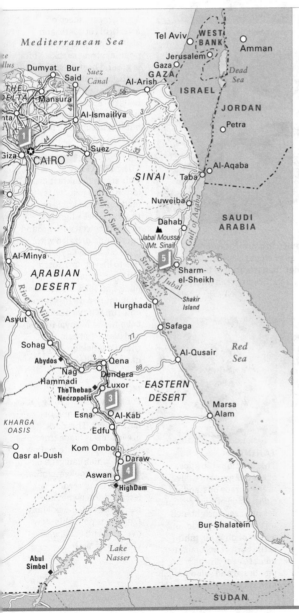

4 **Aswan and Lake Nasser.** Laid-back Aswan is a chance to take a breather after the chaos of Cairo and Luxor, perhaps with a sundowner on a riverside terrace or aboard a traditional felucca sailboat weaving through the islands in the Nile. Aswan's islands and West Bank are the heart of vibrant and welcoming Nubian culture, filled with colorfully painted homes, guesthouses, and markets. Little-visited ancient temples and the famous Abu Simbel line the banks of Lake Nasser, rescued from drowning under the rising waters created by the Aswan High Dam.

5 **Sharm el-Sheikh and the Red Sea Coast.** Full of huge inclusive resorts skirting the stunning coastline, Sharm el-Sheikh and the Red Sea make up Egypt's blissful vacation land. Most visitors are here to worship at the temple of pleasure instead of ticking off the historic sites. Great beaches and balmy weather attract sun-seekers year round. The Red Sea offers exceptional diving, and the mountains hide important Christian monasteries.

What to Eat and Drink in Egypt

TA'AMIYA

Egypt's version of felafel, called *ta'amiya* (or *ta'ameya)*, is made with fava beans instead of chickpeas. Although the patties are bigger and thinner than traditional felafel, they still have golden crispy exteriors, bright green interiors, and that perfect crunch.

KARKADE

There's no better way to cool off after a hot day of sightseeing than with a cold glass of *karkade*, a tea made from hibiscus flowers (you can also drink it hot). The drink is a rich maroon color and tastes sweet and slightly tart. It's full of vitamin C and said to lower blood pressure.

TAHINI

This delicious dip appears at every Egyptian table in the parade of standard sides. Made of finely ground sesame seeds brightened up with lemon, garlic, and a river of olive oil, tahini is the perfect accompaniment to everything from pita bread and salads to fish dishes.

SHAWARMA, KEBAB, AND KOFTA

These three styles of meat make an appearance on nearly every Egyptian restaurant menu. Shawarma and kebab, spiced meats sliced off a vertical rotisserie and stuffed into pita bread, are popular street snacks. Kofta is ground beef seasoned with garlic, parsley, and onion that's formed into balls or rectangular patties. It can be ordered on its own, but it also comes as part of a mixed grill.

FUL MEDAMES

This staple breakfast dish (often called just *ful*) is made of stewed fava beans that have been lightly mashed, spiced with ground cumin, and drizzled with olive oil. Some Egyptians like to kick it up a notch with garlic, parsley, lemon juice, and spicy chilis. Ful is thought to date from pharaonic times (fava beans have been found in royal tombs), and it's still so beloved that it's considered Egypt's national dish.

MOLOKHIA

For many visitors to Egypt, *molokhia* is a love-it-or-hate-it dish. This dark green stew is made from finely chopped jute mallow leaves, which can get a bit slimy when cooked, similar to okra. Its bitterness is lessened somewhat by garlic and coriander. Many Egyptians pour this stew over rice and eat it with chicken or lamb.

Ful medames

PIGEON

Although considered a pest elsewhere, in Egypt, pigeons are raised in dovecotes and served at traditional restaurants. If you order *hamam mahshi*, you'll be presented with a roasted bird (watch out for small bones) stuffed with rice or *freekeh* (cracked green wheat) mixed with onions, pepper, cinnamon, and pigeon liver.

OM ALI

Egypt's national dessert—yes, that's a thing—is a flaky pastry treat that contains milk or cream, cinnamon, pistachios, and heaps of sugar. Though it doesn't contain eggs, it's similar to bread pudding. *Om ali* means "mother of Ali," and the story goes that the wife of Egypt's first Mamluk sultan requested the best dessert her chefs could make, and this was the delicious result.

FITEER

Falling somewhere on the spectrum between a pizza and a crêpe, *fiteer* can be eaten as a dessert or a meal unto itself. Impossibly flaky layers made of flour interspersed with ghee (clarified butter) are baked into a pie. You can order *fiteer* with a huge range of sweet or savory toppings, including Nutella, cheese, ground beef, fruit.

KOSHARY

Koshary, or *koshari*, is the need-to-use-some-leftovers dish that is surprisingly tasty and addictive. A bowl of this popular street food comes piled high with macaroni noodles, rice, lentils, and chickpeas topped with a spiced tomato sauce and crispy fried onions.

Egypt's Top Outdoor Adventures

Hot-air ballooning

HOT-AIR BALLOONING

Drift skywards mirroring the sunrise in an early-morning hot-air balloon over Luxor's West Bank. As you float above the landscape, you'll spot the sand-colored monuments tucked into the desert mountains and witness just how much the Nile transforms the scene from a verdant ribbon of green to the forbidding deserts beyond the river's reach.

RED SEA SCUBA DIVING

In this, the world's northernmost tropical sea, divers of every experience level are guaranteed to spot creatures seen nowhere else. Colorful coral reefs grow close to the shoreline, negating the need for lengthy boat journeys to dive sites. Several well-known shipwrecks, including the *Thistlegorm*, also offer outstanding dive opportunities.

SAILING ON A *FELUCCA*

In many places, you can hire *feluccas*—traditional, single-masted, Nile sailboats—for a few hours. You can also arrange a multiday downriver (north) voyage from Aswan. Regardless of which you choose, your slow-travel journey will be at the mercy of the winds, so you might zip across the water or cruise along languidly with the current.

Donkey, horse, and camel rides

DONKEY, HORSE, AND CAMEL RIDES

Why not travel to ancient monuments in an unforgettable, time-tested manner? You can horseback ride from Giza to Saqqara, and camel rides are offered at the Tombs of the Nobles and St. Simeon's Monastery near Aswan. Guesthouses on Luxor's West Bank also arrange half-day excursions. Check that the animals appear well taken care of before you ride.

FOSSIL-SPOTTING AND DESERT CAMPING IN FAYYUM

Just a few hours' drive from chaotic Cairo is the little-visited oasis known as the Fayyum. Wadi al Hitan, a UNESCO-listed natural area, is often overlooked by travelers who stick to the Nile, but it is an excellent place to spot fossils—the only intact fossil of a prehistoric whale was found here. You can also camp in the desert and gaze at the stars.

SWIMMING IN THE NILE

Don't worry: all the crocs live south of the Aswan High Dam now, so feel free to cannonball into the Nile. Currents can be strong, however, and not all parts of the river are clean, so check locally beforehand. Trips on a *dahabiya*, a traditional, two-masted boat, often include afternoons of swimming—the perfect way to cool off after sightseeing—or you can chill out on the beaches of Gharb Soheil and the Nile islands near Aswan.

WIND- AND KITESURFING IN THE RED SEA

With consistent winds, smooth waters, and ever-pleasant temperatures, the Red Sea coast is a great year-round place to grab a board and a sail. Newbies and professionals alike zip along the water around Hurghada and El Gouna, which has a number of large, shallow bays. Rent equipment for a few hours, or sign up for a weeklong kite-boat safari.

KAYAKING THE NILE

Paddling is a great way to experience the Nile. Join a tour from a beach in Gharb Soheil on Aswan's West Bank, and, soon enough, you'll be riding the mini rapids on the river's cataract currents formed by huge granite boulders. In Cairo, you can paddle out for a unique, water-level view of the capital.

Egypt's Best Historical Sights

PRINCE MOHAMMAD ALI PALACE, CAIRO

A few millennia newer than many of Egypt's historical sites but no less enchanting, this palace (circa 1899) beautifully blends European and Islamic architecture and design. Its tile-covered walls, alabaster fountains, intricate woodwork, and crystal chandeliers make it a royal-worthy retreat from the traffic outside the front gate.

PYRAMIDS OF GIZA

These pyramids, the only of the Seven Wonders of the Ancient World to have survived, are breathtaking. The Great Pyramid was the world's largest man-made structure for almost 4,000 years.

TEMPLES OF ABU SIMBEL

Four colossal statues of Ramses II guard these temples, which UNESCO painstakingly moved to higher ground before Lake Nasser's rising waters swallowed them whole.

SAQQARA

There's old, and then there's really old: the Step Pyramid of Djoser at Saqqara had been standing for more than a century when construction on the Pyramids of Giza began. Today, this great necropolis is one of the country's most active archaeological sites.

TEMPLE OF HORUS, EDFU

Buried in sand for centuries, this Ptolemaic-era temple is one of Egypt's most complete monuments. Beyond the open courtyard, an in-situ ceiling casts hieroglyph-covered walls in shadow. Amid the dimly lighted corridors, it's easy to imagine yourself as one of the worshippers who came to this mighty structure.

TEMPLE OF KHNUM, ESNA

Recent restorations have lifted centuries of grime from the interior on this must-see temple. Bright colors now radiate from its artwork, and researchers have discovered things like previously unknown names of ancient constellations.

TEMPLE OF SETI I, ABYDOS

Legend has it that when the god Osiris was dismembered and scattered by his brother, his head landed in Abydos, which became his cult center. This temple complex also has the Abydos Kings List, the only record of the reigns of Egypt's pharaohs.

Temple of Kom Ombo

VALLEY OF THE KINGS, LUXOR

One of Egypt's star attractions is also its least visible from ground level, and, at first glance, it might leave you unimpressed. But step inside the heavy doors carved into the hillsides, and you'll be bowled over by the beauty of the hieroglyphs and art, the vibrancy of the colors, and the scale of the work covering every available surface. These subterranean chambers were the pharaohs' palaces for eternity, and they had to look the part.

TEMPLE OF KOM OMBO

The fascinating "twin temple" at Kom Ombo is dedicated to two gods in equal measure—the local crocodile god Sobek and Haroeris, a form of falcon-headed Horus— and it's the only one of its kind in Egypt. Don't miss the Crocodile Museum, with more than a dozen mummified specimens, or the back wall's hieroglyphs depicting medical and surgical instruments, such as scalpels, catheters, and even a sponge.

KARNAK TEMPLES, LUXOR

The plural of "temple" hardly hints at the scale of one of the world's biggest religious complexes, which was built over 1,000 years by 30 successive pharaohs. Karnak is Egypt's second-most visited ancient monument after the Pyramids of Giza, but you'll find quiet spots to marvel at the forest-like Great Hypostyle Hall. You can also enter through the "back door" from the Avenue of Sphinxes, opened to visitors in 2021.

What to Watch and Read

DEATH ON THE NILE BY AGATHA CHRISTIE

This endlessly retold whodunit originally published in 1937 still charms murder mystery fans. Its latest incarnation in film came out in 2022, starring Gal Gadot and Armie Hammer, with Kenneth Branagh as the famous detective Hercule Poirot. Even though none of the 2022 release was filmed in Egypt—the temples of Abu Simbel and the wooden cruise boat were entirely recreated on a set in England— it's still a thrill to follow in Christie's footsteps on your own trip around southern Egypt.

THE YACOUBIAN BUILDING BY ALAA AL-ASWANY

Published in Arabic in 2002 and translated into English in 2004, this novel presents a cross-section of modern Egyptian life through characters of different social and economic classes, attitudes, and backgrounds who all live in one Downtown Cairo apartment building. The book, a phenomenal bestseller in the Arab world, spawned a movie and TV series of the same name.

THE SQUARE, DIRECTED BY JEHANE NOUJAIM

This gripping, Emmy-winning and Oscar-nominated 2013 documentary introduces a few of the hundreds of thousands of people who took part in Egypt's Arab Spring and follows the political turmoil that came in its wake.

MOUNTAINS OF THE PHARAOHS: THE UNTOLD STORY OF THE PYRAMID BUILDERS BY ZAHI HAWASS

Hawass, Egypt's most famous archaeologist and the former secretary general of Egypt's Supreme Council of Antiquities, reveals the secrets behind the building of the pyramids in Giza and Saqqara in this 2006 book. He details the reasons for their construction from findings on his own excavation projects in a highly readable narrative account.

THE NILE HILTON INCIDENT, DIRECTED BY TARIK SALEH

This dark, 2017 thriller tracks the story of a female singer murdered at an upscale hotel and the police officer assigned to the case. Despite having a witness and plenty of evidence, many higher-ups want to push the case under the rug and label it a suicide because of the political connections. The film taps into the corruption of Egypt's police on the eve of the Arab Spring.

THE BURIED: AN ARCHAEOLOGY OF THE EGYPTIAN REVOLUTION BY PETER HESSLER

The American author of this fascinating 2019 book decides to move his wife and one-year-old twin daughters to Cairo in 2011 to work for the New Yorker as a Cairo correspondent during the revolution. The eccentric characters Hessler meets and the brilliance of his detailed observations about Egyptian culture and society as he tries to master the Arabic language and explore Egypt's deep and recent history will stick with you on your own adventures around the country.

KOKA THE BUTCHER, DIRECTED BY BENCE MÁTÉ

This short, 2018 documentary captures the behind-the-scenes rivalries of Cairo's pigeon racers who live in Garbage City and the societal pressures that one young fighter faces from his conservative community about whether he can pursue his life's passion.

TAXI BY KHALED AL-KHAMISSI

This 2006 book is a collection of 58 fictional short stories told by the taxi drivers of Cairo. The work highlights the day-to-day frustrations, minutiae, and full range of emotions told in an intimate monologue format.

TICKLING GIANTS, DIRECTED BY SARA TAKSLER

Nicknamed the "Egyptian Jon Stewart," surgeon-turned-comedian Bassem Youssef leaves his job in medicine to document the country's Arab Spring revolution and ends up creating the most successful satirical show on Middle Eastern TV. Despite its high viewership, the show and its regime-prodding jokes invite protests, violence, and legal action and eventually lead Youssef to flee the country. Youssef also autobiographically chronicles this part of his life in his 2017 book, *Revolution for Dummies: Laughing through the Arab Spring*.

THE MAP OF LOVE BY AHDAF SOUEIF

Published in 1999, *The Map of Love* was shortlisted for the Man Booker Prize and has been widely translated. The novel is the tale of an American woman whose discovery of her great-grandmother's love letters leads her to modern-day Egypt to encounter her family's secret history.

UNDERSTANDING CAIRO: THE LOGIC OF A CITY OUT OF CONTROL BY DAVID SIMS

You have to spend all of 30 seconds in Cairo before you experience the chaos of the capital. But simply dismissing the city as chaotic fails to acknowledge how Cairo got to this place. Sims's 2015 book looks into how 18 million Cairenes have had to create and develop their own city in the face of a largely indifferent and negligent government.

MOON KNIGHT, DIRECTED BY MOHAMED DIAB

Egyptian director Mohamed Diab translates ancient mythology for a modern Western audience in this 2022 release from the Marvel Cinematic Universe. Steven Grant works at a museum gift shop and discovers that he has multiple personalities, including Marc Spector, a human who does the bidding of the ancient Egyptian moon god Khonshu. Although scenes in Cairo are actually shot on a set in Hungary because of difficulties obtaining permits, Diab ensures that the series has a distinctly authentic flair.

THE CAIRO TRILOGY BY NAGUIB MAHFOUZ

Nobel Prize–winning Mahfouz is a towering figure in Egyptian literature, a chronicler of Cairo's back alleys and the country's development in the last century. Published in 1956–57, The Cairo Trilogy is made up of the novels *Palace Walk*, *Palace of Desire*, and *Sugar Street*. The books divulge a multi-generational family saga that parallels Egypt's story of colonization, revolution, and progress in the early 20th century.

TERRORISM AND KEBAB, DIRECTED BY SHERIF ARAFA

This 1992 dark comedy takes place in the Kafka-esque Mogamma government administration building in Cairo. A man tries to register for a school transfer for his children but ends up accidentally taking everyone inside the building hostage. He's assumed to be a terrorist, but some people end up joining his cause.

THE CITY ALWAYS WINS BY OMAR ROBERT HAMILTON

Hamilton's phenomenal debut novel, published in 2017, takes readers to the front lines of the Arab Spring alongside a media collective producing a podcast about the revolution in real time. What starts out as a hopeful but uncertain collective outpouring eventually fizzles to a disappointing outcome.

Egypt Today

POLITICS

Egypt had some of the Arab Spring's most visible protests, with hundreds of thousands gathering day after day in central Cairo's Tahrir Square, and the specter of those events still looms large in the Egyptian psyche. The 2011 revolution toppled Hosni Mubarak, Egypt's fourth president who had been in power for three decades, after 18 days of protests.

In 2012, Egypt held its first-ever democratic elections. Mohammed Morsi of the Muslim Brotherhood won the presidency, but protestors returned to Tahrir Square in 2013 on the one-year anniversary of his inauguration, and the army, led by Abdel Fattah al-Sisi, overthrew him days later.

Sisi established an interim government and then won the presidential election in 2014. His presidential term, the second four-year stint, was supposed to end in 2022, but the Egyptian parliament, largely made up of the president's supporters, amended the constitution to allow him to stay in power until 2030.

Sisi governs with a tightening authoritarian grip. Political dissenters are often jailed; freedom of the press and assembly is restricted; security forces have been accused of human rights abuses and extrajudicial killings; and discrimination continues against women, LGBTQ+ people, and Copts.

ECONOMY

Egypt's economy lives or dies by tourism, and political upheaval combined with terrorist attacks against tourists and the COVID-19 pandemic has dealt the country a tough financial blow. Russia's war on Ukraine threatens Egypt financially, too, as the many citizens of those countries who vacation in the beach resorts of Sinai have stopped coming. In addition, Egypt, one of the world's largest buyers of wheat, imports 80% of the crop from Russia and Ukraine and faces record-high prices and potential supply shortages.

In response, Egypt's central bank devalued the currency by 14% in March 2022, good news for foreign travelers because of favorable exchange rates but bad news for locally run accommodations, tour operators, and restaurants, many of which have been forced to close for financial reasons. It's now more imperative than ever that travelers support local businesses on trips to Egypt.

TOURISM DEVELOPMENT

The Egyptian government has embarked on several projects to boost the economy and attract visitors. These include the opening of the Grand Egyptian Museum; continued work on a rail line connecting the Red Sea to the Mediterranean; upgraded Russian-built rolling stock on the existing train network; and the ongoing construction of the as-yet unnamed New Administrative Capital that's supposed to relieve the congestion of Cairo.

In 2021, Egypt impressed crowds with elaborate shows for two big events. The grand Pharaohs' Golden Parade transported 22 royal mummies in an incredible procession of nitrogen containers—fitted onto vehicles designed to look like ancient funerary boats—from the Egyptian Museum on Tahrir Square to their new home at the National Museum of Egyptian Civilization, which opened in 2017. Later in the year, Luxor's Avenue of Sphinxes was unveiled. This ancient pathway connects Karnak Temples with Luxor Temple, and it's now open to modern visitors to walk for the first time.

Kids and Families

Traveling to Egypt brings history to life for children like few other places in the world. Kids will delight in seeing camels, donkeys, and horses, and marveling at the Pyramids of Giza and Egypt's plethora of ancient wonders knows no age limit.

What's more, the family-oriented Egyptians dote on young children, so you're likely to be warmly welcomed everywhere.

HOW TO GET AROUND

Getting around Egypt's larger cities or out on a day trip is usually fastest and easiest with a private car and driver. If needed, check that a car seat is provided or bring your own. For longer journeys, Egypt's domestic flight network out of Cairo can get you to the coast or along the Nile in about an hour. Riding on Egypt's trains gives older kids the chance to see a slice of rural life and meet local people. Just be aware that trains often suffer from hours-long delays.

In cities, Egypt's poorly paved streets can make strollers impractical, so it's best to bring a baby carrier or sling.

WHAT TO BRING

In larger cities and resort towns, disposable diapers and formula are available in grocery stores and pharmacies, though they might not stock brands that have English-language packaging or are familiar to you. Pack sun hats and high SPF sunscreen for the entire family. Stock up your first-aid kit with Band-Aids, hand sanitizer, sterilized wipes, insect repellant, Ibuprofen, and anti-diarrhea pills.

Food hygiene isn't always top notch, and mild food poisoning might strike during your trip. Come prepared with rehydration salts.

For kids, putting together an "explorer's backpack" will get them excited about the trip. Include age-appropriate books about Egypt's ancient history and the pantheon of gods and goddesses that they can read before and during the trip. Pack a flashlight to peek into the dark corners of pyramids and temples.

WHAT TO EAT

Although some Egyptian food might be unfamiliar to you and your children, by and large, the dishes that appear on local tables are crowd-pleasers. *Fiteer*, nicknamed "Egyptian pizza," can be prepared with everyone's choice of either sweet or savory toppings, and mixed grills of chicken and beef are a menu staple that will probably satisfy even the pickiest of young palettes. Before your trip, you can also help your children familiarize themselves with Egyptian flavors by having them sample widely available foods like hummus, tahini, and felafel. In addition, restaurants in large hotels often offer international items like pasta or hamburgers.

WHERE TO STAY

Modern hotels and international chains can be found across Egypt, and they have the same standards and amenities as properties elsewhere in the world. Breakfast is generally included in the nightly rate. Be aware that some of Egypt's older, mid-size hotels have antique elevators, sometimes with no inner doors and only a widely spaced cage guarding the elevator shaft.

CULTURE WRITTEN ON THE TEMPLE WALLS

EGYPTIAN MYTHOLOGY AND HIEROGLYPHS

Religion and mythology played a central role in ancient Egyptian institutions and society, guiding the lives of pharaohs and their subjects. Egypt's bounty of temples and tombs showcases the eternal importance of these deities and how the ancients used them to understand and explain natural phenomena, the cosmos, and the world around them.

Belief in life after death was key to Egyptian religion. The ancient Egyptians thought that the afterlife mirrored their life on earth, so they strove to live honorably. Death was not seen as the end of life, but as the chance to be reborn in an eternal paradise called the Field of Reeds (*a'aru*) ruled by the god Osiris. Mummification was important and widely practiced so that the body would be in good condition for the next life, and tombs were filled with model boats for transport to the afterlife, food, perfumes, and hundreds of *shabti*, small figurines that could be called on to perform work in the afterlife.

As part of this transfer between realms, the soul had to pass a series of tests and a final judgment to be deemed worthy. Standing in the Hall of Truth, the deceased had to confirm that they had not sinned to the 42 Assessors of Maat, the goddess of truth and justice. Heart scarabs placed on the body during mummification often included text from the Book of the Dead urging the heart not to reveal any wrongdoings during this judgment. The heart of the deceased would then be placed on a scale with an ostrich feather, the representation of Maat, on the other side. If the scales balanced, the god Thoth would write down the result and present the deceased to Osiris, but if the heart was heavy with sin, it was eaten by Ammit, a goddess with the head of a crocodile, the front legs of a lion, and the hind legs of a hippo that was called the "Devourer of the Dead."

Wall painting with hieroglyphs

IMPORTANT EGYPTIAN GODS AND GODDESSES

The ancient Egyptians saw the gods as keepers of cosmic order, and they communicated with the common people through the pharaoh, who was also said to be of divine birth. This "divine lineage" that gave the pharaohs their power to rule was justified in the *mammisi,* a small chapel found in temples across the country. Temple decorations show the pharaoh performing daily rituals, though priests would have actually carried out these duties.

Statue of Horus in Edfu Temple

RA

Sun, creation

The worship of Ra, arguably the most important deity, dates from the 2nd Dynasty. Ra was the supreme god, and, beginning in the 4th Dynasty, pharaohs took the title "son of Ra." Ra took on many forms but was usually portrayed with a falcon head topped with a sun disk on a human body. He was identified with the important myths of the solar cycle and daily rebirth. **Cult Center:** Heliopolis, now a suburb of Cairo

AMUN

Air, sun, and self-creation

Amun started as a powerful but invisible god that was symbolized by the wind, which is felt but not seen. He was later conflated with Ra to become Amun-Ra, creator and sustainer of all. So influential was this god that the ancient Egyptian religion nearly became monotheistic —and did so for a short time under the pharaoh Akhenaten, who changed the state religion to worship a single god called Aten. **Cult Center:** Thebes (modern-day Luxor)

MUT

Divine motherhood, sky

The wife of Amun, Mut was the divine mother of creation and was associated with the vulture, the hieroglyph that starts her name. She holds the ankh (key of life) and wears a vulture headdress with the double crown of Upper and Lower Egypt. Mut was seen as the mother of the pharaohs, providing rulers with "divine lineage" and therefore the power and justification to rule over ancient Egypt. **Cult Center:** Thebes

KHONSU

Moon

The son of Amun and Mut was the moon god, depicted as a human with a falcon head or as a mummy with a child's sidelock of hair; in either case he is topped with a moon disk. Khonsu and his parents make up the Theban Triad, the three primary gods worshipped in the ancient capital. The Egyptians used a lunar calendar to determine the timing of religious festivals. **Cult Center:** Thebes

OSIRIS

Afterlife and fertility

Osiris appears in mummified form with a white linen-wrapped body, green skin, and crossed arms holding the crook and flail. Ancient Egyptian myth says that Osiris was killed by his jealous brother Set, who scattered his remains around the country. The goddess Isis, wife of Osiris, put the pieces back together and was impregnated, giving birth to Horus, who avenged his father's death by killing Set. **Cult Center:** Abydos

ISIS

Magic, protection, and mother of the dead

This powerful goddess, often shown nursing her son Horus, was an enduring presence across many pharaonic dynasties, and even the Greeks and Romans who later conquered Egypt worshipped her. Her ability to resurrect Osiris endowed her with magic, and she was thought to protect people with her spells. She later took on traits from other goddesses, including Hathor's cow horns and sun disk. **Cult Center:** Philae, near Aswan

HORUS

Sky

Horus is depicted as a falcon or as a human body with the head of a falcon wearing the double crown of Upper and Lower Egypt. In predynastic times, rulers were called the Followers of Horus. Horus is sometimes merged with Ra, becoming Ra-Horakhty, the god of the rising sun. The four sons of Horus—Imsety, Duamutef, Hapi, and Qebehsenuef—protected the mummified internal organs of the dead stored in canopic jars. **Cult Center:** Edfu

ANUBIS

Mummification

Anubis, shown as a black jackal or as a human with the head of a jackal, was originally the god of the afterlife but was superseded by Osiris. Anubis played an important role in rituals with the deceased, including supervising the Weighing of the Heart ceremony. Paintings in the Book of the Dead show priests wearing Anubis masks as they embalm a mummy. **Cult Center:** Cynopolis (modern-day El Kays)

MAAT

Truth, justice, and cosmic order

Maat personified the essential values of truth and fairness. During the Weighing of the Heart ceremony, the soul of the deceased was judged against the ideal of Maat, represented by an ostrich feather. The vizier responsible for meting out justice was called the Priest of Maat. This goddess was usually depicted holding a scepter in one hand and an ankh in the other, with an ostrich feather on her head. **Cult Centers:** all Egyptian cities

HATHOR

Motherhood, joy, and music

Hathor usually appeared as a cow or as a woman with cow horns that cradle a sun disk. On temple walls, pharaohs and gods are often seen suckling at her breast or udder. She shared characteristics with the goddesses Mut and Isis, but remained important in her own right. She was worshipped outside of Egypt too, as far away as Byblos, in modern-day Lebanon. **Cult Center:** Dendera

PTAH

Craftsmen, creation

This god is usually depicted in mummified form, with green skin and wearing a beard and skullcap that exposes his ears. Ptah was a creator god, described by the priests of Memphis in the creation myth. The name of one of the temples at Memphis, Hut-ka-Ptah (Mansion of the Life Force of Ptah), is thought to be the origin of the Greek name for Egypt, Aigyptos.
Cult Center: Memphis

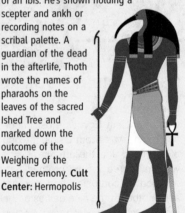

THOTH

Writing, knowledge, and the moon

Thoth, the patron deity of scribes, is depicted as a human's body with the head of an ibis. He's shown holding a scepter and ankh or recording notes on a scribal palette. A guardian of the dead in the afterlife, Thoth wrote the names of pharaohs on the leaves of the sacred Ished Tree and marked down the outcome of the Weighing of the Heart ceremony. **Cult Center:** Hermopolis

HAPI

Fertility and the Nile floods

Hapi was often depicted as a man with blue skin, a protruding belly, and drooping breasts. The Egyptians did not have a god identified exclusively with the Nile, but Hapi was associated with its floods. He carried the papyrus and lotus plants, which are associated with the Nile, and was often shown tying them together, symbolizing the unity of Upper and Lower Egypt.
Cult Center: Elephantine Island, Aswan

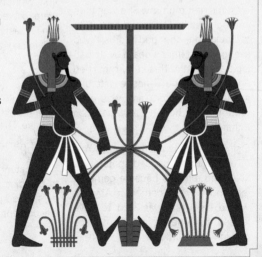

Weighing of the Heart ceremony

OSIRIS AND HIS DOMAIN

THE STORY OF OSIRIS

One of ancient Egypt's most important myths was about Osiris, the god of the dead and the afterlife. Osiris was murdered by his brother, Set, the god of confusion and disorder and another of the nine deities of the creation story of Heliopolis, known as the Ennead ("ennead" comes from the Greek word for "nine"). Set scattered the pieces of Osiris's body throughout Egypt. The goddess Isis, Osiris's wife, gathered all but one of them, and put him back together to form the first mummy. She was then impregnated by Osiris and gave birth to their son, the god Horus, who avenged his father's death by defeating Set in battle. This story remained popular in all the dynasties starting in the Old Kingdom and was even written about by the Greek historian Plutarch.

Osiris thus became the god of resurrection. The supposed spots of his scattered remains became cemeteries, and his cult center at Abydos, where his head was said to have landed, became an important place of pilgrimage and offerings.

By the Second Intermediate Period, Set fell out of favor with most Egyptians, who regarded him as the incarnate of evil and associated him with the invasion of Egypt by the Hyksos from western Asia.

STORY SOURCES

Even though the story of Osiris was endlessly retold in ancient Egypt, no single source contains the entire myth in one place. The earliest explanations of Osiris and the afterlife come from the Pyramid Texts, the first written funerary rituals, which were carved onto the walls of the 6th-Dynasty Pyramid of Teti (2400 BC) in Saqqara. Later texts, including the Book of the Dead, also tell certain aspects of the story.

Ancient Egyptians strove to follow Osiris's example and journey into the afterlife. The god, along with his family of Isis and Horus, represented the struggle against evil, righting injustice, restoring order, and resurrection in paradise. In funerary texts, Osiris acts as judge, allowing only the morally upstanding into the afterlife.

HIEROGLYPHS

Hieroglyphs form a complex system of writing for monumental purposes. On visits to ancient temples, Egyptologist guides can help you decipher the symbols, and you're bound to start noticing repeated motifs and important names encircled in cartouches.

The word "hieroglyph" comes from the Greek for "sacred carvings." Egyptians used hieroglyphs mostly for the walls of temples and mortuary monuments. A simplified form of hieroglyphs, called hieratic, was written with reed pens on papyrus and used for legal, administrative, and literary purposes. Few Egyptians were literate, so the ability to read and write would have been prestigious, allowing access to important jobs in the ancient Egyptian state.

Hieroglyphs consist of three types of symbols: phonetic, logographic, and determinative. Phonetic symbols convey sounds or combinations of sounds, logographic symbols convey meaning, and determinative symbols convey the general concept of the word that precedes it.

The hieroglyphic writing system does not have punctuation or spacing between words. Hieroglyphs could be written horizontally and read from left to right or vice versa—the direction is determined by which way the birds are facing. The symbols could also be written vertically and read from top to bottom.

In 2017, researchers discovered some of the earliest and largest hieroglyphs in El-Kab in southern Egypt. They date back 5,200 years and are about 20 inches tall. In the Old Kingdom (2700–2200 BC), hieroglyphic writing became a completely developed system for decorating monuments, and hieroglyphs remained largely unchanged throughout the pharaonic period.

Hieroglyphs at the Temple of Horus in Edfu

THE ROSETTA STONE

The ability to understand hieroglyphs was lost for more than a millennium until, in 1822, Jean-François Champollion deciphered the Rosetta Stone in Paris. Now housed in the British Museum in London, the Rosetta Stone is one of the most important ancient objects confiscated during colonial rule, and some are calling for its return to Egypt.

Scholars inspecting the Rosetta Stone during the Second International Congress of Orientalists, 1874

Napoléon's first great foreign expedition was to Egypt in 1799. In his first year there, his soldiers found a black granite stela reused in the walls of a medieval fort near the town of Rashid on Egypt's Mediterranean coast. It was inscribed with the same text in three forms (hieroglyphic, demotic, and Greek), so researchers used the section written in Greek, a known language, to decipher the hieroglyphic and demotic writing.

For such an impressive discovery, the actual content of the Rosetta Stone is not that exciting. The text is a royal decree issued at Memphis on the 27th of March, 196 BC. It celebrates the coronation of Ptolemy V Epiphanes, the new king of Ptolemaic Egypt. This slab is part of a larger stela, but none of the other fragments have been found, and none of the texts is entirely complete.

Just two years after the start of Napoléon's campaign in Egypt, he was beaten by the British and had to flee the country. The teams of scientists who returned to France with him documented their findings in a series called *Description de l'Egypte* published between 1809 and 1829. The drawings, paintings, engravings, and maps inspired a wave of Egyptomania as Europeans saw images of the ancient structures and language for the first time.

You can see replicas of the Rosetta Stone in Cairo's Egyptian Museum and the Biblioteca Alexandrina. The original has been on display in London's British Museum for more than 200 years. It's the most visited object in the museum, but some Egyptologists and activists have called for its return to Egypt, especially in light of the opening of the Grand Egyptian Museum (GEM) in Giza.

Zahi Hawass, the former Secretary-General of Egypt's Supreme Council of Antiquities and a well-respected archaeologist, has asked for the stone's return since 2003. However, the GEM's director of archaeological affairs said in 2020 that he doesn't expect it to be returned, instead supporting its place in London as an advertisement to entice people to visit Egypt and see where it came from.

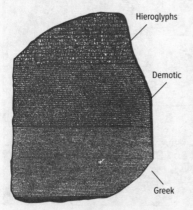

Hieroglyphs

Demotic

Greek

Chapter 2

TRAVEL SMART

Updated by Marnie Sehayek
and Lauren Keith

★ **CAPITAL:**
Cairo

POPULATION:
105,700,000

LANGUAGE:
Official language is Modern
Standard Arabic; de facto
lingua franca is Egyptian
Arabic

$ **CURRENCY:**
Egyptian Pound

COUNTRY CODE:
20

⚠ **EMERGENCIES:**
122

🚗 **DRIVING:**
On the right

⚡ **ELECTRICITY:**
220 V/50 cycles, type C and F
plugs have two round prongs

🕐 **TIME:**
7 hours ahead of New York;
6 hours ahead of New York
during Daylight Saving Time

🌐 **WEB RESOURCES:**
egypt.travel/en
egymonuments.gov.eg
www.sis.gov.eg

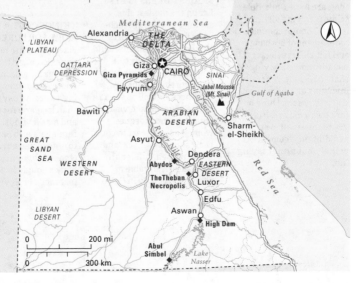

Know Before You Go

Egypt is a land of many wonders but planning a visit here shouldn't leave you wondering what's what. Take some of the mystery out of a trip by keeping a few things in mind.

SECURITY IS A CONSIDERATION

Most visits to Egypt are trouble free, but, as elsewhere in the world, terrorist attacks have occurred, and some have targeted tourists. The government has instituted security measures (e.g., roadside checkpoints, armed guards at some tourist sites), and large hotels scan bags, use metal detectors, and conduct under-car searches. Check your government's travel advice and plan accordingly. In terms of crime, pickpocketing and petty theft are issues, but violent crime involving visitors is rare. Though common, harassment of both male and female travelers is usually more annoying than malicious, generally involving attempts to get you to buy something or fork over *baksheesh* (a tip). Try to take it all in stride, avoiding engagement or politely, but firmly, saying "no."

THINK TWICE ABOUT RENTING A CAR

Independent road trips aren't recommended. Egyptians drive erratically, ignoring traffic laws and speed limits. Road checkpoints are abundant, and security is a concern in certain areas. Parking in major towns and cities is almost nonexistent, and inadequate signage makes navigation difficult. It's best to hire a local guide and driver for short trips or book a multiday excursion with a major operator.

MODEST DRESS IS BEST

Err on the modest side, saving resort- and beachwear for, well ... resorts and beaches. Women should opt for lightweight full-length or capri pants and/or skirts that fall below the knees, as well as shirts with sleeves. When visiting churches and mosques, women need a scarf to cover their shoulders, neck, and hair. For men, full-length pants are preferable to shorts, especially in Cairo, and although you'll rarely be required to don a jacket and tie for dinner in restaurants, plan to wear a shirt with sleeves and closed-toe shoes (not sandals).

CLEAN RESTROOMS ARE HARD TO FIND

Carry wipes or tissues and hand sanitizer. Public restrooms are rarely clean and often don't have toilet paper, as it's common to use water via built-in bidets or hoses instead. Some stalls might have only squat toilets. If there is paper, flushing it is problematic, so there's usually a basket for waste. Urinals are easy to find, but the stench can be unbearable. Your best restroom bets are those in chain restaurants, though you might have to make a purchase. Highway rest stops usually charge LE1 to use their facilities, and it's customary to tip restroom attendants, who might supply toilet paper, at least LE1, even if the facility isn't very clean.

THINGS COST A BIT MORE FOR FOREIGNERS

Fixed prices are nearly nonexistent, so brush up on your bargaining skills and, even after negotiating, expect to pay more than locals do for taxis and market finds. Most foreigners also pay more to enter some attractions. None of this will break the bank, though. In 2022, for instance, the Egyptian/

Arab adult ticket for Cairo's Egyptian Museum cost LE30 (roughly $1.50) as opposed to LE200 (about $10.50) for other nationalities. Not bad, considering that at the same period, an adult nonresident ticket for New York's Metropolitan Museum of Art was $25.

CASH (ESPECIALLY SMALL BILLS) IS KING

Credit cards aren't accepted universally, even in cities, so always carry some cash—preferably in small denominations—for tipping and paying. People in Egypt hoard small bills and LE1 coins, and taxi drivers, tourist attractions, and even hotels and government-run sites sometimes refuse to make change below LE50. ATMs tend to dispense LE200 bills; to get smaller ones, try withdrawing, say, LE2,120 instead of LE2,000. Otherwise, break large bills when patronizing restaurants or convenience stores.

A DATA PLAN MAKES TRAVEL EASIER

Unlocking your phone to use a local SIM card with minutes and data will allow you to navigate winding streets; use ride-hailing apps like Uber or Careem in cities; and communicate with tour guides and hotel staff by phone, text message, or WhatsApp. Note, though, that lines for Cairo airport shops selling SIM cards are usually long,

and staff at non-airport stores might not speak English. Before leaving home, ask your cell provider about roaming plans. These will likely cost more than buying a SIM card and package in Egypt, but they will cut down on the hassle.

IT HELPS TO LEARN A LITTLE ARABIC

Most Egyptians speak some English but knowing a few basic Arabic words and phrases is helpful. So is being familiar with Arabic numerals, especially if you plan to use ride-sharing apps (to check the car's license plate ensuring it's your assigned vehicle and to decipher the total fare). Numbers on buses and trains are also generally in Arabic.

YES, YOU CAN ENJOY A COCKTAIL

Alcohol is available, though you'll sometimes have to search for it. Many restaurants don't serve it and, outside of Cairo, few destinations have a nightlife scene, per se, as Egyptians who stay out late tend to be shopping, drinking coffee at cafés, and smoking *shisha* (waterpipes). International restaurants and large hotels often have bars, and two liquor store chains, Drinkies and Cheers, have locations in Cairo, Alexandria, Luxor, Sharm el-Sheikh, and Hurghada.

EGYPT IS FASCINATING DURING RAMADAN

The Muslim holy month, when the faithful don't eat, drink, or smoke from sunrise to sunset, falls in the ninth month of the lunar-based Islamic calendar, so its dates change annually in the Gregorian calendar. Before the *maghrib* (sunset) prayer, the streets go quiet—even in Cairo, a rare occurrence—as believers head home or to the mosque to pray. *Iftar*, the meal that breaks the day's fast, starts with eating a date and drinking water and is followed by a huge communal feast. People pour into streets decorated with colorful bunting and bright lanterns to shop and socialize, making Ramadan nights noisy and joyous right up until the pre-dawn *suhoor* meal. Visitors aren't expected to fast, but it's respectful not to eat or drink in public during the day. Although some restaurants don't open for lunch, museums and ancient sites could close early, and tour guides might be sleepy, tourism activities proceed as they normally do.

Getting Here and Around

Egypt has always been ruled by the close relationship between the Nile and the desert. Nile waters make the land fertile, and, even today, most Egyptians live within a mile or so of the river. The river was also the major conduit for transport until the arrival of the railways, just over 100 years ago. The country's major rail line follows the river, as does a modern highway.

Since ancient times, the country has geographically been divided into two regions, Upper Egypt and Lower Egypt. Lower Egypt is the northernmost section of the Nile Valley (closest to the Mediterranean Sea), incorporating the oldest Egyptian capital of Memphis, the modern capital Cairo, and the Nile Delta. It's called Lower Egypt because it refers to the lower reaches of the river.

Upper Egypt covers the southern stretches of the country and the ancient capital of Thebes (modern Luxor). The region's name refers to the fact that this part of the country lies around the most upstream sections of the Nile that are within the boundaries of Egypt.

Cairo, the capital since the end of the first millennium AD, is still the country's main transportation hub. From here, you can reach almost any area of the country on a two-hour flight. Overland, the train trip from Cairo to Luxor takes around 12 hours; it's 15 hours to Aswan and two or three hours to Alexandria.

The Red Sea and the Sinai Peninsula are east of Cairo. From the capital, the two main towns—Hurghada on the Red Sea and Sharm El-Sheikh in the Sinai—can both be reached by air (around one hour) or well-surfaced road (around 7 hours to Hurghada and 6 hours to Sharm), though there are U.S. State Department advisories about traveling by car to and within the Sinai Peninsula.

Travel Times from Cairo To:			
	By Air	By Bus	By Tra
Alexandria	½ hour	2½ hours	2–3 hours
Sharm El-Sheikh	1 hour	6 hours	N/A
Hurghada	1 hour	7 hours	N/A

Bear in mind that although road surfa are generally good, signage is poor, and there are numerous hazards, fror slow-moving animal carts to people v ing on the highway. It's probably best not to undertake long journeys by car public bus.

Air

Nonstop flights from New York to Cai are 10 hours. From the West Coast, t minimum flying time is 17 hours (you need to make at least one stop). Cair four hours from Paris, Amsterdam, ar Frankfurt and five hours from London

AIRPORTS

Cairo International Airport is the coun primary gateway and the only one tha has nonstop flights from the United States. Terminal 3 is devoted to all EgyptAir flights and EgyptAir's Europ Star Alliance partners with service fro Europe (Aegean, Austrian, Lufthansa, Ethiopian, Swiss International, and Tu ish airlines). A few scheduled flights f Europe also land at Sharm el-Sheikh, Hurghada, and Luxor.

If you book a package through a trave agent or have prearranged a tour, you airport transfers will almost certainly included in the price. Look for your co pany's sign as you exit baggage claim you book independently, you might ha to take a taxi. ■ TIP→ **Ask your hotel if**

offers airport-transfer service; most hotels do. You will be charged more than the normal taxi fare for this service (some hotels include transfers if you book an executive-floor room), but after a long flight, it's nice to have a stress-free transfer.

Cairo Airport also offers fixed-rate car service (called a limo, although it is generally an average sedan) to all hotels. Private taxis try to charge the same but prices are negotiable. Limo service prices are fixed depending on the destination and the car category. Category A is luxury limousines (e.g., Mercedes-Benz E-Class), Category B is microbuses for up to seven passengers, Category C is midsized cars, and Category D is London Taxis (TX4 vehicles, wheelchair accessible). Pick-up points can be found curbside in front of the terminals. Alternatively, you can take Metro Line 3 from the airport to Embaba Station.

The trip from Cairo's airport to Downtown/Zamalek is about an hour, though it can be just over 30 minutes late at night or early morning. For your flight home, allow a full three hours for international check-in.

FLIGHTS TO AND FROM EGYPT

Only EgyptAir offers nonstop flights to Egypt from the United States (out of New York's JFK and into Cairo). Flights to Cairo on other airlines require a connection in Turkey or Europe.

Most major European airlines and some budget carriers offer flights to Egypt. Note, though, that few airlines have telephone numbers in the country, relying instead on their websites.

FLIGHTS WITHIN EGYPT

To arrange domestic flights after arrival, you'll need to book online, visit a domestic airline office, or work with a reputable travel agent at least one day before you fly. That said, don't expect seats to be available on such short notice, especially in peak season. ■TIP➔ **If possible, book flights within Egypt before your arrival.**

Airlines with domestic service include Air Arabia, AlMasria Universal Airlines, EgyptAir, Nile Air, and Pegasus. EgyptAir, however, offers the most comprehensive service, with flights not only to Cairo, Aswan, Luxor, Hurghada, and Sharm El-Sheikh, but also to Alexandria, Assuit, and Marsa Alam. EgyptAir is also the only airline that flies to Abu Simbel, and these flights fill up fast year round, so book as early as possible.

 ## Bus

Privately owned buses are the cheapest way to get around Egypt. That said, security concerns can be an issue. International authorities discourage independent travelers from using buses on certain routes, specifically from Cairo down the Nile to Luxor and from Luxor east to Hurghada.

Fares are cheap, and buses are generally modern and in good condition, though poor driving standards, video entertainment streamed at high volume, and overzealous air-conditioning can make the journey slightly unpleasant. Note, too, that police checkpoint stops—during which luggage may need to be removed and checked by an officer—can cause delays. If you're planning to incorporate a long-distance bus trip into your itinerary, allow extra travel time.

Cairo's bus terminal, Turgomon, is near Downtown and is the hub for all bus service around the country. You can buy tickets at the station (all ticket windows are labeled with bus company operators)

Getting Here and Around

or via aggregator apps like Tazcara. You can also book and check schedules through proprietary bus company websites or apps, though not all of them have information in English.

High Jet runs from Cairo down the Red Sea Coast. Super Jet, Go Bus, and Blue Bus offer services from Cairo to the Sinai and the Red Sea. EG Bus, though, has the most comprehensive service, including Cairo to the Suez Canal and the Sinai; Cairo down the Nile to Luxor and Aswan and east from Luxor to Hurghada; and routes to Alexandria and along the Mediterranean Coast to the Libyan border and Siwa Oasis.

 ## Car

Driving in Egypt can be stressful and harrowing. Local drivers usually ignore speed limits on open roads and have vehicles that are often dangerous from a structural and mechanical point of view. In the countryside, roads don't have well-defined shoulders, let alone pedestrian walkways, so you must be extremely vigilant, watching out for little children, as well as goats, camels, and oxen. Nighttime driving is particularly problematic, especially as few Egyptian drivers use their headlights after dark, so you can't always see oncoming traffic.

In the city, you'll need to be very mindful of other vehicles and of pedestrians, who can, and do, appear from behind stationary vehicles to cross the street anywhere, including gaps between moving traffic.

Wherever you travel by road in Egypt, you'll encounter police checkpoints, at which foreigners might be required to present passports. Prior to 2008, driving

along the Nile Valley in Upper Egypt required an escort with a guarded traffic convoy. Although this is no longer the case, there are a good number of police checkpoints along this particular route.

CAR RENTAL

For safety reasons, renting a car in Egypt is not recommended, and, with the abundance of affordable guided tour options, it's not really necessary. If, however, you're set on renting a car, you should have no problem booking one at any time of the year. Although most airports have agency offices, it's best to book from home if you want a vehicle for your entire trip. If you decide to rent in a resort, visit the rental office a couple of days before you need the car.

When booking, specify that you want a new car, as many vehicles are at least two years old and have dents and scrapes. Before heading out, check that the car you receive is in good condition, and be sure the agency gives you a 24-hour emergency number to use in case of breakdowns or an accident.

Note that most companies have minimum age limits (normally ranging from 20 to 23) and might charge an extra fee for renters under 26. In addition, you'll need an international driving permit. You'll also be prohibited from driving a car rented in Egypt outside of the country and, while in Egypt, from off-road driving, so avoid dirt roads in the Sinai or desert tracks away from the Nile Valley.

Some but not all car rental companies offer unlimited mileage; for those that don't, car-rental deals tend to offer approximately 100 km (60 miles) per day in the basic rental price. After that, per-day mileage fees can add up quickly, so factor them into your costs.

Most rental companies include full insurance in the quoted rental price, but do check the fine print to make sure you're getting on paper what was agreed to verbally. Insurance does not cover the loss of the car registration document; if you don't return this with the car, you'll be liable for at least $300 to cover loss of income as the vehicle stands idle while the rental agency waits for the replacement document.

If you intend to park a rental car at a hotel between segments of your journey, you'll be asked to hand in the car registration document and your driving license at the security gate, and they will be kept for the duration of your stay. Don't forget the registration card when you leave.

GASOLINE

Gas stations and rest areas are plentiful on major highways, and credit cards are widely accepted. In more remote areas, though, carrying cash to pay for gas is a good idea. It's best to have extra gas and plenty of water with you as well.

Most Egyptian gas stations are full-service, and it's customary to tip the attendant who fills up your car a pound or two. All gas is unleaded and is sold by the liter. Plain unleaded is called *tamanin*, or 80, denoting the level of purity. Higher-quality (and slightly more expensive) gasoline is available as *tisa'in*, or 90, and, occasionally, *khamsa wa tisa'in*, or 95.

Most pumps show amounts in Roman numerals, but you still may find some that use Arabic. ■TIP→ **Watch as the attendant starts the pump to be sure that it reads 000.**

ROAD CONDITIONS

You will find some toll routes in Egypt, the main one being the Cairo–Alexandria road. Generally, road conditions are good, especially in the Sinai and along the Red Sea Coast. That said, there are very few maps available, and signposting—although in Arabic and English—is generally poor.

ROADSIDE EMERGENCIES

Make sure that your car-rental company provides you with contact details, including a 24-hour emergency number to call in case of any problems. If possible, carry a cell phone with you containing these numbers as well as those of police stations and hotels along your route.

If you have car trouble on the highway, pull off the road as soon as possible, then wait and flag down any passing vehicle. Daily buses serve even remote areas, and they will stop for you if they see you.

More worrisome are accidents. Many Egyptian car owners don't have insurance, and disputes tend to be resolved on the scene (be sure to get the license number of the other driver) with more or less fanfare depending on the seriousness of the accident. For accidents in which people have been injured, get emergency help first, and then immediately contact or drive to your embassy. ■TIP→ **In all accident situations, insist on having a senior-level, English-speaking police officer present.**

RULES OF THE ROAD

Speed limits are 60 kph (just under 40 mph) in built-up areas and 90 or 100 kph (55 or 60 mph) on the open road. Although speeds are generally posted at regular intervals, most locals drive as fast as they can, ignoring limits. Lane discipline is nonexistent: drivers will always try to pass, even when visibility is poor, such as on bends or hills. Also be prepared for Egyptian drivers to use their car horns frequently, whether to

Getting Here and Around

communicate regarding right of way or as a complaint or even just as a greeting.

There are restrictions on using cell phones (unless it's via a hands-free system) while driving, and seat belts are compulsory. Drivers, however, regularly flout these laws. Although fines of up to LE500 are the norm, and officers can confiscate your license for dangerous driving practices, enforcement is patchy despite the main towns having numerous traffic officers.

Drunk driving is a serious offense, and perpetrators can be arrested, fined (LE1,000 to LE3,000), and have their vehicles confiscated. Note that the law is not defined by blood-alcohol concentration (officials don't conduct random breathalyzer tests) because most Egyptians don't drink alcohol.

There is no legislation relating to children. Only some rental companies supply car seats for infants; if you have small children, check with the company ahead of time or consider bringing a car seat from home.

Throughout Egypt, expect police checkpoints at intervals of 30 km (20 miles) or so along every highway, as well as at all major intersections and river crossings. At each, be prepared to show your passport to the officers manning the barrier. Note, too, that foreigners are sometimes randomly stopped for no reason other than an attempt by officers to squeeze money from them. If you smile and insist you did not break the law, the officers will usually let you go.

Right turns are permitted on red lights at some intersections—indicated by a flashing light above or to the side of the traffic lane. But not all drivers waiting in this lane want to turn right.

Intersections in parts of downtown Cairo have cameras to catch drivers who cross intersections. It's not uncommon, however, for Cairo traffic lights to be out of service, with traffic controlled by officers using hand movements.

If you want to turn around on a major highway, look ahead for left-side, midstream turning areas, sometimes indicated by signs on the overhead gantry. Just be very careful when using the feeder lanes, which flow directly into the fastest lanes.

Taxi

Taxis are the backbone of transport in Egypt. Fares are cheap and set (in theory) by cities and districts. In Cairo, white and yellow taxis have meters (make sure the driver turns it on when you enter). Black sedans and older taxis may not have a meter, in which case be sure you agree on a fare with the driver before you enter the taxi.

Ask your guide or hotel concierge about realistic fares between destinations before you depart. Note, though, that taking a taxi to or from any hotel will always be more expensive than taking one from the street. Alternatively, you can call a Cairo taxi service or company or use a taxi app. Also, if you take a cab to a tourist site, it's not a bad idea to ask the driver to wait for you outside; the cost will be about LE20 per hour.

Most drivers understand some English. Still, you should familiarize yourself with useful phrases, and, if you're going off the beaten path, have the address of your destination written in Arabic.

Collective service taxis (known as *servees*) or microbuses (*meecros*) operate on a variety of specific routes (e.g., Cairo to Alexandria) and are generally quicker than buses and trains. The very reasonable fares are fixed, though you should confirm the going rate with a hotel concierge or other local. Drivers, however, often weave erratically through traffic to speed up transit times. They're also less likely to speak English.

To catch one of these vehicles, go to the nearest terminal and ask for a servees to your destination. You might also hear drivers shouting *"servees"* to attract passengers. Vehicles will leave once they're full, though passengers will sometimes collectively agree to pay a bit more to leave before it reaches capacity.

Taxis do not typically have ramps or spaces for wheelchair users. If you need such amenities, pre-arrange a car with London Cab Egypt, or book via Tawsila, a taxi service customized for people with disabilities. Carreem Assist, an option that caters to wheelchair users in the popular ride-hailing app, is only available in Alexandria.

RIDE-SHARING

In terms of ride-sharing apps, Uber and Careem (acquired by Uber in 2020) dominate the landscape and are available in most major cities. Indeed, with fixed rates that beat taxi fares and the option to pay with a credit card registered in the app instead of in cash, ride-sharing may be your best choice. What's more, since drivers are subject to a rating system and users have the option to share locations while on a ride, many people feel safer using these platforms than taxis or public transportation.

Careem offers a variety of vehicle options depending on the region. These include sedans, mini-buses, tuk tuks (small, three-wheel vehicles), and even feluccas (small boats often used on the Nile).

Uber also has a single-rider option, as well as a scooter (motorcycle) option. Although the latter is the least-expensive choice, it isn't recommended for long rides, routes that include the highway, or for riders who are faint of heart. Also, most scooter drivers are men, some of whom won't transport women due to the close proximity between driver and rider.

Other popular apps include InDriver, which allows you to set a rate for your trip and search for a driver who will accept it, making the price negotiable, and Swvl, a microbus ride-sharing app.

For any app, you will need a phone with Wi-Fi or roaming (data). It's best to have a local SIM card, so you and the driver can contact each other if you have trouble meeting up in busy areas. Driver tips are appreciated but not expected.

Note that license plate numbers in the apps often appear as alpha numeric, but plate numbers on the vehicles themselves are written in Arabic numerals. Familiarize yourself with Arabic numerals so that you can confirm you're getting in the right vehicle. Also confirm the profile picture of your driver. Finally, don't be surprised if you're dropped off slightly removed from your destination, which is a common practice. Just be prepared to navigate when you arrive.

Getting Here and Around

🚆 Train

There are three types of national trains, the fastest of which is the Turbo or Turbini (also called Special Service or VIP). These air-conditioned trains have first- and second-class cars, as well as refreshments for sale onboard. All tickets are for assigned seats, each of which can be rotated 180 degrees to create a bay of four for groups traveling together.

Although trains often run late, a Turbo trip between Alexandria and Cairo takes between two to three hours and costs up to LE125 for first class. As there are 13 trains per day in each direction, with service between 6 am and 10:30 pm, it's easy to find a seat in your desired time-frame on the day of or the day before a trip.

Turbo trains also travel between Cairo and Upper Egypt. From Cairo to Luxor, a one-way ticket costs between LE171 (second class) and LE254 (first class); from Cairo to Aswan, fares range from LE197 (second class) to LE306 (first class).

Slightly slower and operating with older cars are the Spanish trains (also called Express or AC), which offer similar amenities to Turbini. French trains (also called Ordinary or Ord) move at the slowest speeds, are not air-conditioned, and offer second- and third-class unreserved bench seating. Few visitors use these trains, but, over short distances, they offer a charming experience.

SCHEDULES AND TICKETS

Timetables can be found at all major stations, but it's not uncommon for them to be listed only in Arabic. At some stations, like Ramses Station in Cairo, the departure boards will cycle through Arabic and English. Train numbers are often indicated in Arabic numerals, so familiarize yourself with these. Although schedule and fare information can also be found on the Egyptian Railway's website and app, it's not comprehensive.

You can reserve a seat and buy tickets up to two weeks in advance of your journey via the Egyptian Railway website, but doing so on its app requires an Egyptian National ID card number. As technical difficulties with these services are frequent, many travelers prefer third-party apps like Egypt Trains (available for iPhone and Android) or Train Trip (Android only).

If you haven't made reservations prior to arriving in Egypt, you best bet is to buy tickets at the train station a day or two before your journey. Alternatively, skip the line at the station by using an Egyptian travel agency, many of which sell first-class tickets for a small commission.

SLEEPER TRAINS

Sleeper trains run by the private company Watania make daily trips between Cairo and Luxor or Aswan. These trains have comfortable, air-conditioned sleeping cars—each with an electrical outlet, a sink, soap, and clean towels and bedding—and a lounge car.

Cars tend to fill up, particularly in peak season, so buy tickets several days in advance. Fares, which are higher for foreigners than Egyptian nationals, are in U.S. dollars and include two basic meals—at breakfast time and in the evening—with tea and coffee available at other times for a small price. Tickets range from $84 per person each way for a double cabin to $126 for a single.

You can find schedule and fare information and purchase tickets on the Watania website. In Cairo, the Watania office is at the front of the Ramses Station, next to the main entrance and before security check.

Essentials

Health

There are several minor hazards to be mindful of in Egypt. First, never underestimate the power of the sun. Even in the coolest months, there's a risk of sunburn and sunstroke. Stay out of the sun as much as possible, wear a hat when you are out and about, apply high-SPF sunscreen regularly (international brands are available in pharmacies and supermarkets), and stay hydrated by drinking plenty of fluids (not alcohol).

If you are traveling with children, all this advice goes double. Children may not be aware that they are beginning to suffer from dehydration or sunstroke. Give them plenty to drink even if they don't complain of being thirsty, and keep their heads and skin covered.

In some areas, it's best not to swim in the Nile, and never drink the river water because of the risk of picking up waterborne parasites. Avoid all standing freshwater, as there is the risk of bilharzia (schistosomiasis).

There's little risk of malaria—so no need for antimalarial tablets—but do protect yourself from insects as some carry dengue fever or West Nile virus. Pharmacies and tourist shops sell repellant creams and sprays; some shops also sell coils that burn to give off fumes that repel bugs.

COVID-19
Although COVID-19 brought travel to a virtual standstill for most of 2020 and into 2021, vaccinations have made travel possible and safe again. Remaining requirements and restrictions—including those for non-vaccinated travelers—can, however, vary from one place (or even business) to the next. ■TIP→ **Owing to the pandemic, travel insurance that covers medical needs is mandatory for visitors to Egypt. There aren't any specific coverage requirements except that the plan be valid for the duration of your stay.**

Always travel with a mask in case it's required, and keep up to date on the most recent testing and vaccination guidelines for Egypt. Check out the websites of the CDC and the U.S. Department of State, both of which have destination-specific COVID-19 guidance.

FOOD AND DRINK
Water quality is a concern. Though it's safe to bathe in, never drink water from taps or public fountains, as it may contain microbes that your body isn't used to. Stick with bottled water (*mayya ma'daniya*), which is inexpensive and readily available, for both drinking and brushing your teeth. Just remember to check that the bottle's seal is intact before you open and use it. Alternatively, consider bringing a reusable water bottle with a filter (e.g., Lifestraw or Grayl) to cut down on single-use plastic while staying healthy.

Ice in five-star hotels should be produced using purified water. When in doubt, however, ask for drinks without ice (*min gheir talg*).

To minimize your risk of intestinal issues, make sure the meat you eat is well cooked, avoid unpeeled fruits and vegetables, and avoid dairy products—unless the packaging looks as if it comes from a legitimate factory and you can confirm that it has been stored in a functional refrigerator. Ask about whether the salad in your hotel has been washed in purified water.

Antinal is a locally produced remedy for traveler's diarrhea that's inexpensive and effective. If symptoms become severe, and you cannot keep down liquids (and, thus, run the additional risk of dehydration), call a doctor immediately.

Essentials

HOSPITALS AND PHARMACIES

Medical facilities are not as good as in the United States or Europe, but medical personnel generally speak some English, and many doctors are fluent. Pharmacists are well qualified and able to give advice on common low-risk ailments. They can also sell many medications that are available only by prescription elsewhere, including antibiotics (and even Viagra).

Pharmacies are well stocked, and medications are quite inexpensive by U.S. standards, but not all product names will be the same. For instance, Panadol (generally known as acetaminophen in the United States) is the most common headache remedy.

Pharmacies normally stay open until 10 pm. In major cities you'll also find 24-hour pharmacies, and each town or district has at least one late-night pharmacy, though sometimes these are open in rotation. If you need to find a pharmacy that's open late, inquire at your hotel.

SHOTS AND VACCINATIONS

In addition to ensuring that you're up to date on all routine vaccinations, the CDC recommends a vaccination against hepatitis A; it's also wise to have a vaccination against hepatitis B. The risk of typhoid is generally low, but you should discuss this risk with your doctor, perhaps getting a typhoid vaccination if you intend to take a multiday felucca trip on the Nile. A rabies vaccination is recommended for travelers spending a lot of time outdoors, especially in rural areas.

that hotel management can charge, they don't always equate with ratings that might be used elsewhere. Hence, you might notice a difference in service, as well as in standards of fixtures and fittings in an Egyptian hotel compared with an equivalent hotel at home.

Egypt has a huge selection of five- and one- or two-star properties, but relatively few in the middle range. Properties with ratings of fewer than three stars are basic but usually clean. Most will have a small, en-suite, shower-only bathroom. Amenities at five-star hotels can vary greatly. For instance, those in Cairo, which cater to business clients, tend to have small pools and few, if any, sports facilities, whereas hotels on the Red Sea Coast and in the Sinai have large pools and expansive leisure facilities.

Although you can generally book rooms at the more expensive hotels online, large tour operators often reserve huge blocks of rooms far in advance, so you might not, initially, find a vacancy—even in the off-season. ■TIP→ **It's sometimes easier to book upscale hotels through travel agents, tour operators, and aggregator websites.**

Throughout this guide, hotel reviews have been shortened. For full information, visit Fodors.com. Hotel prices, which are cited in U.S. dollars—commonly used (along with the euro) in price quotes issued by hotels—are the lowest cost of a standard double room in high season.

🛏 Hotels

The Egyptian government awards star ratings to hotels (and cruise ships), with five stars being the highest. Although these ratings dictate the price ranges

💲 Money

The Egyptian pound is written as £E and, more commonly, LE (i.e., *livre égyptienne*, which is the French term for the currency). It is divided into 100 piastres (pt). Bank notes include 25pt, 50pt, LE1, LE5, LE10, LE20, LE50, LE100, and LE200. There are also 25pt, 50pt, and LE1 coins, the latter two being the most common. Don't accept a dog-eared or torn bill, as many vendors will refuse to take it. Just politely give it back and ask for a replacement.

Foreign currency is rarely accepted (and vendors that do accept it probably won't give you a fair exchange rate), and neither are credit cards outside of cruise ships, major hotels and restaurants, and international retailers. Plus, paying with a credit card can incur a 2% to 3% surcharge.

Cash really is king for tipping; buying local merchandise in shops and *souks* (markets); purchasing snacks and beverages in small stores; and paying for taxi, felucca, and carriage rides. LE5 and LE10 are the most useful notes for short taxi rides and small purchases. Smaller notes and coins are handy for tips.

Prices throughout this guide are given for adults. Substantially reduced fees are almost always available for children, students, and senior citizens.

BANKS AND CURRENCY EXCHANGE

It's best to exchange currency on arrival, rather than at home, where exchange rates tend to be less favorable. If you do exchange money prior to traveling, note that there is a LE5,000 import limit.

You can find currency-exchange offices at all airports and most major hotels (where rates often aren't the best), as well as on the street and in major shopping areas. If you've brought traveler's checks, a passport is usually required to cash them. Save the official receipts you're given with each exchange transaction. If you have Egyptian pounds leftover when you

Item	Average Cost
Cup of coffee	LE25–LE50 for American coffee
Glass of wine	LE30–LE200
Glass of beer	LE20–LE125

are ready to leave the country, you may need to show the receipts to exchange the pounds back to your home currency.

In smaller, more out out-of-the-way places, ATMs (*makinat al-flus*) can be difficult to find—or might be broken. In major tourist areas—including Cairo, Luxor, Aswan, and the coastal resorts of Hurghada, El Gouna, and Sharm el-Sheikh—ATMs that accept major bank or international cards (Cirrus and PLUS) are numerous, so you can rely on them to stock your wallet with Egyptian pounds. Screen commands are in Arabic, English, and sometimes French.

Your own bank will probably charge a fee for using ATMs abroad; the foreign bank you use may also charge a fee. Nevertheless, you'll usually get a better rate of exchange at an ATM than you will at a currency-exchange office or even a bank. Plus, extracting funds as you need them is a safer option than carrying around a large amount of cash.

TAXES

On services such as hotel rooms, group travel, and car rental, a 10% tax is levied. Imported goods are highly taxed, but this is included in the ticketed sale price. There is a 14% VAT tax, a service charge of 12% in restaurants and hotels, and a sales tax of 5%–7%. There is no departure tax when you leave the country.

TIPPING

Tipping, or *baksheesh,* is a way of life in Egypt. Everyone who performs a service expects a monetary reward, whether

Essentials

you requested the service or not. Don't be surprised, for instance, if someone engages you in conversation or offers you a "gift"—perhaps a small piece of alabaster or a scarab—and then asks for a little *baksheesh* as you part company.

You should never feel compelled to tip but remember that many Egyptians greatly rely on gratuities to make a living, and the amounts are often nominal. For instance, LE1–LE5 is sufficient for small services, such as a restroom attendant giving you toilet paper. Using the local currency is best. Though coins and small bills can be difficult to come by, try to have them on hand.

In hotels, leave maids LE5–LE10 per night, and give hotel porters LE3–LE5 per bag. In restaurants, it's expected that you leave 10%–15% in cash (even if you're paying the bill with a credit card) for good service. This will be on top of the 12% service charge—which often goes to the restaurant, not the server—that's added to most tabs.

Cabbies don't expect tips for short journeys but add 10% to the agreed upon fee if you engage one to take you to several attractions and wait for you at each. If you hire a guide and driver for a day tour, tip them both: at least LE100 for the guide and another LE50 for the driver. If you listen as temple and tomb guardians point out hieroglyphs, or they give you access to an area or take a photo for you, give them LE10–LE20.

◉ Packing

Cottons, linens, and moisture-wicking fabrics make the most sensible choices for the heat. Collared short-sleeve shirts and lightweight full-length pants not only offer the best sun protection but are also more practical in terms of local attitudes about dress.

A jacket will come in handy on overnights in the desert, where temperatures plummet in the evening. If you travel in winter, pack layers, including a fleece item as well as a jacket. Although men are rarely required to wear a jacket and tie, in Cairo's upscale hotels and nightclubs, the clientele tends to dress up. Both men and women might want to pack at least one fancier outfit.

You'll need a hat, because the sun is hot year-round; sunglasses, because temple facades and rock faces are extremely bright in the daylight; and comfortable shoes, because you'll be walking a lot (sometimes in sand) and navigating awkward stairs at ancient sites. Even in cities, closed-toe shoes are best, as dirty streets make sandals impractical.

Consider packing a small flashlight for visiting dimly lit tombs and temples; lightweight binoculars for close-up views of monumental facades and for bird-watching on the Nile; and antibacterial wipes or gel so that you can clean your hands wherever you are.

You can buy almost anything you need in the cities and main towns, from baby formula and sunscreen to feminine hygiene products and contact lens supplies.

DRESS CODES

Although women aren't expected to wear a headscarf except when visiting a mosque, Egypt is, nevertheless, a majority-Islamic country, where attitudes toward dress are more conservative than in the United States and Europe. Both men and women should pack items of clothing that cover shoulders as well as knees. Wearing less modest clothing is fine at tourist beaches and when on the boat during a Nile cruise.

🌐 Passports and Visas

All visitors must have at least six months validity on their passports to enter Egypt. Citizens of the United States and 44 other countries are eligible to apply online for one of two types of e-visas: a single entry, 30-day visa, or a multiple-entry visa, which is valid for 180 days and allows for multiple stays of up to 30 days within that period of time. The official Government of Egypt portal for e-visas is 🌐 *www.visa2egypt.gov.eg*. Be wary of using other sites: some reportedly charge double the price.

U.S. and EU citizens can also buy tourist visas on arrival in Egypt at any international airport, where windows or kiosks selling them are situated immediately before immigration. Though the process isn't complicated, if you have booked through a tour operator or have arranged a transfer with your hotel, a representative will be waiting for you in the arrivals hall to help with it.

The cost of a single-entry, 30-day visa is $25, payable in U.S. dollars, euros, or pound sterling. To stay longer, you must apply at the Mogamma, a building that serves as the bureaucratic center of the country; it's in Cairo across from the Egyptian Museum.

If you arrive in Egypt via Israel, at Taba, you will not be able to buy a full tourist visa at the border crossing. Officials there will only issue a visa limiting you to the Sinai region that's valid for two weeks; there's no charge for this. To get a tourist visa for travel to other parts of Egypt, visit the Egyptian Consulate in Eilat or obtain an e-visa, if eligible.

🍴 Restaurants

In the countryside, few Egyptians eat out, so restaurants tend to be rudimentary. Establishments in cities and resorts range from street kitchens to gourmet spots with silver service. These destinations also have restaurants—usually in upscale hotels—that serve international cuisine, including Thai, Chinese, and Italian.

Cairo and Alexandria are both well known for their *ahwas* (coffee shops). Today, U.S.–style spots offering caffeine in a range of flavors and styles are joining these traditional cafés.

Vegetarians will always be able to find salads, hummus, and rice to sustain them. That said, fresh vegetables are hard to come by, except in the rather generic cucumber salad, though stewed vegetables (*tabich*) such as *bamia* (okra) are common. Pizza is available in most tourist destinations, as are delicious soups, though some are made with meat-based stocks.

Throughout this guide, restaurant reviews have been shortened. For full information, visit Fodors.com. Restaurant prices, cited in the Egyptian pound (LE), are the average cost of a main course at dinner or, if dinner is not served, at lunch.

MEALS AND MEALTIMES

Most restaurants are open throughout the day. For *fitar* (breakfast), you can do as Egyptians do and indulge in a steaming plate of *ful* (stewed fava beans), accompanied by fried eggs, bread, and pickles. Lighter fare includes croissants and other pastries, bought fresh from the local bakery and topped with cheese or jam. Cairo has a handful of American-style breakfast restaurants, as well as a few 24-hour eateries.

Essentials

The main meal of the day is lunch (*ghada*). It starts with a soup, such as *shorbat'ads* (lentil), for which Egypt is famous throughout the Middle East, or *molukhiyya*, a thick soup made with leafy greens like jute-mallow. This is followed by *mezze* (appetizers), and these can be a meal in and of themselves. You'll taste dips like *tahini* (sesame-seed paste) and *baba ghanoush* (mashed roasted eggplant) as well as dishes such as *wara einab* (stuffed grape leaves) and *ta'amiya* (Egyptian felafel).

Main courses include chicken—grilled or roasted whole in a rotisserie oven—as well as lamb or beef shish kebab (skewered in chunks) or *kofta* (minced lamb on skewers). *Hamam mahshi* (stuffed pigeon) is also popular.

'Asha, or dinner, is composed of a similar menu as at lunch, although many Egyptians partake in only a light evening meal, consisting of fruit and sandwiches. Every meal comes with round loaves of pita-style bread, either *'aish baladi* (coarse-grain wheat) or *'aish shami* (white).

Koshary is a widely popular street food that mixes pasta, rice, and brown lentils, and is topped with a zesty tomato sauce and garlic vinegar, and garnished with chickpeas and crispy fried onions. There are regional differences to the dish, for instance the Alexandrian style uses red lentils, skips noodles, and goes heavy on the cumin. Regardless, *koshary* is a fast, inexpensive, and total comfort food.

Unless otherwise noted, the restaurants listed in this guide are open daily for lunch and dinner.

PAYING

Credit cards are widely accepted in hotel restaurants; less so in private establishments. More places in Cairo and the Red Sea resorts accept cards than in the rest of the country, but they will charge a 2% or 3% processing fee. Wherever you go, it's best to have cash on hand. Small denominations are useful, not only for tipping but also for paying as some restaurants might have trouble breaking bigger bills.

For guidelines on tipping see the Money section.

RESERVATIONS AND DRESS

Make reservations for meals in upscale hotel restaurants, particularly if you are not a guest. Restaurants requiring a jacket and tie for men are rare, with the notable exception of several restaurants in the Sofitel Winter Garden Hotel in Luxor. Diners in upscale Cairo restaurants tend to dress up, however.

⊕ Safety

Egypt has experienced a number of terrorist incidents in the past two decades, including a spate of attacks in Cairo and bombings in the Sinai, where, in 2015, more than 200 tourists were killed as a result of the bombing of Russian Metrojet Flight 9268. Terrorists have targeted diplomatic facilities, tourist locations, transportation hubs, markets/shopping malls, and resorts, as well as religious sites, including mosques, churches, monasteries, and buses traveling to these locations.

Although the government has visibly increased its security presence at tourist locations, the threat of terrorism remains. Safety measures have included providing armed officers to travel with foreigners, creating convoys in certain areas for visitors traveling by road, and ensuring that hotels have guards and X-ray machines to check all incoming bags.

Note that the U.S. State Department does not recommend travel to the Sinai Peninsula (except to the resort town of Sharm el-Sheikh, by air) or the Western Desert. Check its website (⊕ *travel.state. gov*) for the most up-to-date notices and advice.

CRIME

Violent crime perpetrated against foreign visitors is rare, though pick-pocketing and petty theft can be a problem, especially in busy markets and at popular tourist sites or destinations such the Red Sea and Sinai resort areas. (Never leave items unattended on the beach, and lock valuables in your hotel safe before departing from your room.)

If you're threatened in a public place, don't hesitate to yell for help—it will not go unheard. Whatever the emergency, Egyptians will generally go out of their way to assist you. Also helpful are the officers who patrol all the main tourist areas and have brown uniforms with "Tourist Police" on their armbands. Note, though, that not all of them speak English well.

You'll need to report theft to the regular police and get a case number in order to make a claim on your insurance policy. This can be a time-consuming exercise (two or three hours). If you are the victim of a serious crime or accident, contact the U.S. Embassy in Cairo for assistance.

LGBTQ+ TRAVELERS

Although there's no law against homosexuality in Egypt, wide-ranging and ill-defined indecency laws have led to gay men, in particular, being jailed and/ or prosecuted. In addition, homosexuality isn't generally accepted. Hence, the country's LGBTQ+ communities have remained, essentially, underground. It's best to practice discretion.

SCAMS

Be vigilant when dealing with taxi drivers or venders, some of whom try to make easy money off foreigners who are poor at bargaining. Note, too, that you'll be approached for *baksheesh* (tip money) for everything. Young kids will cheerfully greet you as you pass, and then, as you reply, immediately open their hands for money. At major attractions, men may engage you in conversation as you approach a street, stop traffic to help you cross, and then request a cash "reward."

Another possible situation is for a young man to attach himself to your party as you explore the markets, procuring samples of bread or dates for you to try and then eventually asking for "guiding" money. You might also be encouraged to enter a local shop for tea and a chat. Once you're seated and relaxed, however, staffers may press you into purchasing something.

It's important to be aware of these scenarios, but try not to treat everyone with suspicion. Many Egyptians are genuinely willing to help for no reward except the chance to chat with a visitor and practice speaking English.

WOMEN TRAVELERS

Women might find themselves receiving unwanted attention from teenage boys and men. This mainly involves blatant staring or trying to engage in conversation, but it can also include inappropriate comments, which are best ignored.

Assault is not common, but occasionally men will attempt to touch or grope women, particularly in crowded areas. If this happens, make it loud and clear that you find this behavior offensive.

Helpful Arabic Phrases

BASICS

Hello/peace be upon you	salamou alaikom	sah-**lah**-moo aah-**lay**-kom
(reply) Hello/peace be upon you	wa aalaikom essalaam	wah aah-lay-kom ess-sah-**laam**
Goodbye	maa issalameh	maah is-sah-lah-mah
Good morning	sabah elkheir	sah-bahh el-**kheh**-r
Yes	aah, aywa, or naam	aah, ai-wah, or naahm
No	la	lah
Please (man)	min fadlak or law samaht	min fudd-luck or la-wh sah-mah-hht
Please (woman)	min fadlik or law samahti	min fudd-lick or la-wh sah-mahh-tee
Thank you	shokran	shook-run
God willing	Inshallah	in-shaa-al-lah
I'm sorry (man)	asif	aah-siff
I'm sorry (woman)	asfa	ahs-fah
Mr. (Sir)	ostaz	os-taaz
Mrs.	madam	mah-daam
Miss	anissah	**ah-niss-sah**
Pleased to meet you	tsharrafna (or forsa sa'eeda)	ta-shar-ruff-na (or for-sa sa-eed-dah)
How are you? (man speaking)	ezayyak	ez-zai-yack
How are you? (woman speaking)	ezaiyek	ez-zai-yick
Fine, thank you	bi kheir elhhamdilla	bee **kheir** el-**ham**-dihl-lah
How do I get to ...?	ezai arouhh ...	ezz-zai ar-rouhh ...
Let's go	yalla	**yah-lah**

NUMBERS

1	wahed	**wah-hed**
2	itnein	**it-neh-ain**
3	talata	tah-**lah**-ta
4	arbaa	**are-bah-aah**
5	khamsah	**kham-sah**
6	sittah	**seht-tah**
7	sabaa	sab-**ba**-ah
8	tamanyah	tah-mah-n-yah
9	tisaa	**tiss-aah**
10	aashara	**aah-shah-rah**
11	hhdashar	hh-**dah**-shar
12	etnashar	et-**nah**-shar
20	ishreen	iish-**reen**
50	khamseen	kham-**seen**
100	meyyah	**mey-yah**
200	metein	meh-**tein**

DAYS

Today	enaharda	in-nah-har-dah
Tomorrow	bokra	bok-rah
Yesterday	embarehh	ehm-**bah**-rehh
Sunday	el 'hhad	el-hh-had
Monday	el etnain	el ett-**nayn**
Tuesday	ittalaat	it-tah-**latt**
Wednesday	il 'arbaa	il are-**baah**
Thursday	il khamees	il khah-**mees**
Friday	it gomaa'	il gomm-**maah**
Saturday	issabt	**iss-sah-bt**

USEFUL PHRASES

Do you speak English?	Betetkalem ingelizi?	B-tit-**kal**-lem in-geh-**lee**-zee?
I don't understand (man)	mesh fahem	mesh **fah**-him
I don't understand (woman)	mesh fahma	mesh **fah**-mah
I don't know (man)	mesh aarif	mesh **aah**-ref
I don't know (woman)	mesh aarfa	mesh **aahr**-fah
I am American (man)	ana amriki	ah-nah ahm-**ree-kee**
I'm American (woman)	ana amrikiyya	ah-nah ahm-**ree-key**-yah
I'm British (man).	ana breetani	ah-nah **bree-tah-nee**
I'm British (woman).	ana breetaniya	ah-nah **bree-tah-nee**-yah
What is it this?	Eih dah?	eh dah?
What time is it?	Essaa'a kam?	iss-**sah**-'ah cam?
Where is ...	Fein ...	feh-ein (as in feign)
... the train station?	mahhattit ilatr?	mah-hhat-**tit il-att**-r
... the bus station?	mahhattit ilautobees?	mah-**hhat**-tit il-**auto**-bees
... the airport?	el matar?	el mah-**tahr**

... the post office?	el bareed?	el bah-**reed**
... the pharmacy?	el saydaleyyah?	el sigh-dah-**lei-yah**
... the bank?	el bank?	el bahnk
... the embassy?	el seffara?	el sehf-fah-**rah**
... the hotel?	el oh-tail? (or fondo')	el ooh-**tayl** (or fohn-do')
... the cafe?	el ahwa?	el ah-**wah**
... the restaurant?	el mataam?	el **matt-aahm**
... the hospital?	el mostashfa?	el mos-**tash**-fah
... the telephone?	el tiliphon?	el tih-lih-**fohn**
... the restroom?	el hammam?	el hham-**maam**
Police	bolees (or shorta)	boh-lease (or **short**-tah)
Right	yemeen	yeh-mean
Left	shemal	sheh-mahl
Straight ahead	doughri (or tawwali)	doh-ghreh (or taw-wal-lee)
I would like a room	aayez oda	aah-yez **oh-dah**
A little	shwaya (or olayel)	shwai-yah (or o-lai-yel)
A lot	keteer	keh-teer
Enough	kefaya	keh-**fai**-yah
I have a problem	aandi moshkela	aahn-dee **mosh**-keh-lah
I am ill/sick	ana aayan	ah-nah ai-yan
I need a doctor	meh'tag doktor	mehh-**tag dock**-tor
Help!	saadoonee	**saah-doo-nee**
Fire!	hari'a	hhah-**ree**-'ah
Caution/look out	ewaa (or hhaseb)	ehw-**aah** (or **hhaa**-seb)
Turn on the (taxi) meter	shaghal el addadd	shah-ghal el add-dad
Follow the GPS	emshi wara el GPS	emm-she wah-rah el GPS
Ticket	tazkara	tahz-**kahr**-rah

DINING OUT

I would like ...	Aayez	aah-**yez**
... water	mayya	mah-yyah
... bread	aish	ei-sh
... vegetables	khodar	kho-dar
... meat	lahhma	**lahh-mah**
... fruits	fakha	**fahk-hah**
... cake	cakeah	**cake-kah**
... sweets	hhaga helwa (or halaweyyat)	hhah-gah **hhel**-wah (or hah-lah-wei-yaht)
... tea	shay	**shai**
... coffee	ahwa	ah-wah
... a fork	shoka	show-kah
... a spoon	maala a	**maah-lah ah**
... a knife	sekkeena	sick-keen-ah
... a plate	tabaa'	tah-ba'

SHOPPING

I would like to buy ...	aayez ashteri	aah-yez ash-teh-ree
... cigarettes	sagayer	sah-gah-yer
... a city map	khareetit el madeena	khah-ree-titt el mah-dee-nah
... a road map	khareetit el taree'	khah-ree-titt el tah-ree'
How much is it?	bekam?	beh-kam?
It's expensive (man)	ghali	ghah-lee
It's expensive (woman)	ghalya	ghahl-yah
Shop	mahhal	mah-hhal

Contacts

Air

AIRPORT INFORMATION
Cairo International Airport. ✉ *Cairo* ☎ *02/696–6300* ⊕ *www.cairo-airport.com.* **Hurghada International Airport.** ☎ *65/344–2592.* **Luxor International Airport.** ✉ *Luxor* ☎ *95/232–4455.* **Sharm El-Sheikh International Airport.** ✉ *Sharm el Sheikh* ☎ *69/362–3304.*

MAJOR AIRLINES
Aegean Airlines. ✉ *Cairo* ☎ *833/732–8158* ⊕ *en. aegeanair.com.* **Air France.** ✉ *Cairo* ☎ *02/160–0588 in Cairo, 800/237–2747 outside of Egypt* ⊕ *www.air-france.us.* **Austrian Airlines.** ✉ *Cairo* ☎ *02/2580–3500 in Egypt, 800/843–0002* ⊕ *www.austrian.com.* **British Airways.** ✉ *Cairo* ☎ *080/0006–0300 in Egypt, 800/247–9297 outside of Egypt* ⊕ *www. britishairways.com.* **EgyptAir.** ☎ *2/2267–7101 in Cairo, 69/360–3710 in Sharm el-Sheikh, 65/364–3034 in Hurghada* ⊕ *www.egyptair.com.*

Ethiopian Airlines. ✉ *Cairo* ☎ *800/000–963–2800, 800/445–2733* ⊕ *www. ethiopianairlines.com.*

KLM Royal Dutch Airlines. ✉ *Cairo* ☎ *02/160–0599 in Cairo, 800/225–2525 outside of Egypt* ⊕ *www.klm. com.* **Lufthansa.** ✉ *Cairo* ☎ *02/2580–3500 in Egypt, 800/645–3880 outside of Egypt* ⊕ *www.lufthansa. com.* **SAS Scandinavian Airlines.** ✉ *Cairo* ☎ *800/221– 2350* ⊕ *www.flysas.com.* **Swiss International Airlines.** ✉ *Cairo* ☎ *22/580–3500 in Egypt, 833/626-0737 in USA* ⊕ *www.swiss.com.* **Turkish Airlines.** ✉ *Cairo* ☎ *800/874–8875* ⊕ *www. turkishairlines.com.*

BUDGET AIRLINES
Easyjet. ⊕ *www.easyjet.com.* **Pegasus Airlines.** ✉ *Cairo* ⊕ *www.flypgs.com/en.* **Wizz Air.** ⊕ *www.wizzair. com.*

Bus

BUS INFORMATION
Blue Bus. ⊕ *bluebus.com.eg.* **EG Bus.** ⊕ *eg-bus.com.* **Go Bus.** ⊕ *go-bus.com/?lang=en.* **High Jet Transport.** ⊕ *www. highjet-eg.com/en.* **Super Jet.** ⊕ *www.superjet.com.* **Tazcara.** ⊕ *tazcara.com.*

Car

LOCAL AGENCIES
Smart Rental. ☎ *02/2524–3006* ⊕ *www.smartlimo.com.*

MAJOR AGENCIES
Alamo. ☎ *844/354–6962 reservations in the U.S.* ⊕ *www.alamo.com.* **Avis.** ☎ *800/633–3469 in the U.S., 100/107–7400 Cairo International Airport* ⊕ *www.avis.com.* **Budget.** ☎ *800/472–3325 reservations outside the U.S., 800/352–7900 customer service* ⊕ *www. budget.com.* **Europcar.** ☎ *010/6661–1027* ⊕ *www. europcar.com.* **Hertz.** ✉ *Cairo* ☎ *800/654–3131 U.S. and Canada, 800/654– 3001 international* ⊕ *hertz. com.*

🌐 Passport

INFORMATION U.S. Department of State—Egypt International Travel Information. ⊕ *travel.state. gov/content/travel/en/ international-travel/International-Travel-Country-Information-Pages/Egypt. html*. **U.S. Department of State—Passport Information.** ✉ *Cairo* ☎ *877/487–2778* ⊕ *travel.state.gov/content/ travel/en/passports.html*.

🚗 Ride-Sharing

INFORMATION Careem. ⊕ *www.careem.com/ en-ae*. **inDriver.** ⊕ *indriver. com/en*. **Swvl.** ⊕ *www. swvl.com*. **Uber.** ⊕ *www. uber.com*.

🚕 Taxi

INFORMATION City Cab (yellow). ✉ *Cairo* ☎ *19155*. **Tawsila.** ☎ *011/2909–7249 to schedule via Whatsapp, 010/3257–0424 to schedule by phone*.

🚆 Train

INFORMATION Egyptian National Railways. ☎ *15047* Hotline ⊕ *enr.gov.eg*.

SLEEPER TRAINS Ernst–Watania Sleeping Trains. ✉ *Ramses Station, Cairo* ☎ *02/3748–9388* ⊕ *www. wataniasleepingtrains. com*.

🛂 Visa

INFORMATION Egypt E-Visa Portal. ⊕ *www.visa2egypt. gov.eg*.

📍 Visitor Information

BEFORE YOU LEAVE Egyptian Tourist Authority. ✉ *Cairo* ⊕ *www.egypt. travel*.

IN EGYPT Ministry of Tourism and Antiquities. ✉ *Zamalek head office, 3 El Adel Abou Bakr St., Downtown* ☎ *02/2735–4532* ⊕ *egy-monuments.gov.eg*.

ONLINE RESOURCES Cairo Scene. ✉ *Cairo* ⊕ *www. cairoscene.com*. **Egyptian Streets.** ✉ *Cairo* ⊕ *www. egyptianstreets.com*. **Egypt Today.** ✉ *Cairo* ⊕ *www. egypttoday.com*.

Great Itineraries

The Classic Tour of Egypt

10 DAYS

This 10-day tour will give you a whistle-stop introduction to Egypt's big-hitter attractions and ancient sites. The days are full, and you'll constantly be on the move, but the awe and wonder you'll experience make this worthwhile.

CAIRO

1 Day. Hit the ground running with an action-packed day in Cairo's museums, whose artifacts make a great introduction to the ancient sites you'll see later in your trip. Start at the Egyptian Museum (pre-arrange a guided tour). The salmon-pink palace on Tahrir Square opened in 1902, making it the Middle East's oldest archaeological museum.

Have lunch in one of the old-school cafés or restaurants around the labyrinthine Khan el-Khalili market and get tangled up in its narrow streets shopping for the perfect souvenir. Later in the afternoon, get to know the pharaohs at the National Museum of Egyptian Civilization, home to a cache of royal mummies and well-displayed collections of items from throughout Egypt's ages.

Alternatively, you could spend the day in one of the Middle East's newest archaeological museums: the Grand Egyptian Museum, roughly a mile from the Pyramids of Giza. This architecturally significant facility has been designed as a truly modern repository of artifacts culled from other Cairo museums and elsewhere. *(See Ch. 3, Cairo)*

GIZA AND SAQQARA

1 Day. You might have flown over them or spotted them looming on the horizon, but nothing beats seeing the Pyramids of Giza up close. Set on a plateau at Cairo's western edge, these monumental wonders are Egypt's most enduring icons. But they are not the oldest. To see that, head, instead, to Saqqara, a necropolis roughly 20 km (12 miles) south of Giza. It's nearly 50 centuries old and is one of Egypt's most active archaeological sites. *(See Ch. 3, Cairo)*

LUXOR

2 Days. Fly or take the night train to Luxor, which has one of the world's most impressive collections of ancient sites. Spend half a day under the towering canopy of columns at Karnak Temples and then walk the Avenue of Sphinxes to Luxor Temple, still an in-use religious site with a mosque built straight into the temple's foundations.

On the second day, explore the many monuments of Luxor's West Bank. The vividly painted tombs in the Valley of the Kings, the resting place of New Kingdom pharaohs including Tutankhamun, are the unmissable attractions on this side of the Nile, but you'll find plenty more temples and tombs to add to your itinerary, from the modernist-looking Mortuary Temple of Hatshepsut to off-the-beaten-track tombs in Deir el-Medina. *(See Ch. 5, Luxor and the Nile Valley)*

NILE CRUISE FROM LUXOR TO ASWAN

4 Days. There's no better way to experience the Nile than by getting out on the water, and taking a river cruise will also tick a few more temples off your sightseeing checklist. Large Nile cruisers leave from Luxor while traditional two-sail *dahabiyas* depart from the small town of Esna farther south. Float by the lush riverside greenery of palm trees and reeds, watching rural Upper Egypt go by from the pool on the sun deck. You'll stop off at the Temple of Horus in Edfu and the Temple of Kom Ombo before arriving in Aswan a few days later. *(See Ch. 8 Cruising the Nile and Lake Nasser)*

ASWAN AND ABU SIMBEL

2 Days. If you're still hungry for temples, make a beeline to Philae, set on a beautiful island in the Nile between Aswan's two dams. For a more laid-back experience of the city, hire a *felucca*, a small traditional sailboat, to glide among Aswan's Nile islands or head to Elephantine Island or Aswan's West Bank for a taste of Nubian hospitality in cafés painted in cheerful colors.

Make advance arrangements to travel the next morning to Abu Simbel by plane or on an overland tour to see the four mighty colossi of Ramses II guarding the entrance to his temple. Back in Aswan, you can recharge with a drink on a riverside terrace before flying back to Cairo. *(See Ch. 6, Aswan and Lake Nasser)*

Great Itineraries

Egypt in Depth

1 MONTH

The country is packed with ancient temples, tombs, and monuments, but standard itineraries rush you to the big hitters, bypassing less-visited sites that merit exploration. Even in busy cities like Cairo and Luxor, it's easy to take things at a slower pace. More time might even allow for an exceptional experience—like having 3,000-year-old ruins all to yourself.

CAIRO

4 Days. Spend a few days poking around Cairo's major museums and delve deeper into history with visits to the tile-covered Manial Palace, Saladin's historic Citadel, Islamic Cairo's stunning mosques, and the informative Coptic Museum. *(See Ch. 3, Cairo)*

GIZA, SAQQARA, AND DAHSHUR

1 Day. Get your pyramid fix on a day trip west of Cairo. The Pyramids of Giza will take your breath away at first sight, but you can go even deeper in history at Saqqara, where archaeologists seem to discover something new daily. Learn still more about the evolution and refinement of ancient Egyptian pyramid construction at the Red Pyramid and Bent Pyramid in Dahshur. *(See Ch. 3, Cairo)*

ALEXANDRIA

2 Days. Hop on a morning train for the three-hour journey to Alexandria. Fast-forward to Egypt's Greek and Roman eras at the Alexandria National Museum, the eerie catacombs at Kom el-Shoqafa, and Pompey's Pillar, which was erected in honor of the Roman emperor Diocletian, in 298 CE. In the evening, wind down at a seafood restaurant overlooking the Mediterranean. The next day, stroll the seaside Corniche to Fort Qaitbay, a 15th-century citadel, before taking a free tour of the Bibliotheca Alexandrina, the reincarnated library and cultural center from antiquity. In the evening, return to Cairo. From there, travel onward to Luxor by sleeper train or plane. *(See Ch. 4, Alexandria)*

LUXOR

5 Days. Luxor has one of the world's greatest concentrations of ancient monuments, so spend four days exploring both sides of the Nile, a generous amount of time to take in the majesty of the important sites like the Valley of the Kings as well as the quieter areas of Deir el-Medina and the Tombs of the Nobles. On your last day in town, sign up for a day trip tour to Dendera and Abydos to appreciate the lesser-visited temples dedicated to Hathor, the goddess of motherhood and joy, and Osiris, the god of the afterlife. *(See Ch. 5, Luxor and the Nile Valley)*

NILE CRUISE: LUXOR TO ASWAN

5 Days. Spend nearly a week on the water as you chug upriver in a Nile cruiser or sail in a traditional *dahabiya*, making stops at ancient sites along the way. Both types of boats stop at the temples in Edfu and Kom Ombo, but *dahabiya* itineraries usually include additional time in Esna, El-Kab, and other places where larger ships can't dock. *(See Ch. 8, Cruising the Nile and Lake Nasser)*

ASWAN

4 Days. Take laid-back Aswan at a slower pace. The city has plenty for history geeks to explore, including the Nubia Museum and the Temple of Isis at Philae.

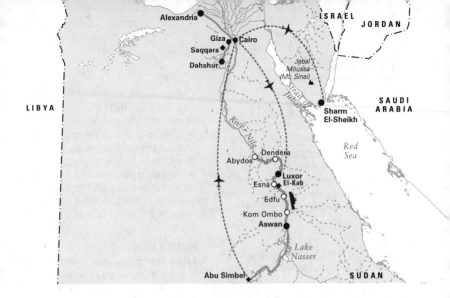

Aswan is also the best place to sail on a traditional *felucca*. Indeed, you must hire a boat of some kind to reach a few of Aswan's Nile islands. If possible, take an overnight *felucca* journey, sleeping on the boat under the stars. On your last day, make sure your phone is fully charged for a photo stroll through the colorfully painted Nubian villages on Elephantine Island and Gharb Soheil. *(See Ch. 6, Aswan and Lake Nasser)*

LAKE NASSER CRUISE: ASWAN TO ABU SIMBEL

5 Days. The temples along the shores of Lake Nasser were rescued from the rising waters by a massive UNESCO project, but they remain firmly off the tourist radar. The only way to see most of them and to get the best view of one of the world's largest man-made bodies of water is aboard a Lake Nasser cruise. The trip ends in Abu Simbel, which you'll be able to enjoy more quietly and at your own pace once the day-trippers have departed. *(See Ch. 8, Cruising the Nile and Lake Nasser)*

SHARM EL-SHEIKH

4 Days. Get a taste of Egypt's wild side in Sinai. Fly from Abu Simbel to Sharm el-Sheikh via Cairo and relax at a resort pool or on the beach after a busy day of travel. Expect to spend most of your time here underwater, diving or snorkeling among the colorful fish and coral in the bountiful Red Sea. *(See Ch. 7, Sharm el-Sheikh and the Red Sea Coast)*

Great Itineraries

Culture and the Coasts

10 DAYS

You can't beat Egypt's historic temples and tombs, but if you want to combine ancient sites with the sea, set out on this itinerary, which takes in the culture of the country's two largest cities before hitting the coast.

CAIRO

2 Days. Dive into Egypt's history in the museums scattered around the capital. If you can't wait to get out on the water, sign up for a kayak tour on the Nile or have dinner on a boat. *(See Ch. 3, Cairo)*

ALEXANDRIA

2 Days. Enjoy Egypt's Mediterranean coast from Alexandria. Make the most of this seaside city by touring the waterfront Citadel of Qaitbay, strolling the crescent-shaped Corniche, and digging into a huge grilled fish dinner at a water-view restaurant. *(See Ch. 4, Alexandria)*

SHARM EL-SHEIKH

3 Days. Start your beach vacation properly by flying to Sharm el-Sheikh via Cairo. Chill out and catch some rays poolside or on the beach before suiting up in diving or snorkeling gear to swim among the flitting fish and beautiful coral reefs near Sharm or in Ras Mohamed National Park. *(See Ch. 7, Sharm el-Sheikh and the Red Sea)*

HURGHADA

3 Days. For Egypt's best diving, take a ferry or flight farther south on the Red Sea to Hurghada. Put on your mask for more diving or snorkeling, or stay above water and ride the wind on a kite- or windsurfing board. *(See Ch. 7, Sharm el-Sheikh and the Red Sea Coast)*

Chapter 3

CAIRO

WITH ABU SIR, MEMPHIS, SAQQARA,
DASHUR, AND THE FAYYUM

Updated by
Monica Gerges

 Sights
★★★★★

 Restaurants
★★★★☆

 Hotels
★★★★☆

 Shopping
★★★★☆

 Nightlife
★★★★☆

WELCOME TO CAIRO

TOP REASONS TO GO

★ **The panoramic view of the Pyramids of Giza:** Gaze out onto the only remaining wonder of the ancient world, and, when you're ready, snap a timeless photograph of the iconic sight.

★ **King Tut:** Come face-to-face with Tutankhamun's gold funerary mask—and other treasures from his tomb—at the Grand Egyptian Museum.

★ **The call to prayer:** Stand in Islamic Cairo at sunset and bask in the resonance of the muezzins' calls from hundreds of minarets in the area.

★ **Bettering your bargaining:** Always pay less than the first asking price for that must-have treasure at Cairo's famous Khan el-Khalili souk.

★ **The nightlife:** Enjoy a cocktail or a cold beer in one of Zamalek's many trendy nightlife spots.

1 Islamic Cairo North. Khan el-Khalili bazaar anchors this area.

2 Islamic Cairo South. A tightly knit district of historic mosques, madrasas, and mansions.

3 The Citadel. For centuries, Egypt was ruled from this lofty fortress.

4 Old Cairo (Coptic Cairo). Cairo's Christian heartbeat emanates from churches here.

5 Downtown Cairo. The city's epicenter is home to the must-see Egyptian Museum of Antiquities.

6 Rodah Island and Garden City. In the 19th and early 20th centuries, expat communities thrived in these districts.

7 Gezira Island and Zamalek. This island neighborhood has popular wine-and-dine spots and the superlative Cairo Opera House.

8 Giza. The plateau famous for its ancient pyramids is now embraced by modern suburbs.

9 Heliopolis. Unique architecture marks this affluent district.

10 New Cairo. Built to alleviate Downtown Cairo's congestion, this fast-growing district has many dining, shopping, and entertainment options.

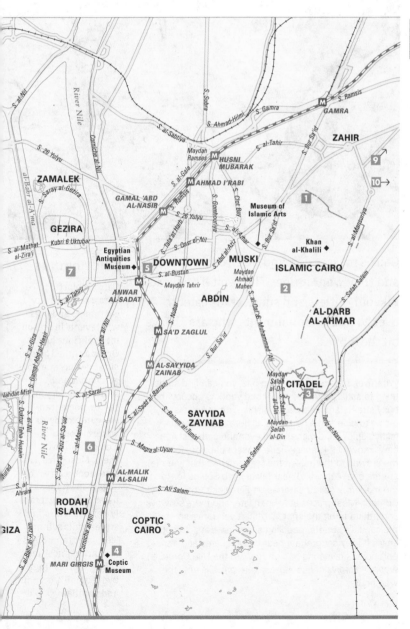

STREET FOOD IN CAIRO

Preparing shawarma

Cairo's masses demand tasty, cheap food, and they want it now. The capital's myriad takeout outlets and snack stalls cater to over 20 million inhabitants who are always on the move.

Wherever, whenever a craving hits, you can find something to satisfy it. An army of food vendors occupy the busy streets and sidewalks, dishing out quick, tasty meals to diners in a hurry. It's all here: grilled meats, felafel, spicy sandwiches, and even the carb-fest in a bowl known as *koshary*. For a feast of choices, follow the crowds to the hole-in-the wall eateries that line the streets of al-Azhar and near Talaat Harb Square, or to the modern-inspired eateries on Zamalek's 26th of July Corridor. Most places stay open late, and there's always something to hit the spot. Pushcart vendors also ply the capital's streets, peddling seeds, sweets, and other snacks. They congregate near busy squares and transport hubs, gravitating at night toward the Nile Corniche, where a carnivalesque atmosphere prevails until the wee hours.

JUICY DRINKS

Cairo's colorful juice bars attract thirsty customers and press whatever is in season into delicious juices. Order a chilled glass of tangerine, mango, guava, banana, strawberry, lemon, carrot, pomegranate, cantaloupe, or watermelon juice—or a combination of them. Most juice bars also stock a forest of sugarcane for making *aseer asab* (sugarcane juice). You'll also find street stalls selling iced *aseer tamr hindi* (tamarind juice) and *sobia* (a refreshing blend of milk, coconut, and vanilla).

FUL MEDAMES

This slow-cooked stew of whole and mashed fava beans and spices—served in a bowl or within a piece of *aish baladi* (Egyptian flatbread)—for breakfast, lunch, or dinner—is considered a national dish. Packed with protein and carbohydrates, it's filling, nutritious (if you go easy on the oil), and affordable.

Tasty variations include *ful iskandarani* (with chopped tomatoes, onions, and coriander) and *ful bil zeit al-harr* (with hot, spicy, flaxseed oil). Watch for *ful naabit,* marinated, ready-to-sprout fava beans often served as bar snacks. Toss the outer skin, and eat the bean—you'll never want to go back to peanuts.

Ful medames

TA'AMIYA

Made from ground fava beans instead of chickpeas, Egypt's version of felafel is mixed with fresh herbs and fried to perfection. It's typically shaped as a patty to perfectly fit inside *aish baladi*, but also comes in *ammatty* (balls), which are served as a side dish, or *eggah*, a plate-sized patty with eggs mixed into the batter. *Ta'amiya* sandwiches typically have lettuce, tomato, and tahini (sesame-seed paste).

SHAWARMA

Marinated lamb, beef, or chicken grilled on a slowly rotating vertical spit is a Middle Eastern favorite. Slices are shaved off and stuffed—along with vegetables and tahini—into flatbread or small buns. Some places also add grilled tomatoes, onions, parsley, and spices.

KOSHARY

The king of Egyptian street food is a fusion of macaroni, rice, noodles, lentils, chickpeas, and crispy fried onions, all crowned with a spicy tomato sauce and a dash of *da'ah* (Egyptian garlic-vinegar sauce). It's cheap, delicious, and will keep you fueled for hours.

FITEER

What's often described as Egyptian pizza is made from flaky phylo-like pastry lightly coated with ghee (clarified butter). It's served plain or with your choice of sweet or savory fillings and toppings—from raisins, coconut flakes, pistachios, honey, jam, and custard to cheese, oriental sausages, and eggs with *basturma* (seasoned, air-dried beef) onions, peppers, and olives. It's made at a specialized bakery known as a *fatatri*, which consists of little more than a brick oven, a rolling board, and a few tables.

The king of Egyptian street food: koshary

The scale of this city can best be described as epic. The traffic, the roughly 21 million people, and the sleepless rhythm all reinforce this impression, threatening to overwhelm you. At its core, though, Cairo is a collection of districts that feel more intimate than the city as a whole, especially if you take your time wandering quiet back alleys and relaxing over mint tea.

Like so much else in Egypt, history is at the heart of Cairo's charm. Many of its areas are made up of the physical remains of a thousand years of being conquered by different groups. The city didn't fully begin, as you might expect, with the pharaohs. They'd quartered themselves in nearby Memphis and Heliopolis, areas only recently overtaken by outward urban sprawl.

The Pyramids of Giza, on the west bank of the Nile, mislead foreigners in their search for the origins of Cairo, which had always been an east-bank city. It's only since the 1960s that the Greater Cairo Metropolitan Area moved faster than the river, leaping the banks and drawing in the endless modern suburbs on the west bank.

Cairo's modern history begins with a Roman trading outpost called Babylon—now known as Old Cairo or Coptic Cairo—at the mouth of a canal that once connected the Nile to the Red Sea. But it was the 7th-century Arab conquerors who were largely responsible for founding the city we know today with their encampment at Fustat, just north of Old Cairo. Under their leader Amr Ibn al-As, the Arabs took over land that had already seen Greek, Persian, and Roman occupation.

In the millennium that followed, the city was ruled by the Fatimids (969–1171), the Ayyubids (1171–1250), the Mamluks (1250–1517), and the Ottomans (1517–1798). It then went through 150 years of French and British colonial administration, culminating in the 1952 revolution, which finally returned power to Egyptian hands.

What makes Cairo unique is that each new set of rulers chose to build a new city upwind from the old one instead of reconstructing what they had conquered. As a result, you can follow the progression of the historic center of Cairo from a bird's-eye view above the Nile. It follows a path from Old Cairo in the south, curving north through Fustat, east to Islamic Cairo, and then west to the colonial Downtown district.

The city now also extends to the Zamalek, al-Manial, and Rodah islands, with districts on both sides including Heliopolis and, most recently, New Cairo. Cairo has settled for the moment, with its historic areas beating the strongest, but the heart threatens to relocate again with the construction of the New Administrative Capital.

Although they've changed since their founding, each of Cairo's districts retains a distinct identity. This can be felt not only in buildings, but also among its residents and their way of life. Pre-Islamic Babylon is, to this day, a predominantly Christian area, and Islamic Cairo is still where families go during the holy month of Ramadan to spend the night eating and relaxing after a day of fasting.

Indeed, one of the joys of Cairo is that its historic areas remain spirited living spaces and not open-air museums. The past here is more a state of mind than a historical fact—and that, ultimately, is the way in which the city is truly overwhelming.

Planning

Planning Your Time

You don't realize just how big Cairo is until you're on your way from the airport to a Downtown Cairo hotel. Drives can take so long that you might think you've changed cities. Amazingly, what you see on the way into town from the airport is only half of the city. Cairo's west-bank sister city of Giza stretches all the way to the Pyramids, miles from Downtown Cairo.

If you are the sort of person who instinctively navigates by compass points, exploring Cairo will be a breeze. The Nile works like a giant north–south needle running through the center of the city. If not, you might find the city bewildering at first.

If you're asking for directions, taxi drivers mainly know major streets and landmarks. And while Egyptians are always eager to help, pedestrians can often be unsure of directions unless they're from the area, so don't count on always being shown the right way. The fact that many streets have old and new names can be confusing as well, so it's best to navigate with a maps application on your phone. Just go with the flow and try to think of every wrong turn as a chance for discovery.

Thankfully, you don't have to conquer all of Cairo to get the most out of it. Much of the city was built in the 1960s, and the new areas hold relatively little historical or cultural interest. The older districts, with the exception of Giza's ancient sights, are all on the east bank and are easily accessible by taxi, ride-hailing applications, or the Metro. These districts become relatively straightforward targets for a day's exploration on foot.

Old Cairo is on the east bank a couple miles south of most of current-day Cairo. Just north of it is Fustat, site of the 7th-century Arab settlement, and east of that is the Citadel. North of the Citadel is the medieval walled district of al-Qahira, which gave the city its name. It's better known today as Islamic Cairo. West of that is the colonial district now known as Downtown Cairo. It is one of several—including Garden City, Heliopolis, and Zamalek—laid out by Europeans in the 19th and 20th centuries. The most interesting sights are in the older districts, while the newer ones have the highest concentrations of hotels, restaurants, and shops.

Although the pyramids are usually at the top of everyone's itinerary, it is more interesting to work your way back through the city's history and end with its pharaonic origins. So start with **Khan el-Khalili**, the great medieval souk, and wander the narrow alleys of nearby **Islamic Cairo** to soak up the texture of life in the city. In a full day, you can explore the surface of Old Cairo, seeing both its Islamic and Coptic core. The **Pyramids of Giza** and the **Sphinx** can be seen in a half day, but also spend a half day at **Memphis** and **Saqqara,** or at the less-visited **Abu Sir** and **Dahshur.** Another day can be spent in **Fayyum,** where you might even enjoy an overnight stay.

When to Go

Cairo weather is uncomfortable for only a couple of months a year. Spring and autumn are gorgeous, with warm days and cool nights, though spring brings the *khamaseen* dust storms that can last a couple of days. Summer is *very* hot but relatively dry, and winter is brief—three months at most—yet chillier than you might expect at night. The city gets a few rainy days a year, mostly in winter.

Ramadan, the holy month of fasting, brings both rewards and inconveniences. The city overflows with hearty cooking, Middle Eastern desserts, and special celebrations—the festivities create an unmatched vibe and make for a great experience. Fasting lasts from sunrise to sunset, with operating hours changing almost everywhere to account for the Ramadan day. Some establishments, mostly bars, also shut down during the month, but foreigners can still enjoy a drink in hotel restaurants and bars.

Getting Here and Around

AIR

Cairo International Airport is the main entry point for flights, and it receives the most international arrivals over any other airport in Egypt. As a result, it's regularly refurbished to expand the capacity of its transit halls. The airport is divided into three terminals: Terminal 1 is exclusive to domestic flights, Terminal 2 is for most international flights, and Terminal 3 is reserved for Egyptair flights and its Star Alliance partners.

Right outside the airport, the luxurious VIP Arrival and Departure Hall welcomes first-class passengers, as well as those who are willing to pay extra for an elevated waiting experience. Here, you can rest in deluxe lounges while your paperwork and luggage are being processed and checked.

AIRPORT TRANSFERS

If your hotel hasn't arranged your transportation to/from the airport, you can take Metro Line 3, which runs to Embaba Station, or you can opt for a taxi, limousine, or ride-hailing service. Cairo taxis are white with a black-and-white checkered line on each side; limousines are all black. The minute you exit the arrivals hall, you'll be inundated with offers from drivers.

Although cabbies should have their meters running, most won't, and this will be your first opportunity to test out your bargaining skills. You should be able to get the price down to around LE200.

If you'd rather ride in a limousine, opt for one of the companies set up in the arrivals hall, or reserve a London Cab beforehand through its mobile application (London Cab Egypt). The fare to central Cairo hotels is about LE400. Ride-hailing companies include Uber, Careem, Indriver, and DiDi, all of which offer reasonable fares.

BUS
TO AND FROM CAIRO

Buses are an affordable and generally safe way of traveling between cities. It's wise to buy your ticket at least a couple of days in advance, especially during peak periods. Long bus rides can be uncomfortable, but, on trips of more than three hours, drivers usually take breaks so everyone can stretch their legs.

■TIP→ **Note that security authorities discourage independent bus travel on routes** down the Nile Valley and prefer that visitors travel by train or plane. Both are modes of travel that can more easily be kept under surveillance by relatively small numbers of officers.

Popular bus companies include Go Bus Egypt, East Delta Travel, SuperJet, and Blue Bus Egypt. Most buses in Cairo depart from the Cairo Gateway Station (previously Torgoman Station) off El-Galaa street, in Downtown Cairo, and have other stops around the city.

WITHIN CAIRO

City buses are usually busy, but they are far and away Cairo's cheapest mode of transportation at LE5– LE15 per ticket. Buses arrive at and depart from stations at Tahrir Square, Attaba Square, Opera Square, Al Haram Street, Ramses Station, and the Citadel. Route numbers aren't always clearly visible on the bus, so it's best to ask where a bus is heading before it departs with you on board.

The Cairo Transport Authority also manages a fleet of air-conditioned buses that are surprisingly convenient and affordable. You can make them out by their yellow color and the "CTA" logo on the side. While buses generally follow a preset course, you can flag them down or ask the driver to let you off at any point along the route.

Mwasalat Misr, which is also considered a public transportation company, offers a well-priced localized experience, and you can use its mobile application to easily view routes, stations, and schedules. Schedules are also available through Google Maps. You'll need to have your app store location set to Egypt so you can download the Mwasalat Misr application.

Airport–Shobra Line, No. 111:
Cairo Airport Bus Station – Airport Bridge – Al Galaa Bridge – Baron Palace – Cairo International Fair – Ghamra Station – Ramsis Railways Station – Dawaran Shobra

Cairo Airport–Bulaq Dakrur Line, No. 381:
Cairo Airport Bus Station – Airport Bridge – Al Galaa Bridge – Baron Palace – El Nour Mosque – Maspiro – Zamalek Central – Geziret El Arab St – Bulaq Dakrur Terminal

Tahrir Square–Fifth Settlement, M5:
Tahrir Square (Abdel Moneim Riad Square) – Ghamra Station – El-Sekka El-Hadeed Club – Downtown Mall – Air Force Specialized Hospital – Dusit Hotel – AUC Terminal – Lotus Terminal

Saray El Qouba–AUC/Fifth Settlement, M6:
Saray El Qouba Terminal – Roxy Square – Administrative Control Authority – Child Park – Central Nasr City – Cairo Festival Mall – Air Force Specialized Hospital – Dusit Hotel – Lotus Terminal

Hadayek Al Ahram–Tahrir Square, M7:
Khafraa Gate – Remaya Square – Mariouteya – Giza Metro Station – Cairo University – Garden City – Tahrir Square (Abdel Moneim Riad Square)

Sixth of October–Tahrir, M10:
October Terminal – October University – Mall of Arabia – Hyper One – Ring Road – Marriott Hotel – Hilton Ramsis – Tahrir Square (Abdel Moneim Riad Square)

Hadayek Al Ahram–Nasr City, M11:
Khafraa Gate – Marriott Mena House – Giza Metro Station – Giza Zoo – Magra Al Eyoon – Salah Al-Din Castle – Al Azhar University – City Starts Terminal

While Cairo's streets are also packed with microbuses—white, privately-owned 12-seaters—we don't recommend them as your first choice. They don't have line numbers and are notoriously difficult to navigate. Alternatively, many ride-hailing applications, most prominently Uber, offer clean, comfortable, and well-timed bus rides with organized routes. These are a far safer option, they are regulated, and they will get you to your destination for a fraction of the price of a taxi or a car ride.

Evening on the Corniche: boats docked along the embankment and views of Gezira, the Nile's largest island.

CAR

Driving in Cairo is not an easy feat. As the local saying goes, if you manage to drive in Cairo, you'll manage to drive anywhere in the world. Even if you are up to the challenge of driving in the city, parking is usually an even greater challenge, and you'll spend a lot of time trying to find a parking space.

While we strongly discourage it, many major car rental agencies have offices in Cairo if you insist on taking the leap. You also have the option of hiring a car and driver.

CAR RENTALS Avis. ⊠ *Cairo International Airport, Cairo* ☎ *10/0107–7400* ⊕ *www. avis.com.* **Budget.** ⊠ *Cairo International Airport, Cairo* ☎ *11/4443–9138* ⊕ *www. budget.com.* **Europcar.** ⊠ *Cairo International Airport, Cairo* ☎ *19348 Hotline* ⊕ *www.europcar.com.eg.* **Hertz.** ⊠ *Cairo International Airport, Cairo* ☎ *10/6505–5558* ⊕ *www.hertz.eg.* **Sixt Rent-a-Car.** ⊠ *Cairo International Airport, Cairo* ☎ *19670 Hotline* ⊕ *www.sixtegypt.com.*

METRO

Although it's overcrowded and oppressively hot in the summer (air-conditioned carriages are available, but you'll have to wait for them), the Metro is reliable and cheap. It runs from 5:30 am to 1 am (2 am during Ramadan), with trains arriving every 2 to 5 minutes. Tickets, sold at booths in stations, cost LE5 for up to 9 stops, LE7 for 10–16 stops, and LE10 for anything beyond that. There are no weekly or monthly passes at the moment.

Three primary lines crisscross the city: Line 1 runs from El-Marg El-Gadidah Station to Helwan Station; Line 2 runs from Shubra El-Kheima station to Giza station; and Line 3 runs from Cairo Airport to Embaba Station. A fourth line, linking central Cairo with the Giza Pyramid Complex, is under construction; two more lines are in the planning stages.

Line maps are available at every station as well as online. Be sure to check them to track your route and determine whether or not you'll need to change lines to reach your destination.

Each train has carriages reserved for women and children, as indicated by signs on platforms. To avoid being hassled or groped, women traveling alone are advised to opt for one of these, especially during rush hour, and to find a comfortable corner away from the crowd when possible. Dressing modestly is a good idea, too.

TAXI

The first rule for taking a white taxi in Cairo is making sure that the meter is on. Otherwise, you'll either fall victim to exorbitant fares, or you'll lose time and energy bargaining with the driver. If you're in a hurry and a meterless taxi is more convenient, bargain the price down before getting in, and always hail a taxi off the street after walking a few meters away from the hotel; it's cheaper. Better yet, opt for one of the many ride-hailing application services available—Uber, Careem, InDriver, or DiDi.

Fares vary according to the time of day and the distance you cover; they increase by some 40%–50% in the very early morning and late at night. During the day and in the evening, a 20-minute ride from Tahrir Square to the Pyramids of Giza should cost about LE80 for one-way; a 5- to 10-minute ride should cost no more than LE20. If you are going a long distance, such as all the way to Saqqara in Giza, the ride should cost about LE120 for one-way. You should also arrange with your driver beforehand to wait for you because it is extremely difficult to get a cab back to the city from there. With waiting, this may push the price up to around LE300–LE350 in total.

When giving directions, name a major landmark near your destination (rather than a street address), such as Tahrir Square or al-Azhar University, and as you get closer to the destination, give more specifics to avoid confusion. If you find a friendly taxi driver who has a clean air-conditioned car, stick with them. Negotiate a day rate of LE150–LE400,

depending on your needs. Tip generously; a good driver can introduce you to many ins and outs around the city that will make your stay more convenient.

TRAIN

All railway lines from Cairo depart from and arrive at Ramses Station, 2 miles (3 km) northeast of Tahrir Square. Trains traveling to and from Alexandria, Nile Delta towns, and Suez Canal cities use tracks 1–7 at the station's main hall. Trains to al-Minya, Luxor, and Aswan depart from platforms 8, 9, 10, and 11 outside the main hall.

There are several daily connections between Cairo and Alexandria, making a trip between the two cities convenient and accessible at all times. Travel times range between 4 to 5 hours and tickets cost LE55–LE70, depending on the class of service you book.

Long-distance and sleeper trains connect Cairo, Luxor, and Aswan. The trains are operated by Abela Egypt, and you should buy your tickets 10 days in advance during peak periods to guarantee your spot. You can purchase them in-person at the station, through a travel agent or a tour company, or online.

CONTACTS Ernst Watania Sleeping Trains. ☎ *12/1183–1987, 12/1184–3479* ⊕ *www. wataniasleepingtrains.com.*

Hotels

Cairo has its fair share of five-star hotels (as rated by the Egyptian Hotel Association) scattered across the city. Since they aim to emulate the modern look and feel of their international peers, they, unfortunately, don't exemplify the distinctive atmosphere of the capital. There are certainly exceptions, and what some lack in traditional character, they make up for in quality. Top-end hotels offer all the facilities and modern conveniences you need to recuperate after a long day of sightseeing and shopping. Outside the five-star range, Cairo's options quickly grow limited, though there are still a few budget-oriented hotels that fit the bill.

Cairo's top hotels are all affordable by international standards, and you can pay premiums for a Nile- or Pyramids-view room at hotels overlooking either. While authorities rate all hotels on a five-star scale, not all of them live up to their stars. High seasons vary; August and September are crowded with Gulf Arabs; December, January, and Easter are peaks for Europeans; and major Islamic holidays see a lot of local and regional guests.

■TIP→ **Many hotels quote prices in U.S. dollars or euros, but if you pay with a credit card, your payment might be charged in the equivalent of Egyptian pounds.**

Hotel reviews have been shortened. For full information, visit Fodors.com. Hotel prices are the lowest cost of a standard double room in high season, excluding taxes and service charges.

What it Costs in U.S. Dollars			
$	$$	$$$	$$$$
HOTELS			
Under $200	$200–$300	$301–$400	Over $400

Nightlife

Cairo's nightlife perfectly reflects the city's general atmosphere—it's vibrant and energetic, and yet it defies easy definition. Most locations move seamlessly from early evening aperitifs to mid-evening dining to late-night dancing. A few embrace more distinct personas, with dive bars, sports bars, cocktail lounges, and nightclubs regularly popping up around the city. The clientele is a cosmopolitan mix of wealthy Egyptians, foreign residents and workers, and international visitors. In the summer, Cairo is a favored destination for Gulf

tourists, many of whom come to enjoy the city's clubs and bars. Popular clubs usually close around 2 am, though some close earlier.

Once a favorite performing art, belly dancing had slowly fallen out of favor over the years with both Egyptians and visitors alike. It's recently been seeing a slow comeback among crowds, especially at weddings. Your best bet if you want to see tame versions of these once risqué performances is to visit nightclubs or parties with scheduled belly-dancing shows. You can also visit one of the five-star hotels in the city, where they usually schedule nightly belly-dancing performances at one of their restaurants, or opt for a Nile cruise that hosts them regularly. In either case, make sure to call ahead and reserve a table.

Performing Arts

Cairo's cultural scene is one of its defining and best attributes. You'll be able to attend a classical Arabic music concert in a restored medieval house one day, take in a performance of *La Bohème* by the Cairo Opera Company the next day, and then watch dervishes whirl in an old palace the day after that. You can then choose to end the week on a club's dance floor hosting a collaboration between a local DJ and a visual artist. One of the best in the Middle East, Cairo's nightlife is known for bars and clubs that attract vacationing Gulf Arabs as well as Western visitors and expats. Occasionally, the two fuse together—a jazz concert of trumpet and *oud* (an Arabic stringed instrument), for example—in a style that is unique to this city. For the latest listings of events, check *Cairo 360, Cairo Gossip, Cairo Nights Out,* or Google "events schedule Cairo," and a list will come up. Always call ahead to double-check performances because arrangements can go awry.

Restaurants

Cairo's restaurant scene has exponentially taken off over the last decade. Eating out is a regular form of entertainment for all Egyptians across the board, with options ranging from a modest day out having street food to an expensive gastronomic experience at a high-end restaurant. Naturally, Egyptian cuisine is still the popular choice among locals, and Cairo is a hub for the best of the country's specialties. Local eateries mainly compete on quality of ingredients, special recipes, and prep time. Other cuisine options have also expanded dramatically over the years to include authentic and fusion versions of Indian, Thai, Chinese, French, Italian, and Japanese.

Local beers, including Stella Premium, Luxor, and Sakara, are served at many restaurants around Cairo. You'll also find locally brewed Heineken and Desperados in most bars. They're often accompanied by a range of local wines that include the top-rate Grand Marquis label; the passable Omar Khayyam, Shahrazade, and Beausoleil; and a much less wonderful Obelisk.

Egyptians eat late; lunch is usually from 1 pm to 3 pm, and dinner often starts at 8 pm or 9 pm. Some restaurants even continue to serve their breakfast menu well past noon. Most restaurants are open daily for both lunch and dinner, and they offer a casual environment where you can kick back and have a relaxed meal. Local beers and wines are not served in all restaurants, but are common enough to find. Expensive imported alcohol, however, is limited to top-end establishments. Although fancier places levy a 12% service charge, it is customary to leave a tip in inverse relation to the size of the bill. Tips range from 8% at expensive places to 12%–14% at cheaper ones.

Restaurant reviews have been shortened. For full information, visit Fodors.com. Restaurant prices are the average cost of a main course at dinner or, if dinner is not served, at lunch, excluding taxes and service charges.

What it Costs in Egyptian Pounds

	$	$$	$$$	$$$$
RESTAURANTS				
	Under LE50	LE50–LE150	LE151–LE250	Over LE250

Shopping

Cairo is a great place to shop for traditional items thanks to the spectacular market Khan el-Khalili, where browsing and bargaining are half the fun. In the Khan, the opening price is *never* the final price. There is no tried-and-true bargaining strategy; just look around, decide how much something is worth to you, and start bargaining lower than that to end up with the price you want. It's also useful to ask around in nearby shops to have an estimate of how much something costs, so you can negotiate from an informed position.

Shopping malls are now an integrated part of Cairo's blueprints. These enclosed, air-conditioned spaces stacked with international brands have revolutionized shopping for residents and visitors. You're also likely to find shops selling a range of the same kinds of souvenirs that you'd find in Khan el-Khalili, though at higher, non-negotiable prices.

Affluent Cairenes not only have the wherewithal to fund their lifestyles, they also have great taste. So, you'll find a wide selection of art galleries, designer shops, and fashion boutiques to indulge your need for retail therapy.

Although most shops today sell reproductions of varying quality, there is a long local tradition in Egypt of connoisseurship in collectibles. This means that there is always the possibility of finding a real gem. Much of the local taste does, however, lean toward ornate French-style furniture and antiques, and Middle Eastern pieces can be rare, but are not impossible to find. There are several nameless antiques shops in Downtown Cairo along Hoda Shaarawy street that are worth looking into. You will most likely not find these family-run stores on your maps, so a walk around that street might lead right to a treasure trove.

Tours

GUIDED TOURS

Cairo is awash with companies offering tours and guides, and it might prove difficult to pick the right one. To narrow your search, look for official tour guides to assure the quality of their services. They have to be licensed by the Egyptian authorities and must undergo a strict program of training and examination before they receive their accreditation. If you intend to visit the sites at Saqqara, Dahshur, Abu Sir, or Fayyum, we recommend you book a guided tour with a well-respected company or an accredited personal guide. This will not only take care of the travel and navigation arrangements, it will also give you access to an expert on hand to answer all your questions during the tour. Booking through a company will also manage any security issues or clearances required with police escorts.

If you are looking for a guided tour, your best bet is to try and set it up with a travel agent. Memphis Tours are a solid choice if you're looking for customized or preset tours around the city. Their diversified background and network of experts put together experiences that cater to all preferences. If you'd rather explore unusual or unfrequented hidden spots around the city, Walk Like An Egyptian is a great choice. They organize walking tours of varying lengths, all designed with Asmaa Khattab's (the founder) love for Egyptian heritage at their core. Bellies En-Route, a food tour service, offers a new and authentic way to experience the capital. Described by founders Mariam and Laila as "small, friendly, and genuine," they organize visits to some of the city's best local dining spots around its many different neighborhoods.

CONTACTS Bellies En Route. ✉ *Cairo* ⊕ *www.belliesenroute.com.* **Memphis Tours.** ✉ *Cairo* ☎ *2/3571–6050* ⊕ *www. memphistours.com.* **Walk Like An Egyptian.** ✉ *Cairo* ⊕ *www.facebook.com/ Walk.Like.An.Egyptian.Page.*

TRAVEL AGENCIES Empire Travel. ✉ *Cairo* ☎ *1205022280* ⊕ *www.empire.travel.*

Islamic Cairo North

Misr al-Mahrousa—a popular appellation that translates to "Egypt the Protected"—is one of the richest troves of Islamic architecture in the world. Cairo had been the capital of Islamic Egypt since its founding, and if the Mamluks hadn't stopped the Mongols' furious advance at Ain Jalut (Palestine) in AD 1260, the city might have been left in rubble. Today, Islamic architectural traditions continue to reverberate between Bab al-Futuh and Bab al-Nasr in the north and the Mosque of Amr Ibn al-As in the south. The areas remain home to a rare concentration of buildings that reflect major parts of the city's exceptional history.

The area is popularly known as Al-Hussein after the mosque (also known as Sayyidna al-Husayn) at the entrance of Khan el-Khalili. Originally built by the Fatimids in the 12th century as a shrine, this mosque is said to contain the head of Husayn, the Prophet's grandson, and is the spiritual heart of the Islamic city.

A view of Islamic Cairo over the massive, 12th-century Sayyidna al-Husayn (aka Al-Hussein) Mosque, one of Egypt's holiest sites.

A visit to this area should figure prominently on your itinerary. Unfortunately, Islamic monuments don't attract as many visitors as pharaonic ones, so, in the past, government funds for restoration were rarely allocated to them. But much of the al-Azhar area has recently undergone a facelift, with serious development, reconstruction, and restoration projects underway.

There's much to experience in the district, from sights and food to shopping and live performances. A walk along these time-honored streets studded with monuments from different eras offers a rare taste of the extravagant beauty that once characterized the heart of the city. It is a visit to the past, light years away from modern Cairo.

You can get a very good feel for the area in half a day, depending on how long you spend at each of the attractions. If browsing and bargaining interest you, it's easy to lose track of time in Khan el-Khalili, so leave enough time for a food break and shopping. Islamic sights are open from about 9 am until 4–5 pm, depending on schedules preset by the Ministry of Tourism and Antiquities. Keep in mind that most of the shops in Khan el-Khalili are closed on Sunday. Friday before noon is also a quieter time in the neighborhood.

 Sights

Al-Aqmar Mosque

MOSQUE | The name of the mosque means "the moonlit" and refers to the way the stone catches the moon's reflection at night. Built in 1125, it's one of a few Fatimid buildings that have escaped major alterations. The shell-like recesses in the stone facade, later to become a common decorative element, were used here for the first time. This little mosque was also the first in Cairo to have an ornamented stone facade, and it was the first to alter its plan according to the existing urban structure, as the street

An ablutions fountain anchors the stately courtyard of the 14th-century Mosque, Madrasa, and Khanqah of Sultan Barquq.

existed before the mosque. ⊠ *Al-Muizz St., Islamic Cairo North* 🖼 *Free.*

Al-Hakim Mosque (*Al-Anwar Mosque*)
MOSQUE | Built outside Cairo's origi-
nal walls (those standing now were
constructed in 1087), this mosque saw
varied usage during its lifetime. During
the Crusades it held European prisoners
of war who built a chapel inside it. Salah
al-Din (1137–1193) tore the chapel down
when he used the structure as a stable.
In the 19th century, Napoléon's troops
used it as a storehouse and fortress;
Muhammad Ali closed part of it off for
use as a *zawya* (small Sufi school); and,
until the establishment of the Museum
of Islamic Arts in 1896, it served as a
repository for Islamic treasures.

Originally built in 1010 by the Fatimid
caliph al-Hakim bi-Amr Allah, this gigantic
mosque was restored under the aegis
of the Aga Khan, spiritual leader of
the Isma'ili Shi'a sect. Al-Hakim was
an eccentric character. Some of the
strangest edicts were declared during his

caliphate, including one ban on *mulokhia*,
a favorite Egyptian dish (he didn't care
for it) and another on women's shoes (to
prevent them from going out in public). He liked riding around town on his
donkey to ensure that his orders were
being obeyed, but one night, he rode
off into the Mokattam hills, never to be
seen again. The Druze claim that he has
vanished only temporarily and will return
to lead them to victory.

Architecturally, the mosque's most
significant elements are its minarets,
which were restored and reinforced
by Baybars II in 1303, giving them that
impressive trapezoidal base. Nevertheless, its scale and history are important,
and its courtyard is large and breezy,
making it a comfortable place to rest or
meditate. ⊠ *Al-Muizz St., Islamic Cairo
North* 🖼 *Free.*

Bab al-Futuh (*the Futuh Gate*)
NOTABLE BUILDING | A small passage to
the left as you enter al-Hakim Mosque
leads to a stairway up to the roof, where

you can access the so-called Gate of Conquests, one of three still remaining in the walls of Fatimid Cairo. It was built by Badr al-Jamali in 1087 under the command of Fatimid Caliph al-Muntasir Billah. Although it was never put to the test, it was designed to protect al-Qahira from the Seljuk Turks who held Syria at the time and were threatening Egypt. This northern gate opens onto busy al-Muizz Street, which eventually leads to Bab Zuweila, the only surviving southern gate of Fatimid Cairo. ⊠ *Al-Muizz St., near Al Banhawi, Islamic Cairo North* 🖃 *Free.*

Bab al-Nasr (the Nasr Gate)

NOTABLE BUILDING | One of the few remaining examples of Islamic military architecture, the impressive Gate of Victory features exceptional craftsmanship and two 65-foot (20-meter) square towers. It was built during the same time and by the same hands as its sister gate, Bab al-Futuh, and wandering along the wall between the two is an interesting experience. An army could defend the city without ever having to leave this wall, which once had 60 gates—connected by tunnels with slit windows—as well as rooms and storehouses built into its girth. On one of this gate's towers is the inscription "Tour Corbin," a memento of the Napoleonic occupation, during which all the gates were renamed after French army officers. ("Tour Junot" and "Tour Perrault" are also carved into Bab al-Futuh.) ⊠ *Bab al-Nasr St., near Al Banhawai, Islamic Cairo North* 🖃 *Free.*

Bayt al-Suhaymi

HISTORIC HOME | With gardens, a well, and a flour mill, this massive, 16th-century merchant's house, considered Cairo's best example of domestic Islamic architecture, seems more like a self-sufficient hamlet than it does a domicile. A charming, evocative little corner of Cairo, the house and adjacent alley have been restored. The entranceway leads to a lush courtyard that is totally unexpected from the outside. On the ground floor are the *salamlik* (public reception rooms); the *haramlik* (private rooms) are upstairs. ⊠ *19 al-Darb al-Asfar St., El-Gamaleya, Islamic Cairo North* 🖀 *2/2787–8865* 🖃 *LE80.*

Complex of Qalawun

NOTABLE BUILDING | A Tartar (Mongol) who was brought to Egypt as a slave, al-Mansur Qalawun became one of the early Mamluk rulers of Egypt. He began building this complex, noteworthy for its workmanship and diverse styles, in 1284. In its heyday, the *bimaristan* (hospital) that Qalawun established here was famous, with a staff that included musicians and storytellers, as well as surgeons capable of performing delicate eye surgeries. The madrasa and mausoleum showcase the complex's impressive street facade. A 194-foot (59-meter) minaret has horseshoe-shaped arched recesses and a corniced overhang, a device used since pharaonic times. The entrance's semicircular arch was the first of its kind in Egypt. Beyond the entrance is a long, tall corridor with the madrasa to the left and the tomb to the right.

The gem of the complex, however, is the mausoleum—the burial place of Qalawun and his son al-Nasir Muhammad. The chamber is dark, cool, and mammoth, and in its center is a wooden grille that encloses the tombs. There is much here to suggest that Qalawun was deeply influenced by what he saw on his exploits in Palestine. The plan of the mausoleum is similar to that of the Dome of the Rock in Jerusalem; it contains an octagon fit within a square. The stained glass and tall proportions have a Gothic quality that are reminiscent of Crusader churches that he saw in the Levant. ⊠ *Al-Muizz St., near Al Banhawi, Islamic Cairo North* 🖃 *LE100, includes access to all al-Muizz St. monuments except the Egyptian Textile Museum, Wekalet Bazaraa, and Bayt Al-Suhaymi.*

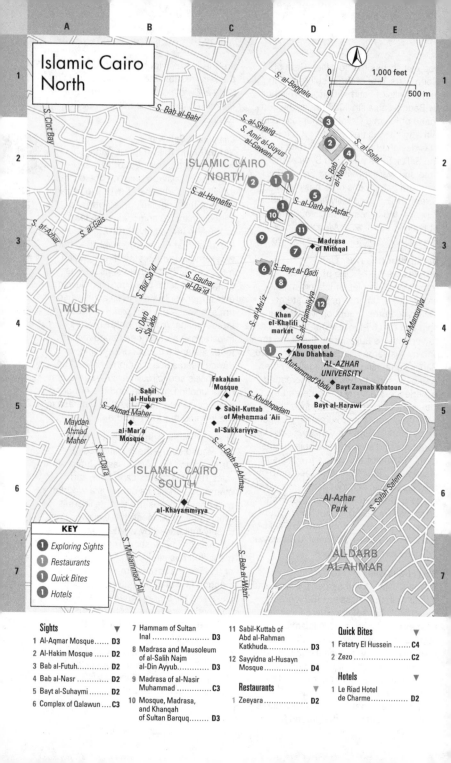

Islamic Cairo North

KEY

- 1 Exploring Sights
- 1 Restaurants
- 1 Quick Bites
- 1 Hotels

The Islamic Day

Muslims pray five times a day, and each prayer usually lasts about 15 minutes. Although times slightly vary by season, each prayer is named after its time of day. This makes it easy to identify what you're hearing the muezzin call for: *Al-Fajr* (dawn prayer); *Al-Dhuhr* (noon prayer); *Al-Asr* (afternoon prayer); *Al-Maghrib* (sunset prayer); and *Al-Isha* (night prayer). Cairo was dubbed "the city of a thousand minarets" for a good reason. Learning when each prayer takes place will enable you to keep track of time, regardless of where you are.

If you happen to visit a mosque during a prayer time, you may be asked to wait outside the main hall until it has finished. This is particularly true during Friday noon prayers, which last longer than others. You might also find a lot of shops temporarily closed during the Friday sermon and noon prayer. Note, too, that mosques often put out prayer mats on the street to accommodate bigger groups of worshippers.

Hammam of Sultan Inal

NOTABLE BUILDING | Public bathhouses were popular back in the day, with more than 80 hammams operating by the end of the 19th century. Commissioned and built in 1456 during the Mamluk period, this one is the only remaining part of a complex that once consisted of a commercial center, a fountain, and two hammams. Located in the Bayn al-Qasrayn area it's one of the few well-preserved monuments of its type. ⊠ *15 Haret Beet Al Qadi, al-Muizz St., Islamic Cairo North* 🎫 *LE100, includes access to all al-Muizz St. monuments except the Egyptian Textile Museum, Wekalet Bazaraa, and Bayt Al-Suhaymi.*

Madrasa and Mausoleum of al-Salih Najm al-Din Ayyub

NOTABLE BUILDING | Though its facade is deceptively regular, this building marks a turning point in Cairo's architectural and political history. The last descendant of Salah al-Din to rule Egypt, al-Salih Najm al-Din al-Ayyub died in 1249 defending the country against the Crusader attack led by Louis IX of France. His madrasa was used by judges to hear cases and issue judgments; punishments were carried out in the street in front of it, in the Bayn al-Qasrayn area, which was the city center for centuries. This madrasa was not only the first in Cairo to have a *liwan* (a vaulted area) for more than one legal school, but it was also the first to have a tomb attached—two traits that became standard features of Mamluk madrasas. Note the minaret's cap, which is shaped like a *mabkhara* (an incense burner), and its keel-arch recess with shell-like ornamentation. ⊠ *Al-Muizz St., Islamic Cairo North* 🎫 *Free* ⊗ *Closed during prayers.*

Madrasa of al-Nasir Muhammad

NOTABLE BUILDING | Considered the greatest Mamluk sultan, al-Nasir ruled on three different occasions between 1293 and 1340 for a total of 42 years, and during his reign, Egypt gained control of the lucrative maritime trade routes that connected England with China. Al-Nasir built more than 30 mosques, the aqueduct from the Nile to the Citadel, and a canal from Cairo to Alexandria. Eight of his sons ruled Egypt in the 21 years following his death. Qalawun's complex has slight Gothic influences, but this, his son's madrasa (built in 1304), contains distinct, Gothic elements. In fact, the entrance was literally lifted from a crusader church in Acre. The minaret, with

its delicate stucco-work, is one of the city's finest. ✉ *Al-Muizz St., Islamic Cairo North* 🎫 *Free* 🕐 *Closed during prayers.*

Mosque, Madrasa, and Khanqah of Sultan Barquq

NOTABLE BUILDING | The first of the Circassian Mamluk sultans, Barquq (whose name means "the plum") rescued the country from the ravages of the Black Death and related famine and political unrest. His complex, established between 1384–1386, includes a school where all four sects of Islam were embraced, a mosque, a Sufi *khanqah* (shrine), and a mausoleum where his father and a number of his wives and sons are buried. It also houses secondary school classrooms, Sufi classrooms, and sleeping quarters with various amenities for the students.

The domed minaret that adorns the entrance facade sets the complex apart. Capitals in the columns attached to the facade's wall feature a stylized ram's head. Inside, the school's four iwans (halls), marble *mihrab* (niche), wooden pulpit, and Qur'an chair are all impressive. Cursive text on the walls depict Qur'an verses, the name of the founder, and the date of construction. The cruciform interior is spacious and austere, and the *qibla* (the direction of Mecca) wall is decorated in marble dado. ✉ *Al-Muizz St., Islamic Cairo North* 🎫 *LE100, includes access to all al-Muizz St. monuments except the Egyptian Textile Museum, Wekalet Bazaraa, and Bayt Al-Suhaymi.*

Sabil-Kuttab of Abd al-Rahman Katkhuda

NOTABLE BUILDING | This 17th-century, Ottoman monument is impressive for its ornate façade, tiled interior, and location at a fork on Islamic Cairo's main street. *Katkhuda* is a Persian word meaning "master of the house," and the powerful gentleman who endowed this building was a patron of the arts and architecture, as befitted his position. Before running water was available to most of Cairo's inhabitants, it was customary for wealthy patrons to build a *sabil* (a public fountain) that provided people with potable water. Often attached to a sabil was a *kuttab* (a basic school) for teaching children the Qur'an and other subjects. ✉ *Al-Muizz St., Islamic Cairo North* 🎫 *LE100 includes access to al-Muizz St. monuments except the Egyptian Textile Museum, Wekalet Bazaraa, and Bayt Al-Suhaymi.*

Sayyidna al-Husayn Mosque (*Al-Hussein Mosque*)

MOSQUE | One of the holiest sites in Egypt, this mosque was originally built by the Fatimids in the 12th century as a shrine and is said to contain the head of Husayn, the Prophet's grandson. Al-Husayn is the spiritual heart of the Islamic city. It is here that the president and his ministers come to pray on important religious occasions. Many of the Sufi orders in the neighborhood perform Friday prayers at al-Husayn. During the *mulid* (celebration) of al-Husayn, held during the Muslim month of Rabi'a al-Akhiri (the fourth month in the Muslim calendar), the square in front of the mosque becomes a carnival. During Ramadan, the area is packed with people from sunset to dawn.

The mosque itself is a 19th-century stone building heavily influenced by the Gothic Revival; only elements of older structures remain. On the south end of the southeast facade stands a partial wall with a gate, known as Bab al-Akhdar (The Green Gate), which probably dates from the Fatimid Dynasty. The mosque is technically closed to non-Muslims. However, while large tour groups are not allowed to enter, there is more leeway for the individual traveler, provided that you avoid prayer times (noon or 1 pm) and Fridays. Women should cover their heads and everyone should cover shoulders and knees. ✉ *Hasan El-Adawy, Islamic Cairo North.*

🍴 Restaurants

★ Zeeyara

$$$$ | MIDDLE EASTERN | On the rooftop terrace of Le Riad Hotel de Charme, Zeeyara serves modernized Egyptian dishes, including a remarkable assortment of hot and cold mezzes and soups and specialties such as boneless stuffed pigeon or lamb with rice, mixed nuts, peas, and cinnamon—a must-try even if you're not a fan of lamb. Desserts are also delicious, and the mocktails are worth a try. **Known for:** phenomenal views; cordial, well-trained staff; sophisticated menu. $ *Average main: LE300* ✉ *114 al-Muizz St., Islamic Cairo North* ☎ *10/5019–5658* ⊕ *www.facebook.com/ zeeyara.restaurant.*

☕ Coffee and Quick Bites

Fatatry El Hussein

$$ | MIDDLE EASTERN | Popular with locals and tourists alike, Fatatry El Hussein (also known as Egyptian Pancake House) specializes in *fiteer,* Egypt's flaky pastry served with your choice of sweet or savory fillings. For one heavenly bite after another, try the mixed-cheese version; dessert options such as custard or cream and honey will surely satisfy your sweet tooth. **Known for:** fast, friendly service; fresh-from-the-oven fiteer; extensive list of savory and sweet fillings. $ *Average main: LE100* ✉ *123 al-Azhar St., El-Gamaleya, Islamic Cairo North* ☎ *2/2593–4844* ▬ *No credit cards.*

Zezo

$$ | MIDDLE EASTERN | The menu at this modest eatery, run by the same family since the 1960s, focuses on thin-loaf sandwiches with meat fillings, some of which are very spicy, though you might consider trying scrambled eggs with *basturma* (seasoned, air-dried, cured beef). In the evening, locals flock here to share a meal with family and friends, so you might have to wait to be seated. **Known for:** specialty honey-and-cream dessert sandwich; sandwiches featuring soft Egyptian fino bread; lively (somewhat chaotic) street-style seating area. $ *Average main: LE50* ✉ *1 Midan Bab al-Futah, El-Gamaleya, Islamic Cairo North* ☎ *11/1912–7150* ▬ *No credit cards.*

🛏 Hotels

Le Riad Hotel de Charme

$$ | HOTEL | Interiors at this intimate hotel are influenced by the great Islamic art and architecture of the surrounding historical streets. **Pros:** homey oasis in the heart of Islamic Cairo; furnished with antiques from around the country; tearoom and rooftop restaurant. **Cons:** breakfast spread has no local flavor; showing some signs of wear; upscale hotel prices without all the upscale hotel amenities. $ *Rooms from: $240* ✉ *114 al-Muizz St., Khan El-Khalili* ☎ *2/2787–6074* ⊕ *www. leriadcairo.com* 🛏 *17 suites* ❗ *Free Breakfast.*

🛍 Shopping

CRAFTS

★ Abd El-Zaher Bookstore

BOOKS | Stop by Cairo's last remaining bookbinding company, in business since 1936, for beautiful, leather-bound and gilt-decorated diaries, sketchbooks, and photo albums. All the items here are hand-crafted using skills that are rare in the 21st century. ✉ *31 Mohammed Abdou St., El-Gamaleya, Islamic Cairo North* ☎ *2/2511–8041.*

MARKETS

★ Khan el-Khalili

MARKET | At this great medieval souk, surrounded by a maze of winding streets and alleys, the air is perfumed with incense, and shopping is a chaotic but thoroughly authentic experience. Everyone, visitors and Cairenes alike, comes here to hunt for traditional items: carpets, gold, silver, clothing, spices, perfumes, waterpipes, jewelry, handicrafts, books, pottery, blown glass, leather, papyrus, pharaonic replicas—you name it. And no one ever buys anything at first price; bargaining is the modus operandi here.

The Khan and its surrounding streets also have lots of places to eat. Look for grilled-meat restaurants on the corner of Maydan al-Husayn and Shar'a Muski and places that specialize in *fiteer,* Egyptian pancakes filled with everything from feta cheese to raisins, between Shar'a Muski and Shar'a al-Azhar.

It's always best to pay using cash, as credit-card purchases can incur a 3% to 6% service charge (ask before handing over your plastic). And if you run out of Egyptian pounds, the Khan has plenty of ATMs. Note that most shops are closed on Sunday and before and/or during Friday prayers (the hour around noon or 1 pm). ⊠ *El-Gamaleya, Islamic Cairo North.*

Islamic Cairo South

Islamic Cairo South is a teeming commercial area that is less geared toward tourism than Islamic Cairo North. Anecdotes abound with regard to Bab Zuweila, the great southern gate of Fatimid Cairo. Some say the severed heads of criminals were displayed there, warning of the perils of breaking the sultan's law; others claim that a troll lived behind the massive gate.

What you can tangibly see today, however, is a wealth of historic monuments on the way to, and beyond, Bab Zuweila. Like Islamic Cairo North, many buildings here are being restored and are closed to visitors, but there are a few gems that you shouldn't miss. The Museum of Islamic Arts is also a must-see.

Although you could cover a good bit of ground here in a half day, a full day allows plenty of time for sightseeing as well as having lunch and doing some shopping. Set aside at least an hour for the Museum of Islamic Arts.

Sights

Al-Azhar Mosque and University

COLLEGE | Built in AD 970 by Fatimid caliph al-Mu'izz, al-Azhar is the oldest university in the world. Although the Fatimids were Shi'ite, the Sunni Mamluks who ousted them recognized its importance and replaced the Shi'ite doctrine with Sunni orthodoxy. Today, the university has faculties of medicine, engineering, and religion. It also has auxiliary campuses across the city.

Al-Azhar's primary significance remains as a school of religious learning. All Egyptian clerics must be certified from it—a process that can take up to 15 years. Young men from all over the world study here in the traditional Socratic method; students sit with a tutor until both agree that the student is ready to go on. The Grand Imam of al-Azhar is not just the director of the university, but also the nation's supreme religious authority. The beauty of al-Azhar, unlike many other monuments, stems in part from the fact that it is alive and very much in use.

Built in pieces throughout the ages, al-Azhar is a mixture of architectural styles, and the enclosure now measures just under 3 acres. After you enter through the **Gates of the Barbers,** a 1752 Ottoman addition, remove your shoes and turn left to the **Madrasa and Tomb of Amir Aqbugha.** Note the organic-shaped mosaic pattern rare to Islamic ornamentation near the top of the recess in the qibla wall (wall in the direction of Mecca).

Back at the entrance, the **Gates of Sultan Qaitbay,** built in 1483, can be seen. The quality of ornamentation verifies this Mamluk leader's patronage of architecture. The finely carved minaret placed off-center is noteworthy. To the right is the **Madrasa al-Taybarsiyya** completed in 1309, and once ranked among the most

Continued on page 94

SHOPPING IN CAIRO

From the mid-1300s Cairo was the center of the world trade in spices controlled by the Mamluks, and the Khan el-Khalili was the major marketplace where these spices were bought and sold. Later, the Khan expanded its offerings to include gold, hand-crafted decorative goods, and other items, thus catering to affluent shoppers hailing from medieval Arabia, Europe, and North Africa. It was one of the world's first shopping malls.

In many ways not much has changed. In the bustling alleyways Cairenes jostle with visitors from around the world, and hundreds of in-your-face vendors play out their well-honed sales pitches: it's a hot and intense experience, but one not to be missed.

(opposite) Night at Khan el-Khalili Market (top) a typical street in the bazaar (right) Dried herbs for sale in the spice stalls.

SHOPPING IN THE KHAN

Opened in 1382 and named after the Khan (an Islamic rest house for travelers and their pack animals) of Emir Djaharks el-Khalili that still stands nearby, Khan el-Khalili is a hodgepodge of lanes and alleyways packed with thousands of small, family-owned stores.

The Khan sits in the heart of historic Islamic Cairo. Shar'a Gawr al-Qayid forms the southern edge with Sayyidna al-Husayn, marked by al-Husayn Mosque, to the east. On the western edge, Shar'a el-Mu'izz with its medieval palaces forms the historical boundary between the Khan el-Khalili and Muski Bazaar, a place where Cairenes shop for their daily needs, buying everything from clay cooking pots to buttons. In practice, the two markets run seamlessly into one another, extending your possibilities for exploration.

A golden array of perfume bottles

In-laid mother of pearl boxes

Bags of beans and corn for sale

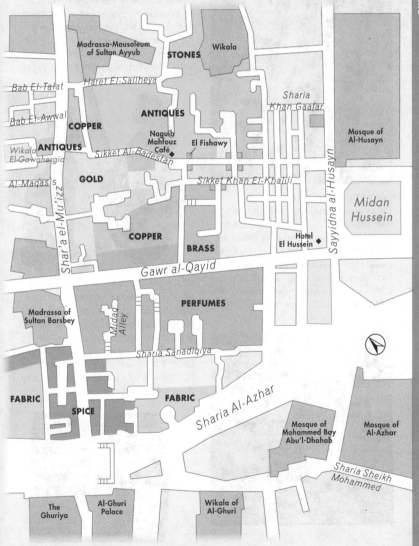

Madrassa-Mausoleum of Sultan Ayyub

STONES

Wikala

Bab El-Tatat

Haret El-Salıheya

Sharia Khan Gaafar

Bab El-Awwal

COPPER

ANTIQUES

Mosque of Al-Husayn

Wikala El-Gawahergia

ANTIQUES

Naguib Mahfouz Café

El Fishawy

Sikket Al-Badestan

Al-Maqasis

GOLD

Sikket Khan El-Khalili

Midan Hussein

Shar'a el-Mu'izz

COPPER

BRASS

Hotel El Hussein

Sayyidna al-Husayn

Gawr al-Qayid

Madrassa of Sultan Barsbey

Midaq Alley

PERFUMES

Sharia Sanadiqiya

FABRIC

FABRIC

Sharia Al-Azhar

SPICE

Mosque of Mohammed Bay Abu'l-Dhahab

Mosque of Al-Azhar

Sharia Sheikh Mohammed

The Ghuriya

Al-Ghuri Palace

Wikala of Al-Ghuri

WHAT TO BUY

You name it, and you can, with a little determination, probably find it in the Khan, from the best in artisan crafts to the kitsch, the fake, and the mass-produced wares shipped from factories thousands of miles from Egypt. To help in your quest for the perfect souvenir of your trip, here's a guide to what's traditional and local.

ALABASTER AND STONEWORK

Carved stonework has been at the heart of Egyptian decorative art since Khufu furnished his first pyramid. Alabaster is a native stone fashioned into many different objects. You'll find exquisite vases that would cost a fortune on Fifth Avenue. Prices start at LE500.

CARPETS AND TEXTILES

The Khan was a major center for carpet sales from the earliest days. The finest come from around the Arab world including Turkey, Iran, and Afghanistan; however, the nomadic peoples of Egypt also produce hand-made carpets from sheep and camel hair, as well as cotton kilims woven on narrow, mobile looms. Prices start at around LE950 for a runner.

MARQUETRY

The workmanship of artisans is extremely high and can be seen in the varied items showing inlaid patterns of different woods, or wood and mother of pearl. Small jewelry boxes are the most portable items, but you can find chess and checkers sets and side tables. Prices for a reasonably good-quality chess set start at around LE3,000.

PERFUMES AND PERFUME BOTTLES

The use of sweet-smelling oils and unguents was well developed in the ancient world and later became a central part of Arabic society. High-quality natural oil–based perfumes are concentrated and heady with scent. Delicate, ornate perfume bottles make the ideal storage vessels, their prettiness designed to highlight the high-value liquids inside. Prices depend on the type of oil but start at around LE150 for half an ounce.

GOLD AND SILVER

Gold and silver are sold by the day's market rate with only a small amount for workmanship, so weight for weight compared to prices in the United States it represents a relatively good value. ■ TIP→ Find out the current price of gold before heading out to shop.

POTTERY AND CERAMICS

Plain terracotta cookware on sale is used in millions of Egyptian homes every day but needs to be sealed before use. Or take home a ceramic plate, bowl, or vase hand-painted with the traditional Arabic pattern. These come in all shapes and sizes. If someone offers to take you to his workshop on the second floor, accept if you have time; most of these crafts are fascinating to see in progress.

METALWARE

Egypt has a tradition of work in various metals, and you have the choice of a whole range of brass and copper decorative items from tables to samovars and pitchers or ornate light fittings incorporating hand-blown glass. The finest of this decoration is still done by hand. Expect to pay around LE1,250 for a small hand-carved serving tray.

SOUVENIRS

Phaoronic-era replicas are always popular souvenirs

It's hard to escape the shadow of the Pharaohs in Egypt even when you are shopping. "Tut-mania" can be seen in thousands of imported mass-produced items, from refrigerator magnets to key rings to coffee mugs, that form the ever-expanding kitsch end of the market.

But it's worth remembering that even the most humble souvenir can resonate to the heart of Egypt's ancient history. Tiny alabaster scarab beetles were placed in the linen wrappings as the bodies of the pharaohs were being mummified to ensure the body passed into the next world, and the ankh was an important symbol for the ancient Egyptians—literally the key of life. Modern versions of both these items are readily available and inexpensive, with prices of less than LE200.

One of the most popular souvenirs of a trip to Egypt is to buy a cartouche (an oblong tablet) of your given name in hieroglyphics, either in gold or silver. Usually a cartouche takes a day or so to make.

HAGGLING

In Egypt, bargaining is not merely a practice designed to confuse visitors, but rather it's a way of life. You'll notice Egyptians negotiating prices for every type of purchase as you stroll around the Khan. Put simply, purchasers use every opportunity to minimize the price they pay, while vendors want the best price possible for their goods. The idea is to arrive at a price that makes both buyer and seller happy. Shop owners will expect you to bargain, so here are a few tips:

■ Show interest in and ask the price of several items before you begin bargaining over the item you like. This gives you an idea of the store's prices in general and masks your intentions.

■ When the merchant quotes a price, make a counteroffer which is around half (or less) of that amount. The merchant will lower his original offer and you raise your offer until you meet somewhere in the middle.

■ Use reasons to counter why the merchant's price is too much (they don't need to be true). These could include the color/size not being quite right or questions about the quality of the material or workmanship. It's not uncommon to say that you prefer an item at another stall but are prepared to take his goods for a lower price.

■ If you are offered refreshment (tea, soda, water) as you bargain, do accept. It is a custom of the vendors, a nicety that doesn't happen in the United States, and it doesn't obligate you to buy anything.

■ If you can't reach an agreement, walking away often results in the merchant lowering his offer price.

■ Shopping early in the morning or later in the evening can mean lower prices. An early sale is considered a sign of a lucky day ahead, while a late sale is a bonus.

SPICES

Spices for sale in the Khan

Many of the most important herbs and spices sold in Cairo are native to this part of the world. Several were important in the pharaonic era, including those for use in the mummification process, but on a more mundane level herbs and spices were used to scent the air, to flavor many dishes, and for the homeopathic treatment of a range of illnesses and conditions from stomach cramps to diarrhea, and from halitosis to water retention. The spice stalls are certainly among the most colorful and fragrant in the Khan. Cooking back home with the spices you buy will bring back great memories of your trip.

WHAT TO BUY

Some of the more common herbs and spices you'll find in the bazaar include anise, caraway seeds, cardamom, chili, cloves, cinnamon, coriander, cumin, fennel, fenugreek, mace, mustard seed, nutmeg, pepper, star anise, sumac, and tamarind. Various curry powders are also sold premixed. The king of all the herbs and spices is saffron. The best saffron will not be cheap, but it's less expensive than in the United States.

You'll also see various items—from powders to dried roots—sold as "Egyptian Viagra." Since it's certain that these haven't been tested under laboratory conditions, treat any claims with healthy skepticism.

KARKADE

The dried flowers of the hibiscus bush are the major ingredient in one of Egypt's staple drinks. The sweet, deep-red infusion is very refreshing served chilled but is also delicious hot. The health benefits of karkade are said include lowering blood pressure and cholesterol.

■TIP→ **Pass on the long strings of sampler packs of spices that many stalls sell.** You'll be buying many spices you'll never use, and you can't be sure how fresh these items are, as this packaging is only for the tourists and may have been hanging in the sunlight for several days or weeks.

Karkade and other spices on display

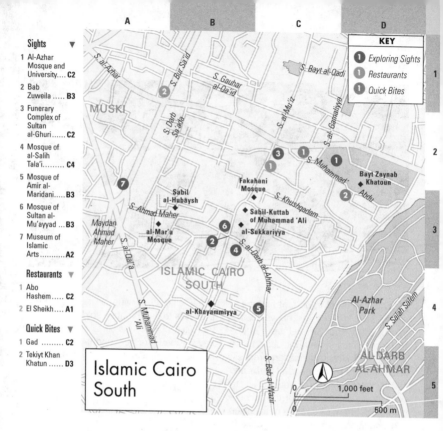

Sights ▼

1 Al-Azhar Mosque and University.... **C2**

2 Bab Zuweila **B3**

3 Funerary Complex of Sultan al-Ghuri **C2**

4 Mosque of al-Salih Tala'i **C4**

5 Mosque of Amir al-Maridani..... **B3**

6 Mosque of Sultan al-Mu'ayyad ... **B3**

7 Museum of Islamic Arts **A2**

Restaurants ▼

1 Abo Hashem **C2**

2 El Sheikh **A1**

Quick Bites ▼

1 Gad **C2**

2 Tekiyt Khan Khatun **D3**

Islamic Cairo South

---

spectacular madrasas in Mamluk Cairo. Only its qibla wall remains, and it's said that the ceiling was once gold-plated.

Qaitbay's gateway opens to a spacious courtyard, quite typical of early Islamic design. Through the keel arches is the entrance to the main sanctuary, which was traditionally a place to pray, learn, and sleep. It's part Fatimid, part Ottoman. The Ottoman extension is distinguished by a set of steps that divides it from the original. The two *qibla* walls, the painted wooden roof, the old metal gates that used to open for prayer, and the ornate stucco work of the Fatimid section are all noteworthy.

To the right of the Ottoman qibla wall is the **Tomb of Abd al-Rahman Katkhuda,** the man most responsible for the post-Mamluk extension of al-Azhar. To the extreme left along the Fatimid *qibla* wall is the

Madrasa and Mausoleum of the Eunuch Gawhar al-Qanaqba'i, treasurer to Sultan Barsbay. It's small, but its intricately inlaid wooden doors, the stained-glass windows, and dome with an interlacing floral pattern are exceptional.

Return to the courtyard. To the right of the **Minaret of Qaitbay** is the **Minaret of al-Ghuri,** the tallest in the complex. Built in 1510, it's divided into three sections like its predecessor but is tiled rather than carved. The first two are octagonal, and the final section, consisting of two pierced rectangular blocks, is unusual, and not at all like Qaitbay's plain cylinder. ⊠ *al-Azhar mosque, al-Azhar St., Islamic Cairo South* 🎟 *Free.*

★ Bab Zuweila

NOTABLE BUILDING | The last remaining southern gate of Fatimid Cairo was built in 1092 and is named after members of the Fatimid army who hailed from a North African Berber tribe called the Zuwayla. The gate features a pair of minaret-topped semicircular towers. The lobed-arch decoration on the inner flanks of the towers in the entrance were used earlier in North African architecture and were introduced here following the Fatimid conquest of Egypt. They are seen in later Fatimid and Mamluk buildings.

The street level here has risen dramatically—what you see as you pass through the massive doorway would have been at eye level for a traveler entering the city on a camel. According to the architectural historian K.A.C. Creswell, the loggia between the two towers on the wall's exterior once housed an orchestra that announced royal comings and goings. The views from the towers themselves are some of the best in Cairo.

Bab Zuweila wasn't always such a lighthearted spot, however. Public executions once took place here. Indeed, the conquering Turks hanged the last independent Mamluk sultan, Tuman bay II, from this gate in 1517. The unlucky man's agony was prolonged because the rope broke three times. Finally, fed up, the Ottomans had him beheaded. ⊠ *Al-Muizz, Islamic Cairo South* ⊠ *LE40.*

Funerary Complex of Sultan al-Ghuri
(al-Ghuriya)

NOTABLE BUILDING | This medieval landmark was the last great Mamluk architectural work before the Ottomans occupied Egypt. Built by Sultan al-Ghuri, who constructed Wikalat al-Ghuri three years later, al-Ghuriya stands on either side of al-Muizz street where it crosses al-Azhar street. The surrounding area was the site of the silk bazaar visible in David Roberts's famous 1839 etching *Bazaar of the Silk Mercers, Cairo.*

On the right side of the street (facing al-Azhar street) is the madrasa, and opposite it stands the mausoleum. Note the unusual design of the minaret—it's

a square base topped by five chimney pots. The mausoleum was rebuilt several times during al-Ghuri's reign. After spending a reported 100,000 dinars on the complex, al-Ghuri was not buried there. He died outside Aleppo, and his body was never found. The bodies of a son, a concubine (both victims of a plague), a daughter, and Tuman bay II (his successor) are interred in the vault. ⊠ *Qasr al-Ghuri, al-Muizz St., Islamic Cairo South* ⊠ *LE60.*

Mosque of al-Salih Tala'i

MOSQUE | Built in 1160, one of the last Fatimid structures constructed outside the city walls is also one of Cairo's most elegant mosques. Like many others, the ground floor housed several shops, which allowed the authorities to pay for the upkeep. Today, these shops are underground because the street level has risen considerably over time.

The mosque has a standard early-Islamic rectangular courtyard plan. The main facade consists of five keel arches on Greco-Roman columns taken from an earlier building that are linked by wooden tie beams. Between each arch, a set of long panels is topped with Fatimid shell niches. The most distinctive architectural feature, however, is the porch-like area underneath the arches of the main facade that creates an open, airy interior court. Inside, the columns are also taken from elsewhere: no two of their capitals are alike. ⊠ *Al-Muizz St., Bab Zuweila, Islamic Cairo South* ⊠ *Free.*

Mosque of Amir al-Maridani

MOSQUE | Featuring fine examples of virtually every decorative art in vogue during the 14th century, this mosque was built by a son-in-law of Sultan Nasir al-Muhammad who died at the tender age of 25. It was then completed under the supervision of the sultan's architect. As you enter the sanctuary behind the fine *mashrabiya* (projected oriel windows made of wood), you'll notice a collection of pillars of pharaonic, Christian, and

Roman origin. The *mihrab* (prayer niche) is made of marble inlay and mother-of-pearl, and the wooden *minbar* (pulpit) is also beautifully carved and inlaid. Above the mihrab are excellent original stucco carvings, unique in Cairo for their naturalistically rendered tree motif, as well as dados of inlaid marble with square Kufic script.

Outside, be sure to admire the first example of a minaret in octagonal form from bottom to top. It is shaped like a pavilion, with eight columns carrying a pear-shaped bulb crown. Note, too, that this mosque is an active community center, so it's open longer than other monuments. ⊠ *Al-Tabbana St., Islamic Cairo South* ⊡ *Free.*

Mosque of Sultan al-Mu'ayyad

MOSQUE | Sultan al-Mu'ayyad was once imprisoned at this location under Sultan Faraj, and he suffered terribly during his imprisonment from fleas and lice. He swore that, if he was ever freed, he would build a mosque there—a sanctuary for the education of scholars. He ultimately assisted in overthrowing the sultan, and became the new sultan within six months. He made good on his promise in 1420 and tore down the infamous jails that once occupied the site.

The mosque's facade is remarkable in that the *ablaq* (the striped wall) is black and white, less common than the usual red and white. The famous entrance of the Sultan Hassan Mosque below the Citadel inspired the high portal. The beautiful bronze-plated door was lifted from the mosque of Mu'ayyad's better-known predecessor. The two elegant identical minarets rest against the towers of Bab Zuweila, which makes them appear to be a part of the gate and not the mosque.

The interior space is well insulated from the bustle of the surrounding district by high walls blanketed in marble panels. The wood and ivory minbar is flanked by a fine columned mihrab with marble

marquetry of exceptional quality. The gilt and blue ceilings are also noteworthy. ⊠ *Al-Muizz St., Bab Zuweila, Islamic Cairo South* ⊡ *Free.*

★ Museum of Islamic Art

ART MUSEUM | Often overlooked, this is one of the finest museums in Cairo, displaying a rare and comprehensive collection of Islamic art and antiquities. You can see woodwork, stucco, intarsia, ceramics, glass, metalwork, textiles, and carpets. Items are arranged according to medium, and every era—from Umayyad to Abbasid, Fatimid, Ayyubid, and Mamluk—is represented. Highlights include one of the earliest Muslim tombstones, dating from AD 652, only 31 years after the Prophet returned to Mecca victorious; a bronze ewer that has a spout in the shape of a rooster and that dates from the time of the Abbasid caliph Marwan II; a series of Abbasid stucco panels from both Egypt and Iraq; frescoes from a Fatimid bathhouse; wooden panels from the Western Palace; carved rock crystal; and an excellent brass-plated Mamluk door, which appears, at first glance, to have standard arabesque decoration but is in fact interspersed with tiny animals and foliage.

The metalwork section contains the doors from the Mosque of al-Salih Tala'i, as well as incense burners, candlesticks, and vases—some items have Christian symbols and some are inlaid with gold and silver. The armor and arms hall is still impressive even though Selim, the conquering Ottoman sultan of 1517, had much of this type of booty carried off to Istanbul, where it is on display at Topkapi Palace. In the ceramics section, pieces from the Fatimid Era and Iran are particularly noteworthy, as are the Mamluk mosque lamps in the glassware collection. ⊠ *Bur Sa'id St., Midan Ahmad Maher, Islamic Cairo South* ☎ *2/2390-1520* ⊕ *www.miaegypt.org* ⊡ *LE120.*

Don't miss the Museum of Islamic Art, where displays showcase textiles and items made of wood, stucco, ceramic, glass, and metal from every era.

🍴 Restaurants

Abo Hashem

$$$ | MIDDLE EASTERN | Although it's been around for more than 120 years, this restaurant remains a hidden gem, nestled amid Islamic Cairo's narrow alleyways. The menu focuses on Egyptian grilled meats, and a typical order for two people consists of ½ kilo (1 pound) of kebab and kofta, which are always served with fresh local salad, tahini, pickles, and *aish baladi* (Egyptian flatbread). **Known for:** sizzling meats served by weight; muyyet salata (salad water), a refreshing, palate-cleansing vinaigrette to sip on while you eat; historical atmosphere. $ *Average main: LE170* ✉ *4 Haret Housh Qadam, El-Darb El-Ahmar, Islamic Cairo South* ✛ *From al-Muizz St., turn right on the narrow street after al-Fakahani Mosque, followed by a left* ☎ *2/2510–4462* 🚫 *No credit cards.*

El Sheikh

$$ | MIDDLE EASTERN | Although you can order grilled kofta, stuffed pigeon, moussaka, or home-style stews served with rice, locals come to this family-run hotspot for Egyptian-style rotisserie chicken that's cooked to golden perfection. The waiters speak minimal English, but the chicken is in ovens on the sidewalk, and many dishes are on display inside, so you can point at what you want. **Known for:** mouthwatering chicken served all day long; the people-watching from lively street-side seating area; daily menu of homestyle stews. $ *Average main: LE150* ✉ *105 Al Qala'a St., off Port Said St., Bab Al Khalq, Islamic Cairo South* ☎ *11/1153–1364* 🌐 *www.facebook.com/elsheikhaboomar* 🚫 *No credit cards.*

☕ Coffee and Quick Bites

Gad

$$ | **MIDDLE EASTERN** | Options at this local street-food favorite range from *ful* (fava bean stew) or ta'amiya (Egyptian-style felafel) sandwiches to beef or chicken shawarma wraps. Most customers order food to go, but seating is available if you need to take a break. **Known for:** inexpensive options for meat-eaters and vegetarians alike; fast, efficient service; open for breakfast, lunch, and dinner. $ *Average main: LE100* ✉ *125 al-Azhar St., El-Darb El-Ahmar, Islamic Cairo South* ☎ *2/2514–5901* 🚫 *No credit cards.*

Tekiyt Khan Khatun

$$ | **MIDDLE EASTERN** | After a day of sight-seeing, this atmospheric, courtyard-style café, set amid buildings that date from the 15th century just south of al-Azhar Street, is a great place to grab a tea or a coffee and a dessert. You can only get here on foot, and it's a little hard to find, but don't worry—the area is safe, and you can ask a local for directions if you get lost. **Known for:** local tea with fresh mint; historical setting; energetic crowd and live (sometimes overly loud) music. $ *Average main: LE100* ✉ *3 Mohammed Abdou St., El-Darb El-Ahmar, Islamic Cairo South* ☎ *12/2127–0366* 🚫 *No credit cards.*

🎭 Performing Arts

Wikalat al-Ghuri

ARTS CENTERS | This handsome, 16th-century building was originally an inn for traders, who stabled their horses and carts in the courtyard and retired to the upper floors. Today it's used as an arts center, and the upstairs rooms now serve as studios for artists specializing in traditional crafts such as carpet weaving, metalworking, and creating *mashrabiyas* (projected oriel windows made of wood). During its restoration, the building was also equipped to host cultural events, including whirling dervish and Arabic music performances. Shows are held every Wednesday and Saturday at 7:30 pm in winter and 8 pm in summer; usually, you must arrive about 30 minutes before the performance starts to guarantee yourself a seat; sometimes, though, shows are canceled due to low attendance numbers, so check ahead. ✉ *Mohammed Abdou St., Islamic Cairo South* ☎ *2/2510–7146* 🆓 *Free.*

🛍 Shopping

SPICES

★ Abd El Rahman Harraz Seeds, Medicinal, and Medical Plants

OTHER SPECIALTY STORE | Founded by its namesake herbalist in 1939, this fantastic family-owned spice shop is one of Cairo's most renowned, with a wide selection of medicinal herbs, traditional beauty aids, essential oils, and cosmetics, mixed in with a few curiosities. The shop is about 0.2 miles (450 meters) from Bab Zuweila, and although its sign isn't in English, you should be able to find it—just look for the stuffed gazelle in the front window. ✉ *1 Ahmed Maher St., El-Darb El-Ahmar, Islamic Cairo South* ☎ *2/2511–1100.*

The Citadel

The view of the huge silver domes and needle-thin minarets of the Mosque of Muhammad Ali against the stark backdrop of the desert cliffs of the Mokattam is iconic. The mosque is just one feature of the Citadel, an immense fortified enclosure that housed numerous power brokers from Salah al-Din al-Ayyub, its founder, in the 12th century, to Napoléon in the 18th century. In the 20th century, it was used as a garrison by British colonial governors and troops until their withdrawal in 1946. It also served as the base of operations for Mamluk slave kings and for a series of sultans and pashas

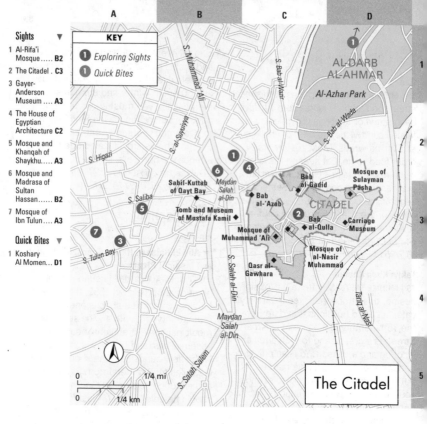

KEY

① Exploring Sights

① Quick Bites

The Citadel

---

with their colorful retinues, including al-Nasir Muhammad's harem of 1,200 concubines.

The Citadel affords wonderful views of the city and is surrounded by impressive monuments, including the grandiose Mosque and Madrasa of Sultan Hassan, one of the largest structures of its kind in the world, and the remarkably calm, austere Mosque of Ibn Tulun, one of Cairo's oldest buildings.

The areas between the three mosques here have been cut by a series of main roads, including modern routes that have attempted to clear paths across the dense historical urban fabric. As a result, this part of the city lacks the coherence and historic charm of districts like Coptic Cairo or the area around Bab Zuweila. Nevertheless, the mosques here are so impressive that if you have time to only see a few of Cairo's Islamic treasures, these should be among them.

◉ Sights

Al-Rifa'i Mosque

MOSQUE | Although it appears neo-Mamluk in style, this mosque was not commissioned until 1869 by the mother of Khedive Isma'il, Princess Hoshiyar. It was completed in 1912 but, from the outside, seems more timeworn and less modern than the 14th-century Mosque of Sultan Hassan beside it. True to the extravagant khedivial tastes, the inside is markedly different from that of its neighboring mosque as well. While the latter is relatively unadorned, al-Rifa'i is lavishly decorated. The mausoleum here contains the bodies of Sufi holy men of the Rifa'i

The Citadel Touring Tips

The Citadel is large and hilly. Be prepared for a strenuous walk to the top from the entrance.

■ **Start at the top.** Work your way down through the attractions to save energy in the hot weather.

■ **Wear comfortable shoes.** There are many uneven surfaces and a sizable incline.

■ **Bring your camera.** Views of the old city and the Cairo skyline from the walls of the Citadel are picture-worthy.

■ **Breathe.** This is one of the breeziest and least crowded parts of Cairo.

■ **Prepare for the sun.** Many parts of the Citadel lack shade, and the sun is still powerful despite the breeze. Take the necessary precautions against sun burn, and wear a hat.

■ **Come early (or late).** Afternoons are busy and often overrun with school groups, so visit in the morning or late afternoon.

order (hence the establishment's name), as well as the remains of many royals. ✉ *Salah al-Din Square, Sayyida Zaynab* 🎫 *LE80, includes entry to Mosque of Sultan Hassan.*

★ The Citadel

CASTLE/PALACE | FAMILY | Local rulers had long overlooked the strategic value of the hill above the city, but, within a few years of his arrival in 1168, Salah al-Din al-Ayyub began creating defense plans with the Citadel at their center. He and his successors built an impenetrable bastion using the most advanced construction techniques of the age, and, for the next 700 years, Egypt was ruled from this hill. Nothing remains of the original complex except a part of the Ayyubid walls—33 feet (10 meters) tall and 10 feet (3 meters) thick—and the Bir Youssef (Youssef Well), which was dug 285 feet (87 meters) straight into solid rock to reach the water table and is still considered an engineering marvel.

In the 1330s, most of the Ayyubid buildings were replaced by Mamluk structures. After assuming power in 1805, Muhammad Ali had all the Mamluk buildings razed and the complex entirely rebuilt. Only the green-domed mosque and a fragment of the **Qasr al-Ablaq** (Striped Palace) remain.

For more than 150 years, the **Mosque of Muhammad Ali** has dominated the City's skyline. Although Ottoman law prohibited anyone but the sultan from building a mosque with more than one minaret, this mosque has two, one of the first indications that Muhammad Ali wouldn't remain submissive to Istanbul. Note the spacious courtyard's gilded clock tower, which was provided by King Louis Philippe in exchange for the obelisk that stands in Paris. It's fair to say that the French got the better end of the bargain: the clock has never worked.

Behind Muhammad Ali stands the **Mosque of al-Nasir Muhammad,** a Mamluk work of art with beautifully crafted masonry, elegant proportions, and a minaret featuring ornate but refined details. Ottomans took much of the original interior decoration to Istanbul, but the space is nevertheless impressive. The courtyard's supporting columns were collected from various sources; several are pharaonic.

Across from al-Nasir's entrance is the **National Police Museum,** worth a quick visit to see the exhibition on Egypt's political assassinations and to enjoy the spectacular view from the courtyard. The enclosure directly below, gated by **Bab al-Azab,** is where Muhammad Ali wrested control from the Mamluk chiefs. (He invited them to a banquet and had them ambushed by a battalion, ending their dominion in Egypt and eliminating all internal opposition in a single stroke.) To the northwest of al-Nasir, the gate known as **Bab al-Qulla** opens to the **Qusur al-Harem** (Harem Palace), now the site of the **National Military Museum**, with somewhat interesting displays of uniforms and weaponry.

Farther west, the **Carriage Museum,** the dining hall of British officers stationed at the Citadel in the early 20th century, now houses eight conveyances used by Egypt's last royal dynasty (1805–1952). In the northwest part of the Citadel is the rarely visited **Sulayman Pasha Mosque** built in 1528. While its plan is entirely a product of Istanbul, the sparse stone decoration shows traces of Mamluk influence.

Before leaving the Citadel, pass by the **Qasr al-Gawhara** (Jewel Palace), where Muhammad Ali received guests. It's now a museum displaying the royal family's extravagance and preference for early 19th-century French style. ⊠ *Al-Qala'a, Salah Salem St., The Citadel* ☎ *2/2512– 1735* 🖾 *LE180.*

Gayer-Anderson Museum

HISTORIC HOME | Also known as Bayt al-Kiritliya (House of the Cretan Woman), the museum consists of two Ottoman houses joined together, restored, and furnished by Major Gayer-Anderson, a British member of Egypt's civil service in the '30s and '40s. The house is adorned with lovely pieces of pharaonic, Islamic, and Central Asian art, and a few oddities here and there. The reception room

features a mosaic fountain at the center of an ornate marble floor, and the courtyard of the east house has the "Well of Bats," the subject of much storytelling in the neighborhood. James Bond's *The Spy Who Loved Me* was partially shot in the reception hall and on the rooftop terrace. The house also inspired Gayer-Anderson's grandson, Theo, to become an art conservationist, and he was involved in the restoration of Bab Zuweila. ⊠ *4 Ahmed Ibn Tolon Square, The Citadel* ☎ *2/2364–7822* 🖾 *LE60.*

The House of Egyptian Architecture

HISTORY MUSEUM | Equally as fascinating as the displays on Egyptian architecture, arranged chronologically, is the 18th-century structure containing them. It's one of the best-preserved Islamic houses in Cairo, greatly influenced by the Ottoman and Mamluk styles. It was originally known as Ali Labib House, but came to be known as the House of the Artists, having been home to many local and international artists, including the renowned Egyptian architect, Hassan Fathi. The museum also conducts workshops and hosts lectures and cultural events. ⊠ *4 Darb Al Labana, El-Darb El-Ahmar, El Khalifa, The Citadel* ☎ *2/2511–7043, 12–02–96–50–78* ⊕ *www.facebook.com/HouseofEgyptian-Architecture2015* 🖾 *LE40.*

Mosque and Khanqah of Shaykhu

MOSQUE | This mosque and *khanqah* (shrine) were built by the commander in chief of Sultan Hassan's forces. The khanqah has a central courtyard surrounded by three floors where 150 rooms once housed 700 Sufi adherents. As in the mosque, classical pillars support the ground-floor arches. Tuman bay II, the last Mamluk sultan, hid here during the Ottoman conquest, so the mosque was badly damaged by shelling. Nevertheless, its *qibla liwan* (hall in the direction of Mecca) still has its original marble inlay work. To the left of it are the tombs of Shaykhu and the first director of the school. Today, this is an active neighborhood mosque. ⊠ *Al Saleeba St., The Citadel* 🎫 *Free.*

★ Mosque and Madrasa of Sultan Hassan

MOSQUE | Constructed between 1356 and 1363 by the Mamluk ruler Sultan Hassan, this is one of the world's largest Islamic religious buildings. Some historians believe it was partially built with stone from the Pyramids of Giza. Regardless, creating it nearly emptied the vast Mamluk treasury.

You enter the complex at an angle through a tall portal that is itself a work of art. The carving on both sides culminates in a series of stalactites above. A dark and relatively low-ceilinged passageway to the left of the entrance leads to the brightly lit main area—a standard cruciform-plan open court.

Unique to this mosque is a madrasa between each of the four *liwans* (halls), one for each of the four Sunni schools of jurisprudence, complete with its own courtyard and four stories of rooms for students and teachers. Also unique is the location of the mausoleum behind the *qibla* wall (wall in the direction of Mecca) which, in effect, forces people who are praying to bow before the tomb of the dead sultan—a fairly heretical idea to devout Muslims. Nevertheless, the mausoleum, which faces Salah al-Din Square, is quite beautiful, particularly in the morning when the rising sun filters through grilled windows.

Of the two tall minarets, only the one to the left of the *qibla liwan* is structurally sound. Have the custodian take you up to get a view of the city, including the Citadel. In fact, this roof was used by several armies, Bonaparte's expedition included, to shell the mountain fortress. ⊠ *Salah al-Din Square, The Citadel* 🎫 *LE80, includes entry to al-Rifa'i Mosque.*

★ Mosque of Ibn Tulun

MOSQUE | This huge congregational mosque was built in 879 by Ahmad Ibn Tulun with the intention of accommodating his entire army during Friday prayers. He was sent to Egypt by the Abbasid caliph in Samarra to serve as its governor. Sensing weakness in Iraq, he declared his independence and began building a new city, al-Qata'i, northwest of al-Fustat and al-Askar. When the Abbasids conquered Egypt again in 970, they razed the entire city as a lesson to future rebels, sparing only the great Friday mosque, but leaving it to wither on the outskirts.

In 1293, emir Lajin hid out in the derelict building for several months while a fugitive from the Mamluk sultan, vowing to restore it if he survived. Three years later, after being appointed sultan himself, he kept his word, repairing the minaret and adding a fountain in the courtyard, the *mihrab* (prayer niche), and the beautiful *minbar* (pulpit). All of this background is secondary to the building itself—you can delight in this masterpiece without even the slightest knowledge of its history. Its grandeur and simplicity set it apart from any other Islamic monument in Cairo.

The mosque is separated from the streets around it with a *ziyada* (a walled-off space) in which the Friday market was once held and where the famous minaret is located. Inside, the mosque covers an area of more than 6 acres. Four arcaded aisles surround the vast courtyard, and the soffits of the arches are covered in beautifully carved stucco—the first time this medium was used in Cairo. The minaret, the only one of its kind in Egypt, is modeled after those in Samarra, with the ziggurat-like stairs spiraling on the outside of the tower. ⊠ *Ahmed Ibn Tolon Square, The Citadel* 🎫 *Free.*

☕ Coffee and Quick Bites

Koshary Al Momen

$ | **MIDDLE EASTERN** | As its name suggests, this restaurant specializes in *koshary*, the street-food favorite that generally consists of macaroni, rice, lentils, and chickpeas topped with a spiced tomato sauce and crispy fried onions. Sit outside, facing a busy intersection, so you can watch life unfold while you eat. **Known for:** a place to satisfy koshary cravings 24/7; delicious rice pudding; oven-baked pasta casseroles and tajines. ⑤ *Average main: LE25* ⌧ *9 Ali Basha St., El-Darb El-Ahmar, The Citadel* ☎ *11/5484–7011* ⊟ *No credit cards.*

Old Cairo (Coptic Cairo)

Coptic Cairo, also known as Old Cairo or as Mar Girgis (Saint George), has a soothing feel compared with Downtown Cairo and other busy districts. The neighborhood is also centuries older than even the city's Islamic areas. It was established when the Roman emperor Trajan (AD 88–117) had a fortress built around a settlement then known as Babylon. At the time, this was a strategic location: the Nile flowed almost 1,300 feet (400 meters) east of its current course and was connected by canal to the Red Sea.

The Copts (an Arabic derivative of the Greek word for Egypt) were the first people in Africa to embrace Christianity when it was introduced by Saint Mark in the first century. They were persecuted harshly for it, and many fled to the desert or south to the Upper Nile Valley. Under Byzantine rule, people came out of hiding; some came to Babylon and began building churches in and around its walls. Unfortunately, the period of peace was short-lived. Serious disputes involving Coptic and Byzantine theology arose, and the Copts, once again, faced persecution.

When the Arabs arrived, the Copts initially welcomed them as liberators from the tyranny of Byzantium. Fustat, the encampment that the Arabs established just outside the walls of Babylon, quickly grew into a major city, leaving the older town as an enclave for Christians and Jews.

Coptic Cairo still has vestiges of all this history: portions of the Roman fortress survive; four churches, a convent, a monastery, and a synagogue that was originally a church; and the oldest mosque in Africa is nearby. The Coptic Museum houses a collection of local Christian art with pharaonic, Hellenistic, and even Islamic influences.

Sites are generally open from 9 am to 4 pm. However, places of worship are closed to visitors during services. This applies to mosques during Friday prayers (noon or 1), churches during Sunday services (7 am–10 am), and temples on Saturday. In churches, it is customary to make a small donation either near the entrance or beside the votary candle stands.

◉ Sights

Church of St. Barbara

CHURCH | One of the largest and finest churches in Cairo was named after a young Nicodemian woman who was killed by her pagan father for converting. First built in 684, it was originally dedicated to Cyrus and John (in Arabic, Abu Qir and Yuhanna, respectively), two martyrs from the city of Damanhour who were killed for not renouncing their Christianity.

The church, which was destroyed by fire and rebuilt in both the 11th and 12th centuries, has the standard layout consisting of a narthex, a nave, side aisles, and three sanctuaries. Technically, there are two churches on the site, as a separate sanctuary was built when the relics of St. Barbara were brought here.

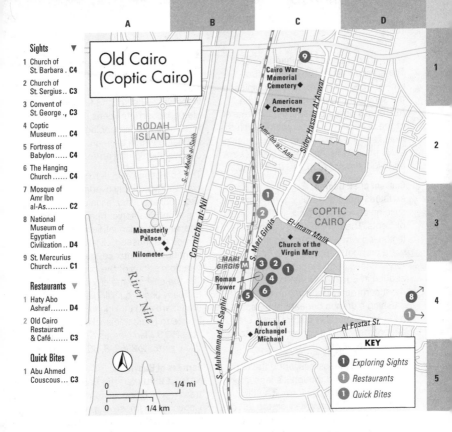

Old Cairo
(Coptic Cairo)

RODAH
ISLAND

Cairo War
Memorial
Cemetery ◆

American
Cemetery ◆

COPTIC
CAIRO

El-Imam Malik

Church of the
Virgin Mary

Manasterly
Palace

Nilometer

MARI
GIRGIS Ⓜ

Roman
Tower

Church of
Archangel
Michael

Al Fostat St.

Corniche al-Nil

River Nile

S. al-Malik al-Salih

S. Mari Girgis

S. Muhammad al-Saghir

Amr Ibn al-Aas

Sidey Hassan Al-Anwar

KEY

① Exploring Sights
① Restaurants
① Quick Bites

0   1/4 mi

0   1/4 km

The sanctuary screen currently in place is a 13th-century wooden piece inlaid with ivory—the original screen is in the Coptic Museum. The icons above the screen include a newly restored Child Enthroned and a rare icon of St. Barbara. To the left of the sanctuary is the chapel dedicated to Cyrus and John, a square structure with a nave, transept, two sanctuaries (one for each saint), and a baptistry. Access to Coptic Cairo's cemetery is through an iron gate to the left of the church. ✉ *Haret al-Qadisa Burbara, Kom Ghorab, Old Cairo* ☏ *12/2744–2733* 🖾 *Free.*

Church of St. Sergius

CHURCH | What's known in Arabic as Abu Serga is considered Cairo's oldest church, originally constructed in the 5th century. Though it was destroyed and rebuilt several times, including during a major restoration venture in the Fatimid era, it is, nevertheless, a model of early Coptic church design. Dedicated to two Roman officers, Sergius and Bacchus, both martyred in Syria in 303, the church sits above a cave where the Holy Family was said to have stayed during their flight from King Herod. Hence, it was once a major pilgrimage destination for 19th-century European travelers. A special ceremony is still held here every June to commemorate the event.

The entrance leads to the side of the narthex, at the end of which is a baptistry. At the ceiling of the nave, 24 marble pillars that were taken from an earlier site and possibly date from the Ptolemaic era (304–30 BC), support a series of arched timbers. Most of the church furnishings are modern replicas of older pieces. The originals are in the Coptic Museum—pieces from a rosewood pulpit and the sanctuary canopy are among the museum's prized possessions. To the left of the sanctuary is the crypt in which the Holy Family is believed to have hidden. ✉ *Haret al-Qadis 'Abu Serga, Mari Gerges, Old Cairo* ☎ *2/2363–4204* ⌨ *Free.*

Convent of St. George

RELIGIOUS BUILDING | This church's namesake holds a special place in the hearts of Copts. The remains of this Roman legionary, who was martyred in Asia, were brought to Egypt in the 12th century. Images of St. George (Mar Girgis) abound in Egyptian Christianity (he's most commonly depicted on a steed crushing a dragon beneath him), so it's no surprise that this district has a church, a monastery, and a convent dedicated to the dragon slayer.

Medieval historians described the complex as huge, and though it's less impressive in its present-day form, it's still worth a visit. The stairway on the left of the courtyard leads down to a structure that dates from the Fatimid era. Inside is a huge reception hall with a beautiful wooden door about 23 feet (7 meters) tall. Behind the door, a shrine contains the icon of St. George and a set of chains used for the chain-wrapping ritual said to represent the sufferings of St. George at the hands of the Romans. ✉ *Haret al-Qadis Girgis, Old Cairo* ⌨ *Free.*

★ Coptic Museum

HISTORY MUSEUM | Opened in 1910 and home to the world's largest collection of Coptic antiquities, this museum traces Coptic history from its beginnings to its full rise, providing a link between ancient and Islamic Egypt, as most of the city's population remained Christian until the 11th century, a half millennium after the Arabs brought Islam to the country.

The insightful displays are more or less arranged by medium. The first floor has carved stone and stucco, frescoes, and woodwork. The second floor includes textiles, manuscripts, icons, and metalwork. In some cases, chronological divisions are made within each grouping to show the evolution of the art form.

The collections also demonstrate how eras can beautifully overlap to produce exceptional artistry, as is evident through the slight Pharaonic, Roman, Byzantine, and Ottoman influences detected across the museum. Many carvings and paintings, for instance, help to trace the transformations of the ancient key of life, the ankh, to the cross. Depictions of the baby Jesus suckling at his mother's breast are also striking in their resemblance to pharaonic suckling representations. ✉ *3 Mari Gerges St., Kom Ghorab, Old Cairo* ☎ *2/2362–8766* ⌨ *LE100.*

Fortress of Babylon

NOTABLE BUILDING | The Babylon Fortress—which now encompasses the Coptic museum, six Coptic churches, and a convent—did not always stand at its current location. The Roman emperor Trajan had it moved here when access to a steady water supply became an issue. At that time, the Nile ran by Old Cairo; it has since changed its course northward by almost 1,300 feet (400 meters). It is also sometimes called Qasr al-Shama'e (Candles Palace) because its towers were illuminated with candles at the beginning of every month. ✉ *Mari Gerges St., Kom Ghorab, Old Cairo* ⌨ *Free.*

The Hanging Church

CHURCH | What's known in Arabic as al-Muallaqah (The Suspended Church) is consecrated to the Blessed Virgin. It sits atop a gatehouse of the Roman fortress, was originally built in the 9th century, and has since been rebuilt several times. Only the section to the right of the sanctuary, above the southern bastion,

The Coptic Museum, opened in 1910, has the world's largest collection of Coptic antiquities, from wooden, carved-stone, and stucco items to icons, manuscripts, and textiles.

is considered original. Nevertheless, it is one of the city's most impressive churches.

The entrance gates open to a flight of stairs that lead onto a covered courtyard, the narthex, paved with glazed geometrical tiles dating from the 11th century. Beyond the narthex is the nave, the main section of the church where services are held. Most columns in Coptic churches were painted with pictures of saints, but few of the paintings survived. Those in the Hanging Church are no exception; only one column still has traces of a figure on it.

Perhaps the most impressive aspect of this space is the marble pulpit. Considered the oldest existing pulpit in the country, it was constructed in the 11th century, though some of its components are older. The pulpit is supported by slender columns arranged in pairs of which no two are alike. Some say this represents the sacraments; others describe

it as being symbolic of Christ and his disciples.

The sanctuary screen is made of cedar and ivory cut in small segments and then inlaid in wood to form a Coptic cross. The top of the screen is covered with icons: Christ is depicted in the center; the Virgin, the archangel Gabriel, and St. Peter are on the right; and St. John the Baptist, St. Paul, and the archangel Michael are on the left. Behind the screen is the sanctuary dedicated to the Virgin Mary. To the right is another screen dating from the 13th century and made of wood and mother-of-pearl. It glows dark pink when a candle is held behind it. Behind this is a small chapel attached to the Ethiopian St. Takla Haymanot Church. A stairway leads from this chapel to one above it, dedicated to St. Mark. This area is probably the oldest part of the church, built in the 3rd century when this was still a bastion of the old Roman fort. ✉ *Mari Gerges St., Kom Ghorab, Old Cairo* 🎫 *Free.*

Exhibits in the new National Museum of Egyptian Civilizations display artifacts both monumental and mundane. Don't miss the interactive Gallery of Royal Mummies, with the remains of 22 rulers.

Mosque of Amr Ibn al-As

MOSQUE | Known as the first mosque on the African continent, it was built by its namesake in 642 following the conquest of Egypt and the founding of Fustat— the first Islamic capital. One of the first companions of Prophet Muhammad, Ibn al-As designated the mosque as a place for communities and troops to come together. Because the original structure probably had mud-brick walls and a palm-thatch roof, it did not survive for long. It was restored and expanded in 673 and again in 698, 710, 750, and 791. Finally, in 827, it was expanded to its current size. The structure's architectural features naturally changed, but there was an attempt in the 1980s to restore its interior to its 827 appearance. ⊠ *Sidey Hassan Al Anwar, Al Kafour, Old Cairo* ⊞ *Free.*

★ National Museum of Egyptian Civilization (NMEC)

HISTORY MUSEUM | Egypt's first museum to focus on all its different civilizations truly takes you on a trip through history.

The collections are designed to tell a story, some chronologically and others thematically. The chronological collections follow the Archaic, Pharaonic, Greco-Roman, Coptic, Medieval, Islamic, modern, and contemporary eras. Thematic collections map a route through the Dawn of Civilization, The Nile, Writing, State and Society, Material Culture, Beliefs and Thinking, and the Gallery of Royal Mummies.

There are currently around 1,600 pieces on display, with plans to display 50,000 artifacts over time, and they range from monumental to the more mundane, like one of the first-ever prosthetics—an artificial toe from the Pharaonic era that predates the Roman Capula Leg. The museum is also the new home of the royal mummies of ancient Egypt. Designed to feel like a tomb, the Gallery of Royal Mummies has the remains of 22 rulers, including 18 kings and four queens. Displays are interactive: you can scan QR codes to learn about each royal.

✉ El-Fustat Road, Ein as Seirah, Old Cairo ☎ 2/2741–2273 ⊕ www.nmec.gov.eg 💲 LE200.

St. Mercurius Church (*Abu Seifein Church*)
CHURCH | Mercurius, or Abu Seifein (Of the Two Swords), is named for a Roman legionary who converted to Christianity after dreaming that an angel gave him a glowing sword and ordered him to use it to fight paganism. He was martyred in Palestine, and his remains were brought to Cairo in the 15th century. Today, this site is of great importance to Coptic Christians; when the seat of the Coptic Patriarch moved from Alexandria to Cairo, Saint Mercurius was the chosen location. The complex actually contains a monastery, a convent, and three churches: Abu Seifein, Abna Shenouda, and a church of the Virgin. ✉ Ali Salem St., off Hassan Al Anwar St., Old Cairo ☎ 2/2531–3538 💲 Free.

🍴 Restaurants

Haty Abo Ashraf
$$$$ | **BARBECUE** | **FAMILY** | At this *haty* (grill room), you can order your tender, juicy meat selection with a chopped salad and a choice of dip (tahina, garlic paste, hummus, baba ganoush) for the side of fresh *aish baladi* (Egyptian flatbread). Abu Ashraf also serves *muyyet salata* (salad water), a vinegar shot that many Egyptians enjoy before a hearty meal to whet their appetites. **Known for:** quirky decor; clean bathrooms; fresh ingredients. 💲 *Average main: LE260* ✉ *New Fustat, Al Fostat St., first neighborhood, Tower # 2/2A, Old Cairo* ✛ *In front of the NMEC* ☎ *10/2278–08219, 2/2742–6083* ⊕ *www.facebook.com/haty.abo.ashraf* 🖃 *No credit cards.*

Old Cairo Restaurant & Café
$$ | **MIDDLE EASTERN** | Thanks to the picture menu, the friendly English-speaking staff, and the free Wi-Fi for customers, this clean, convenient neighborhood restaurant is usually overrun with tourists. The

Middle Eastern dishes are often given a local twist, and the menu includes vegan options as well. **Known for:** delicious ta'amiya; freshly squeezed fruit juices; large portions. 💲 *Average main: LE80* ✉ *Mari Gerges St., Al Kafour, Old Cairo* ☎ *11/0260–7892.*

☕ Coffee and Quick Bites

Abu Ahmed Couscous
$ | **MIDDLE EASTERN** | Unless you happen to walk in the opposite direction from the sites of Coptic Cairo, you're not likely to stumble upon this little hole-in-the-wall kiosk, but it's been around for more than 85 years and is well known to many locals. The specialty is sweet couscous, which you can get with toppings like fresh cream or honey, though nothing beats having it the old-fashioned way—with powdered sugar and nuts. **Known for:** fluffy couscous with a variety of sweet toppings; sells local Egyptian honey and olive oil; a good assortment of Egyptian desserts. 💲 *Average main: LE20* ✉ *70 Mari Gerges St., Old Cairo* ✛ *In front of Mosque of Amr Ibn al-As* ☎ *10/0056–2055* 🖃 *No credit cards.*

🛍 Shopping

The Fokhareen Market (*Fustat Pottery Village*)
CERAMICS | When it comes to unique, handmade pottery, the Fokhareen Market will spoil you for choice. The ancient Egyptians were experts in working with clay, specifically Aswani clay—a product of the Nile's silt—which doesn't secrete toxic substances. It's a tradition that continues today. From sculptures and tiles to bowls and utensils, this pottery village probably has something that will make a gift or a souvenir. Even if you're not looking for something to buy, it's interesting to walk around the village and watch artisans and artists at work. ✉ *The Village of Pottery in Old Cairo, Dar El-Salam, Kom Ghorab, Old Cairo.*

Gold & Jewelery Oriental Gifts (*Old Cairo Bazaar*)

SOUVENIRS | Tucked in an alleyway, down a stairway near the Mar Girgis Metro station, this huge Old Cairo shop brims with merchandise; you'll almost be overwhelmed by the many possible souvenirs. But the atmosphere is calm and quiet, so you can take your time sifting through the items. Though helpful, the owner is relaxed, letting customers make their rounds without pressuring them to buy. ⊠ *Kom Ghorab Ln., Kom Ghorab, Old Cairo* ✛ *Opposite Church of Saint Sergius* ☎ *12/2219–1922, 2/2741–2136.*

Downtown Cairo

In the mid-19th century, Khedive Isma'il had this district laid out according to a Parisian-style urban plan across the old canal from Islamic Cairo, previously the heart of the city. The area soon became a fashionable commercial and residential district—a sort of "Paris on the Nile"—and cafés, jewelers, and major department stores were quick to open.

As districts such as Garden City and Zamalek were developed, Downtown became less residential and more commercial, but it remained, above all else, colonial—near traditional Cairo but self-consciously apart from it. The early 20th century saw a rise of nationalism, and, on Black Saturday in January 1952, much of Downtown was systematically torched during riots, illustrating how greatly colonial architecture was associated with colonial rule.

The riots marked the beginning of the end for foreign control of Egypt. The revolution that overthrew the British-backed monarchy followed within months, and with it all the street names changed to celebrate the new heroes. But it wasn't until the wave of nationalizations in the early 1960s, however, that the colonial chapter in Downtown fully ended. The

foreigners who had stayed on past the revolution lost their businesses, their way of life, and their self-appointed place in a city that never really belonged to them.

Downtown—called Wasat el-Balad in Arabic—is still a beloved district. Its boundary begins at Tahrir Square, famous worldwide as the epicenter of the 2011 protests that led to the ousting of the president at the time. The uprising reinvigorated Downtown Cairo. Its watering holes and modest cafés—long favorites of artists and foreigners—were once again full, this time with young Egyptians from all social classes.

Set at the edge of Downtown Cairo, is the Egyptian Museum, a huge neoclassical structure built of iconic reddish-pink stone. It's a portal to the ancient world, offering a distinct experience from the rest of the neighborhood. Although many of its artifacts are being moved to the new Grand Egyptian Museum in Giza, it still contains an incredible abundance of treasures, making it an essential stop on any trip to Cairo.

Sights

Abdeen Palace Museum

HISTORY MUSEUM | Designed by French architect Léon Rousseau, this massive palace was commissioned by Khedive Isma'il to serve as the official government headquarters in place of the Citadel. Construction began in 1863, and the palace was officially inaugurated in 1874, with a new wing added in 1891. The gardens, however, were not added in until 1921, by Sultan Fuad I before he became king. Much of the palace is closed to the public, but it's worth stopping by to take in the architecture, the well-maintained garden dotted with old-growth trees, and the small museum. The latter occupies just a handful of the massive palace's 500 ornate rooms and has displays of weaponry, silverware once used by the royal family, and other

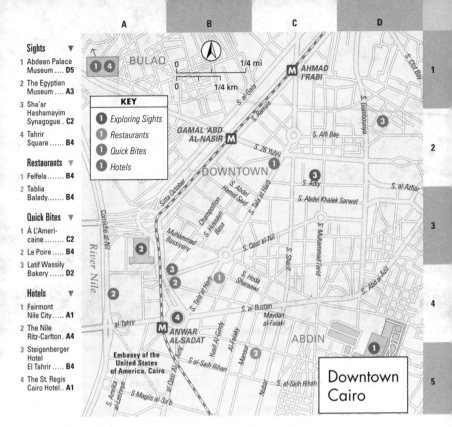

Downtown Cairo

Sights ▼
1 Abdeen Palace Museum **D5**
2 The Egyptian Museum **A3**
3 Sha'ar Hashamayim Synagogue . **C2**
4 Tahrir Square **B4**

Restaurants ▼
1 Felfela **B4**
2 Tablia Balady **B4**

Quick Bites ▼
1 À L'Americaine **C2**
2 La Poire **B4**
3 Latif Wassily Bakery **D2**

Hotels ▼
1 Fairmont Nile City **A1**
2 The Nile Ritz-Carlton .. **A4**
3 Steigenberger Hotel El Tahrir **B4**
4 The St. Regis Cairo Hotel.. **A1**

KEY
1 *Exploring Sights*
1 *Restaurants*
1 *Quick Bites*
1 *Hotels*

items. ⊠ *El-Gomhoreya Square, Rahbet Abdin, Abdeen, Downtown* ☎ *2/2391–6909* 🎫 *LE100* 🕑 *Closed Fri.*

★ **The Egyptian Museum** (*The Museum of Egyptian Antiquities*)

HISTORY MUSEUM | FAMILY | This huge neoclassical building, a Downtown landmark on the north end of Tahrir Square, was masterfully designed by French architect Marcel Dourgnon. It opened in 1902, making it one of the oldest archaeological museums in the Middle East—and one of the largest, with a collection of ancient Egyptian artifacts so vast that it would have taken nine months to complete a tour if you spent just one minute studying each item.

Although some of the museum's treasures have been moved to the National Museum of Egyptian Civilization—and most of the Tutankhamun finds are now in Egypt's newest archaeological repository, the Grand Egyptian Museum in Giza—the breadth here is still staggering. Galleries take you through millennia, from the Predynastic Period (6000 to 3100 BC) through the Greco-Roman Era (332 BC to 313 AD). The Tanis Treasure includes gold masks, jewelry, solid-silver coffins, and other artifacts dating from between 1076 and 945 BC. Don't miss the animal mummy rooms, especially if you have kids in tow, or the Fayyum portraits: done on wood, these very lifelike paintings put you face to face with one individual Roman-era Egyptian after another. ⊠ *Tahrir Square, Downtown* ☎ *2/2579–6948* 🌐 *www.egyptianmuseumcairo. com* 🎫 *LE200; LE50 photography fee (personal use, and without flash).*

Opened in 1902, the Egyptian Museum on Tahrir Square is one of the Middle East's oldest—and one of the world's best—archaeological museums.

Sha'ar Hashamayim Synagogue

SYNAGOGUE | Over the centuries, during Europe's many waves of persecution and expulsion, Jews sought refuge in Muslim lands such as Egypt, where they were protected as People of the Book. The Jewish community lived in peace alongside Muslims and Copts for generations, and it was only in the 20th century, with the founding of the state of Israel and the 1952 revolution's privatization, that political and cultural tensions arose. Although not open to the general public, it's still worth noting this synagogue, an unusual concrete block with a subtle art-nouveau floral motif (the stained-glass windows are rumored to have been done by Tiffany). Financed by some of the Jewish community's most powerful men, it was designed by architect Maurice Cattaui and erected in 1899. ⊠ *Adly St., Downtown* ✛ *opposite Kodak Passage* ☎ *2/2482–4613.*

★ Tahrir Square

PLAZA/SQUARE | After living in Paris, the 19th-century Khedive Isma'il embarked on a mission to create a European-style district in Cairo, both as a way to modernize the city and to cement his political legitimacy. His plans included this square, originally named Ismailia Square, and it became a popular Cairo hub. Although in subsequent decades it lost favor owing to its association with colonial rule, it remained an epicenter for political demonstrations, evolving into a symbol of liberation.

After the 1952 Revolution, its name was changed to Tahrir Square (Liberation Square), and it was a focal point during both the 1977 Egyptian Bread Riots and the 2011 Egyptian Revolution. In 2021, history was made here yet again when the Parade of Mummies passed through the square, in a grand spectacle celebrating the transfer of 22 mummies from the Egyptian Museum to the National

Egyptian Museum Touring Tips

■ **Afternoons are quieter.** Visit the museum in the afternoons after the tour groups have left, though be prepared for heat and humidity since most of the museum is not air-conditioned.

■ **Get guidance.** If you are visiting on your own, hire an official guide (at the museum entrance) to help explain the artifacts in more detail.

■ **Take your time.** Full-day Cairo tours give you a small amount of time in the museum, but it's worth more. In fact, if time permits, visit the museum twice to allow more time to take in the many thousands of items on view.

■ **Travel light.** Bulky bags will be confiscated and held at reception during your visit.

■ **Purchase a photo pass.** It's sold at the door with regular tickets. Buy one even if you're only planning on using your phone's camera. Remember to never use the flash, and keep your pass handy as guards may ask to see it when they see you taking pictures.

■ **Don't touch the artifacts.** Some of the collections are not in glass displays but don't be tempted to touch them. The oils secreted by your hands slowly damage the artifacts and break them down.

■ **Take a guidebook.** Bring your guidebook with you when you visit so that you can relate the artifacts to their geographical sites.

3

Cairo DOWNTOWN CAIRO

Museum of Egyptian Civilization. Today, the obelisk of Ramses II, moved from the Tanis archaeological site, stands tall here. ⊠ *Tahrir Square, Downtown* 🎫 *Free.*

 Restaurants

Felfela

$$ | **MIDDLE EASTERN** | This popular restaurant, built into an alleyway, is a good place to try such Egyptian staples as *shorbat 'ads* (lentil soup), which is tasty with a squeeze of lemon in it; *ta'amiya* (the local version of felafel); and *ful* (stewed fava beans). You can also enjoy a cold beer or a glass of wine with your food. **Known for:** Egyptian-style felafel made from fava beans instead of chickpeas; kebabs by the score; unique decor. ⑤ *Average main: LE150* ⊠ *15 Hoda Shaarawy St., Downtown* ☎ *2/2395–5557* ⊕ *www.felfelaegypt.com.*

Tablia Balady

$$ | **MIDDLE EASTERN** | Home-cooked Egyptian staples are the hallmarks of this side-street restaurant, which is sometimes called Five Ladies, as it's run by five women from the same family. Although the menu changes daily, based on what's fresh and in season, it typically includes *molokhia* (a dish of braised greens with chicken and rice). **Known for:** endearing family vibe and homey decor; open-air dining; surprisingly quiet spot in Downtown. ⑤ *Average main: LE120* ⊠ *8 Abd Magid Al Daramlai St., off Mohammed Mahmoud St., Downtown* ☎ *10/9497–3795* ⊕ *www.facebook.com/ tabliabaldy* ⊟ *No credit cards.*

☕ Coffee and Quick Bites

À L'Americaine

$$ | CAFÉ | Founded in the 1930s, this quaint coffee shop has witnessed most of Downtown's history and was once a favorite spot for its elites and celebrities. Today, people from all walks of life come to enjoy its coffee and desserts. **Known for:** coffee, tea, and sweet treats; lively spot for people-watching; nostalgia-inducing vintage feel. $ *Average main: LE80* ⊠ *7 Emad Eddin St., Downtown* ✛ *on the corner of 26th of July St.* ☎ *2/2591–9666.*

La Poire

$$ | INTERNATIONAL | Conveniently situated a street-crossing away from the Egyptian Museum, La Poire was established in 1975 as a French pastry shop but has expanded its menu to include a variety of savory quick bites and an ever-growing selection of sweet treats. **Known for:** sunny (but air-conditioned) setting; international menu including salads and sandwiches; busy at lunchtime (but the line moves quickly). $ *Average main: LE150* ⊠ *2 Al Bustan St., Qasr El-Nil, Tahrir, Downtown* ☎ *19515 delivery hotline* ⊕ *www.lapoire.me.*

Latif Wassily Bakery

$ | BAKERY | Latif Wassily is a traditional Egyptian *forn* (bakery)—one of the oldest in Downtown. Grab-and-go baked goods include croissants that are generously filled with cheese and breadsticks that are liberally sprinkled with sesame and nigella seeds. **Known for:** items are baked fresh all day; charming facade that transports you to another era; date-stuffed biscuits sold by weight. $ *Average main: LE15* ⊠ *8 El-Mahdi St., Downtown* ☎ *2/2590–3851* ▭ *No credit cards.*

🛏 Hotels

★ Fairmont Nile City

$$$ | HOTEL | Between two towering office blocks overlooking the Nile, this luxury hotel appeals to both business and leisure travelers, with an interior design that looks to the early 20th century for its inspiration. **Pros:** most rooms have Nile views; a mall with a movie theater is part of the complex; roof terrace is a great place to chill out. **Cons:** heavy traffic on the Corniche; large and somewhat impersonal; not really within walking distance of the Downtown attractions. $ *Rooms from: $400* ⊠ *Nile City Tower, 2005 Corniche al-Nil, Bulaq* ☎ *2/2461–9494* ⊕ *www.fairmont.com* ⇨ *542 rooms* ◉| *No Meals.*

The Nile Ritz-Carlton

$$$$ | HOTEL | Great location meets luxury at this hotel, which is a three-minute stroll from the Egyptian Museum and has scenic views of the Nile on one side and of Tahrir Square on the other. **Pros:** excellent restaurants serving an array of cuisines; outdoor pool; 24/7 fitness center and lavish spa services. **Cons:** one of Cairo's most expensive hotels; on-site wedding receptions can get loud; busy surroundings. $ *Rooms from: $900* ⊠ *1113 Corniche al-Nil, Ismailia, Qasr El Nil, Downtown* ☎ *2/2577–8899* ⊕ *www.ritzcarlton.com* ⇨ *381 rooms* ◉| *No Meals.*

Steigenberger Hotel El Tahrir

$ | HOTEL | The efficient staff is eager to please at this hotel, which sits on a corner across from the Egyptian Museum. **Pros:** ideal base for exploring Downtown; excellent value for money; very high standards. **Cons:** nothing special about the room views; traffic is loud; large and somewhat impersonal. $ *Rooms from: $130* ⊠ *2 Kasr Al Nile, Ismailia, Qasr El Nil, Downtown* ☎ *2/2575–0777* ⊕ *www.steigenberger.com* ⇨ *295 rooms* ◉| *No Meals.*

The river views are spectacular from public areas and most guest rooms in the richly decorated Fairmont Nile City hotel.

The St. Regis Cairo Hotel

$$$$ | HOTEL | You can't beat the views of the Nile or the city from this stylish new hotel, which is a mere five-minute ride from the Egyptian Museum and Tahrir Square and which offers valet parking, an airport shuttle, and butler services. **Pros:** close to major sights; luxurious and loaded with amenities; impeccably courteous and friendly staff. **Cons:** luxury comes at a price; heavy traffic on the Corniche; street noise can be an issue. $ *Rooms from: $640* ✉ *1189 Corniche al-Nil, Downtown* ☎ *2/2597–9000* ⊕ *www.thestregis-cairo.com* ➭ *233 rooms* ⦿ *No Meals.*

Nightlife

BARS

Café Riche

CAFÉS | Founded in 1908, Café Riche was once the social headquarters for members of Cairo's theater and literary communities. The historic ambience makes it a great place to enjoy a relaxed drink and, perhaps a French-influenced Egyptian grill dish from a menu that has changed very little in more than a century. ✉ *17 Talaat Harb St., Downtown* ☎ *2/2391–8873.*

★ Carlton Roof Garden

CAFÉS | Locals gather on this beautiful terrace, on the eighth floor of a 1930s family-run hotel, to escape the city's chaotic streets and to take in the incredible skyline views. Staffers are quick on their feet and friendly, and there's a wide range of alcoholic and nonalcoholic drinks. The indoor area, with hardwood floors and large windows, is the place to be when it's chilly. ✉ *21 26 July St., Oraby, Al Azbakeya, Downtown* ☎ *2/2575–5323.*

Carol Tapas Bar

BARS | This low-key Downtown bar, with an eye-catching display of backlit bottles, serves a wide range of cocktails, beer, spirits, and wine to accompany its selection of Middle Eastern mezzes. Nonsmokers take note, though: indoor smoking is allowed. ✉ *12 Kasr El Nil St., Downtown* ☎ *10/2911–1105.*

El Horreya Café and Bar

CAFÉS | This quintessential local bar has been the go-to spot for leftist intellectuals, writers, artists, poets, and expats since the 1930s. You can sip coffee, tea, or a cold beer, all under one roof. ⊠ *2 off Bab El Louq St., El Falaky Square, Abdeen, Downtown* ☎ *2/2392–0397.*

Estoril Bar

BARS | Like many other Downtown spots, this bar is a favorite of political activists and artists. It was established in the 1970s by a Greek couple, and it sits in a passageway between two buildings. The food is hit-or-miss, but the service is excellent, and the bar is lively—often filled with a mix of locals and visitors lingering over bottles of red wine or beer. ⊠ *12 Talaat Harb St., Downtown* ☎ *2/2574–3102.*

Gingko

BARS | The modern, stylish rooftop bar at the Fairmont Nile City hotel serves delicious food to accompany its drinks. You also can't beat the view of the Nile backed by Cairo's skyline. ⊠ *Nile City Towers B, 2005 Corniche al-Nil, Downtown* ☎ *2/2461–9595.*

The Greek Club in Cairo

BARS | Although founded as a Greeks-only establishment in 1906, it became a go-to spot for liberal Egyptians and expats in need of a beer when it opened its doors to the general public in the 1950s. The decor still nods to Greece: tables are topped with blue-and-white checkered cloths, and the outdoor terrace is lined with blue wooden pillars. Although the food isn't anything to write home about, this is still a great place for a casual night out. ⊠ *1 Karim Al Dawla St., Qasr El Nil, Downtown* ☎ *12/2396–6836.*

Le Bistro

BARS | On one of Downtown's hippest streets, this cozy pub and restaurant offers an international menu, a decent selection of drinks, and terrific service.

You can't miss the place: just look for its Art Deco–style facade; inside, though, the decor is less flamboyant. ⊠ *8 Hoda Shaarawy, Downtown* ☎ *10/6487–7776* ⊕ *www.lebistrorestaurant.com.*

 Performing Arts

Access Art Space

ARTS CENTERS | Better known by its former name, Townhouse Gallery, this art space has carved its place in Downtown's cultural landscape by hosting live performances, film screenings, and lectures, as well as contemporary art exhibitions. ⊠ *10 El Nabarawy St., off Champollion St., Qasr El-Nil, Downtown* ☎ *2/2576–8086* ⊕ *www.thetownhousegallery.com.*

Mashrabia Gallery

ARTS CENTERS | Since the early 1990s, this gallery has been a pillar of Cairo's contemporary arts scene, highlighting talented local and international artists. Every month, the gallery organizes temporary exhibitions, performances, discussions, and lectures. It also regularly collaborates with galleries in Switzerland, Italy, Turkey, and Tunisia. ⊠ *15 Mahmoud Bassiouny St., Qasr El-Nil, Downtown* ☎ *2/2578–4494* ⊕ *www.mashrabiagallery.com.*

National Theater

THEATER | Though the current building is a faithful reconstruction of the 1869 original, which burned in a 2008 fire, Cairo's National Theater has remained a symbol of art, culture, and literature in Egypt. The exterior architectural style is Islamic; its interior blends Islamic and traditional Egyptian motifs. ⊠ *Al Bostah St., Abdeen, Downtown* ☎ *2/2591–7783* ⊕ *www. facebook.com/national.theater.eg.*

Shopping

BOOKSTORES

★ Lehnert and Landrock Bookshop

BOOKS | In the early 20th century, travel writers and photographers Rudolf Franz

Lehnert and Ernst Heinrich Landrock explored North Africa, documenting scenes from Bedouin life, before making their way to and settling in Cairo, opening this bookshop in 1924. It's a wonderful place to browse: typewriters, cameras, telephones, and other vintage items are neatly organized within glass cases; the walls are hung with the duo's black-and-white photos; and the shelves are stocked with an international selection of books, many of them on Egypt's history. ⊠ *36 Abd El-Khalik Tharwat St., Abdeen, Downtown* ☎ *2/2393–5324.*

★ L'Orientaliste Books

BOOKS | The Swiss expat who founded this store in the 1950s originally stocked it with used books he gathered from Europeans leaving Egypt. Subsequent owners have continued to maintain a good inventory of books in French and English as well as Arabic. It also sells prints, lithographs, and antique maps and postcards. ⊠ *15 Qasr al-Nil St., Downtown* ☎ *2/2579–4188.*

CRAFTS

Oum El Dounia Gallery

CRAFTS | Located on the first floor of a busy building on an equally busy street, Oum El Dounia—which translates to Mother of the World, a nickname given to Egypt—sells stylish, vibrant items handcrafted by artisans from different parts of Egypt. It also has a section with books, many about the Arab world. ⊠ *3 Talaat Harb St., 1st floor, Downtown* ☎ *2/2393–8273* ⊕ *www.facebook.com/ oumeldouniatahrir.*

JEWELRY

Atef Wassef Silver

JEWELRY & WATCHES | This family-run establishment, in business since the 1960s, is known for its excellent silver items. Most of their limited-edition designs are inspired by Egyptian cultural heritage, but you will also find more contemporary pieces, as well as some inlaid with semi-precious stones. Be prepared to rifle through the collection; the store's inventory is huge, and the hunt is part of the shopping experience. ⊠ *54 Abd El-Khalik Tharwat St., Downtown* ☎ *2/2390–3954* ⊕ *www.facebook.com/ atefwassefsilver.*

 Activities

Mamsha Ahl Misr

HIKING & WALKING | Designed as an entertainment strip, with restaurants and an innovative floating theater that can seat up to 1,240 people, the Mamsha Ahl Misr (The Walkway of Egypt's People) is ideal for a long stroll along the Nile. Phase one, which covers roughly 2 km (1 mile), opened in early 2022; eventually, the walkway will stretch 54 km (35 miles), connecting Cairo and Giza. ⊠ *Corniche El Nil, Downtown.*

Rodah Island and Garden City

Sultan As-Salih Ayyub earmarked Rodah (or Roda) Island in the Nile as a place for the Mamluks and built Al Rodah Castle for them to reside in during his reign (1240–49). Today, the island, which you can see from the Corniche near Downtown Cairo, is accessible via both vehicular and pedestrian roads and bridges.

The island's famous El-Manial district is busy with traffic traveling between Cairo and Giza. Endure the traffic though, because El-Manial is home to Prince Mohamed Ali Palace (Al Manial Palace), an impressive place especially if you love architecture, antiquities, and botany. The Ottoman Manasterly Palace, now part of an arts center, and the Nilometer, one of the oldest Islamic structures in Egypt, stand next to each other near the island's southern tip.

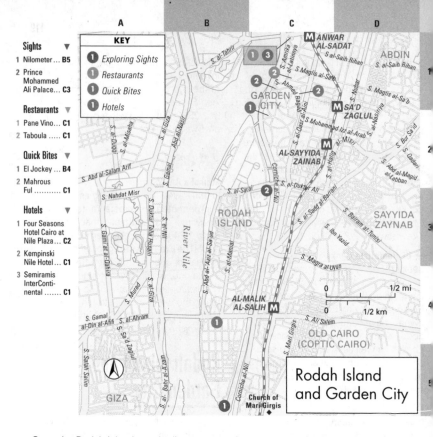

Sights ▼
1 Nilometer... **B5**
2 Prince Mohammed Ali Palace... **C3**

Restaurants ▼
1 Pane Vino... **C1**
2 Taboula **C1**

Quick Bites ▼
1 El Jockey ... **B4**
2 Mahrous Ful **C1**

Hotels ▼
1 Four Seasons Hotel Cairo at Nile Plaza... **C2**
2 Kempinski Nile Hotel ... **C1**
3 Semiramis InterContinental **C1**

KEY
1 Exploring Sights
1 Restaurants
1 Quick Bites
1 Hotels

Rodah Island and Garden City

Opposite Rodah Island—and adjacent to Downtown Cairo—is the quiet and mostly residential Garden City. Planned by private investors and home to many of Cairo's expats during the 19th and early 20th centuries, it's an area with high-end residences, embassies, and such upscale hotels as the Four Seasons Hotel Cairo at Nile Plaza and the Kempinski Nile Hotel.

◉ Sights

Nilometer
NOTABLE BUILDING | At the southern end of Rodah Island, al-Miqyas (The Nilometer) was used from pharaonic times until the completion of the Aswan Dam in the late 1950s to measure the height of flood waters using carved measuring marks. Needless to say, this was something that the populace followed with great interest—and, if the waters were abundant, with great celebration.

Built in 861 on the site of an earlier Nilometer, the present structure is considered the oldest extant Islamic building, though the conical dome is a 1895 restoration. Inside, Qur'an verses that speak of water, vegetation, and prosperity are carved onto the walls. Nearby is a small museum for Umm Kulthum (a famous Egyptian singer-songwriter and actress) that showcases some of her personal effects, including her iconic wardrobes. ☒ Southern tip of Rodah Island, El-Malek El-Saleh St., Rodah Island ☒ LE40.

★ Prince Mohammed Ali Palace (The Manial Palace and Museum)
CASTLE/PALACE | Built between 1900 and 1929 by Prince Mohammed Ali, King Farouk's uncle, the interiors of this palace

are influenced by Ottoman, Moorish, Persian, and European Art Nouveau and Rococo styles, all of which mark also important periods in modern Egyptian architecture. Highlights include the mosque; the sabil (fountain); the clocktower; the Throne and Gold Halls; the tile-adorned Blue Salon; and the hunting and taxidermy museum, which showcases a range of creatures, from insects to mammals. The palace is also renowned for its stunning gardens and distinctive collection of plants. ⊠ *1 Al Saraya St., Rodah Island* ☎ *2/2368–7495* 🖆 *LE100* ⊘ *Closed Fri. and Sat.*

Restaurants

Pane Vino

$$$$ | **ITALIAN** | The ultra-contemporary and fashionable Italian restaurant at the Semiramis InterContinental puts a modern twist on traditional trattoria fare using authentic Italian ingredients. Signature dishes include crispy fried calamari and carpaccio with rocket salad and Parmesan cheese. **Known for:** magnificent Nile views; tempting cocktails and mocktails; a fine yet relaxed setting. ⑤ *Average main: LE300* ⊠ *Semiramis InterContinental, Corniche al-Nil, Garden City* ☎ *2/2798–8000.*

Taboula

$$ | **LEBANESE** | This cozy restaurant, with a highly patterned tiled floor and pale stucco walls adorned with Lebanese crafts, comes alive in the evening. Grilled meats are staples here, as are hot and cold mezze. **Known for:** traditional Lebanese arak (anise liqueur); delectable knafeh (layers of pastry with cheese) that pairs well with mint tea; charming decor that attracts sophisticated crowds. ⑤ *Average main: LE99* ⊠ *1 Latin America St., Garden City* ☎ *2/2792–5261* ⊕ *www. taboula-eg.com.*

☕ Coffee and Quick Bites

El Jockey

$ | **ICE CREAM** | **FAMILY** | This 1930s neighborhood ice-cream shop is a great place to beat the heat, whether you opt for a scoop of chocolate or a fresh-fruit-flavored icy treat. **Known for:** elaborate ice cream cakes; evening people-watching spot; unique Egyptian flavors like mastic. ⑤ *Average main: LE15* ⊠ *30 Roda St., Rodah Island* ☎ *2/2364–7233* ▭ *No credit cards.*

Mahrous Ful

$$ | **MIDDLE EASTERN** | *Ful* (fava-bean stew) carts and restaurants are a common sight in Cairo, but the customers here hail from all over the world thanks to the many nearby embassies and to the freshness and flavor of its offerings. To create the stew, which is served primarily at breakfast but also makes a filling lunch, the beans are slow-cooked in a large metal jug and then mashed and served with tahini and a flavorful oil. **Known for:** vegetarian-friendly feast of ful, salad, pickles, chips, and eggs; pricier than the average ful cart but still very affordable; buzzing 24/7 Cairo street-food experience. ⑤ *Average main: LE50* ⊠ *6 Dr. Mohamed Fawzy St., Garden City* ☎ *11/1146–4714* ▭ *No credit cards.*

🛏 Hotels

Four Seasons Hotel Cairo at Nile Plaza

$$$$ | **RESORT** | **FAMILY** | The attention to detail is evident everywhere, from the proliferation of marble in the vast lobby to the gourmet ingredients used in the restaurants. **Pros:** you'll be surrounded by Cairo glitterati; really large standard rooms; excellent spa. **Cons:** atmosphere is more corporate than resort-like; not all rooms have terraces or balconies; public spaces could be viewed as lacking in character. ⑤ *Rooms from: $500* ⊠ *1089 Corniche al-Nil, Maglis El Shaab, Garden City* ☎ *2/2791–7000* ⊕ *www.fourseasons.com* ⇆ *365 rooms* ❒ *No Meals.*

Did You Know?

As evidenced by its stunning interior, Rodah Island's Nilometer is an Islamic building, but the ancient Egyptians also used such structures to measure the Nile's depth. High flood waters equated to more robust harvests (and greater tax revenues).

Kempinski Nile Hotel

$$ | HOTEL | Comfortable rooms, lots of amenities, and excellent dining experiences—the breakfast buffet at the Italian eatery is particularly good—make it easy to unplug at this luxury hotel on the edge of Garden City. **Pros:** midway between many popular districts; spa, gym, and a rooftop pool; 24/7 private butler service. **Cons:** might feel impersonal to some; room decor is a bit outdated; heavy traffic on the Corniche. ⑤ *Rooms from: $300* ✉ *12 Ahmed Ragheb St., Qasr El Nil, Garden City* ☎ *2/2798–0000* ⊕ *www. kempinski.com* ⇨ *194 rooms* ⑩ *No Meals.*

Semiramis InterContinental

$$ | HOTEL | Rooms at this modern high-rise are spacious, with full-length windows and private balconies that make the most of the city views. **Pros:** close to Downtown Cairo; great lunch buffet; good value for money. **Cons:** some might find it large and impersonal; room decor is a bit plain; heavy traffic on the Corniche. ⑤ *Rooms from: $270* ✉ *Corniche al-Nil, Qasr El Nil, Garden City* ☎ *2/2798–8000* ⊕ *www.intercontinental. com* ⇨ *721 rooms* ⑩ *No Meals.*

Nightlife

BARS

The Bar

BARS | In addition to beer, wine, and cocktails, a relaxed atmosphere and great views of the Corniche are on tap at this bar on the third floor of the luxurious Four Seasons Hotel Cairo at Nile Plaza. If you want something to eat, the hotel's Zaytouni and Bella right nearby. ✉ *Four Seasons Hotel Cairo at Nile Plaza, 1089 Corniche El Nil, Qasr El Nil, Garden City* ☎ *2/2791–6878* ⊕ *www.fourseasons. com.*

Esco-Bar

BARS | Head for the 19th floor of the famous and trendy Cairo Capital Club to enjoy the excellent views while sipping on margaritas and indulging in some high-end Tex-Mex. ✉ *9 El-Moustashar Mohammed Fahmy El-Sayed St., Qasr Ad Dobarah, Qasr El Nil, Garden City* ☎ *12/7133–3388.*

The Kempinski Nile Roof

BARS | The Nile Kempinski's 11th floor is restful: the nicely lit roof-top pool area offers a 360° view of the Nile and the Corniche, and the sounds of the city can barely be heard. Enjoy a drink (or several), a shisha (water pipe), and mezze or sandwiches. Don't plan on using the pool, however—that's a guests-only privilege. ✉ *Kempinski Nile Hotel, 12 Ahmed Ragheb St., Qasr El Nil, Garden City* ☎ *2/2798–0000* ⊕ *www.kempinski.com.*

⊙ Performing Arts

International Center for Arts, El-Manasterly Palace

MUSIC | The setting for this venue, which hosts concerts by notable Egyptian artists, is incomparable: Manasterly Palace is the one remaining part of a complex built by Hassan Fouad Pasha al-Manasterly, former Governor of Cairo, in 1851, and its remarkable architecture adds to the experience of seeing performances here. ✉ *1 El-Malek El-Saleh St., Rodah Island* ☎ *2/2363–1467* ⊕ *www.manasterly.com.*

★ Makan–Egyptian Center for Culture and Arts

FOLK/TRADITIONAL DANCE | Folk music and other performances that reflect Egypt's unique artistic identity are the specialty of this intimate space. Its most famous show is a traditional women's *zar*, a folkloric musical trance and healing ritual that's performed every Wednesday night. Spaces are limited, so it's a good idea to book in advance. ✉ *1 Saad Zaghloul St., Al Munirah, Garden City* ☎ *12/2112–4980* ⊕ *www.egyptmusic.org.*

This bedroom illustrates the mixture of Ottoman, Moorish, Persian, and European Art Nouveau and Rococo styles used to decorate the Prince Mohamed Ali Palace.

🧳 Shopping

ART GALLERIES
Duroub Gallery for Plastic Arts
ART GALLERIES | Duroub Gallery offers a variety of thematic exhibitions throughout the year, and has been operational since 1996. The gallery showcases the works of contemporary artists of all ages, countries, and walks of life. ✉ *4 Latin America St., Qasr Ad Dobarah, Qasr El Nil, Garden City, Rodah Island* ☎ *2/2794–7951.*

CONCEPT STORES
★ Cairopolitan
SOUVENIRS | The whimsical, thoughtfully curated accessories and home decor at this concept store celebrate Egypt's long history—from the ancient to the old to the contemporary. You might find Egypt's signature old quarter incorporated into coasters (or rather, "coinsters," as they're called here) or a pouch shaped like a piece of *aish baladi* (Egyptian flatbread). ✉ *8 Dar El Shefa St., Garden City* ☎ *2/2793–1153* ⊕ *www.cairopolitan.com.*

🏃 Activities

Felucca Ride on the Nile
SAILING | *Feluccas,* the small passenger sailboats found up and down the Nile, are a serene way to soak in the city and separate yourself from it at the same time. They cost between LE100 and LE200 an hour, depending on your negotiation skills and how many people are joining you. A sturdy, popular, and almost historic fleet is across from the Four Seasons Hotel at Nile Plaza on the Corniche of Garden City. The operators usually sell soft drinks and water, but you're welcome to bring your own food and beverages. Make sure to tip the captain at least LE20 before you return to port. ✉ *Corniche el-Nil, Garden City.*

Gezira Island and Zamalek

Gezira Island, which amusingly translates as "Island Island," is small enough to navigate on foot. Although locals usually refer to this affluent Nile islet as "Zamalek," that's actually the name of its primary district. Under Khedive Isma'il, Zamalek was called Jardin des Plantes (Garden of Plants) as it was known for its exotic flora imported from all over the world and incorporated into a landscape planned by the French designer, De La Chevalerie.

Zamalek is home to the iconic Gezira Palace, which was built in 1869 to accommodate foreign dignitaries—including Eugénie, Empress of the French—when they visited to attend the opening of the Suez Canal. It's now the central part of the Cairo Marriott Hotel & Omar Khayyam Casino. Other palaces have also been repurposed as government buildings, museums, and arts centers.

Although some buildings are Art Deco, Zamalek is primarily known for its 19th-century architecture. Many expats and wealthy Cairenes have homes here, so although residential streets are quiet, more commercial areas, with their shops, restaurants, and night spots, seem to never sleep. In addition, the Cairo Opera House, inaugurated here in 1988, helped to establish the island as an arts and culture hub.

Sights

Aisha Fahmy Palace
NOTABLE BUILDING | Beside the Nile near 26th of July Street, Aisha Fahmy Palace is an embodiment of early 20th-century architectural splendor. Designed by Italian architect Antonio Lasciac, it was built in 1907 for Egyptian aristocrat Ali Fahmy, King Farouk's army chief. He left the estate to his daughter, Aisha, and she lived there with her husband, prominent actor and director Youssef Wahbi.

The two-story palace underwent a restoration that lasted more than a decade, and now, in addition to housing the Japanese embassy on the second floor, it serves as a cultural center, with art exhibitions throughout the year. Visitors are welcome to stop by for a look at its Rococo-style interior, featuring silk-clad walls, frescoes, and stained glass; just call ahead to be sure the palace is open. The gardens are also quite serene despite the bustle of neighboring 26th of July Street. ⊠ *1 Aziz Abaza St., Zamalek* ☎ *2/2735–8211* ☑ *Free* ☞ *IDs are checked upon entry.*

Cairo Tower
VIEWPOINT | FAMILY | Designed by Egyptian architect Naoum Shebib and completed in 1961, the Cairo Tower soars 610 feet (187 meters), making it the tallest structure not only in Egypt but also North Africa. Its exterior exhibits pharaonic influences, as evidenced by latticework that is reminiscent of the lotus plant, and its observation deck affords an unprecedented, 360°-view of greater Cairo. Morning visits have their appeal, but sunsets from the tower are phenomenal. ⊠ *Al Borg St., Zamalek* ☎ *2/2736–5112* ☑ *LE200.*

Museum of Modern Egyptian Art
ART MUSEUM | The vast holdings at this museum across from the Cairo Opera House consist of modern works by 20th- and 21st-century Egyptian painters, sculptors, calligraphers, and other artists. Highlights of the permanent collection include sculptures by Mahmoud Mukhtar and paintings by Mahmoud Said, both pioneers of the Egyptian modern art movement in the 1920s and '30s. The museum hosts temporary exhibitions as well. ⊠ *Cairo Opera House, off Mahmoud Mokhtar street, Opera Square, Zamalek* ☎ *2/2736–6667* ☑ *LE20.*

Occupying the Nile's largest island, the Zamalek neighborhood is home to elegant apartment blocks, great restaurants, and the outstanding Cairo Opera House.

🍽 Restaurants

Abou El Sid

$$$ | **MIDDLE EASTERN** | **FAMILY** | You'll feel as if you've entered an Arabian palace when you pass through the portal of this restaurant. The food perfectly complements the decor, with hot and cold mezze and dishes such as moussaka, okra-and-veal-shank stew, and *muammar* (savory rice with cream)—all of it impressive. **Known for:** convenient location in the heart of Zamalek; grilled meats, stuffed pigeon, and other Egyptian classics; branches throughout Cairo and beyond. ⑤ *Average main: LE185* ✉ *157 26 of July Corridor, Mohammed Mazhar St., Zamalek* ☎ *2/2735–9640* ⊕ *www.abouelsid.com.*

Five Bells

$$$$ | **INTERNATIONAL** | Although it's not a fine-dining restaurant, the locally beloved Five Bells has been around for decades and blends a nostalgically proper feel with an easygoing, casual atmosphere. You can sit indoors, where there's a bar, but most people enjoy their Egyptian or international dishes outdoors, under a sizable tent with a central fountain that's surrounded by five bells. **Known for:** remarkable assortment of mezze served with delicious crispy bread; a great place to enjoy a glass of wine; live piano music. ⑤ *Average main: LE300* ✉ *13 Ismail Mohammed St., off Abu Al Feda St., Zamalek* ☎ *10/0113–2181 reservations, 2/2735–8635* ⊕ *five-bells.business.site.*

Le Tarbouche

$$$$ | **MIDDLE EASTERN** | It's hard to decide what's best here—the mouthwatering Egyptian food, the Nile views, the Khedive-style interior, or the excellent service. Indeed, La Tarbouche is one of the restaurants that Cairenes most often recommend to visitors. **Known for:** delicious Egyptian baked rice with pigeon; fall-off-the-bone meat tagines; tranquil oud music. ⑤ *Average main: LE300* ✉ *Saray El Gezirah St., El-Khalig, Zamalek* ☎ *2/2735–6730* ⊕ *www.lepacha. com* ☞ *Children under 10 not allowed after 8 pm.*

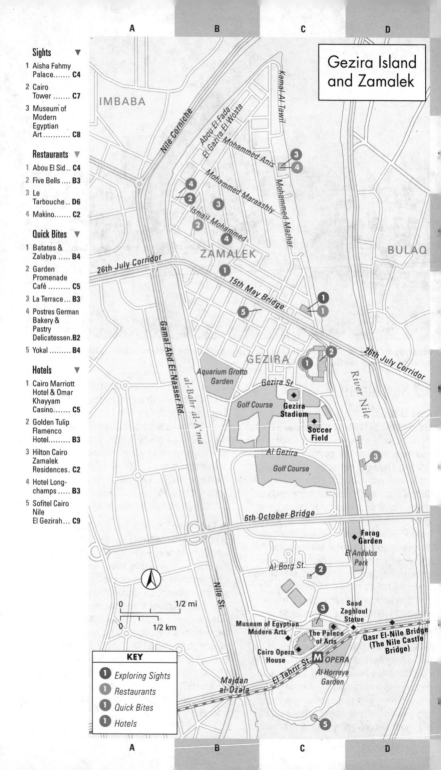

Sights ▼

1 Aisha Fahmy Palace....... C4
2 Cairo Tower C7
3 Museum of Modern Egyptian Art C8

Restaurants ▼

1 Abou El Sid .. C4
2 Five Bells B3
3 Le Tarbouche .. D6
4 Makino....... C2

Quick Bites ▼

1 Batates & Zalabya B4
2 Garden Promenade Café C5
3 La Terrace... B3
4 Postres German Bakery & Pastry Delicatessen.B2
5 Yokal B4

Hotels ▼

1 Cairo Marriott Hotel & Omar Khayyam Casino....... C5
2 Golden Tulip Flamenco Hotel......... B3
3 Hilton Cairo Zamalek Residences. C2
4 Hotel Long-champs B3
5 Sofitel Cairo Nile El Gezirah... C9

Gezira Island and Zamalek

IMBABA

Nile Corniche

Kamal Al-Tawil

Abou El Fada

El Gazira El Wosta

Mohammed Anis

Mohammed Maraashly

Ismail-Mohammed

Mohammed Mazhar

BULAQ

ZAMALEK

26th July Corridor

15th May Bridge

26th July Corridor

Gamal Abd El-Nasser Rd.

GEZIRA

Aquarium Grotto Garden

Gezira St.

al-Bahr al-A'ma

Golf Course

Gezira Stadium

Soccer Field

River Nile

Al Gezira

Golf Course

6th October Bridge

Farag Garden

El Andalos Park

Al Borg St.

Nile St.

Saad Zaghloul Statue

Qasr El-Nile Bridge (The Nile Castle Bridge)

Museum of Egyptian Modern Arts

The Palace of Arts

Cairo Opera House

M OPERA

Al Horreya Garden

Majdan al-Dżala

El Tahrir St.

0   1/2 mi
0   1/2 km

KEY

1 Exploring Sights
1 Restaurants
1 Quick Bites
1 Hotels

Makino

$$$$ | JAPANESE | If you, like many members of the expat community, find yourself craving a warm bowl of ramen or some fresh sushi, head to this small, casual restaurant. The Japanese chefs prefer using only authentic ingredients, some of which can be hard to come by in Cairo, so menu offerings tend to change. **Known for:** authentic ingredients and preparations; one of the only places in Cairo that serves ramen; limited hours and seating. $ *Average main: LE800* ✉ *Hilton Cairo Zamalek Residences, 21 Mohammed Mazhar St., Zamalek* ☎ *2/2737–5163* ⊕ *www.facebook.com/ JapaneseRestaurantMakinoCairo.*

☕ Coffee and Quick Bites

Batates & Zalabya

$ | MIDDLE EASTERN | Batates & Zalabya is a major chain of street stalls that special-izes in two snacks: *batates* (French fries), and, more notably, *zalabya* (Egyptian deep-fried dough balls). Although the classic *zalabya* is served with powdered sugar or sugar syrup, possible toppings here include hazelnut, chocolate, and caramel. **Known for:** freshly fried zalabya with a variety of toppings; practical on-the-go packaging; several quick sweet and savory snack options. $ *Aver-age main: LE25* ✉ *26 July St., on the corner of Shagaret Al Dor St., Zamalek* ☎ *2/2587–3088* ⊕ *www.facebook.com/ Batateszalabya.*

Garden Promenade Café

$$$ | CAFÉ | Seek refuge from Cairo's crowded streets with bite to eat and a drink (alcoholic or not) at this café set in the gardens next to the restored Gezira Palace. Open for breakfast, lunch, and dinner, it serves everything from soups, salads, and sandwiches to pizzas and pastas. **Known for:** charming outdoor setting; a menu with something for everyone; freshly baked local bread. $ *Average main: LE200* ✉ *Cairo Marriott Hotel & Omar Khayyam Casino, 16 Saray El Gezirah St., Zamalek* ☎ *2/2728–3000* ⊕ *www.marriott.com/hotels.*

La Terrace

$$$ | INTERNATIONAL | This eatery on the 11th floor of the President Hotel has several comfortable seating areas and is the perfect place to grab a quick coffee or a relaxed dinner with drinks. You can also enjoy a delicious lunch here, though reservations are a good idea. **Known for:** stylish design and modern vibe; stunning sunset views of Zamalek; gluten-free and vegetarian options. $ *Average main: LE250* ✉ *President Hotel, 22 Taha Hussein St., Zamalek* ☎ *12/7355–1573* ⊕ *www.thepresidentcairo.com.*

Postres German Bakery & Pastry Delicatessen

$$ | BAKERY | Although this eatery is set in Zamalek's Flamenco Hotel, its warm woods, tile work, and selection of baked goods make it feel like a family run bakery in a small European town. It opens at 7 am, so you can enjoy break-fast and coffee while watching Cairenes on their way to work; or come later in the day for a German *brezel* (pretzel). **Known for:** fresh, authentically European baked goods; flavorful cookies and chocolates at Christmastime; cozy and quaint. $ *Average main: LE60* ✉ *2 El Gezira El Wosta St., off Abu Al Feda St., Zamalek* ☎ *10/0188–1836* ⊕ *www.flamencohotels. com.*

Yokal

$$ | MIDDLE EASTERN | Tucked in an alleyway, this hip eatery takes street food to the next level by using premium ingredients in its consistently delicious sandwiches. The bread rolls are addic-tively soft, filled with a variety of meats and generously drizzled with tahini; they come with a side of French fries, too. **Known for:** elevated Egyptian street food; sausages with a dash of ground coffee (talk about secret ingredients!); gloriously soft mini bread rolls baked in-house. $ *Average main: LE100* ✉ *118 26 of July St., Zamalek* ✥ *Back entrance*

This manicured setting beside the Nile nods to a time when Zamalek was called Jardin des Plantes (Garden of Plants), owing to the area being filled with exotic flora.

☎ *11/4449–4466* 🌐 *www.facebook.com/yokal.eg.*

Hotels

Cairo Marriott Hotel & Omar Khayyam Casino
$$ | **HOTEL** | With the resplendent palace built by Khedive Ism'ail in 1869 right in the middle of its grounds, this sizable hotel is considered a prime destination in the bustling Zamalek neighborhood. **Pros:** peaceful, garden-retreat setting; great dining variety; walking distance from many popular attractions. **Cons:** traffic-heavy commutes to other neighborhoods; many rooms don't have a view; busy and a bit impersonal. *Rooms from: $245* ✉ *16 Gezira St., Zamalek* ☎ *2/2728–3000* 🌐 *www.marriott.com* *1122 rooms* *Free Breakfast.*

Golden Tulip Flamenco Hotel
$ | **HOTEL** | **FAMILY** | The family-friendly Flamenco, set amid some of Zamalek's best shopping and dining streets, has spacious rooms that are far more affordable than those at other hotels in this pricey neighborhood. **Pros:** good value for the money; ample breakfast spread; popular happy hour bar. **Cons:** located in the louder part of Zamalek; Wi-Fi doesn't work well; few on-site amenities. *Rooms from: $98* ✉ *2 El Gezira El Wosta St., Zamalek* ☎ *2/2735–0815* 🌐 *www.flamencohotels.com* *176 rooms* *Free Breakfast.*

Hilton Cairo Zamalek Residences
$$ | **HOTEL** | **FAMILY** | Quiet rooms and a convenient location—where you can enjoy nice walks—are among the hallmarks of this well-established hotel. **Pros:** great staff and service; family-friendly; amenities include a spa, a gym, and a pool. **Cons:** decor could use an update; average Wi-Fi service; traffic-heavy commutes to other neighborhoods. *Rooms from: $295* ✉ *21 Mohammed Mazhar St., Zamalek* ☎ *2/2737–0055* 🌐 *www.hilton.com* *164 rooms* *No Meals.*

Hotel Longchamps

$ | B&B/INN | This whimsical bed-and-breakfast on the upper floors of a medium-size tower block offers Old World charm and is a quiet refuge from the city. **Pros:** excellent value for money; friendly, welcoming staff; cozy and quiet. **Cons:** lots of repeat guests can make it difficult to book a room; traffic-heavy commutes to other neighborhoods; no luxury services or amenities. $ *Rooms from: $88* ⊠ *21 Ismail Mohammed St., Zamalek* ☎ *2/2735–2311* ⊕ *www.hotel-longchamps.com* ⌁ *21 rooms* ⍾ *Free Breakfast.*

Sofitel Cairo Nile El Gezirah

$$ | HOTEL | The circular tower of this hotel—on the southern tip of Gezira Island and surrounded by parks and residential districts—has been part the Cairo skyline for well over three decades. **Pros:** quiet and central location; all rooms have a view of the city and the Nile; great patio lounge area. **Cons:** some areas need refurbishing; service can be lacking; noise from the boats can penetrate lower-level rooms. $ *Rooms from: $240* ⊠ *3 El Thawra Council St., Gezira* ☎ *2/2737–3737* ⊕ *www.sofitel.com* ⌁ *433 rooms* ⍾ *No Meals.*

Nightlife

BARS

Aperitivo

BARS | Aperitivo is a great place to dress up and enjoy a night on the town. The modern decor, dark wood, and warm but low-key lighting give it a luxurious, romantic feel; the service is excellent; and the food and drinks, though pricey, are exquisite. ⊠ *157 26 July St., Zamalek* ☎ *2/2735–0543.*

Cairo Cellar (*The Cellar*)

BARS | Though this lively bar is literally in the basement of the President Hotel, the descent into it is far nicer than that into the average cellar. Food (mainly tapas), drinks, and merriment are all on tap. ⊠ *President Hotel, 22 Taha Hussein St., Zamalek* ☎ *2/2735–0652* ⊕ *www.facebook.com/CairoCellar.*

Carmen Pub Bar

BARS | Locals and tourists patronize this relaxed watering hole in the Flamenco Hotel for its draft beer, affordable drinks, and personalized service. The barmen, most of whom have been working here a long time, are exceptionally good at recognizing faces, even those of customers who have visited just once before. ⊠ *Golden Tulip Flamenco Hotel, 2 El Gezira El Wosta St., Zamalek* ☎ *2/2735–0815.*

★ Crimson Bar & Grill

BARS | In terms of location, this rooftop bar won the lottery: it overlooks the Nile from one of Zamalek's quietest streets. No surprise, then, that it's popular, so you need a reservation to get in. The red color scheme is softened a bit by plant walls, wood-and-marble tables, and other fixtures; the food is delicious; and the drinks menu is extensive. Be sure to ask about sizes before ordering, though: sangria is sometimes served in punch bowls—trendy punch bowls, but still. ⊠ *16 Kamal Al Tawil St., Zamalek* ☎ *12/7505–5555* ⊕ *www.crimsoncairo.com* ☞ *Reservations required.*

L'Aubergine

BARS | Head to the candlelit top floor for a cocktail and the ground floor if you want dinner and drinks. The atmosphere is casual, the drinks menu is extensive, and the food menu features innovative dishes. Though it can be a bit dark and a bit loud, and reservations are required, L'Aubergine is open and late and is centrally located. ⊠ *5 Sayed El-Bakry St., Zamalek* ☎ *2/2738–0080* ☞ *Reservations required.*

Monkey Bar & Grill

BARS | Chic decor that mixes rustic with modern, fantastic drinks, and delicious food (the desserts are especially decadent) make for a great experience at this loud, trendy bar and grill. Just remember to make reservations. ⊠ *22 Taha Hussein St., Zamalek* ☎ *10/3349–3330* ☞ *Reservations required.*

Pier 88

BARS | Occupying a docked boat, rather than, as its name suggest, a pier, this upscale restaurant-bar is quiet on most weeknights but comes alive on weekends. Try for a seat in the small outdoor area, where you can enjoy the river breeze. The food is predominately Italian, and the service is generally good—unless it's busy. ⊠ *Imperial Boat, 19 Saray El Gezirah St., Zamalek* ☎ *12/0811–1130* ⊕ *www.pier88group.com.*

CASINOS

Omar Khayyam Casino

THEMED ENTERTAINMENT | The crowd at this upscale casino in the Cairo Marriott Hotel consists only of tourists and expats (by law, Egyptians aren't allowed to gamble). It's open 24/7 and has all the usual games, including roulette, blackjack, and slot machines. All you need to enter is your passport—and perhaps, your lucky charm. ⊠ *Cairo Marriott Hotel & Omar Khayyam Casino, 16 Gezira St., Zamalek* ☎ *2/2728–3000.*

 **Performing Arts**

Cairo Opera House

CONCERTS | This is the beating heart of Zamalek's cultural scene, home to the Cairo Opera Ballet Company, the city's renowned symphony orchestra, and a plethora of performing arts companies. Performances—from the classical to the contemporary, featuring local and international artists—fill the schedules at both the Main and Small halls. Pick an event from the website, book it online, and enjoy the show. You might have to don your Sunday best, though: a jacket and tie are compulsory for men in the Main Hall but not in the others; women can dress more freely, though jeans aren't allowed. ⊠ *Cairo Opera House, off Mahmoud Mokhtar St., Opera Square, Gezira* ☎ *2/2739–0188* ⊕ *www.cairoopera.org.*

 Shopping

ART

Safarkhan Art Gallery

ART GALLERIES | Established in 1968, Safarkhan exhibits, collects, and deals in modern and contemporary Egyptian fine art. The curators highlight the works of some of the country's premier artists, often with an emphasis on up-and-coming talent. The gallery also carries a collection of rare pieces dating back to 1920. ⊠ *6 Brazil St., Zamalek* ☎ *12/7016–9291 sales, 2/2735–3314* ⊕ *www.safarkhan.com.*

CLOTHING AND ACCESSORIES

Sahara Collection

MIXED CLOTHING | **FAMILY** | This store successfully combines high-end fashion concepts with traditional styles in its versatile collections for men and women. What's more, the clothes are locally made and ethically sourced. The same is true of the accessories, which are produced by the brand's sister company, Nomad. ⊠ *13 El-Mansour Mohammed St., Zamalek* ☎ *2/2737–7964* ⊕ *www.thesahara-collection.com.*

Sami Amin Designs

HANDBAGS | Like the colorful and ever-evolving culture of Egypt, Sami Amin's handbags, wallets, jewelry, and other accessories have just the right mix of tradition and modernity. The self-taught designer founded his brand in 1997 and channels his artistic sensibilities into every piece in this endearing little shop. ⊠ *13 El-Mansour Mohammed St., Zamalek* ☎ *12/0401–4016* ⊕ *www.sami-amin.com.*

CRAFTS

★ Mamlouk Gallery

CERAMICS | Although it's tucked away on a side street and has no sign, it's worth making the effort to find this rustic shop that's full to bursting with handcrafted ceramics. It feels like it's from another era—in all the best ways. Its owner is pleasant and helpful but gives you the space to explore the vast selection of unique and colorful items on your own, browsing as long as it takes to find the perfect piece. ✉ *4A Hassan Assem St., Zamalek* ☎ *2/2735–2437.*

HOME DECOR

Caravanserai

HOUSEWARES | Heritage and craftsmanship are the founding pillars of Caravanserai, a store that celebrates both local artistry and cultural fusion in merchandise that ranges from small, minimalistic decorative items to large, elaborate pieces of furniture. ✉ *16 Mohammed Maraashly St., Zamalek* ☎ *10/0167–5855* ⊕ *www. caravanserai-design.com.*

MUSIC

Retrograde

RECORDS | Taking the record store experience a step beyond, Retrograde sells art (including pieces by local artists), used books, and vintage goods—from typewriters to turntables—in addition to vinyl. Note the table in the middle of the shop: many patrons have marked it with messages of love and appreciation. ✉ *33 Ahmed Heshmat St., Zamalek* ☎ *10/9398–4469.*

Sherry's Vinyl

RECORDS | Vintage English and Arabic records feature greatly here, with some French, Russian, and other recordings occasionally finding their way into the mix. Don't know what to look for? Ask the store manager, who has been a collector himself since 1997. You'll also find yourself taken in by the vintage items on display, from gramophones and turntables to off-brand but collectible comic books. Just leave the action figures alone—they're not for sale no matter how hard you try. And be sure to ask for the soup of the day (hint: it's coffee). ✉ *2 Bahgat Ali St., Zamalek* ☎ *12/8843–4858* ⊕ *www.facebook.com/Sherrys.Vintage.*

 Activities

Kayak on the Nile

KAYAKING | A fantastic way to experience the full majesty of the Nile is by kayak. If you're a beginner, guides provide instructions and keep an eye on you. If you have some experience, you can head straight out. ✉ *Zamalek* ☎ *11–17–83–08–01* ⊕ *www.facebook.com/Zamalek.Kayak* 🏷 *LE100* ☞ *Call ahead.*

Giza

It used to be that you approached Giza through green fields. But with Cairo's perpetual expansion, you now must navigate raucous streets full to the brim with buses, vans, taxis, and the odd donkey cart to reach Giza and its ancient sights.

During the second millennium, this area served as a necropolis for many of the pharaohs who ruled ancient Egypt. Although Persian, Greek, Roman, and Byzantine conquests each brought changes, it wasn't until the Muslim conquest of Egypt in AD 642 that the city was founded and given its current name.

Subsequent centuries saw changes, too. The British focused on Giza's urbanization, constructing streets and buildings in the area—an undertaking that's been carried on by subsequent Egyptian governments since 1952. Today, the large concrete towers lining Giza's roads and obscuring the view of the pyramids are indications of an increasingly urban area—one that offers many amenities for those visiting both Cairo and the Great Pyramids.

Until the new Metro line connecting central Cairo to the pyramid complex is completed, the easiest way to reach Giza's main attraction, the pyramids, is to use a ride-hailing app. Some of the bus services that pass by the Giza complex also have apps and charge a fraction of the price, but the ride will take longer.

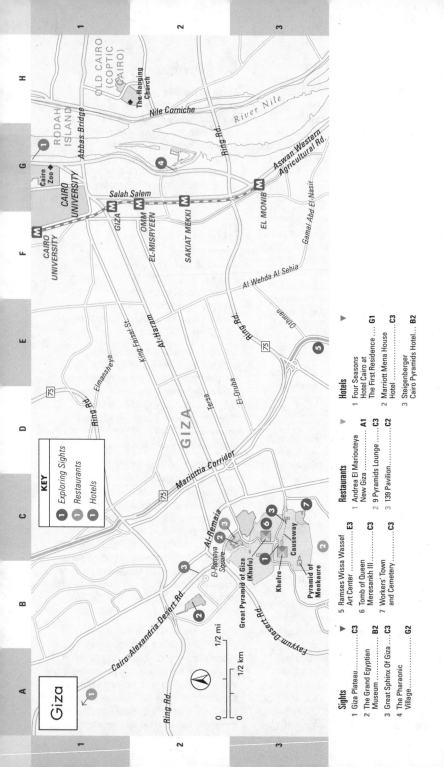

Giza

KEY

- 1 Exploring Sights
- 1 Restaurants
- 1 Hotels

Sights

1 Giza Plateau **C3**
2 The Grand Egyptian Museum **B2**
3 Great Sphinx Of Giza **C3**
4 The Pharaonic Village.............. **G2**
5 Ramses Wissa Wassef Art Center **E3**
6 Tomb of Queen Meresankh III **C3**
7 Workers' Town and Cemetery.............. **C3**

Restaurants

1 Andrea El Mariouteya New Giza **A1**
2 9 Pyramids Lounge **C3**
3 139 Pavilion.............. **C2**

Hotels

1 Four Seasons Hotel Cairo at The First Residence **G1**
2 Marriott Mena House Hotel **C3**
3 Steigenberger Cairo Pyramids Hotel... **B2**

Alternatively, you could hire a white taxi for the day to take you to the pyramids and other nearby ancient sites, but this can be quite expensive.

The most cost-effective option is to use public transit, perhaps dividing up your ride between different modes of transportation. For example, if you ride the Metro to Giza station, you can then use a ride-hailing application or take a Mwasalat Misr bus (including the M7 and the M11 lines) the rest of the way.

To reach the pyramids by bus from central Cairo, take the Mwasalat Misr M7 bus from Abdel Moneim Riad Square Station on Tahrir Square. It has many stops in the general vicinity of the pyramids, including at the Marriott Mena House, which puts you at the foot of the Giza Plateau, as well as stops towards the Chepos, Ahmos, and Khafraa Gates.

Sights

★ Giza Plateau

RUINS | You've seen Giza's iconic super-structures in books or films, but nothing prepares you for the breathtaking, in-re-al-life magnetism of the pyramids. The 4th-Dynasty tombs of three Old Kingdom (2687–2181 BC) rulers that dominate the skyline of the desert plateau to the southwest of Cairo simultaneously inspire humility and awe. The largest and most perfect of them is that of King Khufu (Greek name: Cheops), referred to as the Great Pyramid, followed by those of Khafre (Greek name: Chephren) and Menkaure (Greek name: Mycerinus), his son and grandson respectively.

There is more than meets the eye at the Giza Plateau: each pyramid was built within a complex consisting of cause-ways, temples, a subsidiary queen's pyramid, and a smaller, more symbolic "satellite" pyramid for the king. You can also visit some of the smaller pyramids belonging to female dependents, as well as the *mastabas* (large trapezoidal tombs) of the kings' lesser relatives and courtiers—just ask for details when buying your ticket.

Preparation is key to visiting the Giza Plateau. The walks are long, and the sun is strong year-round, so wear comfortable shoes, a hat, sunglasses, and sunscreen. Be prepared for numerous encounters with souvenir sellers and animal tenders, some of whom overcharge for their products and services—to them, a firm and repetitive *"la shukran"* ("no, thank you") will get the message across. Exploring the interior of one of the pyramids should also be part of your once-in-a-lifetime experience, but brace yourself for a bent back and for tackling some very narrow and sloped corridors.

There's a general admission ticket to the area as well as individual fees for entering the structures that are open to the public and for accessing the Great Sphinx. The evening Great Sphinx and Pyramids sound-and-light show is on the pricey side, and some say it's not worth the money. Still, seeing the monuments lit up at night would be yet another once-in-a-lifetime experience. ⊠ *Giza Plateau, Al Giza Desert, Greater Cairo, Giza* 🌐 *General site admission: LE200. Great Pyramid: LE400. Khafre's Pyramid: LE100. Menkaure's Pyramid: LE100. Sound-and-light show: LE375.*

★ The Grand Egyptian Museum (*GEM*)

HISTORY MUSEUM | One of the most ambitious architectural designs in the new millennium is a fitting home for the mother lode of ancient artifacts excavated in Egypt over the last 150 years. Situated less than 2 km (1 mile) west of the pyramids, the world's largest archaeological museum covers 120 acres (49 hectares) on the Giza Plateau. Although embellished with hieroglyphs, its otherwise modern facade is a clear indication that the interior is state of the art, from the large exhibition halls that welcome

Continued on page 145

THE
PYRAMIDS
OF GIZA

Ascending the throne as a middle-aged man, the ruler Khufu may have personally chosen the plateau in Giza where Egypt's most famous pyramids were built. In antiquity, they would have certainly inspired awe, just as they do today. Indeed, despite the encroachment of the modern city nearby, the only surviving wonders of the ancient world remain resolutely majestic.

"Man fears time, but time fears the pyramids," goes the old adage. Most of the structures on the Giza Plateau, including the main pyramids and the Sphinx, were constructed during the 4th, 5th, and 6th Dynasties (approximately 2613–2181 BC) during the Old Kingdom period. A few monuments date from later. Collectively, however, all are truly wonders of the world—ancient and modern. As such, they've inspired many fanciful beliefs throughout time.

Some ideas about the pyramids have been almost plausible: that they comprised an ancient observatory or a site used in the initiation of priests belonging to a secret order. Others have been less so: that they were devices used to harness spiritual energy or electricity or to facilitate astral projection or the landing of extraterrestrial craft. Still other beliefs have held that within the pyramids, dull razor blades are sharpened, food is preserved, people are healed, and meditation is enhanced.

Egyptologists maintain, of course, that the pyramids were the tombs of great rulers and that their shape was possibly inspired by that of the *benben*, the primeval mound on which the creator god, Atum, stood to bring the world into existence according to ancient-Egyptian creation myths.

HISTORY OF THE PYRAMIDS

At the time of their construction, the pyramids were a great mobilizing force in Egyptian society—each structure easily took a decade or more to build and was a great national project, requiring most of a ruler's workforce. Precisely when and how the pyramids were built remain mysteries. There are, however, several theories about both.

In 2009, a team of researchers led by Abdel-Halim Nur el-Din, a professor of Egyptology at Cairo University, cleverly used astronomy as the basis for determining an exact start date for work on the Great Pyramid. In pharaonic Egypt, major construction projects generally began during the first year of a king's reign and usually at the start of the flood season, considered an auspicious time. This season coincided with the appearance of the star Sothis, or Sirius. By comparing the modern Gregorian calendar with the ancient Egyptian calendar and the cycle of Sothis, the researchers posited that construction commenced on August 23, 2470 BC.

More study is needed to substantiate this theory, which is highly controversial. For instance, many Egyptologists believe, based on other evidence, that Khufu's reign began earlier, perhaps around 2589 BC or so. What is safe to say, however, is that the Great Pyramid is roughly 4,500 years old and that it took about 23 years to build.

Theories about how the pyramids were constructed are even more speculative. One suggests that the builders used an external ramp and/or pulleys to hoist the millions of blocks. Another theory proposes they were built from the inside out, with the architect designing an interior infrastructure of ramps. Regardless, modern engineers still cannot replicate the near-perfect symmetry of a pyramid's base.

Many people assume slaves did most of the work, but the sophistication of both the design and the construction techniques indicates that a great deal of skilled labor was required. Evidence also suggests that many Egyptians considered pyramid construction to be both a profession, one for which they were fed and remunerated, and a great honor.

Laborers were assigned different tasks, including quarrying and transporting the estimated 2,300,000 stones required for the Great Pyramid alone. The sheer weight of these blocks (averaging 2.5 tons each) suggests that they must have been hauled to the site by water. Although desert surrounds the pyramids today, the course of the Nile was different in antiquity, and it probably led directly to the base of the site.

Pyramids of Giza

The Sphinx and Khafre's Pyramid complex.

A workers' village near the pyramids complex supported perhaps 20,000 people and included copper workshops, bakeries, and other businesses. In 2002, archaeologists led by Mark Lehner uncovered sleeping quarters (called galleries) capable of holding as many as 2,000 people at once in beds beneath half-open roofs supported by columns. The workers also ate and drank well—bones found suggest they consumed prime beef, fish, bread, and beer. They additionally had access to medical care, including the treatment of broken bones and other ailments. Clearly, the workers were well-provided for.

Lehner's endeavors could be considered part of the larger, increasingly popular trend of "settlement archaeology." It's important work. Studying everyday ancient Egyptians, as opposed to only their pharaohs, has shown that the pyramids were more than merely monuments to kings. They were also the driving force behind a great civilization.

A NEW HOME FOR OLD FINDS

One of the most ambitious architectural designs in the new millennium is a fitting home for the mother lode of ancient artifacts excavated in Egypt over the last 150 years. Situated just west of the Great Pyramid complex, the world's largest archaeological museum covers 120 acres (49 hectares) on the Giza Plateau. Although embellished with hieroglyphs, its otherwise modern facade is a clear indication that the interior is state of the art.

Some of the estimated 18,000 artifacts—transferred here from Downtown Cairo's Egyptian Museum and other repositories across the country—are on display for the very first time in history. Highlights include the Pharaoh's Royal Solar Boat and much of the Tutankhamun collection.

PYRAMIDS PLATEAU

Access to the most famous three of Egypt's more than 70 pyramids is along one of two routes: the Ring Road (Taree' el-Da'ery) or the Pyramids Road Share' el-Haram). The former affords one of the rare places for a photograph of all three Pyramids of Giza, but, for a good shot, you need a long-focus lens.

Causeway

Valley Temple

Tomb of Queen Khentawes

MASTABAS AND ROCK-CUT TOMBS

Valley Temple

Great Sphinx

Sound-and-Light Show

Sphinx Entrance

Sphinx Temple

Tomb of Meresa

Entrance of mortuary temple in Giza

BASICS

Admission Fees. General site admission: LE200. Great Pyramid (Khufu's Pyramid): LE400. Tomb of Queen Meresankh III: LE50. Menakaure's Pyramid: E 100. Khafre's Pyramid: LE100. Great Sphinx: LE100. Sound-and-light show: LE375.

Hours. Pyramid complexes: Apr.–Sept., daily 8–5; Oct.–Mar., daily 8–4. Last admission is one hour before closing. Sound-and-light show (⊕ *soundandlight.show/en*): two shows nightly at 7:30 and 8:30 pm.

GETTING HERE

Ride-Hailing App or Taxi. Until the new Metro line connecting central Cairo to the pyramid complex is completed, the easiest way to reach Giza's main attraction is to use a ride-hailing app. Some of the bus services that pass by the Giza complex also have apps and charge a fraction of the price, but the ride will take longer. Alternatively, you could hire a white taxi for the day, but this is more expensive.

Public Transit. From central Cairo, take the Mwasalat Misr M7 bus from Abdel Moneim Riad Square Station on Tahrir Square. It has many stops in the general vicinity of the pyramids, including at the Marriott Mena House, which puts you at the foot of the Giza Plateau. You could also mix and match different modes of transportation. For example, take the Metro to Giza station, and take a ride-hail car, taxi, or a Mwasalat Misr bus (including the M7 and the M11 lines) the rest of the way.

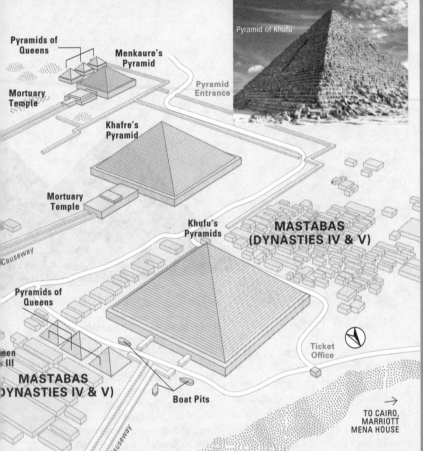

Pyramid of Khufu

Pyramids of
Queens

Menkaure's
Pyramid

Mortuary
Temple

Pyramid
Entrance

Khafre's
Pyramid

Mortuary
Temple

Khufu's
Pyramids

MASTABAS
(DYNASTIES IV & V)

Causeway

Pyramids of
Queens

Ticket
Office

een
III

MASTABAS
(DYNASTIES IV & V)

Boat Pits

Causeway

TO CAIRO,
MARRIOTT
MENA HOUSE

VISITING TIPS

■ You can enter the site via one of two gates: the gate next to side streets filled with horse and camel stables or that across from the luxurious colonial-era Marriott Mena House hotel.

■ Scammers might try to tempt you into venturing off on different roads or buying a ticket before entering the gates. Ignore them and carry on beyond the police checkpoint.

■ You can access the Sphinx via the gate in front of it or down a road from the pyramids. Although the area directly surrounding the colossus is off-limits to visitors, you can marvel at it from the vicinity and take a picture with it in the background. It

is also here, in front of the Sphinx, where you can watch the evening sound-and-light show.

■ For the full experience, visit a pyramid or two, a mastaba, the Sphinx, and, to its south, the town and cemetery of the workers who built the pyramids.

■ Generally, two of the three pyramids can be entered on any given day. If possible, go into the Great Pyramid. The sheer mass of it, pierced by the elegant Grand Gallery leading to the burial chamber, is spectacular.

■ For a truly unique experience, look into the daylong horseback-riding excursions that visit both Giza and sites at Saqqara to the southwest.

THE GIZA PYRAMIDS

Although the three largest pyramids are the main draws, each is part of a complex of smaller subsidiary structures. Courtiers and officials, for example, are buried in nearby masta-bas, a word derived from the Arabic word for "bench," perhaps a nod to their shape (elongated with a flat top and sloping sides). The mastaba is considered a precursor to the smooth-sided "perfect pyramid." The Pyramid of Djoser, built in Saqqara before those at Giza, consisted of a mastaba that was subsequently altered, resulting in its step-pyramid form.

The stairs inside the pyramids are tight (and steep).

MENKAURE'S PYRAMID

Measuring 20 square meters (215 square feet) and 66 meters (215 feet) tall, **Menkaure's Pyramid** is the smallest and last of the main tombs at Giza. It belonged to Khafre's successor, who probably intended to encase the entire structure with red granite, though only the bottom 16 courses were in place when he died. Subsequently, it might have been encased in limestone that was later plundered. Menkaure's successor, Shepseskaf, was responsible for finishing his **mortuary temple** in mud brick. Both it and the pyramid were refurbished during the 26th Dynasty (664–525 BC), when the king's cult enjoyed a renaissance. On the left side, as you climb the ladder to enter the pyramid, a carved inscription notes the restoration and care of the pyramid after its construction. The subterranean granite burial chamber contained a sarcophagus that was lost at sea while being shipped to Britain in the 19th century. The complex also has two **queen's pyramids** and a subsidiary pyramid.

KHAFRE'S PYRAMID

The second-largest Giza pyramid, with an area of 65 square meters (702 square feet) and a height of 143 meters (470 feet), **Khafre's Pyramid** looks taller than the Great Pyramid, but this is only because it sits on slightly higher ground, and its top is still intact. It also retains some of the fine limestone casing at its summit. The complex here includes mortuary and valley temples, a long connecting causeway carved out of rock, and the **Great Sphinx**. The pyramid's two entrances—one of which is on its north side, the other of which is in the pavement on its north side—connect before reaching the underground burial chamber. Here, next to the black granite sarcophagus is a square cavity that, presumably, once contained the canopic chest holding the pharaoh's viscera, which were removed during the mummification ritual. Note that entrance on the pyramid's north side was discovered by Italian explorer, Giovanni Battista Belzoni, in March 1818, an event he cheekily commemorated by scrawling his name in soot along the length of the burial chamber.

KHUFU'S PYRAMID

The **Great Pyramid** measures 70 square meters (753 square feet) and 146 meters (478 feet) high. Its surprisingly modest north entrance dates from the 9th century, when the Caliph al-Ma'mun blasted his way inside to search for treasure. It leads through a curving passage up to a long corridor that opens onto a small landing beyond which is the magnificent **Grand Gallery.** This soars up to the king's burial chamber, containing a sarcophagus robbed of its contents in antiquity. Narrow air passages lead out of the burial chamber. Interestingly, the names of the workers' responsible for building the pyramid, "The Followers of Khufu," were painted on some of the interior blocks. Remnants of the mortuary temple are on the pyramid's east side. Also nearby are the Queens' pyramids and, amid mastabas from the 4th and 5th Dynasties, the **Tomb of Queen Meresankh III**, Khafre's wife and Khufu's granddaughter. Its interior contains colorful low-relief scenes and rock statues of Meresankh, her mother, and her daughters.

THE GREAT SPHINX

The Sphinx

The enigmatic **Sphinx** is part of **Khafre's Pyramid complex** just north of his valley temple. The mythological creature with the head of a human, the body of a lion, and the wings of a falcon, is associated with the sun god, Ra. In this case, the human is believed to be Khafre wearing a *nemes* (the striped headdress worn by pharaohs).

The building with an open court in front of the Sphinx might have been an early sun temple. Khafre and his son, Menkaure, took the title Son of Ra. Much later, during the New Kingdom, Ra was combined with Horus as Ra-Horakhty or Ra-Horus of the Horizon. At that time, the Great Sphinx was worshiped as the image of Horakhty.

The red-granite **stela** between the Sphinx's paws, erected by New Kingdom pharaoh Thutmose IV (1401–1391 BC), tells a fascinating story. When Thutmose was 18, the Great Sphinx promised him the kingship of Egypt if he cleared the sand that was engulfing the colossal statue. Thutmose did so, and, in time, became the pharaoh. The statue subsequently came to be known as Bu Horr (Place of Horus), which evolved into its modern-day Arabic nickname of Abu al-Hol (Father of Terror).

The Sphinx was carved from bedrock, with additional details and its casing made of limestone. Despite several restorations over the millennia, the monument is not complete. Evidence suggests that it once had a uraeus (royal cobra) on its forehead, as well as a full beard. There has been much speculation about the loss of its nose. One story is that Napoleon's troops used it for target practice. Another story relates that, in AD 1478, a religious fanatic became so annoyed by the continued deification of the statue, that he destroyed its nose.

visitors to the storage, research, and restoration areas accessible only to scholars and staff.

At the entrance, a colossal statue of Ramses II towers over all, and a stairway punctuated with royal statuary leads to the upper halls, where some of the estimated 18,000 artifacts—transferred here from Downtown Cairo's Egyptian Museum and other repositories across the country—are on display for the very first time in history. Other highlights of the collection include the Pharaoh's Royal Solar Boat and much of the Tutankhamun collection. ⊠ *Al Giza Desert, Greater Cairo, Giza* ⊠ *LE400.*

★ Great Sphinx Of Giza

RUINS | Carved from an outcropping of limestone bedrock on the Giza Plateau during the 4th Dynasty, this colossal statue of a recumbent Sphinx—a mythological creature generally having the body of a lion and the face of a human—wears a *nemes* (traditional headdress of the pharaoh). It also once had the so-called beard of divinity, as can be seen in royal statues in museums, although that has broken off, as has the Sphinx's nose. Egyptologists suggest that its facial features are those of Khafre's disguised as Ra-Harakhty, a manifestation of the Sun God.

Between the Great Sphinx's paws is the Dream Stele erected by the New Kingdom ruler Thutmose IV. It narrates the story of a young Thutmose, who dreamed about an exchange with the Sphinx whereby, in return for the throne of Egypt, he was asked to clear the sand surrounding the statue. Thutmose happily obliged and became a successful ruler of the 18th Dynasty.

The interior of the Great Sphinx, which consists of small corridors, is off-limits to visitors. Nevertheless, it's hard to resist the opportunity to examine this enigmatic guardian of the necropolis up close—as well as to snap a selfie with it in the background. Note that although there is an evening Sphinx and Pyramids sound-and-light show, it's on the pricey side and some have reported that, for the money, it's underwhelming. Still, if you want a night-time experience at the monuments, it's something to consider. ⊠ *Giza Plateau, Al Giza Desert, Greater Cairo, Giza* ⊠ *General site admission: LE200. Sphinx admission: LE100. Sound-and-light show: LE375.*

The Pharaonic Village

THEME PARK | FAMILY | This open-air living museum takes you on a fascinating voyage through history and is particularly good if you're traveling with children. Although it has dioramas and a museum with educational information and replicas of artifacts that were made using ancient techniques, it's the boat ride through the site that's the main draw. It transports you through a recreated ancient kingdom where actors dressed in period costume go about such day-to-day activities as sculpting statues, making pottery, or even embalming. ⊠ *3 El Bahr Al Aazam St., Giza* ☎ *2/3571–8675* ⊠ *Fees vary.*

Ramses Wissa Wassef Art Center

ARTS CENTER | The namesake founder of this art center near the Giza Plateau was also the architect who designed its mud-brick building featuring distinctive round domes. The center was established in the early 1950s, primarily to teach young Egyptians weaving techniques, and the colorful, elaborate tapestries made here exhibit ancient Egyptian, Coptic, and Islamic influences. You can tour the workshops and see woven works as well as pottery and sculpture. Bring a lunch to enjoy in the lavish gardens. ⊠ *Al Labeini axis, Al Haraneyah, Giza* ☎ *12/2312–1359* ⊕ *www.facebook.com/wissa.wassef. artcenter* ⊗ *Closed Mon.*

★ Tomb of Queen Meresankh III

TOMB | Just east and in the shadow of the Great Pyramid is the tomb of Khafre's wife and the granddaughter of Khufu, Queen Meresankh III. The powerful queen was interred in a large and elegantly decorated *mastaba* (an oblong or rectangular tomb with a flat roof and sloping sides), one of many such 4th and 5th Dynasty tombs in the area. The interior walls depict colorful scenes of full-size figures engaged in key Old Kingdom activities such as baking bread, sculpting, and metal smelting. One scene shows Meresankh's body undergoing mummification on an embalming table beneath a tent. The queen is also shown with her mother, the equally eminent Queen Hetepheres II, on the eastern wall of the chapel. A second chamber contains 10 rock-cut statues of the queen, her mother, and her daughters.

The website of Egypt's Ministry of Tourism and Antiquities has a link that allows you to "visit" this matsaba virtually, but, as you don't stumble upon the tomb of a pyramid owner's wife every day, an in-real-life visit is best. There's a separate admission fee, though, so be sure to ask for a ticket at the entrance. ⊠ *Giza Plateau, Al Giza Desert, Greater Cairo, Giza* ☜ *General site admission: LE200. Tomb of Queen Meresankh: LE50.*

★ Workers' Town and Cemetery

RUINS | In the 1980s, the discovery of the workers' town and cemetery in the southeastern area of the Giza Plateau confirmed that construction of the pyramids was very much an earthly endeavor—requiring the labor of thousands of human beings—and not, as some conspiracy theorists maintain, the result of intervention by otherworldly aliens.

The site consists of the Lower Cemetery of the Workers, containing the remains of laborers, bakers, brewers, draftsmen, and the like; the Upper Cemetery, where high-ranking supervisors and their families were interred; and the so-called Lost City of the Pyramid Builders (Heit el-Ghurab).

Findings in both the cemeteries and the city—an organized grid of streets

with dwellings, storage facilities, and administrative structures—have revealed much about the builders. For instance, archaeologists have determined that although skeletal remains show signs of a life of hard labor, injuries like bone breaks had healed properly, indicating that workers received good medical care. Other findings suggest that workers also had access to both cattle and fish, important sources of protein, and that bread was manufactured on an industrial scale in several large bakeries. ⊠ *Giza Plateau, Al Giza Desert, Greater Cairo, Giza* ☜ *General site admission: LE200. Workers' Town and Cemetery: LE400.*

🍴 Restaurants

Andrea El Mariouteya New Giza

$$$ | **MIDDLE EASTERN** | **FAMILY** | The setting, atop a hill overlooking suburbia and a 20-minute drive from the pyramids, is new, but this Egyptian barbecue restaurant has been in business for more than 60 years. Seated at a wooden table surrounded by stonework, you can feast on mezze, grilled chicken or quail, and the freshest of flatbread—you might even get a glimpse of the women who masterfully prepare it. **Known for:** exceptional bread, freshly baked in natural stone ovens; expansive views; superbly seasoned chicken, grilled to perfection. ⑤ *Average main: LE200* ⊠ *New Giza Road, Cairo-Alexandria Desert Road, Giza* ☏ *10/0353–2000.*

9 Pyramids Lounge

$$$ | **MIDDLE EASTERN** | The Giza Plateau really needed a place like 9 Pyramids Lounge, which is accessed via the Mena House Giza Plateau entrance, where you'll purchase the standard entrance ticket, drive past the pyramids, and be guided to the lounge's parking area. Forego the indoor seating, and head straight to the gazebo-covered outdoor dining area, where you can enjoy Egyptian staples such as *ful, ta'amiya,* and *fiteer* while gazing at the majestic pyramids. **Known for:** accommodating, English-speaking staff; generous Egyptian breakfasts; classic food paired with ancient views. $ *Average main: LE250* ✉ *Giza Plateau, Al Giza Desert, Giza* ☏ *11/1078–8866, 11/1699–9339* ⊕ *www. facebook.com/9PyramidsLounge* ☾ *No dinner.*

★ 139 Pavilion

$$$$ | **INTERNATIONAL** | If you're not already spending a night or two at the Marriott Mena House, start your Giza day trip an hour earlier, and treat yourself to a high-end Pyramids-view breakfast at this restaurant within it. Options in the expansive buffet spread, served from 6 am to 11 am, include international items, and there are both indoor and shaded outdoor seating areas. **Known for:** relaxing atmosphere and pyramid panoramas; attentive, efficient staff; breakfast buffet with international choices like cured and smoked fish. $ *Average main: LE475* ✉ *Marriott Mena House, 6 Pyramids Road, Giza* ☏ *2/3377–3222* ⊕ *www. marriott.com/hotels.*

 ## Hotels

Four Seasons Hotel Cairo at The First Residence

$$$ | **HOTEL** | As you'd expect from the luxury brand, this hotel is superb, with a serene setting, white-glove service, and beautifully appointed guest rooms with marble baths. **Pros:** even standard rooms are spacious; lots of amenities, including a spa and several restaurants; connected to a shopping mall. **Cons:** swimming pool is in shade for much of the day; not as conveniently located as some other hotels; eastward Nile-view rooms also face a residential tower. $ *Rooms from: $370* ✉ *35 Giza St., Giza* ☏ *2/3567–1600* ⊕ *www.fourseasons.com* ⇱ *256 rooms* ✵ *No Meals.*

Marriott Mena House Hotel

$$$ | **HOTEL** | Revered for its proximity to the pyramids, this hotel, which was built in the 19th-century as a khedivial hunting lodge, has hosted many politicians, royals, and celebrities. **Pros:** proximity to the Pyramids and views that can't be beat; original building oozes period charm; excellent food and service. **Cons:** pyramid-view rooms book up months in advance; in-room internet isn't free; far from Downtown, so best for overnights when visiting the pyramids. $ *Rooms from: $373* ✉ *Pyramids Road, Giza* ☏ *2/3377–3222* ⊕ *www.marriott.com* ⇱ *331 rooms* ✵ *No Meals.*

Steigenberger Cairo Pyramids Hotel

$$ | **HOTEL** | Directly opposite the new Grand Egyptian Museum and providing once-in-a-lifetime pyramid views from some of its rooms, this hotel is a solid and relatively affordable choice for visits to Giza. **Pros:** good food and nice outdoor spaces; convenient sightseeing base; kind and helpful staff. **Cons:** traffic noise can be an issue; not close to off-site amenities like shops and restaurants; room decor could use an update. $ *Rooms from: $213* ✉ *Cairo–Alexandria Desert Road, Kafr Nassar, Giza* ☏ *2/3377–2555* ⊕ *www.steigenberger. com/en* ⇱ *132 rooms* ✵ *No Meals.*

 ## Nightlife

BARS

Char Bar

BARS | High ceilings, wooden chairs and floors, and the sweet smell of a burger sizzling are among the things that define the bar on the third floor of the Four Seasons. It's a casual place to unwind with a glass of wine or a cold beer in hand. The signature burgers are delicious but not for the fainthearted (think stacks of potato chips, fried eggs, and loads of cheese); other food offerings include a loaded hotdog and a gooey cookie pan. ✉ *Four Seasons Hotel Cairo at The First*

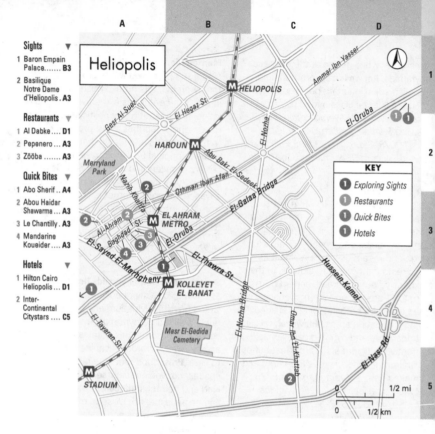

Heliopolis

Sights ▼
1 Baron Empain Palace....... **B3**
2 Basilique Notre Dame d'Heliopolis . **A3**

Restaurants ▼
1 Al Dabke **D1**
2 Pepenero ... **A3**
3 Zööba **A3**

Quick Bites ▼
1 Abo Sherif .. **A4**
2 Abou Haidar Shawarma ... **A3**
3 Le Chantilly . **A3**
4 Mandarine Koueider **A3**

Hotels ▼
1 Hilton Cairo Heliopolis ... **D1**
2 Inter-Continental Citystars **C5**

KEY
1 Exploring Sights
1 Restaurants
1 Quick Bites
1 Hotels

Residence, 35 Charles de Gaulle St., Giza District, Giza ☎ 2/3567–1600 ⊕ www.fourseasons.com/cairofr/dining/restaurants/char-bar ☉ Closed during Ramadan.

Il Giardino Restaurant

BARS | At this lounge and restaurant in the Steigenberger Hotel, you can kick back, relax, and reward yourself with some Italian food and a glass of wine or a cocktail after a day of sightseeing. ⊠ Steigenberger Cairo Pyramids Hotel, Cairo–Alexandria Desert Road, Kafr Nassar, Giza ☎ 2/3377–2555.

🛍 Shopping

JEWELRY

★ Azza Fahmy

JEWELRY & WATCHES | A bib necklace inspired by a maqarnas (an intricate Islamic vaulted ceiling), a lotus cuff

bracelet, or a pair of Eye of Horus earrings would make a wonderfully authentic, if pricey, Egyptian souvenir. Azza Fahmy's statement jewelry, appropriate for both everyday wear and special occasions, has achieved worldwide recognition for its nature- and motif-inspired designs that are sometimes adorned with coral, garnet, lapis lazuli, or other semiprecious or precious stones. In addition to this Giza location, she has a store in the Four Seasons, with outlets elsewhere in Egypt as well as in Dubai, Amman, London, and Washington D.C. ⊠ First Mall, 35 Giza St., 2nd fl., shop 205, Giza ☎ 10/6664–2365 ⊕ www.azzafahmy.com.

Heliopolis

In 1905, Belgian industrialist Édouard Louis Joseph (Baron Empain) bought a swath of land northwest of Cairo and began creating a new, self-sustaining, desert community, with housing, shops, recreational facilities, utilities, and a tram link to the capital. The town he called Heliopolis (City of the Sun) was a hit with upper-class Egyptians and expat movers and shakers. It remained an oasis of the social elite, who lived in mansions and enjoyed cocktail parties and weekends at country clubs, until the 1952 coup d'état.

Although urban development has eliminated some of its green areas, and Cairo, which has sprawled ever closer, is now accessible by concrete roads rather than a tram, Heliopolis has maintained some of its charm. Empain's own early-20th-century palace, modeled on Southeast Asian temples, has been fully restored and now contains a history museum. What was once the grand Heliopolis Palace Hotel is now used as the presidential palace, set behind well-guarded walls.

The heart of Heliopolis, though, is El-Korba, a gentrified district where streets are lined with ornate stoas (covered, colonnaded walkways) and neoclassical or Renaissance-revival buildings featuring Egyptian, Moorish, or Persian elements. It's a lovely place to wander, stopping to shop in jewelry stores or clothing boutiques or to relax in cafés or restaurants.

Sights

Baron Empain Palace
CASTLE/PALACE | Commissioned in 1907 by Edward Louis Joseph Empain, a Belgian baron, this Heliopolis landmark was designed by Alexander Marcel and decorated by Georges-Louis Claude. It's sometimes referred to as Le Palais Hindou (The Hindu Palace), owing to its distinct architecture inspired by Southeast Asian temples. The copper-colored palace is made of reinforced concrete and has a central spiral staircase and elevator that connect its three floors. After being inaccessible for decades, the palace has been restored and now contains a museum with well-curated exhibits detailing the history of Heliopolis. It's worth paying extra for access to the roof, with its incredible 360-degree panoramas. ⊠ *El-Orouba St., El-Montaza, Heliopolis* ☒ *Museum: LE100. Roof: LE50.* ⚠ *No online reservation. Tickets sold at the door.*

Basilique Notre Dame d'Heliopolis
CHURCH | Also known as Our Lady of Heliopolis Co-Cathedral, this Roman Catholic basilica was designed by Alexander Marcel, the designer of the Baron Empain Palace, who modeled it after Istanbul's Hagia Sophia. Hidden beneath its altar is a chamber containing the remains of Baron Empain—a significant figure not only in Heliopolis's history, but in the cathedral's inception—and his family. The church is open to the public (call ahead to confirm hours), but you must prearrange permission from the lay council to access the crypt. ⊠ *Nazih Khalifa crossroad, Al Ahram St., Heliopolis* ☎ *12/2212–5761 Lay Council, 12/2349–9007* ☒ *Free.*

 Restaurants

Al Dabke
$$$$ | LEBANESE | Although the decor is pure Arabian, the cuisine is authentic Lebanese. Fresh bread makes a nice accompaniment to the delicious soups, stews, grilled meats, and hot or cold mezzes. **Known for:** exceptionally friendly service; bread baked in an open oven; plenty of vegetarian options. ⑤ *Average main: LE400* ⊠ *Hilton Cairo Heliopolis, 136 El-Orouba, El-Nozha, Heliopolis* ☎ *2/2267–7730* ⊕ *www.hilton.com.*

The restored, South Asian–inspired Baron Empain Palace, from 1907, has exhibits on the history of Heliopolis and 360-degree rooftop panoramas.

Pepenero

$$$$ | **ITALIAN** | The outdoor seating area of this restaurant in one of El-Korba's historical buildings offers stellar views of the promenade below and is an especially nice place to dine on breezy spring evenings. Mouthwatering dishes on the Italian menu include burrata pizza, gnocchi, and fresh bruschetta. **Known for:** stellar views of El-Korba; Italian salad bar on weekends; casual, intimate setting. $ *Average main: LE400* ✉ *18 Baghdad St., El-Montaza, Heliopolis* ☎ *10/1010–1342* ⊕ *www.instagram.com/pepeneroegypt.*

★ Zööba

$$ | **MIDDLE EASTERN** | **FAMILY** | Known for its relaxed vibe, Zööba offers Egyptian street food featuring modern twists (and slightly higher prices), all of it made with locally sourced ingredients. Be sure to try the *ful* (fava-bean stew) and *ta'amiya* (falafel) with pickled lemons, though the *koshary* (macaroni casserole) is also divine. **Known for:** eclectic decor; delicious rice with sujuk (fermented, spiced sausage); vegetarian and vegan options. $ *Average main: LE75* ✉ *13 Baghdad St., El-Montaza, Heliopolis* ☎ *16082 order hotline* ⊕ *www.zoobaeats.com.*

☕ Coffee and Quick Bites

Abo Sherif

$$ | **MIDDLE EASTERN** | Flakey layers of *fiteer* pastry generously stuffed with your choice of sweet or savory fillings is what Abo Sherif is known for, and every order is made fresh on the spot—you can even watch the dough being flipped, stuffed, and placed in a brick oven. It's customary to take your fiteer to the café across the street and enjoy it with black tea served with fresh mint leaves. **Known for:** crispy, well-balanced sweet kunafa fiteer; unparalleled dough-flipping skills; mixed-cheese fiteer oozing with melted goodness. $ *Average main: LE75* ✉ *64 Damascus St., Heliopolis* ☎ *10/2090–4554* ▭ *No credit cards.*

★ Abou Haidar Shawarma

$ | MIDDLE EASTERN | This Heliopolis landmark, in business for over five decades, often has a line of people waiting to order Egyptian-style beef shawarma, made with a deliciously aromatic marinade and served in a pita or on soft white *fino* bread or fluffy bread rolls. Although there's a small top-floor seating area, this is more of a grab-and-go restaurant. **Known for:** mango juice made with a secret recipe; juicy, well-seasoned beef shawarma rolls; homemade potato chips with the perfect crunch. $ *Average main: LE30* ✉ *13 Ibrahim Al Lakani St., El-Montaza, Heliopolis* ▭ *No credit cards.*

Le Chantilly

$$ | CAFÉ | FAMILY | Favored by locals, Le Chantilly is the perfect place to unwind with a cup of coffee and fresh pastries, seated indoors at a wooden table covered with a checkered tablecloth or in the charming outdoor area. **Known for:** the aroma of freshly baked pastries; sunny outdoor seating; cozy vintage interior. $ *Average main: LE150* ✉ *11 Baghdad St., El-Montaza, Heliopolis* ☏ *2/2415–5620.*

★ Mandarine Koueider

$ | MIDDLE EASTERN | Known for the blue-mosaic niche wall on its facade, this small but beloved branch of Mandarine Koueider is divided into two sections: one side sells Middle Eastern desserts generously stuffed with nuts, and the other sells ice cream in flavors like pistachio, raspberry, or mandarin. The *malban bil eshta* (Turkish delight filled with cream custard that's flavored with mastic) is a must-try. **Known for:** fresh batches of ice cream prepared daily; crisp kunafa (syrup-soaked pastry) with a creamy center; often crowded (but don't let this deter you). $ *Average main: LE30* ✉ *5 Baghdad St., El-Montaza, Heliopolis* ☏ *2/2418–6555* ▭ *No credit cards.*

Hotels

Hilton Cairo Heliopolis

$$ | RESORT | FAMILY | The conveniently located hotel guarantees a relaxed stay with high-end services and all the amenities you expect from a Hilton. **Pros:** wide range of international cuisine options; family-friendly accommodation with a kids pool; only 10 minutes from the international airport, with a free airport shuttle. **Cons:** 45-minute drive to Downtown; no views; food at some restaurants is mediocre for the price. $ *Rooms from: $213* ✉ *El-Orouba, Sheraton Al Matar, El Nozha, Heliopolis* ☏ *2/2267–7730* ⊕ *www.hilton.com* ⇔ *589 rooms* ⦿ *No Meals.*

InterContinental Citystars

$$$ | HOTEL | Amenities here include a health club, a spa that offers customized treatments, indoor and outdoor pools, and restaurants that range from Italian to Japanese. **Pros:** connected to Citystars Mall; pleasant, accommodating staff; comfortable, cozy rooms. **Cons:** no views; a bit outdated; no playground for children. $ *Rooms from: $395* ✉ *Omar Ibn El Khattab St., Heliopolis* ☏ *2/2480–0100* ⊕ *www.ihg.com* ⇔ *490 rooms* ⦿ *No Meals.*

Nightlife

1920s Boutique Hotel & Restaurants

CAFÉS | This beautiful, 100-year old villa has a selection of restaurants, all with bars, that make it a go-to place for a night out. Enjoy Latin dishes at El Barrio, pizza at Il Divino, Middle Eastern at Carlos, sushi at The Smokery, and meat dishes at OX. Reservations at any of them are a good idea. ✉ *58 Beirut St., Heliopolis* ☏ *11/1016–6015, 2/2291–5830* ⊕ *www.1920sboutiquehotel.com.*

★ **Sachi**

COCKTAIL LOUNGES | Sleek black tables and low-hanging lights create an intimate and luxurious atmosphere at this high-end establishment, where the service is stellar, the cocktails are sophisticated, and, if you're peckish, the food is Mediterranean-Asian fusion. ✉ *3 Cleopatra St., Heliopolis* ☎ *12/8090–2028* ⊕ *www.sachirestaurant.com.*

 # Shopping

CARPETS

★ **El Kahhal Carpets**

HOUSEWARES | It's hard not to be impressed by the colorful, floor-to-ceiling displays of carpets at this store, which was founded in 1870 by a young Syrian immigrant who originally set up shop in Cairo's famous market, Khan el-Khalili. Run by the fifth generation of the same family, it's now one of the city's oldest carpet manufacturers, with a wide collection of silk, Persian Heriz, Azerbaijani Shirvan, and modern designs, as well as custom-made carpets, kilims, and tapestries. If you have the time, book the shop's two-hour tour (pick-up and drop-off service from/to anywhere in Cairo can be arranged), which walks you through the history of carpets and enables you to see craftsmen expertly weaving carpets by hand. ✉ *24 Ibrahim Al Lakani, El-Montaza, Heliopolis* ☎ *2/2415–9754* ⊕ *www.elkahhal.com.*

CRAFTS

★ **Fair Trade Egypt**

CRAFTS | With the goal of promoting Egyptian craftsmanship, this boutique offers more than 1,000 products, from leather goods to home accessories, that make fantastic souvenirs. It's the first fair trade–certified organization in Egypt, and it works with more than 2,000 artisans across the country. ✉ *25 Ibrahim Salem, Al Golf, Heliopolis* ☎ *2/2736–5123* ⊕ *www.fairtradeegypt.org.*

Gallery Mabrouka

CRAFTS | Concealed on one of El-Korba's sunny side streets, this nook brims with traditional well-crafted items, including hand-painted plates, meticulous copper-work pieces, and marvelous light fixtures. ✉ *23 Ramses St., off Baghdad St., Heliopolis* ☎ *11/1844–3334.*

SHOPPING MALLS

City Centre Almaza

MALL | One of the newest entertainment complexes in Heliopolis is an all-round crowd-pleaser, with a 16-screen cineplex, a plethora of stores selling regional as well as international brands, a large food court, more than 20 casual sit-down restaurants, and a family entertainment center. ✉ *50M, Sheraton Al Matar, El Nozha, Heliopolis* ⊕ *www.citycentrealmaza.com.*

Citystars Heliopolis (*Stars Center*)

MALL | This massive mall has more than 750 stores selling local and international brands, numerous dining options, and its own version of the Khan el-Khalili bazaar (although prices at this one are higher). ✉ *Omar Ibn El-Khattab, Heliopolis* ⊕ *www.citystars-heliopolis.com.eg.*

Activities

El-Korba Boulevard Walk

HIKING & WALKING | "El-Korba" is derived from *la courbe* (French for "the curve"), a reference to the curve in the district's namesake boulevard, which is a treasured, colonnaded promenade in the heart of Heliopolis. Here, the city's distinct architectural styles take center stage, and shaded arcades house small boutiques, restaurants and cafés. What's the best way to enjoy your walk along the boulevard and its side streets? With an ice cream in hand, of course. ✉ *El-Korba, Heliopolis* ✛ *The junction of Baghdad and Tharwa streets.*

New Cairo

Egyptians debate whether New Cairo is a city or a district, but everyone agrees that it has grown exceptionally fast. The area was established in 2000 in an effort to relieve the epic congestion in its older sibling to the northwest. Although the development continues, many people and businesses have already relocated to New Cairo because of its proximity to the New Administrative Capital, which is being built in phases.

What New Cairo lacks in character, it makes up for in restaurants, entertainment venues, shopping malls, and other amenities, some of them exclusive to the area. It also has some of Cairo's best hotels, which, although distant from the city center, offer luxurious experiences that might just offset the hassle of extra time spent in traffic.

 Restaurants

Asmak

$$$$ | SEAFOOD | Here, you can feast on Egyptian-style seafood, priced by weight and cooked to perfection, without having to visit the coast. The ordering process is streamlined: make your selection from the display, choose how you'd like it prepared (fried, baked, grilled, simmered in a clay tagine), head to a table, and wait for it to arrive. **Known for:** fresh fish brought in daily; very busy at dinnertime; creamy fish roe tagine. $ *Average main: LE500* ⊠ *Concord Plaza, S. Teseen St., New Cairo, Mirage City* ☎ *10/0352–7777.*

Beit Aziz

$$$ | MIDDLE EASTERN | FAMILY | The decor here pays homage to designs used for the *mashrabiya* (a balcony with an elaborate screen-like enclosure), the service reflects Egyptian hospitality, and the portions of Egyptian and Middle Eastern food are generous. Thursday through Saturday, the live traditional music can be quite loud; opt for the indoor seating area or avoid weekends altogether if you want a peaceful meal. **Known for:** live (and often loud) music on weekends; freshly baked fiteer with a variety of fillings; friendly, helpful staff. $ *Average main: LE250* ⊠ *The Park Mall, N Teseen St., New Cairo, Mirage City* ☎ *12/8008–0141.*

Elkbabgi

$$$$ | BARBECUE | FAMILY | Popular with locals and busy on weekends, this family-style restaurant specializes in Egyptian barbecue with the country's traditional staple dishes served on the side. The decor is a little kitschy, but the food is delicious, portions are generous, and the staff is friendly. **Known for:** perfectly baked okra tajine with beef cubes; aromatic, charcoal-grilled beef or lamb; gaudy black, gold, and red-velvet decor. $ *Average main: LE300* ⊠ *N Teseen St., New Cairo, Mirage City* ⊹ *Next to Blom Bank building.*

Marzipan

$$$$ | MIDDLE EASTERN | The sleek, Art Deco–style interior has beautiful mosaic floors and walls adorned with photographs of actors from the 1960s golden age of Egyptian cinema. The food is likewise classic Egyptian; the rice and pigeon tagine and the spicy potatoes with sausage are good bets. **Known for:** baladi bread freshly baked in a brick oven; indoor and outdoor seating; crispy cheese and pastrami phyllo pastry sticks. $ *Average main: LE300* ⊠ *White by Waterway (Waterway 2), N Teseen St., New Cairo, Mirage City* ☎ *10/0647–5932* ⊕ *www.instagram.com/marzipancairo.*

Mo Bistro

$$$$ | INTERNATIONAL | Although it offers delicious seafood, soups, salads, and pastas, Mo Bistro specializes in meat dishes. From juicy, tender flank steaks to slow-cooked beef shanks to bone marrow, everything is expertly seasoned and prepared. **Known for:** flavor and quality in every bite; complimentary basket of fresh bread served with delicious dips; generous, shareable portions. $ *Average* main: LE300 ✉ Garden 8 Mall, Salah El Din Abdel Karim St., New Cairo, Mirage City ☎ 12/7387–8768 ⊕ www.facebook.com/mobistroegypt.

Hotels

Dusit Thani Lakeview Cairo

$$ | **HOTEL** | Known for its sleek, contemporary, Thai-influenced decor and its world-class service, the Dusit Thani is tropical oasis right in the middle of New Cairo. **Pros:** luxurious surroundings; gracious staff; on-site Devarana spa. **Cons:** far from many of Cairo's key sites; you can't go anywhere outside the hotel on foot; arranges expensive cab rides. ⑤ Rooms from: $296 ✉ The LakeView, S. Teseen St., Fifth Settlement, New Cairo, Mirage City ☎ 2/2614–0000 ⊕ www.dusit.com ✈ 467 rooms ⦿ Free Breakfast.

JW Marriott Hotel Cairo

$$$ | **HOTEL** | With on-site amenities like a golf course, a fitness center, and a saltwater "beach" pool complete with sun beds, it's no surprise that this hotel has received raves. **Pros:** just 20 minutes from Cairo International Airport; a great range of amenities; marble baths, luxurious bedding, and soundproof windows are standard. **Cons:** service sometimes lacks attention to detail; the hotel is remote and you won't be able to leave it without a taxi or car; room service food can be a miss. ⑤ Rooms from: $325 ✉ Ring Road, Second New Cairo, Mirage City ☎ 2/2411–5588 ⊕ www.marriott.com ✈ 440 rooms ⦿ Free Breakfast.

Renaissance Cairo Mirage City Hotel

$$ | **HOTEL** | The Renaissance is situated around a massive swimming pool, so all of its spacious, well-equipped, and nicely appointed rooms—featuring dark woods and pops of jewel-tone color—have lovely views. **Pros:** close to Heliopolis; pool is so vast that it feels private even when crowded; free Wi-Fi. **Cons:** though helpful, the staff can be slow to act; far

from central Cairo's sights; you can't navigate the surrounding area on foot. ⑤ Rooms from: $240 ✉ Abbas Al Akad Corridor, Second New Cairo, Mirage City ☎ 2/2406–3333 ⊕ www.marriott.com ✈ 333 rooms ⦿ Free Breakfast.

Royal Maxim Palace Kempinski Cairo

$$$ | **HOTEL** | It's hard not to be taken in by the palatial grandeur of the exterior, the sleek styling of the interior, and the abundance of amenities and creature comforts throughout. **Pros:** on-site Resense spa; a number of fine-dining and drinking options; impeccable service. **Cons:** far from major landmarks; surrounding views aren't the best; you can't go anywhere outside the premises on foot. ⑤ Rooms from: $336 ✉ Ring Road, Second New Cairo, Mirage City ☎ 2/2249–5300 ⊕ www.kempinski.com ✈ 245 rooms ⦿ Free Breakfast.

The Westin Cairo Golf Resort & Spa

$$ | **HOTEL** | Wellness feels like a mission at this golf resort and spa, a hidden gem that's a fantastic getaway from the loud, busy streets of central Cairo. **Pros:** acclaimed spa and wellness services; peaceful property; great views of the 27-hole golf course. **Cons:** a bit impersonal and lacks local flavor; underwhelming dining experiences; housekeeping could use improvement. ⑤ Rooms from: $297 ✉ Katameya Dunes, Road 90, New Cairo, Mirage City ☎ 2/2322–8000 ⊕ www.marriott.com ✈ 177 rooms ⦿ Free Breakfast.

Nightlife

Shinkō

COCKTAIL LOUNGES | This sleek, modern trendsetter has garnered a loyal following thanks to the memorable cocktails created by its talented mixologists. There's also a short bar-food menu. ✉ Swan Lake Compound, 1 Al Zohwer, Second New Cairo, Mirage City ☎ 12/8277–5177 ⊕ www.shinkocairo.com ☞ Reservations required.

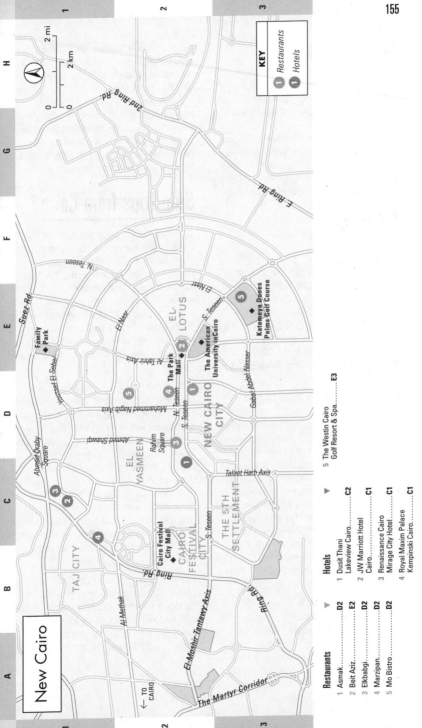

New Cairo

KEY
1 *Restaurants*
1 *Hotels*

155

Restaurants ▶
1 Asmak.............................D2
2 Beit Aziz.........................E2
3 Elkbabgi........................D2
4 Marzipan........................D2
5 Mo Bistro.......................D2

Hotels ▶
1 Dusit Thani
  Lakeview Cairo.............C2
2 JW Marriott Hotel
  Cairo..............................C1
3 Renaissance Cairo
  Mirage City Hotel.........C1
4 Royal Maxim Palace
  Kempinski Cairo...........C1
5 The Westin Cairo
  Golf Resort & Spa........E3

 Performing Arts

The Marquee

THEATER | FAMILY | Part of the Cairo
Festival City shopping and entertainment
complex, Egypt's second-largest arena
can accommodate more than 1,600
people at its local and international con-
certs, dance performances, and theatrical
productions. ✉ *Cairo Festival City, Ring
Road, New Cairo, Mirage City* ☎ *2/2618–
6000* ⊕ *www.festivalcitymallcairo.com.*

Shopping

CONCEPT STORES

Pop Up Shop

OTHER SPECIALTY STORE | You're bound to
find something unique at this lifestyle
concept store, which sells everything
from home-grown decorative items
and local-label clothing to gag gifts. It's
a little hard on the wallet but still well
worth a visit. ✉ *Downtown Mall, Plot A,
S. Teseen St., New Cairo, Mirage City*
☎ *10/2187–3777.*

COSMETICS AND BODYCARE

Nefertari

SKINCARE | The brand that's named after
one of ancient Egypt's most illustrious
queens, Nefertari (whose name means
"beautiful companion"), specializes in
organic, 100% natural, and environmentally friendly body and hair products.
Indeed, it's one of only a handful of Egyptian skincare brands. This stall stocks
most of its products; there are shops and
stalls elsewhere in Cairo as well. ✉ *S1,
Downtown Mall, S. Teseen St., New Cairo, Mirage City* ☎ *12/0517–7227* ⊕ *www.
nefertaribodycare.com.*

SHOPPING MALLS

Cairo Festival City Mall

SHOPPING CENTER | FAMILY | Cairo Festival
City is every shopper's paradise, with
several entertainment venues, a food
court, roughly 300 stores, and myriad
sit-down restaurants—and that's just

inside. Festival Avenue, an outdoor
area that's part of the complex, has still
more cafés and restaurants, as well as a
dancing fountain and an open-air theater.
If you drive here yourself, note your
parking spot and the gate through which
you entered, as the parking facilities are
as vast as the mall itself. ✉ *Ring Road,
New Cairo, Mirage City* ☎ *2/2618–6000*
⊕ *www.festivalcitymallcairo.com.*

Side Trips from Cairo

Just beyond Cairo, on the Nile's west
bank, stand the monuments most closely
identified with Egypt: the timeless
Sphinx and the Pyramids of Giza. Most
of the visitable pharaonic sites in Cairo's
environs, however, date from the Old
Kingdom (2687–2181 BC). If you venture
farther south, you'll find sites from far
more periods of Egyptian history at
Memphis, Abu Sir, Saqqara, Dahshur, and
Fayyum.

Part of the road south follows a canal,
traveling through small villages and amid
palm orchards—scenery that is soothing
compared with that on the drive to Giza.
From central Cairo, the trip to Memphis
takes about an hour (more if traffic is
heavy), and you should allow another
hour for touring its open-air museum.
You can explore Abu Sir in a leisurely
1½ hours. Saqqara, on the other hand
requires at least four hours, though this
active archaeological site merits an entire
day. Allow about two hours for touring
Dahshur.

Fayyum is farther south of Cairo and
requires more travel time. Although it can
be done as a day trip, consider spending
a night in one of its many lodgings so you
have more time to familiarize yourself
with Egypt's largest desert oasis.

Ancient Site Touring Tips

■ **You can visit on your own.**
Although organized tours include Abu Sir, Memphis, Saqqara, and Dahshur, you can visit them independently by hiring a taxi or a car through a ride-hailing app (in both cases, negotiate rates beforehand) or working with your hotel to arrange a car and driver and/or guide. The latter option is best for Saqqara, where good insight is invaluable; ditto for Dahshur, where you must also drive between sites.

■ **Mix and match site visits.** Abu Sir takes about 90 minutes to explore, the museum at Memphis no more than an hour. As they're very close to Cairo and Giza, you can easily tour both on a half-day excursion. Alternatively, combine them with visits to either Saqqara or Dahshur for a day-long outing.

■ **Choose drivers carefully.** If you arrange a taxi or ride-hail car in Cairo, make sure the driver knows his way around the sites; many drivers in the capital don't.

■ **Consider a horseback-riding tour.** You can see Giza and Saqqara on a horseback-riding tour (it's best to book online) offered by stables near the Giza Pyramids.

■ **Take the sun into account.** There's little shade at Memphis and even less at Abu Sir, Saqqara, and Dahshur, so wear sunglasses, hat, sunscreen, and bring lightweight layers to cover arms and shoulders should you need extra protection from the strong rays.

■ **Carry your passport.** You may travel through security checkpoints and be asked to produce a passport, especially if you are not on a guided tour.

■ **Pack provisions.** There are no restaurants, cafés, or convenience stores in the immediate vicinity of Abu Sir and Memphis, and elsewhere they are few and far between; bring your own water and sandwiches or snacks.

■ **Prepare for closures.** Saqqara is an active archaeological zone; on any given day, certain areas might be off limits to visitors, so be mindful of "no entry" signs. Attractions at other ancient sites also temporarily close from time to time.

■ **Don't be tempted by ancient "souvenirs."** On the ground at Saqqara, you might see small, resurfacing artifacts. It's illegal to pocket such "finds," and Egyptian authorities are tough on violators.

■ **When in doubt, ask.** Tourism police stationed at attractions can update you on closures and provide other types of assistance should you need it.

Abu Sir

26 km (16 miles) southwest of Down-town Cairo, 15 km (9 miles) southwest of the Giza Plateau.

Legend has it that Abu Sir is one of the locations where Isis found some of the body parts of her husband, Osiris, who had been dismembered by his envious brother Set. Isis, the goddess of healing and fertility, eventually restored her husband and had a child, Horus, by him. Horus later avenged his father by killing Set, thus restoring order from chaos.

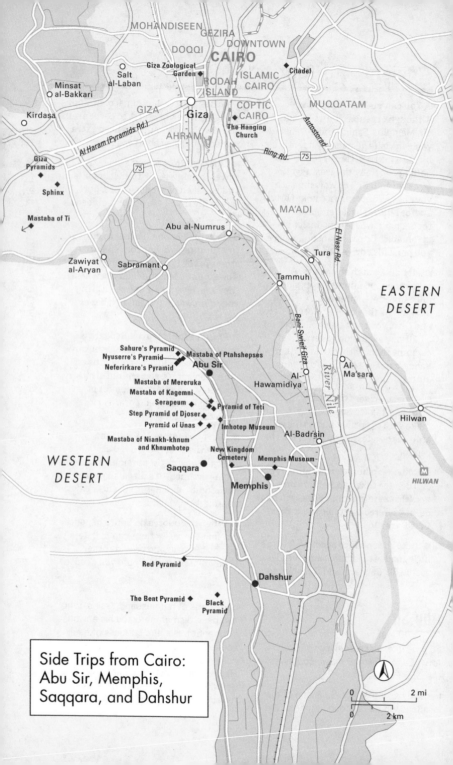

MOHANDISEEN GEZIRA
DOWNTOWN
DOQQI
CAIRO
Giza Zoological
Garden
Salt
al-Laban
RODAH
ISLAND
ISLAMIC
CAIRO
Citadel
Minsat
al-Bakkari
GIZA
COPTIC
CAIRO
MUQQATAM
Kirdasa
Giza
AHRAM
The Hanging
Church
Al Haram (Pyramids Rd.)
Giza
Pyramids
75
Sphinx
Ring Rd.
75
MA'ADI
Mastaba of Ti
Abu al-Numrus
Tura
Zawiyat
al-Aryan
Sabramant
EASTERN
DESERT
Tammuh

El-Nasr Rd.

Bani Swief/Giza

Sahure's Pyramid
Mastaba of Ptahshepses
Nyuserre's Pyramid
Neferirkare's Pyramid
Abu Sir
Al-
Hawamidiya
Al-
Ma'sara
Mastaba of Mereruka
Mastaba of Kagemni
Serapeum
Pyramid of Teti
Step Pyramid of Djoser
Pyramid of Unas
Imhotep Museum
Hilwan
Mastaba of Niankh-khnum
and Khnumhotep
Al-Badrsin

River Nile

WESTERN
DESERT
New Kingdom
Cemetery
Memphis Museum
Saqqara
Memphis
HILWAN

Red Pyramid

Dahshur

The Bent Pyramid
Black
Pyramid

Side Trips from Cairo:
Abu Sir, Memphis,
Saqqara, and Dahshur

0   2 mi

0   2 km

Abu Sir's charm is palpable upon arrival. The site is home to the Sahure, Nyuserre, and Neferirkare pyramids, as well as mastabas, shaft tombs, temples, and causeways, all creating entire complexes and all dating from the 5th Dynasty (2494–2345 BC).

As with many sites in Egypt, excavations here began in the early 20th century, and discoveries are still being made. In the late 1990s, for instance, archaeologists uncovered the intact shaft tomb of an official from a much later period: somewhere between 525 and 340 BC.

You can wander around the exteriors of the structures, many of which are close together, but their interiors are not open. Note, too, that the site itself is sometimes closed to the public. To avoid disappointment, consider incorporating a stop here into an itinerary that includes other ancient sites south of Cairo.

GETTING HERE AND AROUND

It's best to combine a visit to Abu Sir with other area archaeological sites. Although you can drive yourself, it's wiser to book a tour, hire a taxi, or book a car and driver through your hotel. You can also use a ride-hailing service, though you'll need to make arrangements for a pick up later in the day or for the driver to wait. Once you get here, walking is the best way to see the ruins.

Sights

Abu Sir Necropolis

RUINS | The first constructed and northernmost of the pyramids in the Abu Sir region, **Sahure's Pyramid** covers 24 square meters (257 square feet) and is 47 meters (154 feet) tall. It and its surrounding structures comprise a fine example of a 5th-Dynasty royal funerary complex. Alas, this pyramid's poor-quality core masonry collapsed after the Tura limestone casing stones were removed, so

it's in rough shape. Its mortuary temple, however, retains some ancient grandeur, with granite pillars, stairs leading to a now nonexistent second floor, and fine basalt pavement. The causeway linking the pyramid and the valley temple was once decorated with finely carved scenes (now removed from the site) showing archery and fighting. There is much less left of the valley temple itself: a pavement, some doorways, and a scattering of fallen blocks.

At 32 square meters (344 square feet) and an original height of 70 meters (229 feet), **Neferirkare's Pyramid** is the site's largest. The complex in which it's set was meant to be larger than that of Sahure, but Neferirkare (2477–2467 BC) died prior to its completion, leaving him with only the pyramid and a mortuary temple that was posthumously finished using mud brick rather than limestone or granite. The causeway and valley temple were usurped, completed, and appended to the 25-square-meter (265-square-foot) **Nyuserre's Pyramid** belonging to Neferirkare's son, who was pharaoh for 30 years. Although it once stood 52 meters (169 feet) tall, not much is left of this pyramid, as its casing stones were removed, and some of its limestone core was used to create lime in the 19th century.

Between the Sahure and Nyuserre pyramids lies the large family **Mastaba of Ptahshepses,** a vizier and son-in-law of Nyuserre. Although recently closed to the public, check on its status, and visit it if you can. The structure's walls are richly carved with scenes of the vizier's supervisory activities and cargo boats carrying funerary equipment. To the southwest of it is a double room that might have held wooden funerary boats, which were not usually found in tombs of private citizens. ⊠ *Off the Abu Sir village road, Abu Sir* 🖾 *LE80.*

Memphis

33 km (20 miles) south of Downtown
Cairo, 24 km (15 miles) southeast of the
Giza Plateau.

One look at Cairo and you could easily
believe that it has always been the
country's capital. However, a glimpse
into Egypt's early history reveals that the
title was first bequeathed to another:
Memphis.

Memphis was established as the capital
when King Narmer fully united the two
lands of Upper and Lower Egypt, marking
what is considered the start of both the
1st Dynasty and the Early Dynastic Period (3100—2686 BC). Part city, with palaces and temples—the god, Ptah, seems
to have been greatly revered here—part
necropolis, Memphis catered to the living
and dead alike for more than 2000 years.
Although other cities, Thebes (present-day Luxor) and Alexandria among
them, subsequently became Egypt's
capitals, Memphis was long considered a
strategic, economic, and religious center,
losing its importance gradually through
the ages and then more rapidly with the
arrival of Christianity and Islam.

Today, little of the ancient city remains.
Much of the stone from its structures
was stripped away and repurposed
(some of it was even used to build
Cairo), and the modern-day village
of Badrasheen, noted for its palm-rib
furniture industry, sits atop many of the
ancient sites. However, a few of the
artifacts unearthed in area excavations
(some ongoing but not open to the
public) conducted here since the early
20th century are on display in Memphis's
museum in the village of Mit Rahineh.

GETTING HERE AND AROUND
You can easily reach Memphis by hiring a
taxi or a car and driver for an afternoon or
booking a tour. The open-air museum is
walkable and relatively small.

Sights

Memphis Museum (*Mit Rahineh Museum*)
RUINS | Set up like a sculpture garden,
this predominately open-air museum
has a scattered assortment of statuary,
coffins, and architectural fragments
recovered from the area of Memphis.
Highlights include a large Egyptian alabaster sphinx; a sarcophagus that was,
curiously, carved upside down; columns
with interesting motifs; and several statues of Ramses II (aka, Ramses the Great,
1279–1213 BC), including a colossal limestone version of him inside the museum
building. You can view it from ground
level and from a balcony that runs above,
where you can better see finely carved
details like the elaborate dagger at the
pharaoh's waist. Stalls selling souvenir
replicas of Egyptian artifacts are set up
on one side of the garden. Quality varies,
but on the whole, you can find some
attractive items here. ⊠ *Mit Rahineh Rd.,
Mit Rahineh* ✛ *3 km (2 miles) west of
Badrasheen* ⊠ *LE80.*

Saqqara

33 km (21 miles) southwest of Downtown Cairo, 24 km (15 miles) southwest
of Giza, 7 km (4 miles) northwest of
Memphis.

Approached through orchards of flutter-
ing palm trees, dubiously paved roads,
and flocks of waving children welcoming
you, Saqqara is best known for its Step
Pyramid of Djoser, the earliest stone
pyramid constructed in Egypt. But the
plateau also has other pyramids, tombs
of courtiers, and mastabas that, collectively, provide insight on a span of history
that runs from early ancient Egypt to the
Greco-Roman and Coptic periods. All of
this is complemented by the wonderful
Imhotep Museum.

Saqqara is also an active archaeological site for both Egyptian and foreign
teams. Highlights of finds amid the major

Exhibits at the small but superb Imhotep Museum, named for the architect of Saqqara's step pyramid, highlight ancient Egyptian architecture, politics, and religion.

structures include the cheeky Door of the Cats, a catacomb of hundreds of mummified felines; the opulent tomb of Maya, Tutankhamun's wet nurse; the Ka-aper (aka, Sheikh el-Balad) statue, a rare wooden find and a favorite in the Egyptian Museum; and the Serapeum, a space devoted to the burial of sacred bulls.

It is also here that an Old Kingdom official named Wahty found modern-day fame in the 2020 Netflix documentary *Secrets of the Saqqara Tomb*. His tomb is still being excavated and is not open to visitors; you can, however, take a virtual tour of it. The remnants of the Monastery of Apa Jeremiah, which was in operation until the 9th century AD, represent Egypt's Coptic era in Saqqara.

Although you can explore Saqqara's large complexes completely on foot, a combination of walking and driving, with a break in the middle, is best. Depending on what is open at the time of your visit, you could start at the Step Pyramid complex and the Imhotep Museum and then visit the Pyramid of Unas from there on foot. Afterward, return to your car and drive to the Mastaba of Mereruka and the Pyramid of Teti before heading to the Serapeum, where you can also explore the nearby Tomb of Ti and Mastaba of Ptahhotep if you have time.

GETTING HERE AND AROUND

Saqqara is a popular stop on most guided tours, which often include Memphis and, sometimes, Dahshur. Although you can reach the sites via private taxi or a ride-hailing service and explore independently, this is one site where it's best to hire an expert guide or arrange a private excursion to facilitate everything from transportation to buying admission tickets.

If you're feeling really adventurous, you could see Saqqara on horseback (inquire at the ticket office for the pyramids on the Giza Plateau) for about the same price as a taxi. Such excursions traverse the Giza Plateau and then travel through the desert to Saqqara and back.

Sights

★ Imhotep Museum

HISTORY MUSEUM | Named after the architect of the Djoser step pyramid, this relatively small but superb museum brings Saqqara to life, with well-lit artifacts and exhibits that provide background on ancient Egyptian architecture, politics, and religion. Highlights of the collection include a statue of a seated Djoser, the Old Kingdom pharaoh who reigned from approximately 2686 to 2648 BC; a bronze statuette of Imhotep; a Ptolemaic mummy discovered by Zahi Hawass, who is considered Egypt's version of Indiana Jones; the enigmatic "famine" stela; and a set of vibrant blue and turquoise faience tiles that once decorated the interior of Djoser's Pyramid. Note, though, that this museum has experienced temporary closures; keep your fingers crossed that it's open during your visit as it's well worth your time. ⊠ *Pyramid of Djoser Rd., Saqqara* 🚂 *LE180, as part of the Saqqara site's general admission.*

Mastaba of Kagemni

TOMB | No visitor to Kagemni's tomb can ever forget the endearing depiction of a calf drinking its mother's milk or the bewildering one of an underwater battle between a crocodile and a hippopotamus. Both scenes demonstrate the ancient Egyptians' astute observations of the animal world. They are also just two of many scenes expertly carved in the limestone tomb belonging to a chief judge and vizier under the 6th-Dynasty ruler, Teti (2345–2333 BC). Others touch upon daily activities such as fishing, dancing, husbandry, and making food offerings to the tomb owner.

This tomb adjoins the Mastaba of Mereruka to the east. Some presume that a single artist or atelier was responsible for decorating the mastabas in this area because certain scenes—the force-feeding of animals, poultry yards, the tomb owner being carried on a chair—recur.

But they could also be conventional scenes used to decorate tombs at the time.> ⊠ *Saqqara* 🚂 *LE180, as part of the Saqqara site general admission.*

Mastaba of Mereruka

TOMB | The Teti cemetery's largest tomb, with more than 30 rooms, belonged to Mereruka, a wealthy vizier during the reign of the 6th-Dynasty (2345–2181 BC) pharaohs, Teti and Pepy I, and who was married to one of Teti's many daughters. The tomb's significance lies in its renderings of not only its owner but also of Old Kingdom life, with scenes of jewelry-making, scribal recording, herding, and harpooning, among other activities.

In one scene, Mereruka himself can be seen fishing and fowling alongside his family. In another, almost poetic one, the dutiful official is shown as the personification of the three ancient Egyptian seasons: *akhet* (for the flooding), *peret* (for the emergence of fertile land), and *shemu* (for the harvest). In addition, a life-size statue depicts Mereruka stepping forward from the tomb's false door to receive his offerings. ⊠ *Saqqara* 🚂 *LE80.*

Mastaba of Niankh-khnum and Khnumhotep

TOMB | At the end of the walkable section of the Unas Pyramid's causeway is the magnificently decorated and somewhat provocative tomb of the "Two Brothers," namely, Niankh-khnum and Khnumhotep, who were overseers of the Great House manicurists in the 5th Dynasty (2494–2345 BC). As at other tombs, much of the iconography here depicts fishing, carpentry, agriculture, and other everyday activities. But the men's professions are also showcased in precious snippets showing pedicurists and manicurists hard at work.

A remarkable chapel scene of the two interlacing and facing one another has been at the heart of much speculation over the years. Many argue that the men were brothers, perhaps even twins thanks to their similar names. Others note that such intimate ancient Egyptian scenes were usually reserved for husbands and wives, indicating a possible homosexual relationship between the two men, although both had wives and children. Regardless, the two men were close: an inscription above the tomb's entrance reads "joined in life and death." ⊠ *Saqqara* 🎫 *LE140, as part of the New Tombs ticket.*

Mastaba of Ti

TOMB | Ti was a supervisor of the construction of Niuserre and Nefefrikare's pyramids in Abu Sir and was married to Neferhetepes, a priestess of goddesses, with whom he had sons. His recently restored family tomb is exquisitely decorated and painted—the boat-building scenes are particularly noteworthy—with some of its original roof in tact. A statue of Ti, albeit a reproduction, is visible in the *serdab* (a small room specifically for a statue of the deceased), and a large courtyard with a stairway leads to Ti's burial chamber, where you can spot the official's sarcophagus. ⊠ *Athar Saqqara, Saqqara* 🎫 *LE180, as part of the Saqqara site general admission.*

New Kingdom Cemetery

CEMETERY | For more than 3 millenia, Saqqara was used as a burial ground, bearing witness to many mortuary practices along the way. The beautiful non-royal tombs of the New Kingdom (1550–1077 BC) feature underground burial chambers and open, above-ground courtyards with tomb chapels typically surmounted by small pyramids.

South of the Unas Pyramid's causeway are a handful of tombs that belonged to eminent officials of the 18th to 20th dynasties, all lying within one wider complex. Among these officials was 'Aperizia, a vizier of Amenhotep III; Ptahemwia, the "Royal Butler, Clean of Hands" under the rule of Akhenaten and Tutankhamun; Maia, the overseer of treasury; and Meryneith, the scribe. A tomb intended

for Horemheb, the military general during Tutankhamun's reign, also lies within the complex.

The meticulous art etched on the walls of these tombs was done by the best ancient artists and craftsmen, many of whom had practiced in the royal capital of Amarna. Many tombs here were also discovered with stelas and statues of the deceased within, but these artifacts have been moved to museums elsewhere. ⊠ *Saqqara* 🎫 *LE140 ticket for the Noble Tombs and New Kingdom Tombs.*

Pyramid of Teti

TOMB | The son of Unas, Teti was the first pharaoh of the 6th Dynasty (2345–2181 BC), and he's believed to have ruled for a little over a decade. Beyond this not much is known about him. Although his is the northernmost of the royal pyramids, it's not far from the Step Pyramid of Djoser.

Originally, Teti's pyramid was encased in blocks of fine limestone. What remains is a core of smaller blocks of local limestone and debris fill, rendering it less majestic than other structures. You can, however, enter this pyramid through a sloping passageway located at the north face. Inside, an antechamber has a large basalt sarcophagus that might once have contained the pharaoh's body. It's the burial chamber and its pyramid texts (used to guide the soul of the deceased in the afterlife) that are truly captivating, though. Here, long vertical columns are adorned with elegantly carved spells in hieroglyphs, and the ceiling is punctuated by representations of stars set against a dark blue background. ⊠ *Saqqara* 🎫 *LE180, as part of the Saqqara site general admission.*

Pyramid of Unas

TOMB | Unas, sometimes referred to as Wenis, was the last pharaoh of the 5th Dynasty, reigning from approximately 2375 to 2345 BC. At first glance, his pyramid could easily be mistaken for

As ancient graffiti attests, Saqqara's Step Pyramid of Djoser has been an attraction since at least the Middle Kingdom (2130–1649 BC) period.

a topographical feature in the Saqqara landscape. But the slanted case section of Unas's once glorious pyramid reveals a royal tomb that occupies an area of 17 square meters (188 square feet) and originally stood 43 meters (141 feet) tall. It was also the first ancient tomb to have its vaulted burial chamber decorated with resplendent green pyramid texts, meant to safely guide the deceased's soul through the perils of the afterlife. So self-assured was this innovative ruler that his pyramid was called "Perfect Are the Places of Unas" in ancient Egyptian. ⊠ *Saqqara* 🖼 *LE180, as part of the Saqqara site general admission.*

Serapeum

CEMETERY | This underground complex houses the most significant cult animals buried in Saqqara: the sacred Apis bulls, which were considered incarnations of the god Ptah. It is believed that each animal was very carefully selected, with the priests looking for special markings of divinity. In life, the bulls were as well-treated as they were revered. Upon death, they were mummified and placed in great (and extraordinarily heavy) sarcophagi. They were thought to become immortal as Osiris-Apis; over time, the name evolved to Userhapi ("Osorapis" in Greek) and was later associated with the Ptolemaic god, Serapis, resulting in the name of the site. The Serapeum, first used in the New Kingdom (1550–1077 BC), has a niche for each sacred bull; chapels and smaller temples would have been built aboveground. ⊠ *Saqqara* 🖼 *LE150.*

★ Step Pyramid of Djoser

TOMB | The quest for immortality is tangible at what is considered Egypt's first pyramid, so old that it was a great attraction even in antiquity: as the graffiti attests, people came here as tourists and seekers of blessings as early as the Middle Kingdom (2130–1649 BC), if not earlier. It was designed by Imhotep—a great architect who would, in time, become deified and worshiped as the patron god of architects and doctors—for the 3rd Dynasty pharaoh, Djoser, who reigned from approximately 2650 to 2575 BC. Although not much is known about this ruler, Egyptologists surmise that he sent expeditions to Sinai to mine copper and turquoise.

The Step Pyramid was ingeniously erected as a single-level mastaba tomb prior to ending up a a six-step pyramid. It was the predecessor of the "true" pyramid forms, which, like those in Giza have smooth sides. Its interior is a logistical wonder, with almost 6 km (3.5 miles) of passageways and tunnels, as well as chambers. The simple mortuary temple attached to the pyramid is to the north rather than to the east. Djoser also reserved a spot for an Egyptian alabaster sarcophagi belonging to his daughters. After earthquakes destabilized the pyramid, making its interior unsafe, Egyptian authorities embarked on a 14-year, restoration that was completed in 2020 and that cost nearly US$6.6-million. ⊠ *Saqqara* 🖫 *LE180, as part of the Saqqara site general admission.*

Dahshur

38 km (24 miles) southwest of Downtown Cairo, 28 km (17 miles) southwest of the Giza Plateau, 12 km (8 miles) southwest of Saqqara.

Each of Egypt's many archaeological sites adds a piece to the puzzle of ancient civilization, and Dahshur is no exception. Set at the southernmost extension of the Memphite necropolis, the site consists of a few non-royal Old Kingdom (2687–2181 BC) tombs and nine pyramids. Noteworthy among the latter are the Red and Bent pyramids of Sneferu and the Black Pyramid of Amenemhat III. Although lesser-known, the White Pyramid of Amenemhat II and the Pyramid of Senusret III are also worth a stop.

Dahshur is where the famed wooden Ka Statue was unearthed amid other tomb artifacts belonging to the 13th-Dynasty pharaoh, Hor (1777–1775 BC). Depicting the ruler with uplifted arms—representing the hieroglyph for *ka* (spirit)—atop his head, the statue now resides at the Egyptian Museum and is a local favorite.

GETTING HERE AND AROUND
Off the main routes from Cairo or Giza, the road directly to Dahshur travels through mud-brick villages. As with the archaeological sites to its north, Dahshur is included on many tour operator itineraries and can be visited independently by hiring a taxi or private car and driver or using a ride-hailing service.

 Sights

The Bent Pyramid
TOMB | One quick glance at this pyramid, and you can see that something is amiss—some call it a "false pyramid" others refer to its shape as "blunted" rather than "bent." Regardless, it has an unusual silhouette that was the result of an architectural mishap. It was designed for Sneferu (2613–2589 BC), the founder of the 4th Dynasty and the father of Khufu (for whom the Great Pyramid in Giza was built). Only when construction had reached midway did the ancient builders notice that there were flaws—its initial angle was too steep, so, to prevent it from collapsing, they adjusted the angles of its outer face.

Many believe that the Bent Pyramid was the first, albeit unsuccessful, attempt at transitioning from the stepped pyramid to the smooth-sided true pyramid like that of Khufu. Regardless, this is one of Egypt's largest pyramids, standing 105 meters (344 feet) tall and covering an

Fayyum Touring Tips

■ **It's best to visit on an organized tour.** Security concerns may preclude independent travel, and a vehicle of some kind is essential to reach area attractions. Look into private tours as well as larger group tours. Staff at your hotel in Cairo can help.

■ **Plan to stay overnight.** The Fayyum is far enough from Cairo and has enough sites to merit staying more than a day.

■ **Prepare for the sun.** Pack sunscreen, wear comfortable shoes, dress for dry heat and strong sun, and always carry water. Mosquito repellent will also be useful if you're visiting during warmer months.

■ **Don't rely on cell phones to navigate.** Connectivity isn't universal, especially in the national parks, so carry print maps and guidebooks.

■ **Bring cash and ID.** Credit cards aren't accepted everywhere in the Fayyum so always carry some cash. Have your passport with you at all times as well since there might be security checkpoints along the way.

■ **Respect the area.** Don't take anything from the natural parks and reserves, and keep the area clean. It's also best to respect the culture and dress modestly.

■ **Learn key phrases.** Learning a few basic Arabic phrases will not only be appreciated by the locals, but it will also go a long way when you ask for directions or help.

---

area of 52 square meters (599 square feet). It also retains much of its limestone cladding. What's more, Sneferu didn't let this less-than-successful construction project stop him: he went on to commission the neighboring Red Pyramid. ✉ *Al-Haram Dahshur, Menshat Dahshur* 🎟 *LE60, combo ticket for all three main pyramids.*

Black Pyramid

TOMB | Of all the Old and Middle Kingdom pyramids at Dahshur, the one built for Amenemhet III (1844–1797 BC) is, perhaps, the most easily recognizable. It was originally constructed out of black mud brick and encased with fine limestone that was later plundered, leaving it with the darker color that led to its modern-day name. It took an estimated 15 years to build this structure, which measures 31 square meters (344 square feet) and was originally 80 meters (265 feet) tall. Its pyramidion (a pyramid's crowning feature) was fashioned from

black basalt and now resides in the Egyptian Museum.

Nearby are tombs belonging to other members of the court, unlikely to be open to the public. Like Sneferu, Amenemhet III had two pyramids; the other one is in Hawara in Fayyum. ✉ *Al-Haram Dahshur, Menshat Dahshur* 🎟 *LE60 (combo ticket for all three main pyramids).*

Red Pyramid (*North Pyramid*)

TOMB | Named for the pinkish limestone of which it is made, this, like the Bent Pyramid, belonged to Sneferu (2613–2589 BC). It measures 67 square meters (721 square feet) and was originally 104 meters (341 feet) tall, making it only slightly smaller than the Great Pyramid at Giza, later built for Sneferu's son, Khufu. It also marks the first successful attempt at building a smooth-sided "true pyramid." If you can manage navigating the low-ceilinged passage leading down into

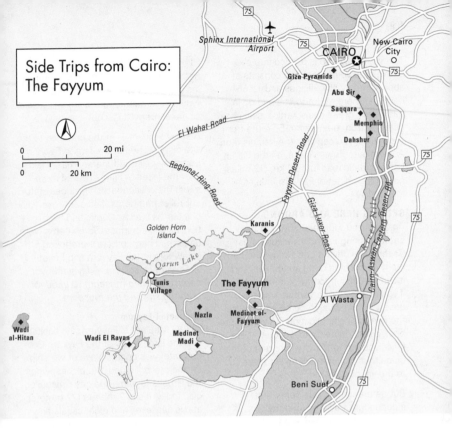

Side Trips from Cairo: The Fayyum

the interior, you can see the pyramid's three magnificent corbelled chambers. You can also see evidence of tomb robbers, who battered the floor of the topmost chamber in search of treasure. Note, too, the graffiti left by 19th-century tourists. ⊠ *Al-Haram Dahshur, Menshat Dahshur* 🎟 *LE60 (combo ticket for all three main pyramids).*

The Fayyum

103 km (64 miles) southwest of Downtown Cairo, 88 km (55 miles) southwest of the Giza Plateau.

The oasis region known as the Fayyum is one of the largest and most fertile in all of Egypt. It's fed by a small river, Bahr Yussef (Waterway of Joseph) that connects with the Nile and splits into a network of secondary canals. "Fayyum" is also used in reference to the region's main city, Medinet el-Fayyum, which was known as Shedet to the ancient Egyptians, Crocodilopolis (Crocodile City) to the Greeks; and Arsinoë to the citizens of the Ptolemaic Kingdom. Its modern name comes from the Coptic *peiom* (meaning sea or lake), but even that can be traced back to ancient Egyptian.

The Fayyum was a key agricultural region during the Middle Kingdom (2130–1649 BC), and, during the Greco-Roman Period (332 BC–AD 395), it provided the Roman Empire with most of the grain. The region's Birket Qarun (Qarun Lake) was once much larger and richer in wildlife. It was also the site of some of Egypt's earliest settlements (circa 6000 BC).

Today, the Fayyum is divided into six administrative centers and consists of approximately 157 villages and 1,565 hamlets. There's a lot to see and do in this warm, green oasis, which is an easy getaway from busy Cairo. En route from the capital, you can visit the Karanis (Kom Aushim) site. Tunis Village, on the Qarun Lake Touristic road just 20 km (12 miles) north of Medinet el-Fayyum, makes an idyllic base.

GETTING HERE AND AROUND

An organized tour might be your best bet for visiting Fayyum because most Cairene taxi drivers don't know the geography of the area or its antiquities, and it can be difficult to navigate especially if you're planning to venture into the desert. Alternatively, you could also use the ride-hailing application SWVL and pre-book a seat on its Cairo–Fayoum route. Once you get to the city, hire one of the ubiquitous pickup-truck taxis to take you to the various sites.

But before setting out, verify that independent travel by foreigners is allowed. This can change on a day-to-day basis depending on the security level. A hotel concierge can help with this in addition to trip planning and arranging transportation.

 Sights

Karanis (*Kom Aushim*)

RUINS | Despite the remains of bathrooms, cooking facilities, and houses, some of which are decorated with frescoes, it's hard to believe that Karanis was once populated by thousands. This Greco-Roman town 25 km (15 miles) north of the city of Fayyum was founded by Ptolemy II's mercenaries in the 3rd century BC. Today, its main attraction is a temple dating from the 1st century BC and dedicated to two crocodile gods, Petesuchs and Pnepheros. At its east entrance, a large square depression is

all that's left of the pool that would have been reserved for the sacred creatures. Inside, niches where mummified crocs would have been interred are still visible, as are some wall inscriptions.

A small >museum at the entrance to the site displays two of the famed Fayyum portraits—painted funerary masks laid over the faces of linen-covered mummies. The collection also includes statuary, relief fragments, and a few everyday objects, as well as Coptic and Islamic textiles and ceramics. Some items were unearthed here, others were found elsewhere in the Fayyum and Egypt. ⊠ *Fayyum Desert Rd.* ⊕ *fayoumegypt. com/kom-ushim-museum* ⊠ *LE60 for both the site and the museum.*

Medinet el-Fayyum

TOWN | Medinet el-Fayyum, the capital and the largest city of the Fayyum Governorate, was once a place of worship for the crocodile god, Sobek, inspiring the Greeks to name the city Crocodilopolis. Today, it sits 7 meters (22 meters) above sea level, and eight canals provide it with water. Traces of ancient Mamluk and Ottoman architecture can be found in some of its downtown mosques, and the lively city center hosts bazaars and markets weekly. The city's iconic attractions, however, are its four waterwheels. They were first introduced during the Ptolemaic Dynasty (305–30 BC), and you can hear them amid the honking of horns and the rush of traffic. There are waterwheels elsewhere in the Fayyum as well. ⊠ *Medinet Fayyum.*

Medinet Madi (*Narmouthis*)

RUINS | Little is known of the town that was originally named Dja and is situated 35 km (22 miles) southwest of the city of Fayyoum. It was founded during the reign of Amenemhat III and Amenemhat IV (1855–1799 BC) and remained extant during the New Kingdom (1550–1077 BC) era, after which it was abandoned.

Revived during the Ptolemaic Dynasty and renamed Narmouthis, the town grew and was occupied even after the Muslim conquest of Egypt, before being abandoned once and for all.

Because Medinet Madi, the so-called City of the Past, is somewhat is isolated it provides an unmatched intimate experience. You can wander its Middle Kingdom temples, some of them remarkably well preserved, dating from the 12th Dynasty and adorned with hieroglyphic inscriptions. ⊠ *Mady Historic City Rd., Fayyum Desert* 🖾 *LE50.*

Nazla

TOWN | The precariously perched kilns that dot the ravine at the edge of this village are a spectacular sight to behold. Specialized pots, such as the *bukla,* a squat vessel with a skewed mouth, are made here, but all are sold at markets in Medinet el-Fayyum. ✛ *From Medinet Fayyum take main road west about 30 km (19 miles) into Nazla; turn onto the road next to mosque.*

★ Tunis Village

TOWN | This small village overlooking Qarun Lake is often referred to as Eastern Switzerland. Evelyne Porret, a Swiss potter, moved to the village in the 1980s and established a pottery school that is still open today. With it, she transformed the villagers' lives. The school, along with a country house, formed a compound that became the center of the town. Today, Tunis Village is home to the workshops of some of the country's best potters, as well as some eco-lodges and contemporary restaurants. ⊠ *Qarun Lake Touristic Rd.*

★ Wadi al-Hitan

NATURE PRESERVE | There are no grandiose temples or legends of conquests here. Instead, you stand in the desert expanse alongside 40-million-year-old whale skeletons. Wadi al-Hitan, or Valley of the Whales, is home to the earliest

prehistoric fossils ever discovered. It provides a glimpse of the land before Egypt ever was. The desert sand is littered with invaluable fossils that tell an evolutionary story.

This UNESCO World Heritage Site located 24 miles (40 km) into the Fayyum desert is best accessed in a private four-wheel-drive vehicle and with a guide who knows the terrain. The on-site Wadi Hitan Fossil & Climate Change Museum explains the geological and paleontological significance of this protected area through a display of fossils and a short documentary. Although named after the whale remains on the site, Wadi al-Hitan is also flush with the remains of other ancient sea creatures including sharks, crocodiles, and turtles. As it's far from the lights of the city, this protected area is sometimes used as a camping site for stargazing trips. ⊠ *Wadi El Rayyan Rd.* 🖾 *Site: LE40. Camping: LE200.*

Wadi El Rayan

NATURE PRESERVE | Surprisingly, Egypt's largest waterfalls stand in the middle of the desert about 65 km (40 mile) southwest of the city of Fayyum. Embodying the region's natural beauty, this national park consists of seven main regions: El Rayan Falls, El-Modawara Mountain, the upper lake, the lower lake, El Rayyan Springs, El Rayyan Mountain, and Wadi al-Hitan. There's a lot to see, so hiring a local guide is encouraged.

Silky sand dunes surround tranquil blue water that is itself framed by flora. El-Modawara Mountain provides breathtaking panoramas. The area's rich wildlife includes Egyptian gazelles and different kinds of foxes. With more than 169 species of birds—some migrants, some local—it's also a bird-watcher's paradise. ⊠ *Wadi El Rayyan Rd.* 🖾 *Site: LE40. Camping: LE200.*

🍴 Restaurants

Blue Donkey Restaurant

$$$$ | MIDDLE EASTERN | Overlooking Qarun Lake, this restaurant in the Lazib Inn Resort & Spa has a cozy, eclectic lounge and serves Egyptian and international cuisine, all prepared with fresh-from-the-garden ingredients. Consider trying one of the Fayyumi dishes; the pigeon is especially noteworthy. **Known for:** fresh and organic ingredients; scenic views; local cuisine. ⑤ *Average main: LE450* ✉ *Lazib Inn Resort & Spa, Youssef El Sedeeq Center, Tunis Village* ☎ *10/0841–3474.*

Ibis Restaurant & Cooking School

$$$ | INTERNATIONAL | With excellent food prepared by Swiss chef Markus Iten, a cozy indoor dining area with a fireplace, and an outdoor terrace with show-stopping views of Qarun Lake, this is the perfect place to fuel up before, during, or after a day of exploring Tunis Village's pottery workshops. The restaurant also offers both pottery and cooking classes. **Known for:** Fresh ingredients; authentic experience; Egyptian and international cuisine. ⑤ *Average main: LE250* ✉ *Izbet, Tunis Village, Qarun Lake Touristic Rd* ☎ *10/6090–6048* ⊕ *www.facebook.com/ibisrestaurantandcookingschool.*

Lummaya Restaurant

$$$$ | MIDDLE EASTERN | The backdrop for the gourmet, Bedouin-inspired dishes at the restaurant in the Remal El Rayan eco-lodge are sand dunes and Qarun Lake. All together it makes for quite a remarkable experience. **Known for:** mandi-style beef, chicken, and duck with rice and spices; rich, authentic dining experience; scenic views. ⑤ *Average main: LE430* ✉ *Remal El Rayan Glamp, Wadi El Rayyan Rd, Al Fayyum Desert* ⊕ *www.instagram.com/remalelrayanglamp.*

🛏 Hotels

★ Lazib Inn Resort & Spa

$$ | RESORT | The spacious suites at this colorful gem, hidden amid greenery in the heart of Tunis Village, have private balconies and terraces. **Pros:** colorful decor; panoramic views of Qarun Lake; spa, heated swimming pool, private whirlpool tubs. **Cons:** limited number of suites; pricey for the area; service can be slow. ⑤ *Rooms from: $213* ✉ *Youssef El Sedeeq Center, Tunis Village* ☎ *10/9073–5328* ⊕ *www.lazibinn.com/en* ⤳ *16 suites* ⦿ *Free Breakfast.*

★ Remal El Rayan

$ | B&B/INN | FAMILY | Amid pristine waterways and endless sand dunes, this eco-lodge's luxurious glamping sites let you spend a night out under the desert stars without foregoing creature comforts. **Pros:** chic stargazing experiences; in the heart of Wadi El Rayan, a national park; eco-friendly stay suitable for the whole family. **Cons:** does not allow alcohol; fairly remote; hard to book accommodations. ⑤ *Rooms from: $160* ✉ *Wadi El Rayyan Rd, Al Fayyum Desert* ⊕ *www.instagram.com/remalelrayanglamp* ⤳ *7 units* ⦿ *Free Breakfast.*

Chapter 4

ALEXANDRIA

Updated by
Cassandra Brooklyn

⊙ Sights	🍽 Restaurants	🛏 Hotels	🛍 Shopping	🍸 Nightlife
★★★★★	★★★★☆	★★★★☆	★★☆☆☆	★★★☆☆

WELCOME TO ALEXANDRIA

TOP REASONS TO GO

★ **Café culture:** Linger over coffee and pastry at the famous Grand Trianon Café.

★ **The seaside promenade:** Stroll along the seafront Corniche, taking in the faded glory of the turn-of-the-20th-century architecture.

★ **A seafood meal:** Order fresh seafood from the tantalizing choices on ice at one of the city's many fine seafood restaurants.

★ **The remains of an ancient wonder:** Climb the parapet of Fort Qaitbay, site of the famed ancient Pharos (lighthouse), for magnificent panoramas of the seafront.

★ **Antiquities on display:** Visit the Greco-Roman Museum to explore artifacts excavated from ancient Alexandria.

Alexandria has grown so rapidly in the last 50 years that it now runs along the coastline from the Western Harbor all the way to Montazah on the Eastern Shore, a distance of more than 16 km (10 miles). It is, nonetheless, a great walking city because the historic Downtown occupies a compact area near the Eastern Harbor, while the ancient sights are a short taxi ride away.

As a rule, addresses are rarely used, and everyone navigates by names and landmarks, but with breezes almost always coming off the sea, orientation is fairly easy—when in doubt, head toward the water and into the wind.

1 Downtown and Raml Station. In the heart of modern Alexandria, the main tram station is on a square surrounded by early-20th-century buildings. Major shopping streets that are always bustling with people cut the district. Nowhere else in the city is its cosmopolitan past more alive. Most of the major sights are a short taxi ride from Raml Station.

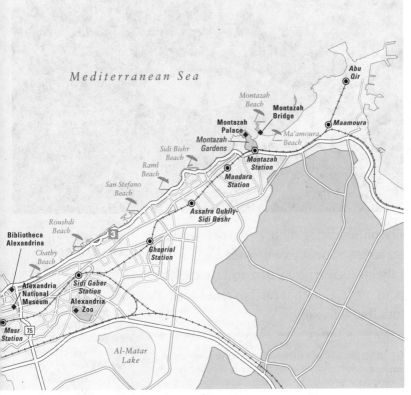

Mediterranean Sea

Abu Qir

Montazah Beach

Montazah Bridge

Maamoura

Montazah Palace

Ma'amoura Beach

Montazah Gardens

Sidi Bishr Beach

Montazah Station

Raml Beach

Mandara Station

San Stefano Beach

Assafra Quhily-Sidi Beshr

Roushdi Beach

Bibliotheca Alexandrina

Chatby Beach

Ghebrial Station

Alexandria National Museum

Sidi Gaber Station

Alexandria Zoo

Masr Station 75

Al-Matar Lake

2 El Anfushi. The westernmost tip of the main bay at the end of the Corniche, this colorful district is home to fishermen, the El Anfushi tombs, and Fort Qaitbay. This was the city's core in ancient and medieval times. Some of the city's best seafood restaurants can be found here.

3 Eastern Shore. A bit of a drive from Downtown, the Eastern Shore encompasses the upscale Montazah district, with its namesake gardens, and is home to several high-end hotels, some of which have beach access.

CAFÉ CULTURE

Coffee served the traditional way

The *ahwa* (coffee shop) is where Egyptian males traditionally go to get their caffeine fix. Part café, part social club, it is an institution that can be traced back hundreds of years.

A traditionally all-male preserve, the *ahwa* is an unpretentious place to while away the hours meeting friends, playing backgammon, or smoking *shisha* (the Egyptian water pipe). The tea and coffee drinking seem almost incidental. Egyptian ahwas can take many forms, from a cluttered hovel at the back of an alley to a spacious salon bathed in faded grandeur. All, however, share three basic ingredients: a drinks counter, a brazier of hot coals for the water pipes that line the walls, and small tin or wood tables that fill the indoor space and might spill outside onto the pavement. While Alexandria's European-style cafés and patisseries exude a sense of sophistication, ahwas are unabashedly proletarian. They are animated yet restful spots frequented mostly by older men sipping tea and puffing shisha over the sound of chatter, slapping dominoes, and Umm Kulthoum's haunting voice.

BLEND WITH THE LOCALS

Tea (*shai* in Arabic) ordered in coffeehouses is typically made with loose tea and served with the dregs. Ask for *shai libton* if you prefer the tea-bag variety. Either way, you'll be asked how sweet you want it. The four options are: *saada* (without sugar), *al-reeha* (lightly sweetened), *mazbout* (medium sweet), or *ziyada* (syrupy).

Café Beverages

COFFEE

Thick *ahwa turki* (Turkish coffee) is brewed using the same Yemeni beans Egyptians have been importing since the Ottoman era. Finer establishments add cardamom to the blend. It is served in small glasses or cups, and you allow the grounds to settle before drinking. Filtered coffee is served in some hotels, and espresso bars are becomingly increasingly popular in the cities.

HERBAL DRINKS

Karkaday, a bright red infusion made from boiled hibiscus flowers, has been popular since the days of the pharaohs. It's usually served chilled, with ice, and is packed with vitamin C. *Helba* is a yellow fenugreek tea said to reduce fever and ease congestion. *Yansoon,* an anise drink, has a medicinal taste but is purported to aid digestion. You can also ask for *irfa* (cinnamon) or *ganzabeel* (ginger) tea, both of which can be served *bi-laban* (with milk).

SOFT DRINKS

Ask for *hagga sa'a* (literally "something cold"). Common offerings include *kakola* (Coke), *bibs* (Pepsi), and *seven* (7 Up). It's not likely you'll find beer, but

A warming "cocktail" of chickpeas, tomato sauce, lemon, and chili

you often come across *Birell,* a locally produced nonalcoholic malt beverage.

LEMON JUICE

Cafés pride themselves on being able to make a perfect *aseer laymoun* (lemon juice). Done right, it should be creamy, not too tart, not too sweet. Many places err on the sweet side, so consider asking for it *sukkar aleel* (lightly sweetened).

CHICKPEA COCKTAIL

On chilly nights ask for *hummus al-sham,* a tummy-warming concoction of slow-cooked chickpeas, tomato sauce, lemon, and chili served in a tall glass. Eat the chickpeas and drink the soup.

MILK DRINKS

Unflavored *zabadi* (yogurt drink) is surprisingly tasty, made better perhaps by requesting it *bil-asal* (with honey). *Rayeb,* however, is soured milk and something of an acquired taste.

SAHLEB

In winter, warm up with a hot cup of *sahleb,* a thick, creamy drink made from orchid root with milk, cinnamon, coconut flakes, raisins, and nuts. Every café has its own recipe.

A cup of creamy, cinnamon-seasoned sahleb

At times, contemporary Alexandria—with its museums and waterfront resorts—feels separate from the ancient city of the same name. Yet the Alexandria of the Greeks, Ptolemy, Cleopatra, Julius Caesar and the Romans, pagan cults, and the Great Library is literally underfoot: the modern metropolis was built atop the ruins of the old.

Overlay a map of the contemporary city with one from antiquity, and you'll see that many of the streets have remained the same: Shar'a al-Horreya runs along the route of the ancient Canopic Way, and Shar'a Nabi Daniel follows the route of the ancient Street of the Soma. Near their intersection once stood the Mouseion, a Greek philosophic and scientific center that had at its heart the collection of the Great Library. Yet only fleeting glimpses of this ancient city peek through the modern crust.

Founded by Alexander the Great in the 4th century BC, Alexandria was capital of Egypt from the 3rd century BC until AD 642, when the Arabs first arrived. By the early 20th century, Alexandria was a wealthy trading port. The merchants were fantastically rich—cosmopolitan without being intellectual—and they enjoyed the sort of idle existence that is born of privilege, a privilege not of high birth but rather of colonial rule, which shielded foreigners from Egyptian law. They lived in villas with extravagant gardens, frequented luxurious shops, gossiped over tea in grand cafés, and lounged on the beach in private resorts. The population was a multicultural mix of Greeks and Arabs, Turks and Armenians, French and Levantines, Jews and Christians—and this spawned a unique atmosphere. It was this city that Greek poet Constantine Cavafy and English novelist E. M. Forster knew.

Then quite suddenly everything changed. The intellectuals and merchants fled, driven out of Egypt by the nationalist revolution of the 1950s, the wars with Israel, and the nationalization of businesses.

It's been six decades since most of the foreigners left, though some Greeks and Armenians remained. But if you take the city as it is today and not as a faded version of what it once was, you will find that Alex (as it's affectionately known) remains an utterly charming place to visit. The Mediterranean laps at the seawall along the Corniche, and gentle sea breezes cool and refresh even in the dead of summer. Graceful old cafés continue to draw lovers and friends—Egyptians now, rather than foreigners—while the streets remain as lively and intriguing as ever. Alexandria is still a great city, even now, shorn of its many pasts.

Planning

When to Go

Alexandria's peak season is summer, when Egyptians flee here for the refreshing Mediterranean breezes. Hotels are also busy on weekends throughout the year. Off-season, Alex is spectacular, as the city settles back into its natural, relaxed rhythm. It rains more here than anywhere in Egypt. Winter is chilly and sometimes windy, which can be a pleasant break from Cairo's annual 360 days of sunshine.

There are a few annual and biennial festivals, and though none would warrant a special trip to Alexandria in itself, some events are worth attending if you're in town when they're on.

FESTIVALS

Held every September at local theaters, **Alexandria International Film Festival** tends to be chaotically organized and is regarded mainly as a chance for Egyptians to see fleeting nudity on screen (there's censorship the rest of the year). The festival occasionally showcases interesting art films.⊕ *alexmcff.com.*

The **Alexandria Song Festival** is a competition for international and local singers, songwriters, and composers usually held in late July at the Alexandria Opera House.

Planning Your Time

Three days in Alexandria is ample time to see the main sights. A visit to the Alexandria National Museum will give you some historical context, and you can see the ruins of the original Pharos at Fort Qaitbay. The great Library of Alexandria was destroyed but its modern replacement is one of the world's most ambitious collections of printed and electronic media. Leave time to browse in the Attarine market and to walk along the Corniche. Don't miss the wild European/Middle Eastern palace of the former *khedive* (prince) in Montazah; the gardens here are also beautiful. If you have any extra time, take a day trip and head west along the coast to explore the memorials on the El Alamein battlefields, reminders of sacrifices made during World War II; you can do this by taxi or with a car and driver hired through your hotel.

Getting Here and Around

AIR

There is an airport in Alexandria about an hour from the city center, but flights between Alex and Cairo are infrequent and typically include layovers in other countries. Even with direct flights, flying between the two cities usually winds up taking longer than catching a train or bus, which is why so few people do it. Taking into account ground transport to and from the airports, frequent flight delays, and having to get to the airport an hour before scheduled takeoff, the half-hour flight doesn't save any time. If flights resume between Alexandria and Sharm el-Sheikh and Hurghada, flying would make sense since trains do not run to those cities and bus rides are extremely long.

CONTACTS EgyptAir. ⊠ *Saad Zaghloul Sq., Raml Station* ☎ *03/0900-70000* ⊕ *www. egyptair.com.*

BUS

If you want to travel between Cairo and Alexandria by bus, Go Bus, Super Jet, and the West Delta Bus Company run air-conditioned deluxe buses approximately every hour from 5 am to midnight. Buses depart from many locations in Cairo, including Almaza, Tahrir Square, and Giza. In Alexandria all buses arrive to and depart from the Mohram Bey bus terminal, which is approximately a 25-minute taxi ride from Downtown.

Families like to stroll and picnic in the Montazah Gardens, which surround a lavish palace.

Although most local bus routes are too convoluted to bother with, a constant stream of minibuses runs along the Corniche night and day. Flag them down anywhere, using a hand signal to point the direction you want to go, then pile in. They are shockingly cheap and, if anything, too fast. There are two catches to minibus travel: first, you have to know the name of the district to which you are traveling (Manshiya, Sporting, Montazah, and so forth), because you need to shout it in the window to the driver, who lets you know if he goes there. Second, you have to know what your destination looks like so you can tell the driver to stop. It's easier than it sounds, and your fellow passengers always help out.

Alexandria's new Big Red Bus just might be the most scenic way to explore the waterfront area. These air-conditioned, double-decker buses cost only LE15 and run along the Corniche from Montazah Gardens to Fort Qaitbay. For the best views, grab a seat on the top deck. There's no official, reliable schedule, but

buses run about once an hour and you can hail them down anywhere along the Corniche, assuming there's sufficient space for the bus to pull over. There's no phone or official website, but you can pay on board.

CONTACTS Go Bus. ⊠ *Alexandria* ☎ *128/7299–999 WhatsApp, 2/19567 in Egypt* ⊕ *gobus-eg.com.* **Super Jet.** ⊠ *Alexandria* ☎ *2/2575–1313 in Cairo, 3/543–5222 in Alexandria.* **West Delta Bus Company.** ⊠ *38 Mohammed Talaat Noe-man, Alexandria* ☎ *2/2575–2157 in Cairo, 2/2575–9751 in Cairo.*

CAR
Unless you plan to continue on to remote areas of the Mediterranean coast west of Alexandria, there is little reason to come by car. Taxis within the city are inexpensive, and parking is so difficult that a car is more trouble than it's worth. On top of that, the two highways connecting Cairo and Alexandria—the Delta and Desert roads—are both plagued by fatal car crashes. If you still want to come by car, the Desert Road, which starts near

the Pyramids in Giza, is the faster route, taking roughly three hours. Avoid driving at night.

If you are brave enough to drive to Alex, you'll find traffic to be slightly more orderly compared to that of Cairo. Streets are less crowded, and drivers are a little bit better about obeying traffic regulations.

The main road in Alexandria is the Corniche—technically 26th of July Street, but no one calls it that—which runs along the waterfront from Fort Qaitbay all the way to Montazah. East of Eastern Harbor, the Corniche is mostly called Tariq al-Geish. Unless you park on a hill, be sure to leave your car in neutral, because people will push it around a bit to maximize parking space.

If you'd like to rent a car (with or without a driver), speak with your hotel to arrange it.

TAXI AND RIDE-SHARE

Taxis are the best way to get around Alexandria. They are very inexpensive, and you can flag them down almost anywhere. If you're alone and male, you're generally expected to sit in the front; women and couples can sit in the back. The reason for the men-in-front rule is that the driver might try to pick up another passenger en route—it's standard practice, so don't be surprised.

Drivers don't use their meters, so you have to guess at the appropriate fare. A ride within Downtown should be LE50 to LE100; from Downtown to Montazah (15–30 minutes), roughly 6 km (10 miles), about LE100–150. If you look rich, expect to pay a bit more—elderly widows often pay little, whereas prices double, at a minimum, if a driver picks you up at a five-star hotel. There are no radio taxis in Alexandria, but major hotels always have taxis waiting.

Uber works reasonably well in Alexandria, though it sometimes has problems with re-routing, delays, and canceling rides. The rates that appear in Uber are often significantly cheaper than standard taxi rates, which is why some Uber drivers may cancel the ride. If you do use Uber, a cash tip is recommended so that drivers are fairly compensated and encouraged not to cancel future rides.

TRAIN

Trains are by far the most comfortable and convenient option for getting to and from Alexandria, and the travel time and ticket prices are the same in either direction. Turbo trains are the fastest (average journey time is about three hours), and tickets for these services cost LE150 for first class and LE100 for second class. Tickets for the slower Express services are LE80 for first class and LE60 for second class but the trains are extremely slow, lack air conditioning, and are not recommended for tourists.

The European-style train station in Alexandria was the first train station in Africa and, at the time of writing, is undergoing renovations to add a café, improve Wi-Fi in the station, and improve train speeds. Due to the renovation, trains are delayed and are running significantly slower than normal (trips to or from Cairo can take 5–6 hours), but once the work is complete (expected date in 2023), train speed and reliability should improve significantly.

Be sure to confirm the scheduled departure times in advance. Currently, trains depart approximately every hour from 6 am to 8 pm. Seats are reserved, and tickets are best bought a day in advance—a laborious process that requires a trip to the station. If you take your chances, there are almost always seats available for same-day travel (except on the morning Turbo services), though travel on summer Fridays out of Cairo and Sundays out of Alexandria can be booked up. When arriving in Alex, do not get off at the first station in the city, Sidi Gabr, though many of the passengers will; the main station is Misr Station, one stop farther, which is the end of the line.

TRAM

Picturesque and cheap, Alexandria's trams are likely to take four to five times longer to get where you're going than a taxi would. The main station is Raml, near Maydan Sa'd Zaghlul. Riding the tram to the library is quick, fun, and a great way to see the city but riding it all the way to the Jewelry Museum or other farther-out sights will take at least an hour. Buy tickets onboard.

The numbers of the trams (which are marked in Arabic on cards in the front windows) and colors of the routes can change, so for the most recent information, check the station maps. To orient yourself and determine which way you're going, locate the sea, which is to the north (you'll certainly feel the breeze blowing from it).

Beaches

The beaches along Egypt's Mediterranean coast differ greatly in character from those along the Red Sea and in the Sinai. Waves can be strong and persistent in fall, winter, and spring, helped by stiff offshore prevailing breezes. This wave action and water movement affects underwater visibility, making diving less enjoyable here than in the Red Sea. The beaches along the Corniche in Alexandria are narrow but composed of fine sand. Many are formed from shallow coves interspersed with rocky outlets. The character of the public beaches in the city is much less cosmopolitan than at, say, Sharm El-Sheikh or Hurghada, and they are frequented far more by local and Cairene families than international visitors. For this reason you should dress modestly (no skimpy bikinis), though the atmosphere is not oppressive. On hotel beaches, such as at the Four Seasons, there is no problem with beachwear, and you will be able to sunbathe without attention.

Hotels

Hotels in Alexandria are located in two clusters that are roughly 30 minutes apart. Upscale resort hotels are all out along the eastern shoreline in Montazah, close to or even within the manicured khedivial palace gardens—but not convenient to the city or the historic sights. Lower-budget hotels are almost all Downtown, much more convenient but less tranquil.

In truth, with the exception of the Four Seasons, the luxury hotels in Alexandria are mostly drab, generic places not worth what they charge. Fortunately, a couple of mid-range hotels, including the surprisingly elegant Metropole, make attractive alternatives in the city center. Summer is a busy season, when advance reservations are essential. In spring and fall you may find hotels fully booked on weekends, when residents of Cairo head to Alexandria for some downtime. Outside peak summer season, most hotels discount their prices by 30% to 40%.

■ TIP → **Many hotels quote prices in U.S. dollars or euros, but if you pay with a credit card, your payment might be charged in the equivalent of Egyptian pounds.**

Hotel reviews have been shortened. For full information, visit Fodors.com. Hotel prices are the lowest cost of a standard double room in high season, excluding taxes and service charges.

What it Costs in U.S. Dollars			
$	$$	$$$	$$$$
HOTELS			
Under $70	$70–$130	$131–$200	Over $200

Nightlife

The joke among foreign residents in Alexandria is that if you want nightlife, go to Cairo. Things aren't quite that dire, but you'll still find that your nocturnal activities lean toward the wholesome rather than the iniquitous. Alexandria is a conservative town, so there's no bar scene to speak of, and most restaurants don't serve alcohol. If you want to enjoy a drink in convivial surroundings, head to the five-star hotels, which have a selection of international and local brands.

Performing Arts

The arts scene in Alex lags behind Cairo, but there are some beacons of interest. The main venues for music, theater, and exhibitions are the cultural centers attached to foreign consulates because they can fly under the radar of censors. Their programs are often very interesting and they connect you with the cosmopolitan side of Alex that is often invisible in the city at large. To find out what's happening, call the individual consulates for their schedules; pick up *Egypt Today*, which occasionally lists events; or look for advertisements at expatriate hangouts.

INFORMATION American Cultural Center.
✉ *3 Pharaana St., El Azarita* ☎ *03/486–1009* ⊕ *alexandria.usconsulate.gov.*
British Council. ✉ *11 Shar'a Mahmoud Abou El Ela, Kafr Abdou* ☎ *03/545–6513* ⊕ *www.britishcouncil.org.eg.* **Cervantes Institute.** ✉ *101 Shar'a al-Horreya, Alexandria* ☎ *3/392–0214.* **French Cultural Center.**
✉ *30 Shar'a Nabi Daniel, El Attarin* ☎ *3/392–0804* ⊕ *institutfrancais-egypte. com.* **German Cultural Center.** ✉ *10 Shar'a Batalsa, El Azarita* ☎ *3/487–9870* ⊕ *www.goethe.de.* **Greek Cultural Center.** ✉ *18 Shar'a Sidi al-Metwalli, El Attarin* ☎ *3/482–1598* ⊕ *www.hfc.gr.* **Russian Cultural Center.** ✉ *5 Shar'a Batalsa, El Azarita* ☎ *3/482–5645.*

Restaurants

Alexandria's culinary gift is extraordinary seafood, drawing on the best of the Mediterranean and the Red Sea. The preparation tends to be simple: grilled or fried, perhaps laced with garlic, herbs, or butter, and typically served with tahini (sesame paste) and a couple of salads on the side. The ingredients are so fresh that anything more elaborate would obscure the flavors. Most places display their offerings of fish, shrimp, crab, calamari, and mussels on ice, and you pay by weight or per serving. The price includes preparation and everything else—there are no hidden costs. If you need help choosing, there will always be someone on hand to guide your selection.

Because the focus is on fresh seafood, restaurants in Alexandria (especially the good ones) tend to be informal and quite inexpensive for the quality of what they serve. Naturally, many are near the water, some of them appropriately weathered, while others consist of no more than a few tables in an alley. A few places will levy a service charge, but most will not. In all places a tip of 10% is appropriate. Do not expect alcohol to be served in most restaurants.

Off-season, Alexandrians eat meals at standard times: 1 to 3 for lunch and 8 to 11 for dinner. But in summer dinner often begins much later. There is nothing more Mediterranean about Alexandria than the pace of dinner in the summer: after an evening siesta, have a *shisha* (water pipe) around 11, arrive at a waterfront restaurant after midnight, then wrap up the meal with an early morning espresso at an outdoor café nearby. You don't have to eat so late, of course, but you might be surprised how seductive it is.

Restaurant reviews have been shortened. For full information, visit Fodors. com. Restaurant prices are the average cost of a main course at dinner or, if dinner is not served, at lunch, excluding taxes and service charges.

What it Costs in Egyptian Pounds			
$	$$	$$$	$$$$
RESTAURANTS			
Under LE50	LE50– LE100	LE101– LE150	Over LE150

Shopping

Alexandria isn't really a shopping city. There's little to buy here that you can't do better finding in Cairo, where the selection is much greater. If you're looking for chain stores, head to the city center or the San Stefano Mall (15 minutes east of Downtown by taxi).

Visitor Information

The maps and brochures at the Tourist Information Center are good and detailed and the multilingual staff is easily one of the most helpful of any government office in the country. The visitor center is open until 6 pm and you can get a city map here.

CONTACTS Tourist Information Center. ✉ *Maydan Sa'd Zaghlul, Raml Station* ☎ *3/485–1556.*

Downtown and Raml Station

Nowhere is Alexandria's cosmopolitan past more evident than Downtown, where its Italianate buildings house French cafés, Armenian jewelers, and Greek restaurants. Because so few buildings survived the British bombardment in 1882, it is no surprise that what stands today reflects the late-19th-century European city that rose from the rubble. There are a few historical and cultural sights,

including the Roman Theater, the Greco-Roman Museum, and the resurrected Great Library.

 ## Sights

Alexandria National Museum
HISTORY MUSEUM | A small but high-quality collection of artifacts includes items found under the waters of the Western Harbor during recent marine archaeological projects. The display galleries cover every era of the city's long history and include Christian pieces, Islamic arts and crafts, and more recent information about Alexandria's colonial era. The early-20th-century Italianate palace that houses the museum, designed by a French architect, is a prime example of this colonial past. ✉ *110 Shar'a el Horreya, El Shallalat* ☎ *3/483–5519* 🎟 *LE100.*

★ Bibliotheca Alexandrina
COLLEGE | **FAMILY** | This monumental $190 million UNESCO-sponsored project began with an instinctively appealing idea: to resurrect the Great Library of ancient Alexandria, once one of the world's major centers of learning. Its location near the Silsileh Peninsula, on the edge of the Eastern Harbor, has tremendous symbolic resonance, having been the royal quarters in ancient times and one of several possible locations of the original library.

The modernist Norwegian-designed building is in the form of an enormous multitier cylinder tilted to face the sea, with a roof of diamond-shape windows that allow controlled light into the seven cascading interior floors. The most impressive feature, however, is the curving exterior wall covered in rough-hewn granite blocks from Aswan that have been engraved with letters from ancient languages.

With an aim to promote intellectual excellence, the library is a repository for the printed word—it holds millions of books including rare manuscripts—but

183

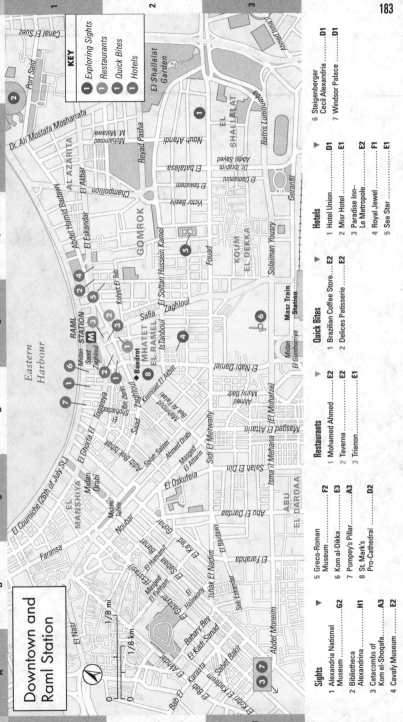

Downtown and Raml Station

Sights ▶

1 Alexandria National Museum G2
2 Bibliotheca Alexandrina H1
3 Catacombs of Kom el-Shoqafa ... A3
4 Cavafy Museum E2
5 Greco-Roman Museum F2
6 Kom al-Dikka E3
7 Pompey's Pillar A3
8 St. Mark's Pro-Cathedral D2

Restaurants ▶

1 Mohamed Ahmed E2
2 Taverna E2
3 Trianon E1

Quick Bites ▶

1 Brazilian Coffee Store ... E2
2 Delices Patisserie E2

Hotels ▶

1 Hotel Union D1
2 Misr Hotel E1
3 Paradise Inn–Le Metropole E2
4 Royal Jewel F1
5 Sea Star E1
6 Steigenberger Cecil Alexandria D1
7 Windsor Palace D1

is also a facility to store knowledge in all its forms, from audio tape recordings to electronic media. It is a robust academic organization with seven specialist research centers and has the Virtual Immersive Science and Technology Applications (VISTA) system, which transforms 2D data into 3D simulations so researchers can study the projected behavior of theoretical models. The library also acts as a forum for cross-cultural academic discussion and is home to more than 10 institutes. Membership allows you to explore the archive and use the Internet for research, but don't expect to be able to use the facility like an Internet café.

Once you've enjoyed the view of the vast interior from the mezzanine gallery, there's little to hold you in the main hall, but the library has several small museums and exhibitions. The **Manuscripts Museum** has a large collection of rare documents, parchments, and early printed books. The **Impressions of Alexandria** exhibition features paintings and sketches of the city dating from the 15th to the 19th centuries and photographs taken in the late 19th and early 20th centuries. The **Antiquities Museum** on the basement level has a collection of finds from Pharaonic, Roman, and Islamic Alexandria. Examples of monumental Roman statuary include *Huge Forearm Holding a Ball* (nothing else remains of the immense piece), and a finely chiseled bust of the Emperor Octavian (Augustus). Egypto-Roman artifacts include the mummy of Anhk Hor, governor of Upper Egypt, and several 2nd-century funerary masks showing the prevalent cross-styling between the classical Egyptian and Roman Egyptian styles. A planetarium and IMAX theater are the latest additions to the complex, offering a range of science- and astronomy-based activities including stargazing and constellation identification as well as interactive museum displays. ⊠ *63 Shar'a Soter, Chatby* ☎ *3/483–9999* ⊕ *www.bibalex.org* 🏛 *Library LE70, Antiquities*

Museum LE50, Manuscripts Museum LE30, Planetarium and IMAX shows LE50 ⊗ *Closed Fri. until 3pm.*

★ **Catacombs of Kom el-Shoqafa**
HISTORIC SIGHT | This is the most impressive of Alexandria's ancient remains, dating from the 2nd century AD. Excavation started in 1892, and the catacombs were discovered accidentally eight years later when a donkey fell through a chamber ceiling. A long spiral staircase leads to the main hall. The stairs run down the outside of a shaft, which excavators used to transport the bodies of the dead. The staircase leads to the rotunda, which, like all but the lowest chamber, is undecorated but striking for the sheer scale of the underground space, supported by giant columns carved out of the bedrock.

A few rooms branch off from the rotunda: the Triclinium was a banquet hall where relatives and friends toasted the deceased, and the Caracalla Hall has four lightly painted tombs and a case of bones. The next level down contains a labyrinth of smaller nooks for storing bodies and leads to the lowest excavated room, which is framed by columns and sculpted snakes. Casts of two statues stand here—the originals are in the Greco-Roman Museum—and three tombs are of interest for their mix of pharaonic and Greek imagery. ⊠ *Shar' El Shenity*

The Ancient Library of Alexandria

Relatively little is known about the ancient library itself, beyond its reputation for scholarship. It was founded by Ptolemy I in the 4th century BC and is said to have held a collection of 500,000 volumes—at a time when books were rare, costly commodities all written by hand. Succeeding pharaohs gathered existing knowledge from around the Greek world but also invited scientists and scholars to conduct research, ensuring that Alexandria was at the cutting edge of learning.

Theories about its destruction abound, but most assume it stood for roughly 500 years before being consumed by fire. What is known is that the Great Library—and the complex of lecture halls, laboratories, and observatories called the Mouseion, of which it was part—was a source of literary and scientific wisdom that changed the world. It was here, for example, that Euclid set forth the elements of geometry still taught in schools today, and Eratosthenes measured the circumference of the earth. And it was here, too, that the conqueror Julius Caesar had a new, more accurate calendar drawn up—the Julian calendar—that became the framework for the measurement of time throughout the Western world.

Abu Mandour, Karmouz ☎ *3/482–5800* 🎫 *LE80 (includes Pompey's Pillar).*

Cavafy Museum

HISTORIC HOME | Constantine Cavafy was ignored during his lifetime but has received international recognition since his death in 1933. His poetry, which focused on such themes as moral dilemmas and uncertainty about the future, resonated with the Greek-speaking community around the Eastern Mediterranean and has been widely translated. His poems, which include "The God Abandons Antony," and, most famously, "The City," are suffused with melancholy and a sense of alienation.

The small flat where Cavafy spent the last years of his life has been turned into a museum. Half of it is given over to a re-creation of his home, with a period-piece brass bed and some reputedly genuine Christian icons. On the walls is a collection of portraits and sketches of Cavafy that only the most vain of men could have hung in his own apartment. The other half of the museum houses newspaper clippings about the poet's life and a library of his works, in the many languages and permutations in which they were published after his death—a remarkable legacy for a man who lived so quietly. There is, as well, a room dedicated to a student of Cavafy named Stratis Tsirkas, who lived in Upper Egypt and wrote a massive trilogy set in the Middle East. And there is one last curiosity: a cast of Cavafy's death mask lying cushioned on a purple pillow. ✉ *4 Shar'a CP Cavafy (formerly Shar'a Sharm El-Sheikh), Mahatet El Raml* ☎ *3/468–1598* 🎫 *LE40* ⊙ *Closed Mon.*

Greco-Roman Museum

HISTORY MUSEUM | This museum was founded in 1895 and contains the best of the pieces found at Pompey's Pillar—including a statue of the Apis Bull—and two statues from the catacombs at Kom el-Shoqafa. This is Egypt's finest museum covering the period from Alexander the Great's conquest in 332 BC to the third Persian occupation in AD 619. There are a great many pharaonic pieces here as well; indeed, the most impressive thing

The curvaceous, rough-hewn granite exterior of the Bibliotheca Alexandrina is engraved with letters from ancient languages.

about the museum is that it shows the scale of cross-fertilization between pharaonic culture and the Greek and Roman cultures that followed. Highlights of the collection include early Christian mummies, remnants of a temple to the crocodile god Sobek, and a courtyard full of sun-drenched statuary. ⊠ 5 Shar'a al-Mathaf el Romani, Raml Station ☎ 3/483–6434 🎫 LE50.

Kom al-Dikka (*Roman Theater*)
HISTORIC SIGHT | The focal point of this excavated section of the ancient city is a well-preserved amphitheater—the only one of its kind in Egypt—originally constructed in the 4th century AD, then rebuilt in the 6th century, following an earthquake. At that time a large dome was added (only its supporting columns still stand), and the theater went from being a cultural venue to a forum for public meetings of the City Council—a change deduced from ancient graffiti promoting various political parties.

The other half of the site is the ancient baths and living quarters, although much of this area is best seen through the fence from the side near Pastroudis Café, where the cisterns and walls are clearly visible. The red bricks mark the location of the heated baths—warmed by an elaborate underground system—which complemented the adjacent cold and steam baths. The whole area fell into disuse after the 7th-century Persian conquest of Egypt. One noteworthy site in the residential section is a Roman house known as the **Villa of the Birds**, so named for its colorful floor mosaics depicting birds in several forms. The colorful and detailed craftsmanship shows a high level of sophistication. The mosaics, now restored, are protected by a modern structure. Operas are sometimes performed here in the summer. ⊠ Kon al-Dikka ✛ Off Maydan El Shohada, opposite the Misr train station ☎ 3/486–5106 🎫 LE80.

Dating from the 2nd Century AD, the Catacombs of Kom el-Shoqafa drop down more than one level beneath modern Alexandria.

Pompey's Pillar (*Serapium Oracle*)

RUINS | One of Alexandria's most iconic sights is this 88-foot-tall, hilltop, granite pillar surrounded by ruins. Known in Arabic as *al-'Amud al-Sawiri* (Column of the Horseman), the pillar was misnamed after Pompeius (106–48 BC) by the Crusaders. In fact, it dates to the 3rd century AD, when it was erected in honor of the emperor Diocletian on the site of a Ptolemaic temple to Serapis.

Helpful signs on the ruins name each virtually empty spot as a "pool" or "bath," which to the untrained eye look like indistinguishable rocks. The late-model sphinxes lying around on pedestals add a little character. The most interesting element, ironically, is that from the hill you can get a glimpse inside the walled cemetery next door, as well as a view of a long and busy market street. ⊠ *Corner of Amoud El Sawary and El Shenity Abou Mandour, Karmouz* ☎ *3/960–1315* ✉ *LE60 (includes the Catacombs of Kom el-Shoqafa).*

St. Mark's Pro-Cathedral

CHURCH | After St. Mark visited Alexandria in AD 49, the city became an early Christian outpost, building its first cathedral by AD 282. This church, constructed in 1855, was one of the few buildings undamaged during the shelling of the city by British warships in 1882. It exhibits an odd mix of Western, Moorish, and Byzantine design elements that somehow manage to blend together harmoniously. The soft yellow stone and colorful stained-glass windows are particularly exquisite in the early morning sun. The walls are lined with plaques, some of which date back almost a century, commemorating members of the Anglican community for their years of long service to the church. A passport (the actual passport, not a copy) is required for entry. ⊠ *Maydan Ahmed Orabi, Manshiya* ☎ *3/487–9927* ✉ *Free but a donation of LE30-50 is appropriate.*

🍴 Restaurants

★ Mohamed Ahmed

$$ | **MIDDLE EASTERN** | What began as a kosher restaurant in 1940 is now the best place in Alexandria to find felafel and Egypt's national dish, *ful* (fava beans). International royalty and celebrities have dined here, but on an average day you're likely to be surrounded by locals getting their fill of vegetarian staples like roasted eggplant with tomatoes, tahini, chopped salad, baba ganoush, and pickled vegetables. **Known for:** very affordable food; the best ful and felafel in town; extremely fast service. ⑤ *Average main: LE50* ✉ *17 Sharia Shakaur, Alexandria* ☎ *3/487–3576* 🚫 *No credit cards.*

Taverna

$$ | **PIZZA** | **FAMILY** | This is more a pizzeria than a real Greek taverna, but the pizza is delicious, assembled in front of you and baked in an oven to the left of the entrance. The baladi oven to the right is used for *fiteer,* a kind of Egyptian pizza than can be sweet or savory; it's also often fairly oily—ask them to go light on the ghee (clarified butter) by telling them "*semna khafeef.*" The menu also includes fish and shrimp dishes. **Known for:** the best shawarma in town; hand-stretched pizza crusts; casual atmosphere. ⑤ *Average main: LE100* ✉ *1 Maydan Sa'd Zaghlul, Raml Station* ☎ *3/485–4004.*

Trianon

$ | **EUROPEAN** | One of Alexandria's most stylish institutions and one of its oldest coffee shops is also the city's most gorgeous restaurant, with high ceilings, elaborate carved wooden chandeliers, and swirling art nouveau murals. The food is enjoyable but unspectacular; try avocado salad and *gambari konfa* (fried shrimp pastry) for appetizers, and main courses of *fattah* (lamb) or *kebab samak* (fish with green rice). **Known for:** one of the oldest coffee shops in the city; desserts in the café; historic ambience. ⑤ *Average main:*

LE45 ✉ *52 Maydan Sa'd Zaghlul, Raml Station* ☎ *3/483–5881.*

☕ Coffee and Quick Bites

Brazilian Coffee Store

$$ | **CAFÉ** | Little has changed since this stand-up espresso bar opened in 1929, as you can see from the foot-traffic patterns worn into the tile floor. The ancient roasters are visible to the right—if you're lucky they'll be roasting beans when you walk in, and the café will be filled with plumes of aromatic smoke. **Known for:** the largest coffee chain in town; you'll smell the coffee from a block away; great place to relax and people watch. ⑤ *Average main: LE60* ✉ *44 Shar'a Sa'd Zaghlul, Mahatet El Raml* ☎ *3/482–5059* 🌐 *www.facebook.com/Brazilian.coffee.stores.*

Delices Patisserie

$$$$ | **MIDDLE EASTERN** | Delices Patisserie is a great place to pick up traditional Egyptian pastries or stop in for a snack, a drink, or a quick bite. If the weather is nice, skip the indoor dining room and grab a seat on the outdoor patio. **Known for:** fabulous people-watching from the outdoor patio; the most extravagant fresh juice cocktails around; large portions and a hugely varied menu. ⑤ *Average main: LE180* ✉ *46 Saad Zaghloul, Al Mesallah Sharq, Alexandria* ☎ *3/486–1432* 🌐 *www.facebook.com/DelicesGroup* 🚫 *No credit cards.*

🛏 Hotels

Hotel Union

$ | **HOTEL** | Don't be misled by the dingy entrance and modest common area: this is one of the best inexpensive hotels in the city. **Pros:** walking distance to sights and eateries; excellent value for money; sea views. **Cons:** noise from the Corniche won't please light sleepers; not all rooms have private bathrooms; some facilities in need of a little TLC. ⑤ *Rooms from: $24* ✉ *164 Corniche, Raml Station*

☎ 3/480–7312 ▭ No credit cards ⇨ 46 rooms ◉ No Meals.

Misr Hotel

$ | HOTEL | FAMILY | On the 9th floor of Alexandria's first skyscraper, built in 1930, is one of the nicest budget hotels in town. **Pros:** well-located and across the street from a popular food court; Wi-Fi signal reaches the rooms; excellent views of the city and Mediterranean Sea. **Cons:** street noise may be bothersome to light sleepers; rooms and decor are fairly basic; the building is old and could use some TLC. ⑤ *Rooms from: $48* ✉ *21 Amin Fekry, Al Mesallah Sharq, Al Attarin, Alexandria Governorate, Egypt, Raml Station* ☎ *3/481–4483* ▭ *No credit cards* ⇨ *12 rooms* ◉ *Free Breakfast.*

Paradise Inn–Le Metropole

$$ | HOTEL | The best value in Alexandria, the turn-of-the-20th-century Le Metropole has an elegance few other hotels can match. **Pros:** delightful period atmosphere; one of few hotels that serves alcohol; excellent location for exploring Downtown on foot. **Cons:** with only one elevator, there's often a wait; some traffic noise in rooms overlooking the main street; rooms sizes can vary dramatically. ⑤ *Rooms from: LE90* ✉ *52 Shar'a Sa'd Zaghlul, Raml Station* ☎ *3/486–1467* ⊕ *www.paradiseinnegypt.com* ⇨ *66 rooms* ◉ *Free Breakfast.*

Royal Jewel

$$$ | HOTEL | FAMILY | What started as a 19th-century British Bridge Club and then served as a rest house for Egyptian King Farouk in the 20th century is now one of the most unique places to stay in Alexandria. **Pros:** prices tend to be less expensive than comparable hotels; prime location for exploring the Downtown area; guests have access to the unique, on-site library. **Cons:** no alcohol is served (but you can bring your own); no pool or beach access; the first-floor nature of the hotel makes it especially noisy. ⑤ *Rooms from: $159* ✉ *Alexandar Akbar*

St, Alexandria ☎ 3/485–7333 ⇨ 38 rooms ◉ Free Breakfast.

Sea Star

$ | HOTEL | A rather basic hotel, Sea Star's greatest appeal is its location. **Pros:** clean option for the price; the large suites are an affordable option for groups; location means you're in the heart of the action but on a quieter side street. **Cons:** no on-site restaurant; prices can change on a whim, so make sure to negotiate; very ordinary decor. ⑤ *Rooms from: $26* ✉ *24 Shar'a Amin Fikhry, Raml Station* ☎ *3/487–1787* ▭ *No credit cards* ⇨ *46 rooms* ◉ *No Meals.*

Steigenberger Cecil Alexandria

$$$ | HOTEL | FAMILY | With the Cecil, you're paying for history more than creature comforts, but if atmosphere is what you want you'll find it here in spades. **Pros:** excellent location for exploring Downtown on foot; cozy historic hotel; no-smoking rooms. **Cons:** no pool or beach access; small bathrooms; rooms are overpriced for the size. ⑤ *Rooms from: $159* ✉ *16 Maydan Sa'd Zaghlul, Mahatet El Raml* ☎ *3/487–7173* ⊕ *www. steigenberger.com* ⇨ *95 rooms* ◉ *Free Breakfast.*

Windsor Palace

$$ | HOTEL | Erected on the Alexandria Corniche in 1906, the Windsor Palace retains a period look and feel thanks to its furnishings, tapestries, and oil paintings. **Pros:** new Skyroof disco and lounge on the roof; excellent location on the Downtown Corniche; one of few hotels serving alcohol. **Cons:** no pool or beach access; on-site facilities are limited; although grand in scale, the lobby has a soulless quality. ⑤ *Rooms from: $95* ✉ *El-Gaish Rd., El Gondy El Maghool Square, Raml Station* ☎ *3/480–8700* ⊕ *www.para-diseinnegypt.com* ⇨ *71 rooms* ◉ *Free Breakfast.*

Nightlife

Cap d'Or (Sheikh 'Ali)

BARS | A modest place, Cap d'Or is blessed with a gorgeous old art nouveau bar that serves a range of Stellas (the primary Egyptian beer brand) along with some cognacs. Drinks will arrive with snacks that may be charged for—ask before you start nibbling. The bar is on the small street that runs south from Sa'd Zaghlul; it is usually open until 2 am. ⊠ 4 Shar'a Adib, Manshiya ☎ 3/487–5177.

Elite

CAFÉS | This Raml Station café and restaurant popular among expats is a good place to find out about local performances and other cultural events. ⊠ 43 Shar'a Safiya Zaghlul, Mahatet El Raml ☎ 3/482–3952.

Monty Bar

BARS | The Cecil's bar was named after General Montgomery, who commanded the Allied troops in the Battle of El Alamein. Monty Bar is a suitably conservative, wood-paneled venue. The clientele is a mixture of expat workers and sophisticated Cairenes. There's regular live music, but Monty's is too small to take the volume levels, so conversation can become impossible. ⊠ Steingenberger Cecil Hotel, 16 Maydan Sa'd Zaghlul, Alexandria ☎ 3/487–7173 ⊕ www.steigenberger.com.

Sky Roof—Windsor Palace Hotel

BARS | Located on the roof of the Windsor Palace Hotel, the appropriately named Sky Roof is a relaxed bar, lounge, and restaurant where local and exclusively selected international DJs start spinning around 9 pm. You can hear the music from the outdoor lounge, which is made up of comfortable, cushy sofas and tables but if the wind picks up at night (and it often does), head inside to continue the party. Supposedly reservations are required and staff must first approve your social media profile before a reservation is granted but we did not find this to be the case. ⊠ El-Gaish Rd., El Gondy El Maghool Square, Alexandria ☎ 3/480–8700.

Sky View

BARS | Equal parts restaurant, bar, and lounge, Sky View comes alive on top of the Paradise Inn-Metropole Hotel each night with live entertainment. Enjoy dinner or drinks and watch the sun set over the Mediterranean Sea or grab a seat at one of the inviting couches on the patio. Note that the space can get extremely windy at night and there is sometimes an order minimum (LE100–LE200) that isn't posted at the entrance. Supposedly reservations are required and staff must first approve your social media profile before a reservation is granted but we did not find this to be the case. ⊠ 6W22+83F, Al Mesallah Sharq, Al Attarin, Alexandria Governorate, Egypt ☎ 3/484–0910.

Spitfire Bar

BARS | This is a real sailor's bar: banknotes and bumper stickers from all over the world cover the walls, and among the other decorations are a yellowing advertisement for the marines—a fairly tame poster of a woman in a wet T-shirt. But the atmosphere couldn't be more congenial—it's almost sedate—and there isn't a hint of sleaze to be found. The Spitfire is just north of Shar'a Sa'd Zaghlul on Shar'a Ancienne Bourse and is open until midnight. ⊠ 7 Shar'a Ancienne Bourse, Manshiya, Alexandria ☎ 3/480–6503.

Performing Arts

Alexandria Opera House

MUSIC | Alex's opera house is also known as the Sayed Darwish Theatre. The 1921 edifice reopened after a full renovation project early in the 21st century. It offers a season of eclectic performances plus the occasional visiting company. ⊠ 22 Shar'a al-Horreya, Alexandria ☎ 3/480–0138.

New Finds

Active archaeology continues in the shallows of the Eastern Harbor, thought to be the location of Cleopatra's palace and the heart of Ptolemaic Alexandria. Since 1990, a team led by Franck Goddio has been mapping the harbor floor and discovering artifacts including coins and many other items. In 2010, several cat statues brought to the surface indicated the site of a temple of Bastet, protector of Lower Egypt, who was depicted in feline form.

Given the importance of the site and the impossibility of raising the monumental structures, the Egyptian Government and UNESCO have reached an agreement to move forward with an imaginative project currently called the "Alexandria Underwater Museum," which will allow visitors to view the remains of the city where they lie.

Innovative architect Jacques Rougerie has produced a spellbinding design for the new structure, incorporating an underwater tunnel that would allow tourists to come face to face with Cleopatra's city. However, the project is still at the embryonic stage.

🛍 Shopping

MARKETS

The **Attarine Market** is the best, if slightly informal, source for reproduction furniture and antiques. Outside, used books are sold at the street market on Nabi Daniel near al-Horreya, although it's mostly school textbooks. **Manshiya Market** is good for clothing, textiles, and spices. All three markets are great places to experience authentic life in Egypt.

Other markets in Alexandria tend to be more basic and practical, selling kitchen items or cheap clothing, and are aimed almost exclusively at locals. Both the Attarine and Manshiya markets are near the harbor and cruise ship port and are open from about 11 am until midnight Monday through Saturday.

Attarine Market

MARKET | This area acquired a reputation in the 1960s as the place to find high-quality antiques, sold by fleeing foreigners. Those days are long gone and there are only a few true antiques stores left in the area, but it's fascinating nonetheless to see the tiny workshops where reproduction French-style furniture so popular in Egypt originates. Almost all the workshops will be happy to sell direct if you find a piece that appeals to you, but consider the challenge of shipping it back home before you give in to temptation. The market actually consists of a series of alleyways, the sum of which feels less established—and far less touristy—than Cairo's Khan al-Khalili bazaar. ⊠ *Alexandria* ✛ *To find the market, walk 1 block west of the Attarine Mosque and cross Shar'a al-Horreya to the alley between the café and the parts store, El Attarine.*

Manshiya Market

MARKET | The Manshiya Market, which is also known as the "Downtown" or "old city" market, is basically a flea market near the Attarine Market. Here, clothing, textiles, spices, and jewelry are sold in the streets west of Maydan Orabi. Perhaps the most visually interesting market in Alexandria is the produce section of the market, which begins near the Raml Tram Station and runs west for a mile.

El Anfushi

Somewhere—really, everywhere—under Alexandria lies a wealth of archaeological remains, but little of it has been excavated. As a result, the city's ancient and medieval remnants exist in scattered pockets. The most central sights are the Greco-Roman Museum and the Roman Theater, but none of the rest are more than a 15-minute taxi ride from Raml Station in the El Anfushi, Karmouz, Koum El Dakka, and El Shallalat districts.

 Sights

Abu al-Abbas al-Mursi Mosque
MOSQUE | This attractive mosque was built during World War II over the tomb of a 13th-century holy man, who is the patron saint of the city's fishermen. The area surrounding it has been turned into Egypt's largest and most bizarre religious/retail complex, with a cluster of mosques sharing a terrace that hides an underground shopping center. Intruding on the space is a horrific modernism-on-the-cheap office building (with yet more shops) that is as pointed and angular as the mosques are smooth and curved. If you are dressed modestly and the mosque is open, you should be able to get inside. If so, remove your shoes and refrain from taking photos. ⊠ *Corniche, al-Anfushi, El Anfushi.*

Anfushi Tombs
CEMETERY | These 3rd-century-BC Ptolemaic tombs are built on a smaller scale than the Catacombs at Kom el-Shoqafa, but this necropolis has more extant decoration, including paintings on the limestone walls that simulate marble and include various images from the pantheon of pharaonic gods. The tombs are on the spit of land (which at one time was an island) separating the Western and Eastern harbors, roughly a third of the way between the Palace of Ras al-Tin on the western point and Fort Qaitbay on the eastern point. ⊠ *Shar'a Ras El Tin, El Anfushi* 🕾 *LE60.*

Fort Qaitbay
MILITARY SIGHT | This sandstone fort lies on the very tip of the Corniche, dominating the view of the Eastern Harbor. It was built on the site of Alexandria's Pharos lighthouse, one of the seven wonders of the ancient world, and incorporates its remains—much of which are still visible—into the foundation. A Greek named Sostratus in the 3rd century BC constructed the lighthouse in the Ptolemaic period. Standing about 122 meters (400 feet) high and capable of projecting a light that could be seen 53 km (35 miles) out to sea, it was one of the most awesome structures created by ancients. The base of the four-tiered Pharos was thought to have contained some 300 rooms, as well as a hydraulic system for lifting fuel to the top of the tower.

In the centuries that followed, the Pharos was damaged and rebuilt several times, until it was finally destroyed in the great earthquake of 1307. It lay in ruins for two centuries until the Mamluk Sultan Qaitbay had the current fortress constructed in 1479. Recently, a French team found what are thought to be parts of the Pharos in shallow waters just offshore, rekindling local interest in the ancient monument—there is even talk of an underwater museum, although that is unlikely to materialize anytime soon.

The outer walls of the fort enclose a large open space, and the ramparts' walk affords magnificent views of miles and miles of coastline. The fort also encourages romance—the arrow slits built into the ramparts that were once used to defend the fort now shelter Egyptian couples enjoying the chance to court each other in semiprivacy. The interior of the building within the fort, by comparison, is exceptionally dull, housing an undecorated mosque, a patriotic mural of President Jamal 'Abd al-Nasir (Nasser) reviewing a fantastically outfitted Egyptian navy, and

Although it looks like an older landmark, the elegant Abu al-Abbas al-Mursi Mosque was actually built during World War II.

a kitsch historical model of "the fleet of Senefroo." Upstairs are the iron bullets, swords, bombs, and shards of pottery recovered from Napoleon's ship *l'Orient*, which the British sank off Abu Qir, several miles east.

During the summer months, look out for evening musical performances and concert series at the fort. ✉ *Corniche (far western end), El Anfuṣi* ☎ *3/480–9144* ⬚ *LE60.*

The Battlefield and Monuments of El Alamein

CEMETERY | The desert west of Alexandria was the field of one of the decisive battles of World War II. In 1942, the British Eighth Army led by General Montgomery attacked the German Afrika Corps led by Field Marshal Rommel (the famous "Desert Fox") and sent them into a retreat, which would eventually clear Axis troops from the whole of North Africa. Soldiers from Great Britain, Australia, New Zealand, Canada, South Africa, India, and other countries were buried here if they died on the battlefield. Otherwise, their bodies were transferred to the hospital in Alexandria and buried in the Commonwealth Cemetery that still exists in the city.

Three carefully tended military grave sites hold the remains of Allied, Italian, and German soldiers—each with a suitably somber monument. The gardens of El Alamein's museum display an array of military hardware used in the battle. Inside the museum, galleries offer background information on the forces involved and explain how the campaign in North Africa developed and how the decisive battle played out. The museum has also collected a wealth of personal items, including letters and photographs from soldiers on all sides that layer a compelling human story on top of the military records. The sites are about an hour west of Alexandria along the coastal road. Renting a taxi for the morning is the most convenient way to see the museum, monuments, and graveyards. Local tour companies also organize guides and

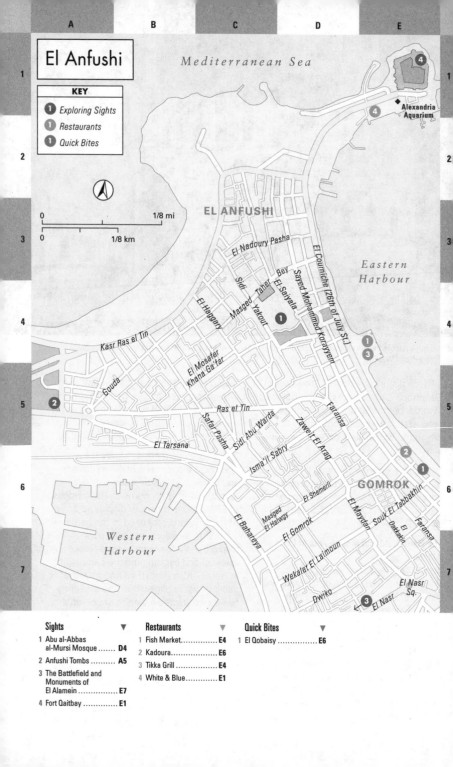

El Anfushi

KEY

- **1** *Exploring Sights*
- **1** *Restaurants*
- **1** *Quick Bites*

Mediterranean Sea

EL ANFUSHI

Eastern Harbour

El Nadoury Pasha

El Corniche (26th of July St.)

Sayyed Mohammad Korayyem

Sidi

Masged Taher Bey

El Saiyala

El Haggary

Masged Yakout

Kasr Ras el Tin

El Mosafer Khana Ga'far

Gouda

Ras el Tin

Safar Pasha

Sidi Abu Warda

El Tarsana

Isma'il Sabry

Zaweit El Arag

Faransa

Western Harbour

El Bahateya

Masged El Halwgy

El Gomrok

El Shemerli

El Maydan

GOMROK

Souk El Tabbakhin

El Dakakin

Faransa

Wekalet El Laimoun

El Nasr Sq.

Dwiko

El Nasr

♦ **Alexandria Aquarium**

Sights ▼	Restaurants ▼	Quick Bites ▼
1 Abu al-Abbas al-Mursi Mosque **D4**	1 Fish Market............... **E4**	1 El Qobaisy **E6**
2 Anfushi Tombs **A5**	2 Kadoura.................... **E6**	
3 The Battlefield and Monuments of El Alamein **E7**	3 Tikka Grill **E4**	
4 Fort Qaitbay **E1**	4 White & Blue............. **E1**	

transportation. ✉ El Alamein ✛ 96 km (60 miles) west of Alexandria ☎ 46/410–0031 🖰 LE100.

Restaurants

Fish Market

$$$$ | **SEAFOOD** | **FAMILY** | On the waterfront side of the Alexandria Corniche, this is probably the biggest fish restaurant in the city and sees a regular crowd of locals who know they'll get excellent but simply cooked seafood plus a great view out across the harbor. The catch is priced by kilogram, and rice and salads are included. **Known for:** fantastic views across the harbor; great place to dine with locals and have an authentic experience; very high food and hygiene standards. Ⓢ *Average main: LE700* ✉ *Corniche (near the Abu al-Abbas al-Mursi Mosque), Gomrouk* ☎ 3/480–5114.

Kadoura

$$$$ | **SEAFOOD** | **FAMILY** | Kadoura is a nationwide chain that got its start in Alexandria in 1950, and lucky for hungry visitors, it's every bit as good as its reputation. Fish is grilled with a delicious fresh tomato, garlic, and herb purée; calamari come lightly fried, tender, and tasty. **Known for:** all sides and drinks are included with the meal; fresh food and fast service; a relaxed and inviting atmosphere. Ⓢ *Average main: LE400* ✉ *47 26th of July St. (the Corniche), Gomrouk* ☎ 3/480–0967 ⊕ *kadoura-restaurants. com* ▭ *No credit cards.*

Tikka Grill

$$$$ | **MIDDLE EASTERN** | **FAMILY** | Alexandrians swear by this place, and it's packed with families in the early evenings and an older crowd later on. It has surprisingly elegant decor and a magnificent setting next to the water, though the atmosphere can be a little manic as waiters rush around with trays full of food. **Known for:** late-night hours; a lively, family-friendly atmosphere; great views across the harbor. Ⓢ *Average main: LE200* ✉ *Corniche (near Abu al-Abbas al-Mursi Mosque), Gomrouk* ☎ 3/480–5114.

White & Blue

$$$$ | **INTERNATIONAL** | **FAMILY** | Just before the entrance to Fort Qaitbay and the city's famous Citadel, you'll find the Greek Nautical Club, commonly referred to as the "Greek Club." Head to the White & Blue restaurant on the second floor, where you'll find some of the city's best views of the Mediterranean Sea and the harbor. White & Blue manages to pull off an upscale atmosphere while remaining accessible and unpretentious. **Known for:** phenomenal views of the sea and harbor; one of the few restaurants serving alcohol; a classy vibe. Ⓢ *Average main: LE500* ✉ *Qaitbay Str. Alexandria 21599 Egypt, El Anfushi* ☎ 12/7588–8836 WhatsApp ⊕ *www.instagram.com/white-andblue.eg.*

Coffee and Quick Bites

El Qobaisy

$ | **MIDDLE EASTERN** | A small palace of marble decorated with piles of colorful fresh fruit, El Qobaisy is one of the most incongruous places in Alexandria. It's a casual juice bar, but the uniformed staff look as if they could grace a fine-dining establishment and the mango, hibiscus, coconut, and strawberry juice is mouthwateringly fresh. **Known for:** superfast service; the freshest juice in town; amazing coconut juice, especially popular during Ramadan. Ⓢ *Average main: LE30* ✉ *50 26th of July St., the Corniche, Gomrouk* ☎ 3/486–7860 ▭ *No credit cards.*

Performing Arts

Alexandria Center of Arts

ARTS CENTERS | This performing arts center has a theater, plus galleries and workshop space. They run a varied program of arts performances, films, and exhibitions throughout the year. ✉ *1 Shar'a al-Horreya, Alexandria* ☎ 3/495–6633.

Did You Know?

The views are fantastic from Fort Qaitbay, which was built in 1479 atop the site of the enormous Pharos Lighthouse, one of the seven wonders of the ancient world, whose light was thought to be visible 53 km (35 miles) from shore.

The Royal Jewelry Museum's palatial setting perfectly complements the wearable treasures on display.

Eastern Shoreline

The Eastern Shoreline area, about a 30-minute drive from Downtown, is where you'll find most of the higher-end hotels, many of which have beach access. There are few sights and attractions in the area aside from Montazah Gardens and the Royal Jewelry Museum but there is plenty of good food. Large shopping malls are concentrated here but travelers seeking authentic markets and handmade souvenirs should look elsewhere.

Sights

Montazah Gardens

CASTLE/PALACE | FAMILY | When the descendants of Mohammed Ali became khedives (princes) of Egypt in the mid-18th century, they began to surround themselves with the trappings of a royal lifestyle, and this included the lavish El Montazah palace, built outside Alexandria in the 1890s by Khedive Abbas Hilmi Pasha. During the era of Egyptian Royalty (1922–1952) the palace, enlarged in ornate Italianate style by King Faoud and surrounded by acres of lush gardens, played host to lavish parties. It was from here that Faoud's son King Farouk made his last journey on Egyptian soil after his abdication in 1952. He went into exile in Rome and died there in 1965. Today the palace is part of the presidential property portfolio. The formal gardens, with their flower beds, lawns, and beaches, offer a shady place to stroll or picnic and are very popular with local families.

At the time of writing, the majority of the grounds are under renovation and unable to be visited but they are expected to re-open in 2024. ✉ *Corniche al-Nil, Montazah* 💷 *LE25.*

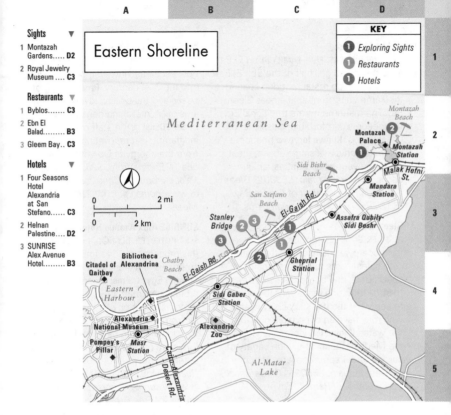

Eastern Shoreline

KEY

1 Exploring Sights
1 Restaurants
1 Hotels

Mediterranean Sea

Montazah Beach

Montazah Palace

Montazah Station

Malak Hefni St.

Sidi Bishr Beach

Mandara Station

San Stefano Beach

El-Gaish Rd.

Assafra Qubily-Sidi Boshr

Stanley Bridge

Bibliotheca Alexandrina

Chatby Beach

Gheprial Station

El-Gaish Rd.

Citadel of Qaitbay

Eastern Harbour

Sidi Gaber Station

Alexandria National Museum

Alexandria Zoo

Pompey's Pillar

Masr Station

Cairo-Alexandria Desert Rd.

Al-Matar Lake

0 — 2 mi
0 — 2 km

Royal Jewelry Museum

ART MUSEUM | One of the newest arrivals to Alexandria's museum scene is the stunning Royal Jewelry Museum in the Zizenia neighborhood. It houses an impressive collection of 19th- and 20th-century jewelry from various royal and elite members of society. Inside a former palace that seamlessly blends European and Islamic styles, the building's gilded ceilings, fine paintings, and elaborate mosaics are as stunning as the jewels themselves. While you'll certainly find sapphire-studded necklaces, emerald-encrusted broaches, and many other extravagant wearable items, you'll also find gold-plated and gem-coated dinnerware, chess sets, and scepters. ☒ 27 Ahmed Yehina St. ☎ 3/582–8348 ⊕ www. instagram.com/royal.museum ☞ LE100.

🍴 Restaurants

Byblos

$$$$ | MEDITERRANEAN | The signature restaurant of the Four Seasons, Byblos serves excellent Lebanese and Syrian dishes that you can mix and match depending on your mood or order as a prix-fixe. Start with a selection of hot and cold mezze, then try *sheikh al manshee* (eggplant stuffed with minced beef and tomato sauce) or *kebbeh bel laban* (lamb meatballs smothered with yogurt sauce and mint). **Known for:** the classiest decor in the entire city; impressive selection of beer and wine; personalized romantic dinner arrangements are available. ⑤ *Average main: LE900* ☒ Four Seasons Hotel, 399 El Geish Rd., San Stefano ☎ 3/581–8000 ⊕ www.fourseasons.com/ alexandria/dining.

★ Ebn El Balad

$$$$ | MIDDLE EASTERN | FAMILY | Ebn El Balad is the mixed grill half of the Ebn El Balad–Ebn Hamido restaurant duo sharing the same waterfront space near Gleem Bay. The maritime-meets-traditional-Egyptian decor is comfortable, classic, and unassuming. **Known for:** two phenomenal restaurants in a single space; great meat and vegetarian options; unique decor. $ *Average main: LE300* ⊠ *Gleem, Alexandria* ✛ *just west of Gleem Bay* ☎ *12/2855–5909* ▭ *No credit cards.*

Gleem Bay

$$$$ | ECLECTIC | Gleem Bay is a waterfront boardwalk hangout dotted with cute cafés, pasta purveyors, seafood specializers, and burger joints. It's easy to stroll from one restaurant to another to see what the day's specialty is and who may have an open table right by the water. **Known for:** incredible views of the Mediterranean Sea; wide variety of cuisine; great spot for a late night bite. $ *Average main: LE500* ⊠ *Glime Beach, San Stefano, El Raml 1, Egypt.*

Hotels

Four Seasons Hotel Alexandria at San Stefano

$$$$ | HOTEL | The opening of the Four Seasons in 2007 gave Alexandria its first world-class, five-star property. **Pros:** high-quality furnishings throughout; a good choice of restaurants and cafés; spectacular two-story spa. **Cons:** 10-minute taxi ride to Downtown; beach is closed in winter; you must traverse a tunnel under the Corniche road to get to the beach. $ *Rooms from: $422* ⊠ *399 El Geish Rd., San Stefano, Alexandria* ☎ *3/581–8000* ⊕ *www.fourseasons.com/alexandria* ⮐ *118 rooms* ⫶○⫶ *No Meals.*

Helnan Palestine

$$$$ | HOTEL | FAMILY | Set amid royal gardens, between the old palace and a private cove, this modernist hotel was built in 1964 to house visiting heads of state attending an Arab summit; its interior space has, however, been brought into the 21st century. **Pros:** setting offers peace and tranquillity; lovely surroundings of Montazah gardens; private beach. **Cons:** some staff members are indifferent; last renovation was 2002; far from the energy of Downtown Alexandria. $ *Rooms from: $265* ⊠ *Montazah Palace grounds, Montazah* ☎ *3/547–3500* ⊕ *www.helnan.com* ⮐ *216 rooms* ⫶○⫶ *No Meals.*

SUNRISE Alex Avenue Hotel

$$$ | HOTEL | FAMILY | On a delightful bay, this modern hotel has international-style amenities and a resort setting not often seen in Egypt. **Pros:** friendly, helpful, professional staff; private sandy beach; three excellent on-site restaurants. **Cons:** far from the city center; the wing above the nightclub can be noisy; rooms are furnished more simply than most 5-star hotels. $ *Rooms from: $160* ⊠ *Corniche Road, Roshdi, Montazah* ☎ *3/522–6001* ⊕ *www.sunrise-resorts.com* ⮐ *167 rooms* ⫶○⫶ *Free Breakfast.*

Activities

SPAS

Fours Seasons Hotel Spa and Wellness Center

SPAS | This upscale spa is one of the biggest in Egypt; there are excellent fitness facilities, as well as massage and body treatments, and separate sauna, Jacuzzi, and steam-room facilities for men and women. ⊠ *Four Seasons Hotel, 399 El Geish Rd., San Stefano* ☎ *3/581–8000* ⊕ *www.fourseasons.com/alexandria/spa.*

Chapter 5

LUXOR AND THE NILE VALLEY

Updated by
Lauren Keith

 Sights   🍴 Restaurants   🛏 Hotels   🛍 Shopping   🍸 Nightlife

★★★★★   ★★★☆☆   ★★★★☆   ★★☆☆☆   ★☆☆☆☆

WELCOME TO LUXOR AND THE NILE VALLEY

TOP REASONS TO GO

★ **Valley of the Kings:** Follow the story of the pharaoh's journey to the afterlife through the vividly painted walls and ceilings in the tombs of this royal necropolis.

★ **Karnak Temples:** Stand in awe below the "petrified forest" of columns in the Great Hypostyle Hall before visiting the many temples and monuments in one of the world's largest religious complexes.

★ **Tomb of Nefertari:** Admire the electric colors and quiet atmosphere of this regal tomb—arguably the best in the entire country—made specially for Ramses II's favorite queen.

★ **Cruising the Nile:** Make the river your home for a few days aboard a traditional wind-powered *dahabiya* or a large river cruiser as your floating room ferries you to the ancient monuments.

★ **Temple of Horus:** Scope out the architectural perfection and dark, atmospheric interior of Edfu's temple dedicated to the falcon-headed god.

As a former ancient capital, Luxor has the lion's share of the region's temples and tombs, but fascinating historic sites are dotted all along the Nile south to Aswan and beyond.

North of Luxor are impressive temples in the small towns of Abydos and Dendera, visitable on a day trip. The ancient sites south of Luxor are most easily visited on a Nile cruise, but it's also possible to go by road or train.

1 Luxor. Ancient Thebes is one of Egypt's busiest tourist destinations, and its West Bank is dotted with vast mortuary temples and rock-cut tombs painted floor to ceiling in immaculate artworks. The city has the widest selection of hotels and restaurants in the southern Nile valley.

2 Dendera. The Greco-Roman Temple of Hathor marks the cult center of the goddess of motherhood and love.

3 Abydos. Exquisite reliefs and well-preserved paint are highlights of a temple started by (and named for) Seti I and finished by his son, Ramses II.

4 Esna. The Temple of Khnum gleams with renewed brilliance thanks to the work of an Egyptian–German conservation team.

5 El-Kab. Rock-cut tombs with preserved carvings and paintwork are in the vicinity of this town, which has been settled since 3100 BC.

6 Edfu. Built during the Ptolemaic Dynasty (305–30 BC), the Temple of Horus is one of ancient Egypt's most intact—and magnificent—temples.

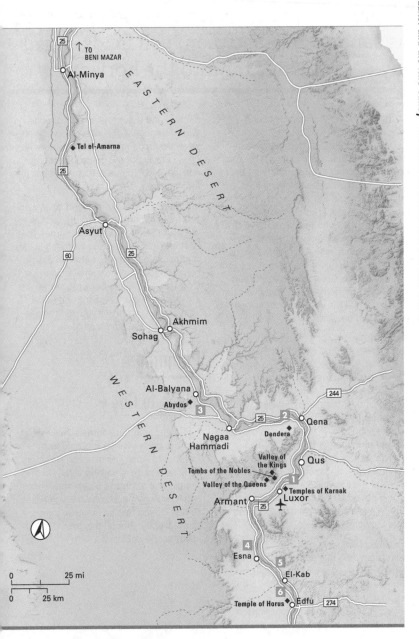

For proof that Egypt is a gift of the Nile, take a hot-air balloon flight over Luxor. From the air, the thin blue ribbon of river is sandwiched between lush fields edged by desert sands far into the horizon.

If the Nile didn't provide this bounty of water, the harsh, sun-baked landscape would have been left to the scorpions and snakes. Since antiquity, the Nile has been a superhighway connecting Egypt's most important cities for merchants, the military, and the monarchy. Then, as today, the river's eternal importance is on full display, with the Nile's network of glorious temples and tombs that were erected within easy reach of the life-giving water. You can still sail it and see for yourself. Start by anchoring yourself in Luxor, the modern city built atop ancient Thebes, until the river's magnetic pull carries you onward.

Luxor has plenty of sites along both sides of the Nile. On the city's East Bank, the new Avenue of the Sphinxes connects the incredible Karnak Temple Complex, one of the world's largest religious sites and built over thousands of years, with Luxor Temple, which was also developed and expanded over time. As the sun sets in the west (before being reborn again in the east), it seemed fitting for the New Kingdom pharaohs, courtiers, and nobles to build their tombs on Luxor's West Bank, beyond the fertile areas closest to the Nile and hidden amid, and beneath, the secluded desert.

Reached by dusty potholed roads filled with zippy tuk-tuks and donkey carts laden with the day's harvest, the grand temples at Dendera and Abydos are a short distance north of Luxor but a world away. They were once major religious centers and today feel slightly at odds with the modest agricultural towns that have grown up nearby. Now the temples draw pilgrims of the guidebook-toting sort, a bit less pious perhaps, but still just as entranced.

Wonderful ancient tombs and cities also line the riverbank south from Luxor all the way to Egypt's southern border. The best and easiest way to see these places is aboard a Nile cruise, either on a large boat or a traditional two-mast *dahabiya*. Only dahabiya itineraries stop at the smaller sites, such as Esna and El-Kab, so research carefully if you want to see specific temples and tombs.

Planning

When to Go

High season in the southern Nile valley is in the cooler winter months, from October to April. The heat can kick in as early as March, rendering early-morning temple and tomb tours essential. Fortunately, summer evenings are significantly cooler. During Ramadan, Luxor slows down slightly, though this tourist hub is never entirely quiet.

Planning Your Time

If you're in town to sail up the Nile to Aswan, remember that some cruises schedule only a single day in Luxor, and this major city deserves more time. You'll need at least a day to visit the West Bank mortuary temples and tombs, another day to visit the temples at Karnak and Luxor, and a third day if you want to explore Abydos and Dendera.

Getting Here and Around

AIR

EgyptAir links Luxor to Cairo with four flights a day. In the busy winter season, some European and Middle Eastern airlines operate nonstop flights to Luxor from Brussels, Doha, Istanbul, Jeddah, London, Milan, and Zürich, but these routes are not flown daily.

Luxor Airport is about 9 km (5.5 miles) southeast of town. Taxis from the airport to downtown take about 20 minutes and cost LE250. For less hassle, book your airport transfer through your accommodations.

BOAT

Luxor is the start and end point for Nile cruises, and the most popular direction for departures is going south (upriver) from Luxor to Aswan. Most *dahabiya* (traditional two-masted sailing vessel) journeys begin in Esna instead of Luxor, negating the need to bypass the Esna Lock.

If you want to take a *felucca* (small traditional sailboat) on an overnight trip, it's better to do this from Aswan. Feluccas are entirely wind-dependent, and it can take days to go a short distance, so captains are unlikely to take you far beyond Luxor city limits.

For more information, see Ch. 8, Cruising the Nile and Lake Nasser.

BUS

You can reach Luxor by bus from Cairo, but the journey times are long and departures are often overnight. Most travelers opt for a flight or the train.

If you do decide to travel by bus, Go Bus and Blue Bus are the most comfortable options. Tickets cost about LE300 (more for "deluxe" vehicles with more amenities), and the travel time is 10 to 11 hours.

The coastal Red Sea city of Hurghada is the nearest tourist destination to reach by bus from Luxor. Companies have daytime departures, and the journey takes about four hours.

TRAIN

Egypt's main railway line runs from Cairo to Luxor and Aswan, spanning nearly the entire country. Trains operate day and night, and Egyptian National Railways has a variety of classes and carriages to choose from.

Egyptian National Railways has an array of services. Daytime options include Special Service OD (carriages built in 2015 with air-conditioning and specific seat reservations), Speed AC Spanish (older air-conditioned carriages from Spain, hence the name), and Ordinary trains, which do not have reserved seats or air-conditioning and are best left for short journeys.

Special Service OD and Speed AC Spanish trains offer first- and second-class tickets. Ordinary trains run second- and third-class only. Foreigners who don't speak Arabic are unlikely to be able to buy third-class tickets. Some Ordinary trains have been upgraded to new air-conditioned carriages that were delivered from Russia in 2021.

Before reaching Luxor from Cairo, trains stop in Giza, Asyut, Al Balyana (for Abydos), and Qena (for Dendera).

WATANIA SLEEPING TRAINS

Egypt has one of the Middle East's few sleeper train services, and an overnight ride on the Ernst Watania Sleeping Train is sure to be a memorable experience. From Cairo, the sleeper train has a nightly departure at 7:45 pm, and one or two additional departures are added in the peak winter season. The carriages, built in East Germany in the 1980s, are dated but clean and comfortable enough.

You might be able to buy tickets online (though the website often has technical glitches that will render that impossible); otherwise, book in person at the train station or through a local travel agency. Tickets cost $120 for a two-berth room and include a simple dinner and breakfast.

Hotels

Accommodation prices are much lower in the heat of summer (May to September). All hotels and guesthouses include breakfast in their rates, and some offer half-board (breakfast and dinner) options, especially on the West Bank where there are fewer restaurants. Accommodations can arrange tours and transfers.

Some hotels open their pools to nonguests for a fee. The best option is Hilton Luxor, which offers a day pass for LE430.

■TIP→ **Many hotels quote prices in U.S. dollars or euros, but if you pay with a credit card, your payment might be charged in the equivalent of Egyptian pounds.**

Hotel reviews have been shortened. For full information, visit Fodors.com. Hotel prices are the lowest cost of a standard double room in high season, excluding taxes and service charges.

What it Costs in U.S. Dollars

	$	$$	$$$	$$$$
HOTELS				
	under $50	$50–$75	$76–$100	over $100

Restaurants

Luxor offers the widest range of restaurant cuisines in the southern Nile valley, but as with most places around the country, you'll more often be feasting on a table full of Egyptian mealtime essentials, including soups, salads, hot and cold appetizers, grilled meats, and *tagines* (slow-cooked vegetables and meat in a spiced tomato-based stew), especially on Luxor's West Bank and in smaller towns.

Confusingly, the taxes and service fees vary by restaurant but should be indicated on the menu. Ask before ordering if you don't see it written down. The combined additional charges can tack on an extra 25% or more.

Consider tipping about 15% even if a service charge is included. Restaurant staff are not well-paid, and the courtesy will be appreciated. Bring cash: restaurants outside of major hotels do not accept cards. Hotel restaurants are generally open to non-guests, but reservations are recommended.

Restaurant reviews have been shortened. For full information, visit Fodors.com. Restaurant prices are the average cost of a main course at dinner or, if dinner is not served, at lunch, excluding taxes and service charges.

What it Costs in Egyptian pounds

	$	$$	$$$	$$$$
RESTAURANTS				
	under LE100	LE100–LE125	LE126–LE150	over LE150

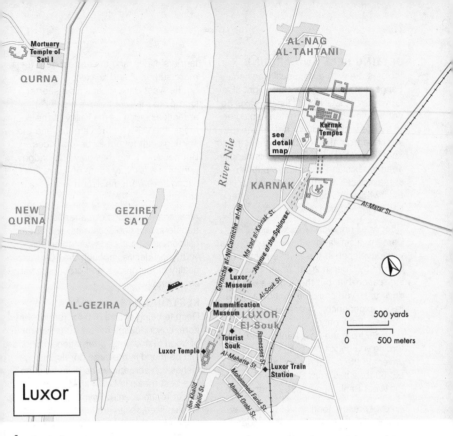

Luxor

672 km (418 miles) south of Cairo, 214 km (133 miles) north of Aswan.

One of the planet's oldest continuously inhabited cities, Luxor has been known by many names throughout its long history. Its modern moniker comes from the Arabic *al-Uqsur* (the palaces), but it was known in antiquity as Thebes.

Luxor is touted as the world's greatest open-air museum, and both its East and West banks have plenty on display, from the larger-than-life sandstone temple at Karnak to the valley necropolises's once-hidden, treasure-filled tombs that have art so astounding that they look like the painters finished yesterday.

Luxor lives—or dies—by tourism. After a decade of volatile politics and a global pandemic, travelers are returning to the city's ancient sites, but even at quieter times, the hassle from touts and would-be tour guides can be fierce, overwhelming, and off-putting to visitors.

As ancient as it is, this city doesn't stand still. Archaeologists continue to open excavated sites and make new finds, including the huge 2021 discovery of a "lost golden city" from 3,400 years ago on the West Bank, and the grand opening of the Avenue of Sphinxes between the temples of Karnak and Luxor, walkable by modern travelers for the first time.

What will never change is Luxor's spellbinding atmosphere. No matter how well-worn the paths to every sight might be, the thrill and appeal of this city's cache of ancient art and historic monuments is undeniable.

GETTING HERE AND AROUND

Luxor is rife with taxis, usually ancient Peugeot station wagons that might also be worthy of a UNESCO listing. Taxis do not have fixed rates or meters, so agree to a price with the driver before you get in. A ride from the southern hotel strip to Karnak costs about LE85. Hotels happily arrange taxis and sometimes publish set taxi prices, but these are higher than what you'd pay on the street after a bargaining session.

Uber does not work in Luxor, but Careem, a similar ride-hailing service that was developed in the Middle East and bought by Uber in 2020, does. Prices are reasonable, but the app has a lack of drivers, so you could be waiting a while. In our experience, Careem worked on the East Bank only, and drivers would not take you from the East Bank to the West, forcing you back to haggling with cab drivers in the street. Expect to pay about LE250 for a taxi from Downtown Luxor to the West Bank, about a 30-minute drive.

An ever-present long line of horse-drawn carriages called *calèches* can be found outside Luxor Temple and along the Corniche. The constant din of shouts and hassle from the drivers is one of Luxor's most unpleasant experiences. Many of the animals are not well taken care of, and it's better to skip a ride.

Feluccas (small traditional sailing vessels) float along the Nile, a beautiful way to see the sunset or spend an afternoon on the water. A sunset sail costs about LE200 for two people.

HOTELS

The heart of the city—and all the convenience and hassle that come with it—is on Luxor's East Bank. The train station and airport are on this side of the river, as are all the major hotel chains, Luxor's two main temples, and most of restaurants.

Luxor's West Bank is a breath of fresh air from the chaos of the East Bank. Low-rise guesthouses crop up among farmers' fields, and the atmosphere feels more authentic and relaxed. Staying on the West Bank means it's a shorter journey to many of Luxor's big-ticket attractions, such as the Valley of the Kings, the Valley of the Queens, and the starting point for hot-air balloon rides. But because Luxor has only one bridge (which is a fair way south of town), it's a long drive from the airport or the train station.

All accommodations can arrange airport transfers, tours, felucca trips, and hot-air balloon rides, and nearly anything else your heart desires, though the cost, quality of the guides, and group size vary considerably.

RESTAURANTS

Despite being such a hub for foreign visitors, Luxor doesn't have a huge variety of good restaurants. International options can be found in the large hotels, but dishes can sometimes be disappointing. The best meals in Luxor are the ones closet to the source: Egyptian street-food staples like *koshary* (macaroni, rice, lentils, and chickpeas, topped with a spiced tomato sauce and crispy fried onions).

Restaurant options on the more rural West Bank are limited, and many people opt to eat at their accommodations. Home-cooked feasts at West Bank guesthouses can be especially memorable.

Outside of hotels, you're unlikely to find alcohol on the menu, and most restaurants do not take credit cards.

TOURS
GUIDED TOURS

To see the sights of Luxor, joining a tour or hiring a guide and driver is best. Signage at the ancient sites ranges from poor to nonexistent, and hearing the history will greatly enhance your visit.

Magic Carpet Travel is highly recommended for tours around Luxor and further afield. The company has clean,

Luxor Pass Pros and Cons

Launched in 2016, the **Luxor Pass** is an excellent companion if you're staying in town for a few days and plan to do a lot of sightseeing. The Luxor Pass comes in two options: Standard (US$100) and Premium (US$200). Both offer free, skip-the-line access to every museum and archaeological site on the East and West banks, but the Premium Pass also includes entry to the tombs of Seti I (otherwise LE1000, about US$55) in the Valley of the Kings and Nefertari (LE1400, about US$76) in the Valley of the Queens. The Luxor Pass is valid for five consecutive days. If you purchased the Cairo Pass for sightseeing there, you can get a 50% discount on the Luxor Pass, even on the Premium version. Students also receive a further 50% discount.

Tickets to the sites in Luxor can add up quickly, especially if you visit the two top-price tombs. The Luxor Pass is also a good idea for independent exploring in lesser-visited areas, such as the Tombs of the Nobles, which otherwise require visitors to purchase tickets at an office miles away.

The only downside of the pass is getting a taste of Egyptian bureaucracy—it's a hassle to buy and sometimes, even, to use. The Luxor Pass is not available online (there's no official government website), and it can be purchased only at Karnak or the Valley of the Kings.

You must purchase the pass with the exact amount of cash in U.S. dollars or euros (not Egyptian pounds), and you're also required to show your passport, plus provide a copy of your passport and a passport-style photo of yourself. Sorting the paperwork at the ticket office can take anywhere from 15 minutes to half an hour or more, and the employees sometimes run a scam telling you that they need extra money for more photocopies. Be firm, and if necessary, suggest calling in the tourist police—only one passport copy and one photo is required. Bringing a tour guide with you could be helpful.

Even though the Luxor Pass was announced several years ago, not all site guards are familiar with it, so even if there's no line at the entrance (and these days there rarely is), you might still be waiting while they call the main office to ask about it.

new-model cars and works with knowledgable male and female Egyptologist guides.

Haytham Ramadan runs Egypt Customized Tours and has fascinating outings around both the East Bank and West Bank sights, plus an unmissable food tour to introduce you to Luxor's best eats.

Luxor also makes a good base for day trips to Abydos, Dendera, and Esna, none of which are included on big boat cruise itineraries.

CONTACTS Egypt Customized Tours. ✉ Luxor ☎ 10/0003–7743 ⊕ www.facebook. com/egyptcustomizedtours. **Magic Carpet Travel.** ✉ Nefertiti Hotel, El Sahaby St., Downtown ☎ 15/5499–9050 ⊕ magiccarpetegypt.com.

HOT-AIR BALLOON RIDES

Luxor is the most popular place in Egypt for hot-air balloon flights, a peaceful way to get an early-morning aerial view of the West Bank. Rides start as the sun is rising, and you spend about an hour gliding over the temples and tombs.

Karnak Touring Tips

■ **Know your limits.** Karnak is a huge complex, and if you're pressed for time or worn out by temple hopping in the heat, focus your sightseeing on the route that leads east from the main entrance's Avenue of Ram-Headed Sphinxes.

■ Alternatively, enter via the Avenue of Sphinxes "back door." After the 2021 opening of this pedestrianized route from Luxor Temple, it's possible to enter from Karnak's quiet southern entrances. The Avenue of Sphinxes forks into two paths: one leads to the Gate of Euergetes and the Temple of Khonsu to the west, and the other heads past the Mut Temple Enclosure to the Tenth Pylon.

■ **The early bird gets the temple.** Karnak opens at 7 am, and it's best to visit first thing. The morning light brings the reliefs into beautiful focus. Huge tour groups start to arrive around 9 am, and the afternoon heat can put off even the most ambitious explorer.

More than 10,000 balloon launches happen in Luxor every year, but the city has seen a number of accidents, some fatal. Research carefully and choose a reputable operator.

CONTACTS Paradise Balloons. ✉ *Luxor* ☎ *10/9211–3366* ⊕ *www.facebook. com/paradiseballoon.* **Sindbad Balloons.** ✉ *37 Abdel Hamed el-Omda St., Luxor* ☎ *10/009–5500* ⊕ *www.sindbadballoons. com.*

East Bank

The East Bank of Luxor has plenty of history to keep you occupied for at least a day, with two magnificent temples linked by the walkable Avenue of Sphinxes—fully opened in 2021—and two museums when you need some air-conditioning.

◉ Sights

★ Karnak Temples

RUINS | One of the world's largest religious sites, Karnak is not just one temple but a giant complex of massive story-telling pylons; a huge hypostyle hall that's a forest of columns; and a scattering of seemingly countless temples, chapels, and obelisks. Some 30 pharaohs—as well as the Greek Ptolemies and early Christians—stamped their style and erased past names from Karnak over thousands of years, resulting in a hodgepodge of structures and designs. As a rule, the farther you walk into the complex, the more ancient the constructions.

Karnak is divided into three precincts dedicated to important gods of ancient Thebes—Amun-Ra, Mut, and Montu—but the Precinct of Amun-Ra is the only area that's fully open for visitors. Fortunately, it's also the most fascinating.

Although you can access Karnak from the Avenue of Sphinxes, its main entry is via the **Avenue of Ram-Headed Sphinxes**, which leads to the Precinct of Amun-Ra, the major part of the Karnak. The **First Pylon** was actually the last one built and was left unfinished by the pharaohs of the 30th Dynasty. Walk through the pylon and spot the remains of the ancient mud-brick ramp used to build it.

In the **Great Forecourt**, a solitary 69-foot-tall column with an open papyrus capital is all that remains of the **Kiosk of Taharqa** (690–664 BC), an Ethiopian pharaoh of

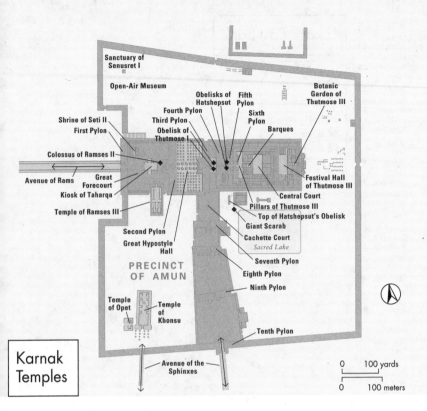

Sanctuary of
Senusret I

Open-Air Museum

Obelisks of   Fifth
Hatshepsut   Pylon

Botanic
Garden of
Thutmose III

Fourth Pylon
Third Pylon

Sixth
Pylon

Shrine of Seti II
First Pylon

Obelisk of
Thutmose I

Barques

Colossus of Ramses II

Avenue of Rams

Great
Forecourt

Festival Hall
of Thutmose III

Kiosk of Taharqa

Central Court

Temple of Ramses III

Pillars of Thutmose III
Top of Hatshepsut's Obelisk

Giant Scarab

Second Pylon

Cachette Court

Great Hypostyle
Hall

Sacred Lake

Seventh Pylon

PRECINCT
OF AMUN

Eighth Pylon

Ninth Pylon

Temple
of Opet

Temple
of
Khonsu

Tenth Pylon

Avenue of the
Sphinxes

Karnak
Temples

0   100 yards

0   100 meters

the 25th Dynasty. The small temple to the left of the forecourt entrance is the **Shrine of Seti II** (19th Dynasty), which has three small chapels that stored the sacred barques (boats) for the gods during the Opet processions and are depicted on the walls. In the southeast portion of the Great Forecourt, two colossi representing the king front the **Temple of Ramses III** (20th Dynasty), which follows the standard New Kingdom design of pylon: the open-air courtyard has arms-crossed statues in the form of Osiris (god of the afterlife), and a hypostyle hall. Like the wider Karnak temple complex, this temple has three chapels for each god of the Theban Triad.

Constructed during the reign of Horemheb (18th Dynasty), the **Second Pylon** was built with blocks recycled from dismantled monuments from Akhenaten, who

changed the state religion and was seen as a heretic. The blocks were usurped and reused again by Ramses I and Ramses II.

The second pylon opens onto the **Great Hypostyle Hall**, a towering forest of 134 columns in 16 rows. The tallest reach nearly 80 feet into the sky, but originally this hall had a roof. The colors and hieroglyphs are remarkable. The 12 columns alongside the processional way have open-papyrus capitals, while the other columns have papyrus-bud capitals and are smaller. The New Kingdom pharaoh Seti I built much of the elaborate hall, and it was completed by his son, Ramses II.

Amenhotep III (18th Dynasty) constructed the **Third Pylon,** which leads to a handful of obelisks, including the 70-foot-tall **Obelisk of Thutmose I** (18th Dynasty) and, past the Fourth Pylon, the

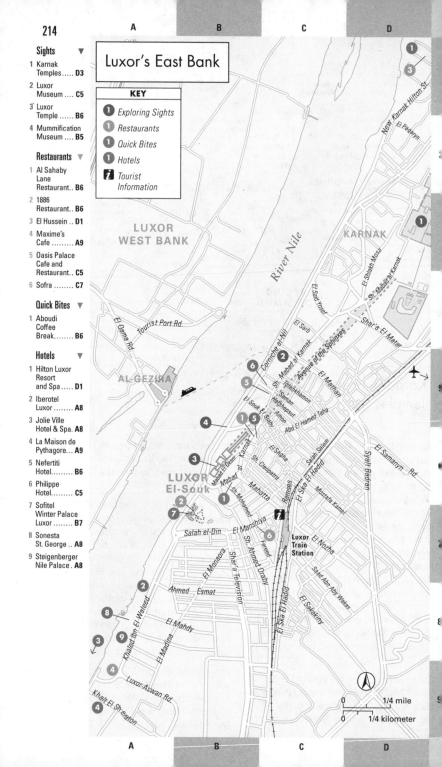

Sights ▼

1 Karnak
  Temples..... **D3**

2 Luxor
  Museum **C5**

3 Luxor
  Temple **B6**

4 Mummification
  Museum **B5**

Restaurants ▼

1 Al Sahaby
  Lane
  Restaurant.. **B6**

2 1886
  Restaurant.. **B6**

3 El Hussein .. **D1**

4 Maxime's
  Cafe **A9**

5 Oasis Palace
  Cafe and
  Restaurant.. **C5**

6 Sofra **C7**

Quick Bites ▼

1 Aboudi
  Coffee
  Break........ **B6**

Hotels ▼

1 Hilton Luxor
  Resort
  and Spa **D1**

2 Iberotel
  Luxor **A8**

3 Jolie Ville
  Hotel & Spa. **A8**

4 La Maison de
  Pythagore... **A9**

5 Nefertiti
  Hotel......... **B6**

6 Philippe
  Hotel......... **C5**

7 Sofitel
  Winter Palace
  Luxor **B7**

8 Sonesta
  St. George .. **A8**

9 Steigenberger
  Nile Palace . **A8**

Obelisk of Hatshepsut. The lower part of her obelisk is well preserved because Thutmose III, Hatshepsut's stepson and successor, encased it within a brick wall, probably not to preserve it but to hide its presence.

Beyond the Fifth Pylon and Sixth Pylon, look for the two **Pillars of Thutmose III** carved with papyrus and lotus plants representing the union of Upper and Lower Egypt. Nearby are elegant statues of the gods Amun-Ra and Amunet, carved during the reign of Tutankhamun. Philip III Arrhidaeus, the half-brother and successor of Alexander the Great, built a red granite **Sanctuary** on the site of an earlier temple destroyed by the Persians.

At the end of Karnak's east–west axis is the **Festival Hall of Thutmose III**, erected to commemorate the pharaoh's military campaigns in Asia. The unusual columns are representations of tent poles used when traveling to battle. Behind the hall is the "botanical garden," a vestibule with reliefs showing plants and animals that the pharaoh brought back from his expeditions. Spot the graffiti that indicates that this hall was later used as a church.

Several monuments and courtyards also run along Karnak's north–south axis, which begins between the third and fourth pylons. The **Cachette Court**, at the northernmost part of the axis, was so named because of the thousands of statues and bronzes found in it in 1903. To the south lie the seventh through tenth pylons, separated by courtyards. Archaeological work continues in this area, and not all locations are accessible. A path continues southbound outside the Precinct of Amun to the Avenue of Sphinxes, which links to Luxor Temple.

The **Sacred Lake** is near the Cachette Court, and it's where priests purified themselves before rituals and where you can take a break in the waterside café. At the northwest corner of the lake, a large scarab statue dates from the reign of Amenhotep III. Farther to the northwest lie the fallen remains of the other Obelisk of Hatshepsut (its partner is back between the fourth and fifth pylons).

Karnak is home to plenty more temples, chapels, and pylons that are less visited but still impressive. The **Open-Air Museum** north of the First Pylon contains the small **Chapel of Senusret I**, which dates from 1971 BC but was dismantled by Amenhotep III and used to fill the Third Pylon about 600 years later. The chapel contains high-quality reliefs that show the pharaoh being crowned and the deities of provinces around Egypt. The nearby **Red Chapel of Hatshepsut** was used to keep sacred boats for festivals.

Karnak has a **Sound and Light Show** (LE300) that includes a walk through the gradually lit complex, ending at the sacred lake, where you take a seat and the second part begins. For the steep ticket price, the display gets mixed reviews and feels outdated. ✉ *New Karnak* 🖃 *LE200.*

★ **Luxor Museum**

HISTORY MUSEUM | One of Egypt's best museums outside of Cairo houses a bounty of statuary, with a particularly great selection from the New Kingdom, over several floors. The displays have thorough descriptions, a rare find in Egypt. Many of the pieces were unearthed around Deir el-Bahri, the area just across the Nile from the museum that includes the Mortuary Temple of Hatshepsut.

The **ground floor** has several masterpieces from the New Kingdom, including carvings of Thutmose III and crocodile-headed Sobek giving life to Amenhotep III. A newer wing, called **Glory of Thebes' Military and Technology Gallery,** showcases the royal mummies of Ramses I and Ahmose I in darkened rooms along with New Kingdom chariots and weapons of war on two levels.

Hieroglyphs depicting a mummy and gods highlight the importance of preserving the body for the afterlife.

On the **upper floor**, look for carved stones from Amenhotep IV's temple at Karnak before the pharaoh changed his name to Akhenaten, created a new monotheistic religion—the world's first—and moved the capital from Thebes to his new city of Tell el-Amarna. The stone blocks were discovered inside Karnak's Ninth Pylon in the 1960s, reused there by later rulers attempting to erase the "heretic" pharaoh's legacy. Other artifacts include ushabti (small servant statues), a wooden model boat from King Tut's tomb in the Valley of the Kings, tombstones from the Christian era, and Islamic-period pottery.

Near the museum entrance is the **Cachette Gallery**, which shows New Kingdom statues unearthed from Luxor Temple in 1989, hidden to protect them from destruction by later rulers. ⊠ *Corniche el-Nile St., Corniche* ☎ *LE140.*

★ Luxor Temple

RUINS | An astounding contrast with the modern city right outside its gate, Luxor Temple is a mostly New Kingdom construction started around 1390 BC. The temple was the southern counterpart to the temples of Karnak. During the annual Opet festival, statues of the gods were paraded down the Avenue of Sphinxes from Karnak to Luxor. For nearly 35 centuries, this religious complex has been a place of worship—from the ancient Egyptian pantheon to the mosque built into the temple's foundations that is open to the local community.

Like Karnak, Luxor Temple was adapted and expanded over millennia. Likely built over a Middle Kingdom predecessor, the largely 18th-Dynasty temple was developed by Amenhotep III and expanded by Ramses II, Nectanebo I, Alexander the Great, and the Romans. The Romans transformed the area around the temple into a military camp, and after the 4th-century AD Christian ban on pagan cults, several churches were built inside the temple.

A towering obelisk and a series of seated and standing statues of Ramses II guard the 79-foot-tall **First Pylon** and entrance to the temple. Originally, it was a pair of

Luxor Temple Touring Tips

■ **Start in the east.** The ticket office is off Mabad el-Luxor Street. There's no entrance to the temple from the Corniche.

■ **Visit after dark.** Luxor Temple is open until 8 pm, and it has a completely different atmosphere after the sun goes down. A stroll along the illuminated Avenue of Sphinxes is a beautiful way to arrive.

■ It's still a place of worship. Time your visit to coincide with one of the calls to prayer to hear the adhan from the minaret of the Abu al-Haggag Mosque echo through the hypostyle halls. The mosque is built into Luxor Temple's foundations, but it's now accessed from the modern ground level, more than a story higher than the temple floor.

obelisks, but Muhammad Ali Pasha, the ruler of Ottoman Egypt, gifted the other to the French in 1830, and it's still in Paris. The pylon shows war scenes from the Battle of Kadesh, a campaign that Ramses II waged against the Hittites in modern-day Syria.

Heading off in the other direction is the 3-km (2-mile) **Avenue of Sphinxes** that leads to the Karnak temple complex. Its full length was opened in 2021 to pedestrians for the first time in thousands of years, and you can walk to a "back door" entrance to Karnak after exploring Luxor Temple.

Beyond the First Pylon lies the **Court of Ramses II**, encircled with a double row of papyrus-bud columns. Wall carvings show the pharaoh making offerings to the gods, as well as a list of some of his sons' names and titles. To the right of the entrance is a triple shrine built by Hatshepsut but taken over by her stepson successor, Thutmose III, who took credit for the monument by removing her cartouches and writing in his own. The shrine is dedicated to the Theban Triad: Amun-Ra in the middle, Mut on the left, and Khonsu on the right. To the left of the court entrance, well above the temple's floor level, is the still-open **Mosque of Abu al-Haggag**, built atop a Christian church.

Al-Haggag was a holy man from Baghdad who died in Luxor in AD 1245.

The **Colonnade of Amenhotep III** consists of two rows of seven columns with papyrus-bud capitals. The wall decoration, completed by Amenhotep's successors, illustrates the voyage of the statue of the god Amun-Ra from Karnak to Luxor Temple during the Opet festival. On each side of the central walk are statues of Amun-Ra and Mut, carved during the reign of Tutankhamun, which Ramses II later usurped.

The colonnade leads to the **Court of Amenhotep III,** where a cachette of statues hidden by the Romans was found in 1989; it's now on display in the Luxor Museum. Double rows of remarkably elegant columns with papyrus-bud capitals flank this peristyle court on three sides. A **H ypostyle Hall** with even more columns lies to the south. Between the last two columns on the left as you walk to the back of the temple is a Roman altar dedicated to the Emperor Constantine.

South of the hypostyle hall are **chapels** dedicated to Mut and Khonsu. The first antechamber originally had eight columns, but they were removed during the 4th century AD to convert the space into a Christian church. The Romans plastered over the ancient Egyptian carvings, but

Sunset at Luxor Temple, the southern counterpart to the Karnak Temples.

one still intact scene shows an entourage of Roman officials awaiting the emperor.

Behind the chapels is the **Offering Hall,** with access to the inner sanctuary. On the east side, a doorway leads to the **mammisi** (chapel showing divine birth), used to prove that Amenhotep III was the son of the god Amun-Ra and to strengthen the pharaoh's position as absolute ruler. The symbolic birth scenes are spread over three registers on the left wall, showing goddesses suckling children, the pharaoh's birth in front of several gods, and Hathor (the goddess of motherhood) presenting the infant to Amun-Ra. ⊠ *Mabad el-Luxor St., Corniche* 🖾 *LE160.*

Mummification Museum

HISTORY MUSEUM | The Egyptians began mummifying their dead more than 4,500 years ago, and while they weren't the first ancient civilization to start this practice, they are the best known. This museum walks you through the process of preparing the body both physically and spiritually for the afterlife, using modern drawings before showcasing the actual results. The museum has just one human mummy but several mummified animals, including a cat, an ibis, and a baboon. Displays also show the tools of the trade, canopic jars, heart scarabs, and a vial of "liquid residue" from a stone sarcophagus.

■ TIP→ **The ticket price is high for this disappointingly small museum (just one room!). Skip it if you've already visited the museums in Cairo.** ⊠ *Corniche el-Nile St., Corniche* 🖾 *LE100.*

 Restaurants

Al Sahaby Lane Restaurant

$$$ | **MIDDLE EASTERN** | Perched atop the Nefertiti Hotel, Al Sahaby opened in the 1930s and has been serving incredible Egyptian dishes to visitors and locals for generations. You can't go wrong with anything on the menu, but consider trying the succulent camel meat pot, served with sides of roasted vegetables and *freekeh,* a grain that comes from

The Avenue of Sphinxes

After more than 70 years of excavations, Luxor's 3,000-year-old **Avenue of Sphinxes** was opened in November 2021 to huge fanfare and an extravagant show put on by the Egyptian government. For the first time, modern travelers can walk the ancient path between the Karnak complex and Luxor Temple, lined with hundreds of sphinx statues in the shape of lions, rams, and humans. About one-third of the original 1,057 sphinx statues have been unearthed, and the search and excavation for more continues.

The opening ceremony in 2021 reenacted the Opet Festival, an ancient annual celebration that paraded statues of the gods from temple to temple along this 2.7-km (1.7-mile) route. Entry to the avenue is included with tickets for Karnak and Luxor temples, and walking it is an excellent alternative way to enter Karnak through a quiet "back door," far from the busy main way in.

durum wheat. **Known for:** rooftop dining; beloved enough to have a street named in its honor; classic dishes. ⑤ *Average main: LE150* ✉ *Nefertiti Hotel, El Sahabi St., Downtown* ☎ *95/225–6086* ⊕ *nefertitihotel.com.*

1886 Restaurant
$$$$ | FRENCH | Step back into an elegant era beneath the Venetian crystal chandeliers of the dining room at 1886, where you'll feast by candlelight reflected on the heavy silver plates and thick linens. Dishes are French-inspired, and the menu has quite a bit of seafood. **Known for:** luxurious surroundings; vegetarian options; dressing up for dinner. ⑤ *Average main: LE400* ✉ *Sofitel Winter Palace Luxor, Corniche el-Nile St., Corniche* ☎ *95/238–0422* ⊕ *all.accor.com* 👔 *Jacket and tie required.*

El Hussein
$$$$ | MIDDLE EASTERN | Don't let the stained tablecloths at this upper-story dining room put you off: communal eats can be a messy business. Standard mixed-grill items share the lineup with less common offerings such as turkey, duck, quail, and rabbit, which must be ordered before arriving. **Known for:** authentic dining; wide selection of meats; molokheya, a thick, green, gelatinous soup made from jute leaves. ⑤ *Average main: LE250* ✉ *Hilton St., New Karnak* ☎ *10/0008–0960.*

Maxime's Cafe
$ | MIDDLE EASTERN | A surprisingly good find at the southern end of Luxor's East Bank hotel strip, Maxime's has a menu of burgers and fries, as well as Middle Eastern staples. The relaxing atmosphere makes it a great spot to while away an evening. **Known for:** hookah pipes; crowd-pleasing favorites; open-air courtyard. ⑤ *Average main: LE80* ✉ *Khaled Ibn el-Waleed St., Luxor South* 🚮 *No credit cards.*

Oasis Palace Cafe and Restaurant
$$ | INTERNATIONAL | In one of the few remaining 19th-century mansions in town, this relaxed restaurant decorated with old-school photos and furnishings lives up to its name. The menu runs the gamut from respectable pasta dishes to decent sandwiches. **Known for:** reliable go-to spot; good selection of vegetarian dishes; a bit of history. ⑤ *Average main: LE100* ✉ *Dr. Labib Habashy St., Corniche* ☎ *12/7941–6951* 🚮 *No credit cards.*

★ Sofra

$$ | MIDDLE EASTERN | In a tile-decorated 1930s house with an airy upstairs dining space, this restaurant lets you take a culinary tour of Egypt. Dishes range from oven-roasted rabbit with *molokheya* (a dark green gelatinous soup made from the jute mallow plant) to *hamam mahshi*, herby rice-stuffed pigeon. **Known for:** one of the best restaurants in Luxor; mezze platter you can make a meal out of; offers cooking classes. $ *Average main: LE125* ⊠ *90 Mohamed Farid St., al-Manshiya* ☎ *95/235–9752* ⊕ *www.sofra.com.eg.*

Coffee and Quick Bites

Aboudi Coffee Break

$ | FAST FOOD | The best of the fast-food cafés near Luxor Temple, Aboudi is indeed a welcome break from the chaos outside its front doors. The menu is full of basic sandwiches and grilled meats. **Known for:** stand-out fast-food joint; fast, reliable Wi-Fi; large selection of smoothies and lemonades. $ *Average main: LE60* ⊠ *Mabad el-Karnak St., Downtown* ☎ *10/1060–7702* ⊕ *www.facebook.com/ Aboudi.Restaurant.Break.*

🛏 Hotels

★ Hilton Luxor Resort and Spa

$$$$ | RESORT | One of the top places to stay on Luxor's East Bank, this riverside Hilton property is a treat to return to after a dusty day of temple-touring, and you can enjoy spectacular views (best seen with a discounted happy-hour drink in hand) of the Nile from the heated pools or unwind in the thermal bath area. **Pros:** gorgeous bar and swimming area, including an infinity pool; self-service sauna and steam room; reliable, functional Wi-Fi. **Cons:** balconies are very small; overpriced food and drink (except during happy hour); secluded location and no shuttle service to Downtown. $ *Rooms from: $127* ⊠ *New Karnak* ☎ *95/239–9999*

⊕ *www.hilton.com* ⤳ *236 rooms* ⦾ *Free Breakfast.*

Iberotel Luxor

$$ | HOTEL | Ideally situated at the southern end of the Corniche, this blocky, white, Nile-front hotel offers the necessities without pretension. **Pros:** nice garden area between the hotel and its Nile frontage; swimming pool floats in the Nile; good location for riverside strolls to Luxor Temple. **Cons:** slow Wi-Fi; street-side rooms have poor soundproofing; bathrooms could use a refresh. $ *Rooms from: $63* ⊠ *Khaled Ibn el-Waleed St., Corniche* ☎ *95/238–0925* ⊕ *www.jazhotels.com* ⤳ *185 rooms* ⦾ *Free Breakfast.*

Jolie Ville Hotel & Spa

$$$ | RESORT | FAMILY | Set on its own island linked to Luxor by a bridge, Jolie Ville is a beautiful place to disconnect and recharge after a long day out, and it's a good choice for families, too. **Pros:** lovely, lush grounds; lots of amenities, including a spa, tennis courts, and yoga classes; perfect Nile views from the riverside infinity pool. **Cons:** lots of mosquitoes; golf cart or long walk required to reach golf facilities from some rooms; far from city center. $ *Rooms from: $97* ⊠ *Kings Island, Luxor South* ☎ *95/227–4855* ⊕ *www.jolievilleluxor.com* ⤳ *550 rooms* ⦾ *Free Breakfast.*

La Maison de Pythagore

$$ | B&B/INN | Set in a traditional mud-brick home, the only guesthouse on the East Bank guarantees an authentic, personal touch. **Pros:** delicious home-cooked meals; authentic, cozy space that's the antithesis of nearby chain hotels; garden and roof areas to relax. **Cons:** alleyway is too narrow for a taxi to drive down, so you'll have to walk; tough-to-find location and no sign on front door; no Wi-Fi. $ *Rooms from: $65* ⊠ *Gazirat al-Awameyah, Luxor South* ☎ *10/0210–5656* ⊕ *www.lamaisondepythagore.com* ⤳ *7 rooms* ⦾ *Free Breakfast.*

★ Nefertiti Hotel

$ | HOTEL | The Nefertiti Hotel ticks every essential travel box—clean rooms with comfortable beds, enviable central location, no-request-is-too-much service, and a top-notch rooftop restaurant—and it all comes at an unbeatable price. **Pros:** affiliated with an excellent tour company, which operates out of the lobby; excellent location overlooking Luxor Temple; highly recommended restaurant on the roof. **Cons:** shower doesn't have basin, so the floor gets wet; no elevator; Wi-Fi barely works. ⑤ *Rooms from: $33* ⊠ *El Sahabi St., Downtown* ☎ *10/0032–9991* ⊕ *www.nefertitihotel.com* ⇆ *30 rooms* ⦿ *Free Breakfast.*

Philippe Hotel

$ | HOTEL | The Philippe has seen better days, but it's still a decent budget stay in a good location. **Pros:** good value for a short stay; conveniently situated between Luxor and Karnak temples; rooftop has pool. **Cons:** needs renovation; lots of street noise; no Wi-Fi in rooms. ⑤ *Rooms from: $28* ⊠ *Dr. Labib Habashy St., Corniche* ☎ *95/237–2284* ⊕ *www.philippeluxorhotel.com* ⇆ *69 rooms* ⦿ *Free Breakfast.*

Sofitel Winter Palace Luxor

$$$$ | HOTEL | Built in 1886, this famous hotel has seen its fair share of history and still maintains elegant period fixtures and features, from afternoon tea in the Victorian lounge with original Venetian chandeliers and parquet flooring to the posh, suit-jacket-required restaurant. **Pros:** one of Egypt's grand hotels; historic features still in place throughout the property; gardens are quiet despite the central location. **Cons:** hot water takes a while to arrive to the shower; have to enter annoying code to connect to Wi-Fi; some rooms are a bit scuffed up. ⑤ *Rooms from: $195* ⊠ *Corniche el-Nile St., Corniche* ☎ *95/238–0422* ⊕ *all.accor.com* ⇆ *194 rooms* ⦿ *Free Breakfast.*

Sonesta St. George

$$$ | HOTEL | Outfitted with marble surfaces, dark wood, and rich, ruby-colored fabrics, the Sonesta St. George has a stately air that extends from its grand lobby to the sleek rooms upstairs. **Pros:** home to the only Japanese restaurant in Luxor; large Nile-side outdoor area; classy mahogany bar area with Nile views. **Cons:** pool area looks tired and in need of an update; only two on-site restaurants; in-room Wi-Fi isn't free. ⑤ *Rooms from: $85* ⊠ *Khaled Ibn el-Waleed St., Downtown* ☎ *95/238–2575* ⊕ *www.sonesta.com* ⇆ *320 rooms* ⦿ *Free Breakfast.*

Steigenberger Nile Palace

$$$$ | HOTEL | Sandwiched among other chain hotels on Luxor's southern strip, this cream-colored, art deco–style hotel has the resort-y feel of being a city within the city, with stacks of rooms, restaurants, and entertainment options. **Pros:** Turkish hammam is the only one in the city; Nile-view rooms are worth the upgrade; choice of 10 on-site restaurants. **Cons:** hotel-arranged tours and taxis are expensive; lots of late-night noise in patio-view rooms because of hotel activities in the courtyard; pool is small for the number of rooms. ⑤ *Rooms from: $105* ⊠ *Khaled Ibn el-Waleed St., Downtown* ☎ *95/236–6999* ⊕ *www.steigenberger.com* ⇆ *304 rooms* ⦿ *Free Breakfast.*

🍸 Nightlife

Luxor stays up late, though the city has only a few bars, and there isn't a nightlife scene as such. For an evening outing, take a post-dinner stroll along the Corniche or the illuminated Avenue of Sphinxes.

Kings Head Pub and Restaurant

PUBS | The logo—the face of the "heretic" pharaoh, Akhenaten, dressed in the regalia of a historic British king—gives an indication of the cultural meld at this quirky pub, across from the Lotus Hotel and up two flights of stairs. The

As elsewhere in Egypt, bargaining is the norm in the colorful markets of Luxor.

easygoing atmosphere is conducive to a social game of pool, enjoying a couple drinks with new friends, or just admiring the eclectic decor, which includes coasters from around the world, mosque lamps, and plenty of English flags. A small blackboard announces the cocktail of the week (Sex in a Felucca, for instance). ✉ *Khaled Ibn el-Waleed St., Khaled Ibn El Waleed* ☎ *10/6510–2133* ⊕ *www.facebook.com/ KingsHeadPubAndRestaurant.*

Royal Bar

BARS | If sipping a classy cocktail in the elegant bar of a grand old hotel is your thing, you'll love this spot. The half-wall of bookshelves is a nod to the space's previous use as a library, and its decor of rich red walls, damask fabrics, and mahogany woodwork lends it a sophisticated air. A musician plays classical piano music every evening. ✉ *Sofitel Winter Palace Luxor, Corniche el-Nile St., Corniche* ☎ *95/238–0422* ⊕ *all.accor.com.*

Shopping

Shopping in Luxor is a high-pressure game, with lots of cajoling and hassle if you so much as glance at a shop for longer than a split second. Be prepared to bargain hard if you spot something you want to take home.

El-Souk

MARKET | Running for several pedestrianized blocks and covered with sun-shading lattices, Luxor's main tourist market is a cacophony of catcalling. It's the most overwhelming shopping experience this side of Cairo's Khan el-Khalili. The wares—brass trays, buckets of spices, leather poufs, jewelry, and racks of brightly colored cotton scarves—are pretty much the same as what you'll see at tourist attractions the country over. There is nothing local about this market, but if you've had your eye on a specific souvenir, this place is as good as any to pick it up. ✉ *Abd el-Hameed Taha, Downtown.*

The Scarab

One of the least expensive souvenirs you can bring back from your trip to Egypt is a small scarab beetle carved from stone. The scarab, or dung beetle, had a special place in the ancient Egyptian belief system. Just as the humble beetle pushes a ball of dung, the god Khepri rolls the sun across the sky each day, an ongoing cycle of creation and renewal. Khepri is often pictured with a man's body and a scarab for a head.

Scarab amulets first appeared during the Old Kingdom's 6th Dynasty (around 2650 BC) and remained powerful more than 1,000 years later. By the time of the New Kingdom (1550 BC), heart scarabs were essential amulets to include with mummies, and they were inscribed with names or verses from the Book of the Dead, pleading with the heart not to betray the deceased during the final judgement. The dung beetle rises out of the Earth when it hatches in the same way that ancient Egyptians hoped to emerge into the afterlife. That's why the image of a scarab is often seen in tombs.

★ **Gaddis & Co.**

BOOKS | Behind the old-fashioned painted signage, Gaddis & Co. is a treasure trove of books and maps, but the black-and-white mounted photos make excellent souvenirs. Attiya Gaddis was one of Egypt's first local photographers, and he opened this studio in 1907. His photos document the changing scene of Luxor at the turn of the 20th century, as Europeans began excavations around the Valley of the Kings. The Gaddis family still runs this shop, as well as the budget Gaddis Hotel on the southern end of Luxor's hotel strip. ⊠ *Winter Palace Shopping Arcade, Corniche el-Nile St., Corniche* ☎ *95/237–2142* ⊕ *www.facebook.com/gaddisandco.*

★ **Habiba Gallery**

CRAFTS | One street and a world away from the tourist market, Habiba Gallery is a peaceful little shopping oasis. This no-hassle store sells beautifully made handicrafts from around Egypt at fixed prices, a relief if you're tired of bargaining. ⊠ *Andrawes Pasha St., Downtown* ☎ *10/0306–2229* ⊕ *www.facebook.com/habibagalleryluxor.*

West Bank

Every night, the sun sets in the west and is reborn the next morning in the east. By the same principle, the ancient Egyptians thought of the West Bank of the Nile as the realm of the dead, while the land of the living was in the east. Less than 3 km (2 miles) from the riverside, the verdant, long-cultivated land abruptly transforms into desert, and it's here that the Egyptians constructed their extensive necropolis.

New Kingdom pharaohs (1570–1069 BC) built their tombs in the seclusion of these desert hills, with the goal of making them less accessible than the Old and Middle Kingdom royal tombs, which had been robbed even by the time of the New Kingdom. The pharaohs had their sepulchers hollowed out underground, and the artisans who carved and painted them were required to live in their own village nearby, isolated from the East Bank, so as to not disclose the tombs' locations. To further celebrate their own greatness, most New Kingdom rulers constructed huge mortuary temples,

where the namesake deceased pharaoh was worshipped in perpetuity.

But the West Bank is not just a vast royal graveyard reserved for the sovereigns and their families. Important courtiers and members of the nobility also have a number of tombs in the area.

Luxor's West Bank is home to Egypt's largest concentration of ancient monuments, so pace yourself and space out your visits over several days to fully absorb and appreciate their splendor. Although it's not essential to hire a tour guide, signage is utterly lacking so having a guide will greatly enrich your understanding of the sites you're seeing.

GETTING HERE AND AROUND

A public ferry leaves from a dock near the Luxor Museum on the East Bank and drops passengers off near Al Qurna Road on the West Bank. Tickets cost LE2. Ferries leave when they are nearing capacity, which means you could be waiting for passengers. If you want a quicker departure, bargain for a private motorboat (about LE25). To reach the West Bank sights from the river, you'll need a taxi or a bicycle.

A one-way taxi from the West Bank dock to the Valley of the Kings runs about LE70 but going on a tour with a guide and driver is a better option. Yes, it costs more, but you'll also gain an understanding of the sites, and you won't be hassled by other would-be guides.

A handful of places a short walk from the dock, as well as some West Bank guesthouses, rent bicycles for about LE70 per day. Cycling is a fascinating, slower-paced way to visit the West Bank, but check the quality of the bicycle before you set off and, as always, keep an eye on the temperature and bring plenty of water.

To travel even more slowly, you can go by donkey, best arranged through accommodations on the West Bank.

Sights

Colossi of Memnon

RUINS | Standing (sitting, actually) nearly 18 meters (60 feet) tall, these statues of Amenhotep III once guarded his mortuary temple, which is slowly being excavated to the northwest. Alongside the legs of the colossi are standing figures of the king's mother and his queen, Tiye. Relief carvings on the bases of the colossi depict the uniting of Upper and Lower Egypt.

These colossi were well known to the ancient Greeks and Romans, and after an earthquake fractured one of the monuments in 27 BC, it was said to sing softly at dawn. For the Greeks, that sound recalled the myth of Memnon, who was meeting his mother Eos (the goddess of dawn) outside the walls of Troy when Achilles killed him. In the 3rd century AD, Roman Emperor Septimius Severus had the statue repaired and accidentally silenced the song.

The Colossi of Memnon are usually a perfunctory early-morning stop for tour groups to the West Bank. ⊠ *Thebes* 🎫 *Free*.

Deir el-Medina (Workers' Village)

CEMETERY | In its own small valley, Deir el-Medina is where the artisans in charge of building and decorating the royal tombs lived. The site includes the stone walls of their otherwise ruined houses, small but vibrantly decorated tombs, and a small temple. The workers showed off their skills in their own burial chambers, applying the technical and artistic mastery they used on their employers' projects to their own.

■ TIP→ **Claustrophobes beware: these tombs are much more compact than the royal tombs and have low ceilings that some people will not be able to stand upright in. They're also accessed by incredibly steep staircases and narrow corridors.**

One of the most astonishing burial spaces in this area is the **Tomb of Sennutem** (TT 1), who was an artist during the reigns of Seti I and Ramses II. The paintings on the walls of the burial chamber look as if they were just completed. A striking scene is the god Anubis tending to a mummy on a lion-headed bed surrounded by texts from the Book of the Dead. On the ceilings are several depictions of the deceased, kneeling in adoration before the gods.

The **Tomb of Inherkha** (TT 359) has beautifully painted ceilings of a repeating cow head and sun disk motif, as well as scenes from the Book of the Dead and the Book of the Gates. Inherkha was chief workman for Ramses III and Ramses IV, and he's shown making offerings to rows of seated pharaohs.

The **Family Tomb** is the most complex of the group and consists of three connected chambers for Amennakht (TT 218) and his two sons Nebenmaat (TT 219) and Khaemteri (TT 220). Popping out from the lemon yellow background are mummified figures, larger-than-life birds, palm trees, and column after column of text. The chamber for Nebenmaat is incredible to behold: the unusual monochromatic hieroglyphic script is just as eye-catching as the colorfully painted gods.

A five-minute walk to the northeast is the **Temple of Deir el-Medina**, dedicated to a plethora of gods, including Hathor and Maat. The temple was founded during the reign of Amenhotep III (18th Dynasty), but the current structure dates from more than 1,100 years later, from the reign of Ptolemy IV. Coptic Christians later turned the temple into a monastery, which gave this place its name (Deir el-Medina means "Monastery of the City"). Look out for the judgement scene of a heart being weighed against Maat's feather of truth and justice. If the heart is heavier, it has committed bad deeds during its time on earth and will not go on to enjoy the afterlife. ✉ *Thebes* 🖼 *LE100*.

Medinet Habu

RUINS | Medinet Habu is an impressive complex that was successively enlarged from the New Kingdom to the Ptolemaic period. Hatshepsut constructed the oldest chapel (which has been undergoing restoration and might be closed), but Ramses III (1186–1155 BC) built the main part of the structure, which functioned as his mortuary temple and an administrative center for the West Bank.

The second king of the 20th Dynasty, Ramses III hugely admired his grandfather, the great builder and military man Ramses II, so he copied his predecessor's architectural style and decorative scheme. Following Ramses II's example a century before him, Ramses III consolidated the frontiers of Egypt and led successful campaigns against the Libyans and the so-called "Sea People," whose origin still isn't known.

Enter the complex through the huge fortress-like gate, called a *migdol* or Syrian Gate, a two-story structure with expansive views out over the courtyard. On the **First Pylon**, Ramses III displays his full military might and his victories over Egypt's enemies. The back of the pylon shows the enemies' severed hands and genitals piled up in front of the pharaoh. At the **Window of Appearances**, on the western side of the **First Court**, ancient visitors would have been able to see the living pharaoh when he presented himself from his palace.

Through the **Second Pylon**, the **Second Court** is decorated with scenes of religious ceremonies. The colors and reliefs in the court are well preserved. The remains of the hypostyle hall and the smaller chapels that surround the second court are less complete, but ongoing restoration work could see them brought to life. ✉ *Thebes* 🖼 *LE100*.

Mortuary Temple of Hatshepsut

RUINS | Appearing like a modern mirage, the Mortuary Temple of Hatshepsut is a

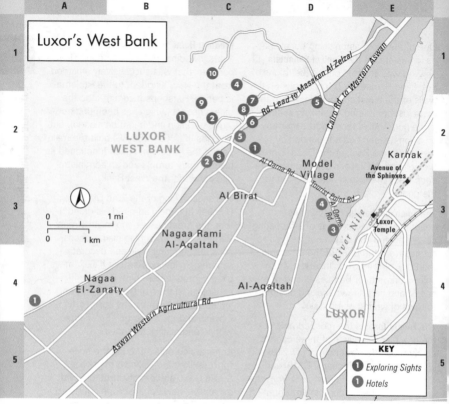

Luxor's West Bank

LUXOR WEST BANK

Al Birat

Nagaa Rami Al-Aqaltah

Nagaa El-Zanaty

Al-Aqaltah

Aswan Western Agricultural Rd.

Model Village

Karnak

Avenue of the Sphinxes

Luxor Temple

LUXOR

River Nile

Rd. Lead to Masaken Al Zelzal

Cairo Rd. to Western Aswan

Al-Qarna Rd.

Tourist Point Rd.

Al Qarna Rd.

0 — 1 mi
0 — 1 km

KEY

- ① Exploring Sights
- ① Hotels

Tomb Numbering

All tombs on the West Bank are numbered based on a system developed by English Egyptologist John Gardner Wilkinson in 1827. He painted numbers at the entrances of the tombs that could be seen at the time, 1 to 21 starting at the entrance and heading south. Tombs found later are given a number based the order of their discovery and have an abbreviation for their area: KV for Valley of the Kings, QV for Valley of the Queens, and TT for Theban Tomb at other burial sites. The Valley of the Kings tomb list currently ends with KV 65, discovered in 2008 but as yet unexcavated. King Tut's tomb, discovered in 1922, is KV 62.

sublime piece of architecture, consisting of three colonnades rising on terraces that melt into the foot of soaring limestone cliffs.

Hatshepsut was the most important woman to rule Egypt as pharaoh (1479–1458 BC). Instead of waging war to expand Egyptian territory like her predecessors, she chose to consolidate the country, build monuments, and organize expeditions to the land of Punt—modern scholars still debate its actual location—to bring myrrh, incense, and offerings for the gods. Before acting as pharaoh, she served as regent for her (then young) successor, Thutmose III. As soon as Thutmose III came of age to rule over Egypt, he began a program of erasing her name and images from monuments across the country, but some of them were preserved, perhaps by priests or temple workers loyal to Hatshepsut.

The reliefs inside the **First Colonnade** are damaged, but they include a detailed scene of transporting the queen's granite obelisks on boats from Aswan to Karnak. Take the large ramp that leads to the second courtyard. The **Hathor Chapel** on the left is dedicated to the goddess of motherhood and love, whose head tops the columns. To the right of the chapel starts the **Second Colonnade**, which shows expeditions to Punt, and the variety of goods brought back from there.

The colonnade to the right of the ramp is devoted to the divine birth of Hatshepsut, and Hatshepsut's mother is seated with the god Amun-Ra between the first and second columns. By showing that she was of divine origin, Hatshepsut validated her right to rule over Egypt as pharaoh. The **Anubis Chapel** at the end of the colonnade is better preserved and still has a good amount of colored paint. Wall scenes show offerings given to the god of mummification.

The ramp continues to the **Upper Terrace**, where a line of crossed-arm statues of Hatshepsut as Osiris, god of the afterlife, hold court. The carvings in this terrace's hypostyle hall depict celebrations and coronation rituals, including the Beautiful Festival of the Valley, when the sacred boat (barque) of the sun god Amun-Ra visited the tombs and temples of deceased pharaohs on the West Bank. Priests carry barques with statues of the gods and pharaohs followed by musicians and dancers. Cut into the rock at the back of the terrace is the **Sanctuary of Amun**, with a star-painted ceiling and offering scenes.

A golf-cart-style tram can whisk you the quarter of a mile from the end of the tourist market to the start of the temple complex for LE5. The Mortuary Temple of Hatshepsut is a common stop on tours before or after visiting the Valley of

The Temple of Ramses III (20th Dynasty) exemplifies New Kingdom design.

the Kings. This whole area is called Deir el-Bahri (Monastery of the North), but the tombs and other mortuary temples are closed or not worth visiting because they are in ruins. ⊠ *Thebes* 🎫 *LE140.*

Mortuary Temple of Seti I

RUINS | Of all of Seti I's grand building projects—the captivating temple at Abydos and his tomb in the Valley of the Kings, the longest, best decorated, and most expensive to visit—his mortuary temple is a little lackluster. Constructed toward the end of the pharaoh's reign, this structure was unfinished when he died, and Ramses II saw it to completion. The temple has been damaged by floods, both in antiquity and modern times, as well as colonies of bats. The pillar-fronted temple facade and the hypostyle hall are the only massive parts of the temple still standing. But because it's left off from big-group tour itineraries, it's a quiet spot to enjoy at a slower pace.

■ TIP→ **Tickets cannot be purchased on-site and must be bought at the Antiquities Inspectorate ticket office 3 km (1.8 miles) away on the main road into the valley.** Tour operators and taxi drivers know this and will stop there beforehand, but this requirement makes an independent visit more challenging. ⊠ *Wadi el-Melok Rd., Thebes* 🎫 *LE60.*

Ramesseum

RUINS | The mortuary temple of Ramses II is one of the many monuments built by the king who so prolifically used architecture to show his greatness and celebrate his divinity. The temple is a typical New Kingdom construction, with two pylons, two courtyards, and a hypostyle hall, followed by chapels and a sanctuary. Between the first and second courtyards, track down the broken colossus of the pharaoh that would have been 18 meters (62 feet) tall when it stood. This figure is said to have inspired Percy Bysshe Shelley's poem "Ozymandias," though he never saw the statue himself.

Big tour groups often skip this spot, leaving you to wander through the columns of the hypostyle hall in peace.

■ TIP→ **Tickets cannot be purchased**

How to Make a Mummy

The Egyptians prepared well for the afterlife, building furniture and figurines never used in their real lives and instead piling them into beautifully painted tombs. They believed the preserved body provided a permanent house for the soul in the afterlife. The human body also needed to emerge into the next realm in life-like condition, so they used mummification to preserve the features of the deceased. The ancient Egyptians did it so well that it's possible to see what royalty and nobility from 3,000 years ago looked like during their lives, sometimes even down to the color of their hair.

Mummification removes all the moisture from the body, leaving dried remains that are resistant to decay. To start the ritual, a priest made a slit in the left side of the body to remove the lungs, liver, stomach, and intestines. The heart, believed to be necessary for rebirth, was left in place. The organs were mummified separately from the body, wrapped, and placed either in canopic jars or back in the body cavity before burial. The embalmer inserted a hooked tool up the nose and through the ethmoid bone to poke, prod, and punch the brain before it was teased out of the nostril.

The body was washed and then covered and packed with natron, a mixture of salt and carbonate. This process was repeated a few times over the course of 40 days. Afterward, the body cavity was emptied, packed with linen, and sewn up. The body was adorned with amulets and jewelry and wrapped elaborately in bandages while the priests prayed.

The whole procedure for a good-quality mummy took 70 days. Starting in the First Intermediate Period (2181 BC), a funerary mask made of cartonnage (linen or papyrus covered in plaster) or gold (like that of Tutankhamun) was placed over the head and shoulders of the mummy. This practice continued until the Roman era.

The body package was then put into a wooden coffin, which, in turn, was placed in a sarcophagus (larger than a coffin and usually made of stone) before being placed in the tomb. The organ-filled canopic jars were buried next to the body. Sometimes a funerary text containing spells to help the deceased in the afterlife was written on papyrus and placed within the coffin.

on site, so get yours at the Antiquities Inspectorate ticket office before you visit. ⊠ *Thebes* 🖾 *LE80.*

Tombs of the Nobles: Nakht, Menna, and Amenemope

CEMETERY | Nakht was a scribe and astronomer under Thutmose IV, and his T-shaped tomb (TT 52) is somewhat small. Only the vestibule is decorated with vivid colors, but they show incredibly detailed scenes of Nakht hunting, fishing, and farming. To the right is a false door with a beautiful painting of eight men and two women presenting offerings.

The Tomb of Menna (TT 69) has colorful paintings of his family, including his wife and five children. Menna was a scribe and overseer of fields, and he's supervising a farm for eternity on one of the walls. Overhead, a patch of painted patterned ceiling is particularly vibrant.

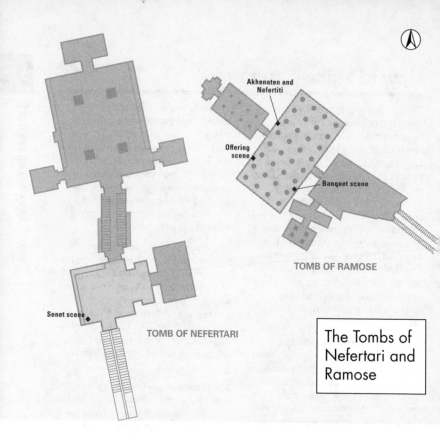

Akhenaten and Nefertiti

Offering scene

Banquet scene

TOMB OF RAMOSE

Senet scene

TOMB OF NEFERTARI

The Tombs of Nefertari and Ramose

Most of the corridor is now inaccessible to visitors, but from a distant angle, you can admire the well-preserved colorful roof and see funerary scenes, such as the Opening of the Mouth ceremony and Weighing of the Heart.

Much has been damaged in the Tomb of Amenemope (TT 148), partly because of the poor quality of the stone in this area. But the quality of the decor for Amenemope, a priest under successive generations of Ramses, is high, and the walls of painted reliefs—not just flat paint on the wall—are rare and indicative of his stature. 📧 *LE60*

Tombs of the Nobles: Ramose, Userhet, and Khaemhet

CEMETERY | The **Tomb of Ramose** (TT 55) is one of the finest in the area. Ramose was a governor of Thebes and vizier during the reign of Amenhotep III and

Akhenaten. It's so large that it has a hypostyle hall, a pillared hall, and a chapel, though some of the columns are modern reconstructions. Near the entrance are unpainted reliefs, but look out for Ramose and his wife, whose eyes and eyebrows are outlined in black, the only pigment on the entire wall. The left wall has two registers painted, one in good condition, and the scene shows a dozen crying women. Near the entrance to the pillared hall is a carving of the Aten sun disk, the sole god worshipped in new monotheistic religion started by Akhenaten that lasted only 20 years. The tomb was left unfinished.

In life, Userhet worked as a royal scribe and "Counter of Bread," and his **tomb** (TT 56) is in an inverted T-style, with a wide antechamber leading to a long, slender burial chamber. Scenes in the

Valley of the Queens Touring Tips

■ **Take the path less traveled.**
While other visitors are packed into the Valley of the Kings, come to the quieter Valley of the Queens instead.

■ **It's worth paying to see Nefertari's tomb.** With its impeccable artistry, bright colors, and paint that looks like it dried yesterday, the tomb of Nefertari will leave you in awe. Yes, the ticket is expensive, but it might just be the best ancient site you see on your trip to Egypt.

■ **Tipping at the tombs.** The tombs are manned by guardians who sometimes point out features on the walls or lead you through with a flashlight. Be aware that if you let them show you around, baksheesh (a tip) is expected as you exit. Tour guides are not allowed inside any of the tombs.

---

antechamber depict Userhet's earthly responsibilities: counting boxes of grain and overseeing the distribution of bread rations to the Egyptian army. The ceilings are painted in a bright rug-weave pattern, and the inner chamber has vivid scenes of Userhet hunting and fishing.

A scribe and Overseer of Granaries under Amenhotep III, Khaemhet had a well-decorated space to send him into the afterlife. His **tomb** (TT 57) has both raised and sunken reliefs, and scenes depict his life's work of supervising the harvest and measuring grain supplies. Much of the art is damaged, including a pair of statues at the back of the tomb representing Khaemhet and his wife, but it's still an evocative space. *LE60*

Tombs of the Nobles: Rekhmire and Sennofer
CEMETERY | The **Tomb of Rekhmire** (TT 100), who was a vizier during the reigns of Thutmose III and Amenhotep II, is well preserved, with nearly complete scenes of daily life that reveal much about day-to-day activities of the ancient Egyptians. The walls explain Rekhmire's work duties, including inspecting the construction of temples and tax collection. He also records tributes from foreign countries, and Nubians arrive with leopards, giraffes, and cattle, and the Syrians bring vases, a chariot, horses, a bear,

an elephant, and human captives. The paintings inside the chapel reveal how jewelry and sculptures were made and helped archaeologists understand the techniques used at the time.

The **Tomb of Sennofer** (TT 96) is nicknamed "Tomb of the Vineyards" because the ceiling is painted with swirling grapevines thanks to Sennofer's job as Overseer of Granaries and Gardens. A short but steep walk is required to enter the tomb. Inside you'll see scenes of Sennofer heading to the afterlife with servants carrying his belongings. The burial chamber has colorful paintings of Sennofer and his wife worshipping Anubis and Osiris and Sennofer and his family making a pilgrimage to Abydos where the deceased has his heart weighed to ensure he is worthy of entrance to the afterlife. *LE40*

Valley of the Kings
CEMETERY | Once a burial location for New Kingdom pharaohs known only to a select few, the secret of the Valley of the Kings has long been out. Every year, 1.5 million visitors come to see a rotating selection of the 65 tombs that have been discovered, ranging from the unknown and unexcavated to an underground gallery displaying the pinnacle of art and architecture of ancient Egypt.

Visiting the Tombs of the Nobles

Spread out over a large area between Deir el-Medina and Deir el-Bahri, the Tombs of the Nobles are little visited but still have impressive paintwork and are a delight to see. More than 400 tombs have been found and numbered, and nobles, priests, and government officials were buried here.

Most of the tombs date from the 18th to 20th Dynasties (1550–1077 BC), but some were reused during the 25th and 26th Dynasties (747–525 BC). Unlike the royal burial chambers in the Valley of the Kings and Valley of the Queens, these tombs show scenes of everyday life, festivals, and the deceased hard at work.

■ TIP→ **The tombs are grouped into pairs or trios for tickets. You must pay at the Antiquities Inspectorate ticket office before visiting; you cannot buy tickets on-site.** It's helpful to have a guide for these tombs because they are spread over a wide area that's not well signposted.

The well-publicized, 1922 discovery of Tutankhamun, Egypt's short-lived "boy king," still draws many visitors, but it's actually one of the least splendid tombs in the valley, completed in a rush because of his untimely death and emptied of its gilded grave goods, which were relocated to Cairo museums. You might not have seen the names of Ramses V and VI (KV 9) or Seti I (KV 17) in your school textbooks, but you'll certainly want to know more after seeing the beauty and detail of the scenes that accompanied them into the afterlife.

The tombs in the Valley of the Kings are some of Egypt's greatest treasures, but their existence is threatened just by visitors coming to see them. The hot temperatures in the valley actually bring in moisture—in the form of sweat and humid breath from tourists—that damages the 3,000-year-old art painted on fragile rock walls and ceilings. Dehumidifiers and glass screens have been installed in some of the busiest underground areas, and guides are not allowed inside any tombs to cut down on crowds. ⊠ *Thebes* 🚋 *LE240 for three tombs. Additional tickets: LE1,000 for Seti I, LE300 for Tutankhamun, LE100 for Ramses V & VI.*

Valley of the Queens

CEMETERY | The Valley of the Queens was the final resting place for pharaohs' wives, royal children, and members of the nobility for nearly 500 years, from the 18th to 20th Dynasties. Archaeologists have discovered more than 90 tombs, but only four are open to the public, clustered together a short walk from the entrance. The undisputed highlight of the Valley of the Queens is standing in awe of the artwork in the incredible Tomb of Nefertari. Don't let the eye-wateringly high price of entry—this is the single most expensive ticket for any tourist attraction in Egypt—prevent you from entering. It's worth noting, though, that most of the other tombs in the Valley of the Queens are less elaborately decorated but also less frequently visited, meaning that you might even have them to yourself.

The **Tomb of Nefertari** (QV 66), the most beloved of Ramses II's many wives, has the largest tomb in the Valley of the Queens. It also has some of the most vivid surviving decorations of any ancient Egyptian tomb, with paintings covering

Continued on page 245

Valley of the Kings

VALLEY OF THE KINGS

Hoping to prevent tomb robberies, pharaohs from the zenith of ancient Egypt's power chose to be interred in the remote Valley of the Kings, rather than in elaborate pyramids, starting around 1550 BC.

Archaeologists have discovered 65 New Kingdom tombs in this royal necropolis. The last complete tomb found, that of Tutankhamun, was opened in 1922, but the search for others continues. Most tombs have a long, sloping corridor leading to a burial chamber, but the artwork and state of preservation vary from one tomb to the next. Unlike nonroyal tombs, which show scenes from daily life, pharaohs' tombs have exclusively religious texts and scenes. Spells, notably from the Book of the Dead, aided the journey to the afterlife, where, as divine beings, the pharaohs were guaranteed a special place.

Valley of the Queens

HISTORY OF THE VALLEY

Starting from the 11th Dynasty (around 2130 BC), pharaohs ruled from Thebes, modern-day Luxor, building their mortuary temples and tombs on the West Bank of the Nile. **Amenhotep I** (1525–1504 BC) also founded the royal tomb-workers' village of **Deir el-Medina** on the West Bank. He and his mother, Ahmose-Nefertari, were the patrons of this village, and they were deified and worshipped there after their deaths. Amenhotep I is also believed to have been the first pharaoh to separate his mortuary temple from his actual tomb, which possibly sits near the summit of the range of cliffs behind Deir el-Medina, above the southern end of the Valley of Kings.

TOMB BUILDING BEGINS

Amenhotep I inspired his powerful successor, Thutmose I (1506–1493 BC), father of Queen Hatshepsut, to separate his mortuary temple from his burial spot, too. Thutmose I apparently took the advice of a noble named Ineni (who is buried in the necropolis of Sheikh Abd el-Qurna) to select an even more remote spot than the one chosen by Amenhotep I—the area now known as the Valley of the Kings.

Thutmose I established his tomb (KV 20) with great secrecy inside the desolate valley, away from the tombs of most of his predecessors in Thebes and hundreds of miles from the great necropolises of Memphis and Giza.

VALLEY OF THE QUEENS

As a rule, in the 18th Dynasty (1550–1292 BC), only the pharaohs—or queens who ruled as pharaohs—constructed tombs in the Valley of the Kings. Close relatives joined the pharaohs in their tombs, and sometimes a favorite vizier or noble was permitted a small rock chamber near his ruler. Ramses II (KV 7) buried his favorite wife, Nefertari, in a separate valley, now known as the Valley of the Queens.

BUILDING THE TOMBS

Construction of the tombs in the Valley of the Kings probably began at the ascension of the pharaoh with the selection of fine, untouched rock. Tunneling proceeded with great speed, as shown by the size of tombs of those who reigned for relatively short periods.

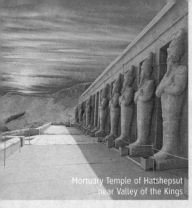

Mortuary Temple of Hatshepsut
near Valley of the Kings

Tomb of Ramses V and VI

A distant view of the entrance to
the tomb of Ramses V and VI

Deir el-Medina

Valley of the Queens

Tomb of Ramses IX

MAJOR SIGHTS IN THE VALLEY OF THE KINGS

A Valley of the Kings Visitor Center. Before heading to the tombs, spend some time at the visitor center, which offers interesting background on the valley's archaeological discoveries and excavation techniques. A fascinating 3-D scale model shows the positioning of the tombs (which sometimes collide with one another) above and below ground and gives you a sense of the site's immensity. The center also has a film about the discovery of King Tutankhamun's tomb.

B Tomb of Ramses IV (KV 2). Ramses IV (1155–1149 BC), the son and successor of Ramses III, is considered the first in a series of weak pharaohs whose declining power brought about the end of native kingship in Egypt. The tomb's first striking scene is the sun disk containing a scarab and the sun god Ra in his ram-headed form, with Isis and Nephthys kneeling on either side.

Much of the tomb contains spells from numerous religious books that provided the god-king with the means to pass into the afterlife. The third corridor, for example, is dedicated to the Book of Caverns, which relates the journey of Ra through realms of the underworld, illustrating the ancient Egyptian concept of hell. The sun god is later depicted in the burial chamber passing

Tomb of Ramses IV

through the 12 gates of the underworld, each guarded by a dreadful serpent.

In the third division of the underworld, a serpent organizes 12 goddesses in two rows of six, representing the six hours before and after midnight. The goddess Nut is represented with the constellations of the heavens on her body. Ramses IV's sarcophagus is still inside the tomb, its lid broken in half by robbers. The tomb also has graffiti from the Ptolemaic and Coptic periods.

C Tomb of Ramses IX (KV 6). This tomb held the body of one of the last great pharaohs of the 20th Dynasty and the New Kingdom, both of which ended around 1077 BC. Three corridors depict spells from several religious

Tombs on Luxor's West Bank are all numbered; the higher the number, the more recent the discovery. Abbreviations are used for locale, so, KV, indicates Valley of the Kings; QV the Valley of the Queens; and TT the Theban Tombs at other burial sites.

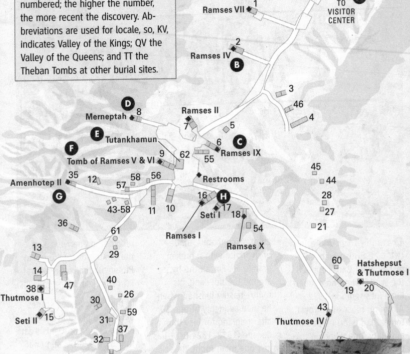

Ramses VII 1  TO VISITOR CENTER A

Ramses IV 2 B

3

46

4

Merneptah 8 D

Ramses II 7

5

Tutankhamun E

6

Ramses IX C

Tomb of Ramses V & VI 9 F 62 55

Restrooms

45

44

Amenhotep II 35 12 58 56

28

G 57 27

43-58 11 10 16 H 17 Seti I 18

21

36 Ramses I 54 Ramses X

61 29

13 60 Hatshepsut & Thutmose I

14 40 19 20

38 47 26

Thutmose I 30 59 43

Seti II 15 31 Thutmose IV

37

32

42

33

I 34

Thutmose III

books. Most notably, the third corridor contains passages from the Amduat (Book of What is in the Underworld) with a row of tied-up, kneeling captives in a long row above the floor. Two partially decorated chambers precede the burial chamber. Nut is represented on the ceiling as part of the Book of the Night. The tomb does not contain a sarcophagus.

D Tomb of Merneptah (KV 8). Five corridors and many chambers and side chambers make up the tomb

of the fourth pharaoh (1213–1203 BC) of the 19th Dynasty and the successor of Ramses II. The left wall in the first corridor shows the king before the god Ra-Horakhty. It's followed by three columns of the Litany of Ra, and it ends with a disk surrounded by a crocodile and a serpent, adjoining the rest of the Litany. The wall opposite is completely devoted to the Litany.

On both sides of the second corridor are figures of gods with texts from the Book of the Gates and the

Amduat. The jackal god Anubis is accompanied by Isis on the left and Nephthys on the right. Most of the subsequent chambers are decorated with passages from the Amduat. The eight-pillared burial chamber contains the red granite inner lid of the sarcophagus, decorated with scenes from the Book of the Gates.

Tomb of Merneptah

Tomb of Seti I

E Tomb of Tutankhamun (KV 62). British archaeologist Howard Carter thrilled the world when he opened King Tut's tomb in 1922. Although most other royal tombs had been robbed in antiquity, Tutankhamun's treasure was largely intact, and it toured internationally for decades. Most of it is now in Giza's new Grand Egyptian Museum.

Tut's mummy, the only one on display in the Valley of the Kings, lies without its wrappings in a climate-controlled glass case in the burial chamber, which also contains the original

Tomb of Tutankhamun

outer sarcophagus, made of quartzite with a broken granite lid. For all the hype around the boy-king, his tomb—hastily finished when he died suddenly at age 19, after reigning for less than a decade (1332–1324 BC)—has just one main room, the burial chamber, which is the only space that's decorated. One of the scenes, from the Amduat, shows the god Khepri in a sacred boat, followed by three registers, each with four baboons.

F Tomb of Ramses V and Ramses VI (KV 9). During the construction of this beautiful, albeit unfinished, tomb, builders broke through to other tombs accidentally and had to reroute. It was started for Ramses V (1149–1145 BC) but finished by Ramses VI (1145–1137 BC), who usurped some of the decorations and cartouches of his predecessor. Robbers raided the tomb shortly after Ramses VI's death, which was

recorded on papyrus, and the tomb remained open in Ptolemaic times (Greek graffiti can be seen on the walls).

In the first corridor, scenes depict the pharaoh with Ra-Horakhty and Osiris. Past that on the left, a sun boat is between the 12 hours of the night and 12 hours of the day. The second corridor has a picture of Osiris enthroned with nine figures approaching him, with a sun boat above. The holy apes of Ra-Horakhty drive a pig, representing a wicked being, from the boat. Past that is a third corridor, followed by a chamber, and then a four-pillared hall. The pillars are decorated with pictures of various gods, as is the ceiling. Above the door at the end of the chamber, the pharaoh burns incense before Osiris.

Next, two corridors precede an antechamber with a chapter from the Book of the Dead. The unfinished burial

Tomb of Ramses V and VI

chamber at the end has lovely astronomical figures on its ceiling. On its right wall, a sun boat has Khepri, the scarab-faced god of the rising sun, standing with the ram-headed god representing the setting sun. Two lions support the boat, drawn across the sky. Two birds with human heads, a typical depiction of the soul, worship the sun as he passes.

G Tomb of Amenhotep II (KV 35). This impressive tomb was kept in a secret location known by high priests, who, in the 9th century BC, moved other mummies there for safeguarding. About 2,800 years later, in 1898, excavators found 13 royal mummies inside it. The entrance has a set of steps, followed by a sloping corridor. Another set of steps descends to a corridor containing a well, now covered with a bridge. The deep well was built to protect the tomb from floods—and to lead robbers astray. The tomb builders cut a small chamber into it for deception.

The entrance on the other side was also filled with plaster. On its other side, an undecorated, two-pillared hall leads to another set of stairs to throw off robbers. At its end is the real burial chamber. A decorated, two-level hall goes down to the sarcophagus of Amenhotep II (1425–1400 BC). His mummy was moved from Cairo's Egyptian Museum to the National Museum of Egyptian Civilization in 2021.

H Tomb of Seti I (KV 17). Arguably the most impressive tomb in the entire Valley of the Kings—and the one commanding an eye-wateringly high extra ticket price—is the Tomb of Seti I (1290–1279 BC). It is absolutely worth the added expense to explore the valley's longest, deepest, and most finely decorated tomb, which set precedents for future burial chambers.

Every surface—in all seven corridors and 10 chambers—is covered in beautifully painted bas-relief, a fitting tribute to the pharaoh who restored ancient Egypt to its former glory and ushered in an artistic and cultural high point. Not only does this tomb show the full program of ancient Egypt's religious texts on its walls, but it was also the first with a vaulted burial chamber.

I Tomb of Thutmose III (KV 34). The tomb was built for the 18th-Dynasty successor (1458–1425 BC) and stepson of Hatshepsut (1479–1458 BC), who ruled as pharaoh and served as his co-regent while he was a child. Note the cartouche-shaped burial chamber: first found in this tomb, it was replicated in later constructions. The burial chamber's walls list divinities described in the Amduat, scenes from which decorate the sarcophagus chamber. The sarcophagus and lid, made of quartzite, are still in the tomb.

TOMB ROBBING

Tomb robbing was commonplace in ancient Egypt, and even the pharaohs themselves usurped the tombs of their predecessors for their own burials. Accounts from antiquity describe confessions from robbers who broke into tombs in the Valley of the Kings, tore jewelry from the bodies of the kings, and burnt their coffins. It's no surprise, then, why the pharaohs took great care to keep the locations of their tombs secret, although once they were known, they sometimes stood wide open. In the 21st Dynasty (1069–945 BC), robbery became so common that priests moved 13 royal mummies to the secret tomb of Amenhotep II; the mummies were discovered only in 1898.

PLANNING YOUR VISIT

Tomb of Ramses IV

Weather and Timing: The Valley of the Kings is hot year-round and scorching in summer. Outside of the tombs, there's precious little shade. Protect yourself from the sun by wearing a hat or light scarf and applying sunscreen. Ideally, arrive as early as possible (the site opens at 7 am) and allow the better part of a day to explore it. Water in plastic bottles (including reusable and more environmentally friendly options) is allowed, and there's a cafe on site.

What to Expect: One of Luxor's most popular attractions can see up to 1.5 million visitors a year. The valley is vast, and the crowds can be large, particularly at the tombs that are open closest to the visitor center. You can linger in each tomb for as long as you like. Note, though, that tour guides cannot give lectures inside the tombs, so they explain each before you enter.

If you have specific interests and are visiting with a tour guide, let him or her know in advance what you'd like to see. Your admission ticket allows you access to three tombs (excluding those that have extra charges), so you'll need to purchase additional tickets if you'd like to visit more.

Extra-Charge Tombs: Despite the pharaoh's renown, some people do not recommend paying for the extra ticket to enter the tomb of Tutankhamun because it's small and sparsely decorated. However, it is the only tomb here that contains an intact mummy. The tombs of Seti I and Ramses V & VI, which also require paying an extra fee, are far more interesting.

Photography: Inside the tombs, you can take photos on your cell phone for free. To shoot with a larger camera, you must purchase a photography pass at the visitor center for LE300 when you buy your entry tickets. At each tomb, guardians might ask to see your photography pass when they notice that you have a camera. Flash photography is not allowed for any camera type.

TOMB ACCESS

The main admission ticket allows access to three Valley of the Kings tombs; a few have extra entrance fees as well, though, and not all tombs are open all the time. Every few months, officials rotate their openings and closures to mitigate damage to the ancient art by moisture and carbon dioxide—from the air outside and the sweat and breath of visitors. Some tombs are closed for much longer (years, even) owing to restoration works or excavations. On arrival, stop by the visitor center to see what's currently accessible.

🎫 LE240 for three tombs. Extra-cost tickets: LE1,000 for Seti I, LE300 for Tutankhamun, LE100 for Ramses V & VI.

⊙ Daily 7–5.

every wall and the entire ceiling. The tomb is accessed by a staircase that leads into an antechamber, painted with chapters from the Book of the Dead and offering scenes to Anubis, the jackal-headed god of mummification, and Osiris, god of the afterlife. White stars that resemble starfish dot the dark-blue ceiling. Another set of stairs drops down to the column-supported burial room where the sarcophagus and mummy were once located (alas, the tomb was robbed of its many treasures in antiquity). You're allowed just 10 minutes inside the tomb.

The **Tomb of Amun-her-Khepshef** (QV 55) was built for a son of Ramses III, and the prince died when he was about 15 years old. The tomb has a simple linear design, and the wall paintings maintain their bright and lively colors. Scenes show the pharaoh introducing the prince, as a child with a side-lock of hair, to various gods, and an uninscribed sarcophagus rests in an undecorated burial chamber at the back. The tomb also contains an unusual item inside a glass case: the mummified remains of a fetus (not the prince).

The cruciform **Tomb of Titi** (QV 52), a queen of the 20th Dynasty, is well preserved. Her family history isn't well known, but it's thought that she might have been a wife of Ramses III and the mother of Amun-her-Khepshef, whose tomb is nearby. The corridor is decorated on both sides with a kneeling winged figure of Maat, the goddess of truth and justice, and the queen standing in front of different deities. In the chamber on the right is a double representation of Hathor, the goddess of motherhood and love, depicted as a sacred cow coming out of the mountain to receive the queen and then as a woman accepting offerings from Titi.

The **Tomb of Khaemwaset** (QV 44), a prince who was a young son of Ramses III, has fine workmanship and decoration on the walls. The scenes represent the prince,

either with his pharaoh father or alone, making offerings to the gods. Hieroglyphic text from the Book of the Dead accompanies the paintings. Look out for the prince wearing a long translucent garment, showing the masterful skill of the ancient painters. ✉ *Thebes* 🔤 *LE100. Additional LE1,400 for Tomb of Nefertari.*

Hotels

Al Moudira Hotel
$$$$ | HOTEL | One of Luxor's most luxurious places to stay, Al Moudira is so enchanting you might not want to leave to go sightseeing. **Pros:** peaceful oasis away from the chaos of Luxor; individually decorated rooms with exquisite attention to detail; top-notch service. **Cons:** bathrooms could use an update; food menu feels limited if you're staying for more than a couple days; in a remote part of the West Bank, far from the Nile, ferry, and attractions. ⑤ *Rooms from: $230* ✉ *Hager Al Dabbeya, Luxor West Bank* 🕾 *12/2325–1307* ⊕ *www.moudira. com* 🛏 *54 rooms* ❍❙ *Free Breakfast.*

Beit Sabee Guesthouse
$ | B&B/INN | Overlooking Medinet Habu, this charming guesthouse in a three-story mudbrick house is decked out in colorful Nubian textiles and traditional decor. **Pros:** rooftop dining area has views of temple ruins and the Theban Hills; quiet residental-rural location; excellent home-cooked lunch and dinner available. **Cons:** no swimming pool; hard to find and no signage; taxi required to reach many sights and restaurants. ⑤ *Rooms from: $42* ✉ *Luxor West Bank* ⊕ *www. nourelnil.com/guesthouse* 🛏 *15 rooms* ❍❙ *Free Breakfast.*

El Gezira Garden Hotel
$$ | HOTEL | FAMILY | Relaxed and welcoming, Gezira Garden Hotel is a little oasis on the West Bank, and all rooms come with balconies to soak up the flower-filled, tree-shaded scene. **Pros:** verdant, quiet grounds; staff are helpful and

The Amarna Era

Amenhotep IV turned ancient Egypt upside down when he came to the throne around 1353 BC. Early in his reign, he greatly reformed the state religion, which would later get him branded as a heretic and erased from history until the 19th century.

He changed his name to Akhenaten and declared that all the Egyptian gods—including Amun, the main god—were to be usurped by Aten, represented by a sun disk with rays emanating from it and an *ankh* symbol depicting the gift of life. The reason for this major religious change is unclear. The pharaoh was the only person allowed to have close contact with the god, a regulation that highlighted the pharaoh's divinity and reduced the power of the priesthood. To create even more distance from tradition, Akhenaten moved the country's capital from Thebes to his brand new city of Tell el-Amarna.

Akhenaten revolutionized the art of the era by adopting more relaxed poses, such as scenes of him kissing his children and sharing affection. In statues and carvings, the pharaoh wanted himself shown with an androgynous body form, long face, wide hips, drooping belly, protruding breasts, and long fingers.

Preoccupied with religion and the building of his own capital city, Akhenaten had little concern for maintaining Egypt's borders. Sensing weakness, the country's opportunistic enemies sent raiding parties and took territory.

Akhenaten reigned for 17 years, and, when he died, so did his new religion and capital. Priests moved to reinstate Thebes and its temple to Amun as Egypt's religious heart. Akhenaten and his successors were excised from the official records, one of the reasons why the tomb of Tutankhamun, Akhenaten's son who was originally named Tutankhaten after his father's preferred god, lay undiscovered for so long.

friendly; short walk from the East Bank ferry. **Cons:** air-conditioners are noisy; Wi-Fi sometimes drops out in the rooms; rooms could use a cosmetic touch-up. ⑤ *Rooms from: $50* ✉ *El-Bairat, Luxor West Bank* ☎ *95/231–2505* ⊕ *www. el-gezira.com* ↪ *28 rooms* ❍ *Free Breakfast.*

Embrace Hotel

$$ | **HOTEL** | A beautiful blend of traditional architecture and modern amenities, Embrace Hotel channels good vibes into an environmentally thoughtful property that runs on clean energy, has a swimming pool without chemicals, and offers organic toiletries and meals. **Pros:** peaceful West Bank location; eco-conscious approach; welcoming staff. **Cons:** water takes a long time to warm up, and there isn't much of it; Wi-Fi doesn't work in all areas; rooms are dark. ⑤ *Rooms from: $55* ✉ *Gezirat al-Bairat, Luxor West Bank* ☎ *10/0840–2999* ⊕ *www.facebook. com/Embrace.Hotel* ↪ *24 rooms* ❍ *Free Breakfast.*

Marsam Hotel

$$ | **HOTEL** | Originally constructed in the 1920s as a dig house for the University of Chicago's archaeological expeditions, the Marsam Hotel maintains its simple historic charm with mud-brick rooms, locally made furniture, and traditional decor. **Pros:** local garden-grown ingredients used for meals; archaeologists still stay here, too; you can sleep in a historic space, such as Howard Carter's

Temple of Hathor Trivia

■ **Turbulent times.** As you walk around the temple, watch for empty cartouches. Usually, these oval-shaped insignias encircle the name of the pharaoh, but, during the chaotic time of the Ptolemies, the ruler was replaced before the carvers could finish their work.

■ **Light in the darkness.** In the small crypt area, find the relief that has been dubbed the "Dendera Light," showing a snake emerging from a lotus flower in a long oval. Some say that it shows that the ancient Egyptians had modern lighting technology like arc lamps and cathode ray tubes.

■ **Could the Dendera Zodiac return to Egypt?** In 2020, Zahi Hawass, the famous outspoken archaeologist and the former Egyptian antiquities minister, launched a campaign to return some of Egypt's priceless artifacts from American and European museums, including the Dendera Zodiac (in Paris), the Rosetta Stone (in London), and a bust of Nefertiti (in Berlin).

Workroom. **Cons:** popular lunch stop for large tour groups; no swimming pool; on the way to the Valley of the Kings, but otherwise remote. ⑤ *Rooms from: $53 ⊠ Luxor West Bank ☎ 10/0342–6471 ⊕ marsamhotelluxor.com ⊘ Closed mid-May–mid-Sept. ⇄ 20 rooms* ⫮◯⫮ *Free Breakfast.*

🛍 Shopping

Shop Sandouk

CRAFTS | On a quiet West Bank backstreet, Shop Sandouk is a hassle-free spot to shop for fair-trade handicrafts—from clothing and hand-woven fabrics to alabaster pottery and wooden jewelry boxes. The owner will likely offer you a hot or cold drink before leaving you to browse in peace. ⊠ *Luxor West Bank ⊹ In the ferryboat area ☎ 10/0093–4980 ⊕ shopsandouk.com.*

Dendera

84 km (52 miles) north of Luxor.

The prime point of interest in Dendera is the Temple of Hathor. Although the site was occupied from at least the Old Kingdom (2687–2181 BC) onward, it's the remains of structures from the Late Period (664–332 BC) and the Greco-Roman Period (332–30 BC) that are highlights here.

GETTING HERE AND AROUND

Many travel agencies in Luxor offer trips to Dendera, usually combined with a visit to Abydos to make a full day out. The drive takes about 90 minutes from Luxor. You'll need to provide your passport to the tour company to scan and send to the traffic police at least 24 hours in advance.

To visit independently, you can get a train to Qena and then a taxi to the temple.

Sights

Temple of Hathor

RUINS | Set back 2 km (1.8 miles) from the Nile on the edge of the desert, the Temple of Hathor at Dendera is mostly a Greco-Roman Period (332–30 BC) construction, but this location has been a holy place since the Old Kingdom (2687–2181 BC). Dendera was the cult center for Hathor, the goddess of motherhood

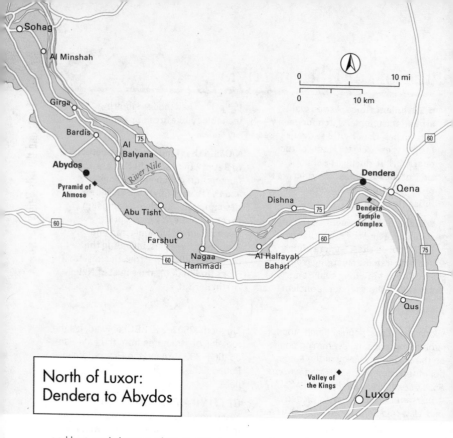

and love, and she was often depicted as a cow or as a woman with cow horns.

Enter the temple grounds through the mud-brick wall. The gated doorway leads to the **Outer Hypostyle Hall**, overwhelmingly decorated with beautiful art on every surface. The hall consists of 24 huge columns with Hathor-head capitals, some of which were defaced during the Christian era. Look up at the immaculately carved and painted ceiling, recently cleaned and restored, which shows diagrams of the night sky and signs of the zodiac. The sky goddess Nut is seen swallowing the sun disk, and it passes through her body so she can give birth to it the next morning.

The next room is the six-column **Inner Hypostyle Hall**. Six small rooms open off this hall, and the carvings show what was stored in them, such as ritual perfumes, jewelry, and the bounty of the harvest. Walk on to the **Sanctuary**, where the statue of the goddess would have been kept. Below the sanctuary are several **Crypts** that held additional statues of Hathor brought out on festival days. Some of the crypt rooms can be visited; to gain access, though, you might have to give the temple guardian a *baksheesh* (tip). Claustrophobes beware: the steps down are steep, and the rooms are small, but the reliefs have incredible detail that would have only been seen by a select few.

Stairways on either side of the sanctuary lead to the **Roof**, the walkways' walls carved with priestly processions wending their way up the sides. Head to the chapel in the northeastern corner to see the **Dendera Zodiac**, a circular bas-relief that

Egyptian Revival under Seti I

Seti I, one of the great pharaohs of the New Kingdom, oversaw a renaissance of art and design in ancient Egypt, a high priority after the Amarna era of Akhenaten, who replaced the traditional pantheon of deities with a single god. Seti I sought to restore the glory of Egypt, leading the country through an economic and cultural high point.

He started the incredible Great Hypostyle Hall at Karnak and the temple at Abydos, among many other projects, and his tomb in the Valley of the Kings is the longest and the first to feature painted reliefs on every surface. Seti I's mummy—part of the Pharaohs' Golden Parade in 2021 that transferred 22 royal mummies from the Egyptian Museum to the National Museum of Egyptian Civilization in Cairo—is one of the best preserved.

Descended from a noble military family, Seti I worked to re-establish Egypt's borders and land that had been lost under Akhenaten. He fought wars with the Nubians and Libyans and even took control of the city of Kadesh, in modern-day Syria, from the Hittites. Battle scenes are etched into the walls of the Great Hypostyle Hall in Karnak.

shows zodiac signs and constellations that's the only known complete map of the ancient sky. Sadly, the one here is a plaster recreation—the original is at the Louvre in Paris. A metal staircase leads to the highest part of the roof, reopened in 2020, which offers a panoramic view of the temple grounds. Again, though, you might have to give the temple guardian a *baksheesh* to be able to climb up.

Back on ground level, walk around the temple building to see lion-headed gargoyles. On the back of the temple, find the **scene of Queen Cleopatra VII**—yes, the famous one who was involved with Julius Caesar and Mark Antony and was Egypt's last pharaoh—presenting her son, Caesarion, to the gods as the next ruler of Egypt.

Nearby, behind the main temple, is the small **Temple of Isis,** which is strangely oriented both east–west and north–south. Walls show scenes of the divine birth of Isis. As in the main temple, the early Christians defaced a number of the images of the ancient Egyptian gods. To the west is the **Sacred Lake**, once used in rituals but now a sandpit with a few palm trees.

Back toward the complex entrance are the mud-brick remains of the **Sanatorium**, where religious pilgrims came to bathe and be healed. Two of the buildings to the north are **Mammisi**, chapels that depict the birth of a god and were used to "prove" the divinity of the king. Nectanebo I (379–361 BC) built the southern chapel, but the Ptolemies decorated it. The mammisi closest to the complex entrance is from the Roman era, built mainly by Trajan (AD 98–117). It celebrates the birth of the god Ihy, son of Horus and Hathor, as well as the divinity of the pharaoh. The sanctuary is surrounded by an ambulatory, the outer portion of which is partially decorated.

Between the mammisi lies a 5th-century **Coptic Basilica**. It no longer has a roof, but the trefoil apse and several shell niches are still visible from its hall. ✉ *Mabed Dendera* 🎫 *LE120.*

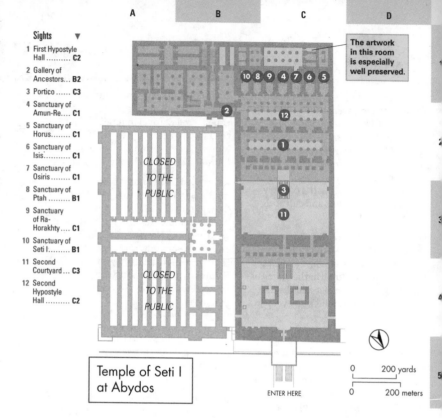

The artwork in this room is especially well preserved.

CLOSED TO THE PUBLIC

CLOSED TO THE PUBLIC

Temple of Seti I at Abydos

ENTER HERE

0 — 200 yards

0 — 200 meters

Abydos

175 km (109 miles) northwest of Luxor.

For the afterlife-obsessed ancient Egyptians, Abydos was one of the most sacred sites. It's the main cult center for Osiris, god of the afterlife, because it's where they thought the god's head landed after he was cut into 14 pieces and scattered around the country by his jealous brother Set. Ancient Egyptians strove to make a pilgrimage to Abydos at least once in their lives. These grounds were also used to bury the dead for more than 4,500 years.

GETTING HERE AND AROUND

It's easiest to visit Abydos on a day trip from Luxor. Travel agencies arrange guides and drivers, and the visit is usually combined with a stop at the temple in Dendera. The journey to Abydos takes about three hours from Luxor. You'll need to provide your passport to the tour company to scan and send to the traffic police at least 24 hours in advance.

If you'd rather visit under your own steam, you can get the train to Al Balyana and then a taxi to the temple.

Sights

★ Temple of Seti I

RUINS | Seti I initiated construction of this temple complex but died before its completion, which left his son, Ramses II, to finish it. Today it remains one of the most fascinating temples in Egypt because of its exquisite reliefs, unique chapel design, and preserved paint.

To reach the temple, walk up a ramp through two mostly destroyed courtyards

The carvings are very detailed in the Temple of Seti I in Abydos, which has the Abydos Kings List documenting the reigns of some of the pharaohs who preceded Seti.

built by Ramses II. The temple's facade features a carved and partially painted **Portico**, half a modern reconstruction, with scenes of Ramses II making offerings to the gods. Inside the central door is the **First Hypostyle Hall**, which has 12 pairs of sandstone columns with papyrus-bud capitals. Unlike many temples, the roof is in situ, giving the space a dark, mysterious atmosphere. The column placement creates seven aisles that lead to seven sanctuaries set in the back wall of the second hypostyle hall. The walls are carved with images of Seti I making offerings to Amun-Ra, the creator god, and preparing and dedicating the temple building.

Seti I almost completed the decoration of the **Second Hypostyle Hall**, and the exquisite quality of these reliefs stands in stark contrast to the cruder work commissioned later by Ramses II. The **Seven Sanctuaries** at the back of the hall are rare features in Egyptian temples. They are dedicated to Horus, Isis, Osiris, Amun-Ra, Ra-Horakhty, Ptah, and the deified

Seti I, and each is decorated with scenes of the king making offerings to the gods and the gods giving symbols of life and kingship in return. Osiris's sanctuary is the most impressive and leads to two further halls and chapels for Isis (his wife) and Horus (his son).

The relationship between Osiris and Isis is seen in more graphic detail east of the sanctuaries, where a chamber has a scene of the conception of Horus. The story goes that Isis flew around Egypt to gather all the pieces of Osiris but was missing one—we'll let you guess which. She fashioned one for Osiris, added a bit of magic, and conceived Horus.

Along the corridor away from the sanctuaries, the **Gallery of Ancestors** contains the Abydos Kings List, an important table that records the previous 76 kings of ancient Egypt being read out by the future Ramses II as he is watched over by his father Seti I. These rows of cartouches are the only source of the order and names of some Old Kingdom pharaohs,

Abydos Trivia

■ It's a bird, it's a plane, it's a... hieroglyph? Across a stone ceiling beam in the hypostyle hall, look for the famous helicopter hieroglyphs, which purportedly show shapes that look like an airplane, a UFO, and a submarine among the ancient writing. They've actually been created by plaster that fell out of usurped royal inscriptions.

■ Excavations are ongoing. Abydos was used as a burial ground from about 4000 BC to AD 600, and many of the earliest pharaohs were buried here to be as close as possible to the god of the afterlife. Excavation areas are off-limits to visitors, but you might see archaeologists at work.

■ Beer's the thing. In 2021, archaeologists unearthed what could be the world's oldest brewery at Abydos. It's thought to date from 3100 BC and might have been used for funerary rituals while burying royalty. It had a production capacity of 6,000 gallons.

though it does rewrite history by not including rulers considered illegitimate, including Hatshepsut and Akhenaten.

An upward sloping interior corridor has a scene of a young Ramses II and his pharaoh father lassoing a bull and then offering it as a sacrifice to the gods. This corridor leads outside to the sunken **Osireion**, which is off-limits to visitors and can only be viewed from above, which precludes getting a good look at the reliefs. This sandstone and granite monument was thought to be the tomb of Osiris. Its architectural style is reminiscent of Old Kingdom construction, but it was actually built by Seti I.

Just northwest of Seti I's temple lies the **Temple of Ramses II** (1279–1213 BC). Its roof and most of the upper portions of its walls are missing, but enough of it remains to give a feeling of its layout and decoration. What's left of the decoration shows that this temple—unlike the inferior work that Ramses commissioned to complete his father's temple—is close in style and quality to the work done during the reign of Seti I, and the walls retain some vibrant reds, yellows, and greens. ✉ *Abydos Rd.* 🎫 *LE100.*

Esna

58 km (36 miles) southwest of Luxor.

Esna's main attraction, the Temple of Khnum, has been brought back to life by an Egyptian–German conservation team that started cleaning and restoring it in 2018. By 2022, the work was about half complete, showing just how much dirt, soot, and bird poop had accumulated and obscured the colors and designs.

GETTING HERE AND AROUND

Esna is the starting point for many *dahabiya* (traditional, two-masted boat) sailings so that they don't have to pass through the Esna Locks, and a stop at the temple and a walk through town might be included on the itinerary before you board the boat. Large cruise ships do not usually stop at Esna, but it's an easy half-day trip from Luxor, best booked through a tour company.

 Sights

Temple of Khnum

RUINS | Surrounded by Esna on all sides and set 9 meters (30 feet) below the modern street level, the Temple

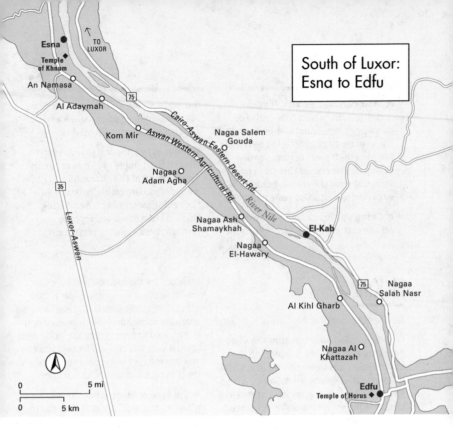

of Khnum might not have the grand approach or huge footprint of other sites, but its interior makes it worth a visit. In 2018, an Egyptian–German conservation team began cleaning and restoring the temple, revealing the vibrant colors of its artwork, which was done in ink rather than in relief, and had previously been hidden by layers of grime.

Started under the Ptolemies and finished by the Romans, it was one of the last temples of ancient Egypt, even though it's dedicated to one of the country's earliest-worshipped gods. Ram-headed Khnum was the god of the source of the Nile and created other deities and humans on a potter's wheel.

Today, the hypostyle hall is the only part of the temple that's visible and visitable (the rest is likely buried under the town).

Holding up the roof are four rows of 12-meter (40-foot) columns with remarkable capitals: covered in a unique array of beautifully painted, colorful palm leaves and flowers, they resemble lush gardens. While your neck is still craned, note the incredible illustration of the phases of the moon on the ceiling of the temple's northern side. Roman signs of the zodiac are shown on the southern side. The walls display festive celebrations, offerings to gods, and highly interesting everyday scenes, such as fishing in the Nile and hunting migratory birds from Europe. The work of the conservation team was only half complete as of 2022, so there's still more scenic color to uncover. ⊠ *Esna* 🎟 *LE80.*

Edfu Trivia

■ **Your carriage awaits.** If you're arriving in Edfu on a Nile cruise or dahabiya (traditional sailing vessel), the usual way of getting to the temple is by horse-drawn carriages called calèches. The cost of this transport is included with the cruise, but a tip is expected (about LE50 per carriage).

■ **Going up.** Priests once showed off the statue of Horus from the roof during festivals. You can partly follow in their footsteps up the staircase, but the roof itself is not accessible.

■ **Defaced but not destroyed.** Even though the Temple of Horus is mostly intact, many of the pharaohs and gods were defaced by early Christians, and the ceilings were blackened during this era from arson attempts to remove these pagan depictions.

El-Kab

86 km (53 miles) south of Luxor.

Originally called Nekheb, after the vulture goddess, Nekbhet, who protected the town, El-Kab has been settled since 3100 BC and was originally enclosed by a massive mud-brick wall. A handful of rock-cut tombs in the area have some preserved paintwork and carvings.

GETTING HERE AND AROUND

El-Kab is a stop on some *dahabiya* trips, but not for large cruise ships because they don't have a place to dock. Travel agencies in Luxor don't offer this trip as standard, but you could work with one to build your own itinerary and combine a visit to El-Kab with a stop at the temple in Esna. El-Kab is about 90 minutes from Luxor by road.

◉ Sights

El-Kab Tombs

CEMETERY | Just northwest of the town of El-Kab are several rock-cut tombs from different dynastic periods. The walls of the **Tomb of Ahmose, Son of Ibana,** tell a biographical story emphasizing the military campaigns of the owner, when he was an admiral in the ancient Egyptian navy.

Look out for the hieroglyph of a chariot, the earliest surviving depiction in this script. The space was likely used as a chapel to remember the deceased and not an actual tomb where the body was kept. It was left unfinished, and you can see the red grid lines that the painters used to plan and design the scenes.

In the **Tomb of Renni**, who was a provincial governor and high priest during the reign of Amenhotep I (1541–1520 BC), you can admire paintings of the harvest, family banquets, and checkerboard-patterned ceilings. At the back of the tomb is a niche that once held a statue but is now nearly destroyed.

The grandson of Ahmose, the naval commander buried nearby, **Paheri** had his tomb decorated with scenes of his work as a scribe and regional governor, counting livestock, receiving tributes of gold, and supervising the wine harvest.

The **Tomb of Setau**, a high priest during the reign of Ramses III (1186–1155 BC), is heavily damaged, but its walls are decorated with a few interesting scenes of celebrations for the pharaoh's 30th year on the throne and the goddess Nekhbet (considered the protector of El-Kab) in her sacred boat guarded by a vulture while sailing down the Nile. ⊠ *Athar al-Kab* ⌂ *LE60.*

Built during the Ptolemaic Dynasty (305–30 BC) of the Greco-Roman Period, the Temple of Horus in Edfu is one of Egypt's most intact sanctuaries.

Edfu

109 km (68 miles) south of Luxor, 111 km (69 miles) north of Aswan.

Edfu's temple, dedicated to the god Horus, is magnificent. It's one of the finest examples of Ptolemaic Dynasty (305–30 BC) construction in Egypt.

GETTING HERE AND AROUND

Both large cruise ships and *dahabiyas* (traditional, two-masted sailing vessels) stop at Edfu. To reach the temple, you'll be shuffled into a horse-drawn carriage for a short ride to the ticket office.

If you're not on a cruise, you can visit Edfu on a day trip from Luxor or Aswan. It's about a 2.5-hour drive from either city, but be aware that most of your day will be spent in the car instead of sightseeing.

The railway line from Cairo to Luxor and Aswan stops in Edfu. The train station is on the city's East Bank, and you can get a taxi to the temple.

Sights

Temple of Horus

RUINS | Edfu's magnificent Temple of Horus is one of ancient Egypt's most intact temples, thanks to dry desert sand burying it for centuries, and it's a breathtaking sight. Built during the Ptolemaic Dynasty (305–30 BC) of the Greco-Roman Period, the temple rests on much earlier foundations.

The enormous, 37-meter-tall (120-foot-tall) **Pylon**, fronted by a pair of granite statues of Horus as a falcon that look miniscule in comparison, leads into the open **Courtyard** with a single row of columns on three sides. At the far end, in front of the **Hypostyle Hall**, are two more statues of Horus. The column capitals come in a wide variety of floral motifs, including palm leaves, lotus, and papyrus. A library was once located on the eastern side of the Hypostyle Hall, and hieroglyphs on the walls list the names of the books.

Beyond the Hypostyle Hall is a series of side chapels and chambers encircling the sanctuary. Carvings on the walls detail the construction of the temple, down to the specific day that work on it began: August 23, 237 BC. The inner rooms of the temple are dark and atmospheric and were originally illuminated only by shafts of light from narrow slits in the ceiling, which are still in place, today helped by modern lights along the floor. The once richly colored walls, decorated with scenes of pharaohs making offerings, would have shone and glimmered like jewels in the half-light, and it's easy to imagine priestly processions passing through the temple, chanting and praying amid clouds of incense. One of the side rooms, dubbed the **Laboratory**, lists the ingredients and recipes for perfumes and essences used in temple rituals.

In the **Sanctuary** is a reproduction of a barque, the sacred boat used to transport the statue of Horus for festivals and downriver to Dendera to be reunited with his wife, Hathor. A large granite shrine made during the reign of Nectanebo II (358–340 BC), a relic from the previous building and the oldest part of the temple, looms eerily at the back of the Sanctuary.

A stone enclosure wall wraps around the back half of the temple, and it has carvings of Horus defeating the god Set, who killed Horus's father Osiris. This area is one of the few places where this myth is illustrated. Set is shown as a small hippo, easily conquered by the huge figure of falcon-headed Horus.

On the eastern side of the temple is the **Nilometer**, a gauge used to measure the height of the Nile and to calculate taxes. If the river level was high, the harvest would be bountiful and so would the tax revenues. ✉ *Edfu* 🖼 *LE180*.

ASWAN AND LAKE NASSER

Updated by
Lauren Keith

WELCOME TO ASWAN AND LAKE NASSER

TOP REASONS TO GO

★ **Abu Simbel:** Stand in awe of the colossal statues of Ramses II at Egypt's southernmost temple complex.

★ **Philae:** Soak in the atmosphere of this island temple dedicated to the goddess Isis, where the last ever hieroglyph inscription was carved.

★ **Sail on a felucca:** Take to the Nile on a traditional sailboat and glide around Aswan's river islands and cataracts.

★ **Toast the sunset:** Grab a sundowner on the terrace of the historic Old Cataract hotel or a laid-back waterside café.

★ **Gharb Soheil:** Get to know the rich Nubian culture and endless hospitality in this amazingly colorful village.

For sights in and near Aswan, tours organized through a local company or your accommodations are the easiest way to get around. You can also travel independently without a guide by negotiating a rate with a private taxi, but the lack of signage means you'll miss a lot of the history and detail.

Philae, Aswan High Dam, and the dock for Lake Nasser cruises are south of Aswan. Abu Simbel is even farther south—the temples and village are a 45-minute flight from Aswan or a 3½-hour drive one way.

1 Aswan. A perfect base for exploring, Aswan is much more laid-back than Luxor or Cairo. Go with the flow sailing on a *felucca* (small, traditional boat) on the Nile and get to know the friendly Nubians in their island and West Bank villages.

2 Kom Ombo. What was the crossroads of ancient trade routes has a unique, split-personality temple.

3 Daraw Camel Market. Hundreds of camels await their fate at this market, a fascinating sightseeing alternative when you tire of ancient history.

4 Philae. Here the draw is the gorgeous Temple of Isis, set on an island in the Aswan Dam reservoir, just south of the city and just north of the Aswan High Dam.

5 Lake Nasser. A cruise on one of the world's largest man-made lakes will introduce you to a clutch of little-visited temples.

6 Abu Simbel. Four 20-meter-tall (65-foot-tall) colossi of Ramses II front his temple; smaller—relatively speaking, at 10 meters (33 feet) statues of him and his queen, Nefertari, front her temple.

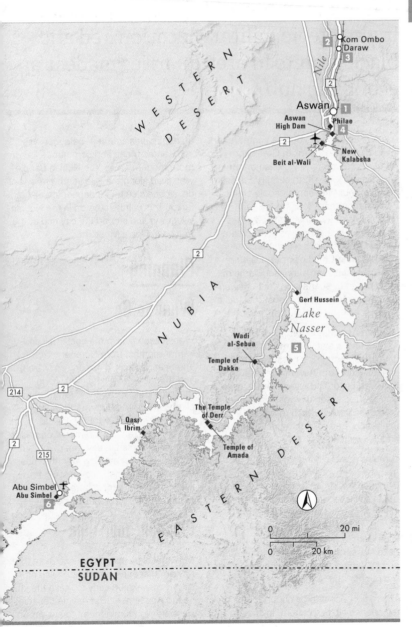

For thousands of years, Aswan was the Egyptian empire's "Southern Gate." Cataracts and islands in the Nile made it a strategic military location; red and black granite in area quarries made it an economic hub.

Aswan has also long been a winter resort loved by Europeans, from Greek and Roman conquerors to Victorian-era Brits. Thomas Cook, the 19th-century English entrepreneur who some people credit with starting mass tourism in Egypt, brought visitors by the boatload—first on his luxurious *dahabiyas* (two-masted sailing vessels) and later on steamer ships. Agatha Christie wrote *Death on the Nile* about such a trip, and some of the story's key scenes are set in Aswan's Old Cataract, the sumptuous Cook-built hotel where she penned her novel.

North of Aswan, the Temple of Sobek at Kom Ombo is a stop on many Nile cruise itineraries, though it's possible to see it on a day trip from Aswan or as a stopover between Luxor and Aswan on the overland route. Lesser known is the camel market at Daraw, which remains a local institution, free of both tourist trappings and conveniences.

Temples line the banks of the Nile all the way to Egypt's southern frontier. Between Aswan and the northern shores of Lake Nasser are a handful of popular sights. The most impressive are the Temple of Isis at Philae and the Aswan High Dam. A five-day cruise around Lake Nasser takes in several little-seen archaeological sites before concluding at the mighty Abu Simbel.

The region also affords opportunities to experience Nubian culture. In ancient times, Egypt's southern neighbor was sometimes friend and sometimes foe. In more modern times, the Nubian people who lived along the Nile south of Aswan developed a culture independent of Arab Egypt. This culture lives on in the Nubian villages in and around the city and at the must-see Nubia Museum.

Planning

When to Go

High season falls in the cooler fall and winter months, from October to April. The heat can kick in as early as March, and the furnace will definitely be in full force by May. As the thermometer climbs in summer (when the average high temperature is 108°F), life slows considerably, and accommodation prices plummet. Ramadan days are quiet, but joining locals for evening *iftar* (the meal that breaks the fast) and enjoying the lively after-dark atmosphere of the market streets are wonderful experiences.

Planning Your Time

Most travelers spend only one night in Aswan to see the temple at Philae or simply to wake up early to make the journey to Abu Simbel. But Aswan deserves a couple nights minimum: to set sail on a *felucca* (small traditional sailing vessel), stroll through a dazzlingly painted Nubian village, and relax with a coffee or cocktail on a Nile-side terrace.

Getting Here and Around

AIR

EgyptAir operates a handful of direct flights daily between Aswan and Cairo, as well as between Aswan and Abu Simbel. The journey time to Cairo is about one hour and 20 minutes. Some private and budget carriers, such as Nile Air and Air Cairo, have infrequent service, usually limited to one or two days a week.

AIRPORT TRANSFERS

Aswan's airport is about a 45-minute drive southwest of town. A taxi to/from Downtown will cost about LE250. For minimal hassle, book your airport transfer through your accommodations.

BOAT

Aswan is the start or end point for Nile cruises. Local tour operators such as Aswan Individual offer overnight and multi-day felucca trips from Aswan, a highlight of a visit here. Traveling by felucca is blissfully slow and entirely wind-dependent. For example, it will take a full day or more to reach Kom Ombo, 40 km (25 miles) to the north.

For more information on Nile cruises and felucca trips, see Ch. 8, Cruising the Nile and Lake Nasser.

BUS

It's not worth getting the bus to Aswan. The bus station is only a few miles north of Aswan's center, but the city is well served by trains from Luxor and Cairo.

TAXI

From Aswan, you can hire a taxi for day trips into the wider region.

TRAIN

Aswan is the southern terminus of Egypt's passenger rail line. Trains arrive in Aswan from Cairo via Luxor and several smaller towns along the way, including Kom Ombo. Services operate throughout the day and even overnight. At 1,561 km (970 miles) long, this train route crosses nearly the entirety of Egypt, and the journey takes upwards of 14 hours, not factoring in the inevitable hours-long delay that affects nearly every service. Keep your arrival plans flexible.

Egyptian National Railways has an array of services. Daytime options include Special Service OD (carriages built in 2015 with air-conditioning and specific seat reservations), Speed AC Spanish (older air-conditioned carriages from Spain, hence the name), and Ordinary trains, which do not have reserved seats or air-conditioning and are best left for short journeys.

Special Service OD and Speed AC Spanish trains offer first- and second-class tickets. Ordinary trains run second- and third-class only. Foreigners who don't speak Arabic are unlikely to be able to buy third-class tickets. Some Ordinary trains have been upgraded to new air-conditioned carriages that were delivered from Russia in 2021.

WATANIA SLEEPING TRAINS

Egypt has one of the Middle East's few sleeper train services, and an overnight ride on the Ernst Watania Sleeping Train is sure to be a memorable experience. From Cairo, the sleeper train has a nightly departure at 7:45 pm (theoretically arriving in Aswan at 9:25 am), and one or two additional departures are added in the peak winter season. The carriages, built in East Germany in the 1980s, are dated but clean and comfortable enough.

You might be able to buy tickets online (though the website often has technical glitches that will render that impossible); otherwise, book in person at the train station or through a local travel agency. Tickets cost $120 for a two-berth room and include a simple dinner and breakfast.

Hotels

Aswan is a logical base for exploring the city as well as the wider region; it's easy to arrange day trips to Abu Simbel, Kom Ombo, and Daraw. Lodging options in the city range from a historic grande dame hotel to small guesthouses run by Nubian families. Note, too, that some of the city's island hotels operate free ferry services to and from town.

As elsewhere in Egypt, hotels in this region are often a little scuffed up and have poor or nonexistent Wi-Fi, even at high-end properties. Similar to restaurants, most accommodations charge VAT, city tax, and service fees above and beyond the price of the room. It's standard for breakfast to be included in the room price.

■TIP→ **Many hotels quote prices in U.S. dollars or euros, but if you pay with a credit card, your payment might be charged in the equivalent of Egyptian pounds.**

Hotel reviews have been shortened. For full information, visit Fodors.com. Hotel prices are the lowest cost of a standard double room in high season, excluding taxes and service charges.

What it Costs in U.S. Dollars			
$	$$	$$$	$$$$
HOTELS			
under $50	$50–$100	$101–$200	over $200

Restaurants

What the restaurant scenes in Aswan and the southern Nile Valley lack in variety they make up for with decent local eats. For international options, make a reservation at one of Aswan's five-star hotels, such as the Old Cataract or Mövenpick Resort.

Confusingly, the taxes and service fees vary by restaurant but should be indicated on the menu. Ask before ordering if you don't see it written down. The combined additional charges can tack on an extra 25% or more.

Consider tipping about 15% even if a service charge is included. Restaurant staff are not well paid, and the courtesy will be appreciated. Bring cash: restaurants outside of major hotels do not accept cards. Hotel restaurants are generally open to nonguests, but reservations are recommended.

Restaurant reviews have been shortened. For full information, visit Fodors. com. Restaurant prices are the average cost of a main course at dinner or, if dinner is not served, at lunch, excluding taxes and service charges.

What it Costs in Egyptian Pounds			
$	$$	$$$	$$$$
RESTAURANTS			
Under LE120	LE 120–LE 135	LE 136–LE 150	over LE 150

Aswan

876 km (544 miles) south of Cairo, 239 km (149 miles) south of Luxor.

Life glides along at a relatively slow pace in Aswan, the smallest of the Nile's three major hubs, after Luxor and Cairo. Many visitors arrive on a Nile cruise and leave after just a day, but the city merits a longer visit—to fully experience Nubian culture on Elephantine Island and the West Bank, as well as to simply unwind.

GETTING HERE AND AROUND
Aswan is the best place in Egypt to travel on the Nile, and some sights are accessible only by boat.

Feluccas (small traditional boats) sail around Aswan's islands and to the West

Bank. You can bargain with a captain along the East Bank Corniche to take you on a 90-minute sunset ride (about LE200) or a half-day sightseeing voyage (about LE500). Although you can cross the Aswan Dam by taxi to Gharb Soheil, a Nubian village on the West Bank (LE150 one way), the journey by boat is much more scenic and far shorter.

Motorized public ferries cross from Aswan's East Bank to two places on Elephantine Island as well as to the Tombs of the Nobles. Each route costs LE5 one way.

You'll have no trouble finding a taxi in Aswan, and drivers often solicit for passengers along the riverfront Corniche. The cars are usually ancient Peugeot station wagons, and the price of your trip depends on your bargaining skills. Agree on terms before you get in. Prices start at LE20 for short journeys, and a taxi from the train station to any hotel on the East Bank shouldn't cost more than LE50.

Horse-drawn carriages called *calèches* also tout for business along the Corniche. The animals aren't always well taken care of, so it's better to avoid this transport option.

TOURS
GUIDED TOURS
Aswan's attractions have little signage, so visiting with a tour company will ensure you fully understand and appreciate what you're seeing. All hotels in Aswan can arrange guides to the main sights, but quality and group size vary.

Aswan Individual is a highly recommended travel company offering tours to the area's top sights by car or felucca as well as build-your-own trips to off-the-beaten-track spots, such as Daraw's camel market. Ask about its overnight and multi-day felucca trip, an unforgettable sailing experience with local Nubian captains. Aswan Individual prides itself on fair prices, working with locals and not

taking visitors to papyrus, perfume, or spice shops—a breath of fresh air.

CONTACTS Aswan Individual. ⊠ *Aswan* ☏ *0100/250–9588* ⊕ *www.aswan-individual.com.*

The East Bank

Aswan was originally constructed on the east bank of the Nile, laid out along the riverside Corniche. Then, as now, the East Bank hums along. It's also where you'll find Aswan's large hotels.

Sights

Aswan Market
MARKET | Though you'll see some of the standard tourist shop offerings, Aswan's market feels more local than others in Egypt. Stretching for several downtown blocks, some pedestrianized, along Sharia el-Souk (Market Street), it's mildly busy by day but absolutely packed come evening. Traders hawk such wares as spices, carpets, clothing, herbal remedies, and fresh fruits and vegetables, and although they are persistent, they are mercifully less aggressive than elsewhere. Restaurants and cafés can be found along the route and the side streets when you need a break. ⊠ *Saad Zaghloul St., Downtown.*

Nubia Museum
HISTORY MUSEUM | An effort to preserve the Nubian history that was on the verge of being lost because of the construction of the Aswan High Dam, the Nubia Museum houses more than 2,000 artifacts that highlight the culture and heritage of these people and the land. Arranged chronologically, the museum walks you through prehistory, the Kingdom of Kush when Nubian kings ruled Egypt, and onward through the Christian and Islamic periods.

Artifacts range from larger-than-life statuary to a small game of backgammon.

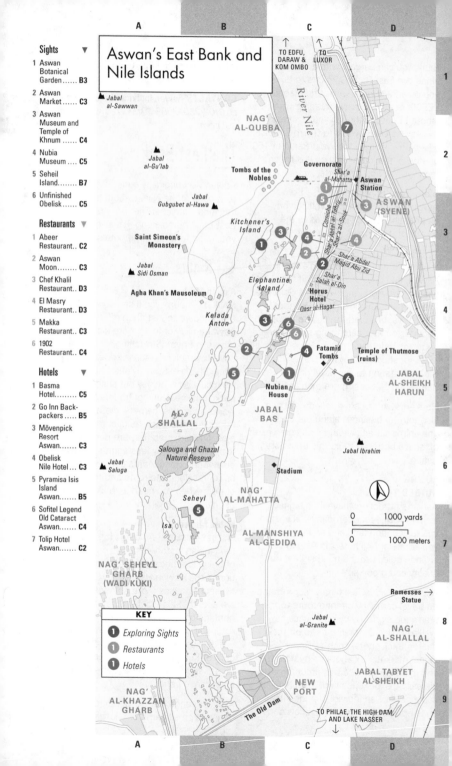

A diorama presents scenes of rural Nubian life, informative if you don't have time to visit one of the villages yourself. Outside, the museum's grounds include a water feature representing the Nile, a reconstruction of a Nubian house, a cave with rock inscriptions, and part of a Fatimid-era cemetery. Allow about two hours to do it all justice. ⊠ *Al Fanadek St., Aswan South* ⊑ *LE140.*

Unfinished Obelisk

MONUMENT | High-quality granite from Aswan is used in temples, monuments, and obelisks across Egypt, and this failed extraction was instrumental in figuring out exactly how the ancients cut such huge pieces of stone from the quarry. The stonemasons discovered a flaw in this massive obelisk-to-be, and it was left imprisoned in the bedrock. Had it been raised, it would have stood 42 meters (138 feet) tall—larger than any other obelisk—and weighed 1,168 tons.

◼ TIP→ **This site is often included on Aswan tour group itineraries, but unless you're particularly interested in ancient stonework, save your precious vacation time for more interesting sites.** ⊠ *Sheyakhah Oula, Aswan South* ⊑ *LE80.*

 Restaurants

Abeer Restaurant

\$\$ | **MIDDLE EASTERN** | Abeer does a roaring trade in barbecued meats, as evidenced by the inevitable (but fast-moving) line. Meals come with sides of rice, salad, and soup, and the staff is friendly and helpful even if there's a language barrier. **Known for:** generous portions; a local favorite; efficient service. ⑤ *Average main: LE120* ⊠ *Abtal el-Tahrir St., Downtown* ▭ *No credit cards.*

Aswan Moon

\$ | **MIDDLE EASTERN** | The food at this part-café part-restaurant won't knock your socks off, but if you're in the area, the Nile-side view and the laid-back atmosphere are worth pulling up a chair. The menu covers the Egyptian standards and throws in some international dishes as well. **Known for:** serves beer and wine; mixed grills, kofta, and shawarma; pizza and pasta. ⑤ *Average main: LE100* ⊠ *Corniche Al Nile, Corniche* ☎ *12/8790–7845* ▭ *No credit cards.*

Chef Khalil Restaurant

\$\$\$\$ | **SEAFOOD** | Step off the pedestrianized market street and into this small restaurant for fresh seafood. Take your pick of the catch, and the staff will tell you the price and cook it how you like it. **Known for:** central location; heaping seafood platters; dishes served with sides of rice, salad, and small plates. ⑤ *Average main: LE250* ⊠ *Saad Zaghloul St., Downtown* ☎ *97/231–0142* ▭ *No credit cards.*

El Masry Restaurant

\$\$\$ | **MIDDLE EASTERN** | Escape the Downtown bustle with a meal stop at this refuge from the rigors of the market. The menu is a parade of the usual suspects, primarily grilled meats, and the service is good. **Known for:** well established eatery; vegetarian options; pricier than similar area restaurants. ⑤ *Average main: LE150* ⊠ *Matar St., Downtown* ☎ *106/877–6644* ▭ *No credit cards.*

Makka Restaurant

\$\$\$ | **MIDDLE EASTERN** | Makka serves such local fare as grilled meats and *molokheya* (a thick, green, often garlicky soup made with jute leaves). As usual, dishes are accompanied by plenty of small plates. **Known for:** you won't leave hungry; Egyptian staple dishes; stuffed pigeon. ⑤ *Average main: LE150* ⊠ *Abtal el-Tahrir, Daraw* ☎ *97/244–0232* ▭ *No credit cards.*

1902 Restaurant

\$\$\$\$ | **INTERNATIONAL** | Don your best outfit (casual wear isn't allowed) and have a seat in the red-and-white, keyhole-arched dining room, originally opened in 1902 for dignitaries to celebrate the inauguration of the Aswan Dam. The atmosphere is unforgettable, and the French-inspired

The Nubia Museum's many artifacts are arranged chronologically, from prehistory to the Kingdom of Kush, when Nubian kings ruled Egypt, to the Christian and Islamic periods.

menu is heavy on seafood. **Known for:** fancy dining; grandiose decor; historic destination. ⑤ *Average main: LE600* ✉ *Sofitel Legend Old Cataract Hotel, Abtal el-Tahrir St., Aswan South* ☎ *97/231–6000* ⊕ *all.accor.com* ⋔ *Jackets required.*

 ## Hotels

Basma Hotel

$$ | HOTEL | Occupying a promontory above Aswan, the Basma has an artsy vibe and is accented with murals, stained glass, and sculptures, many made by local artists. **Pros:** large swimming pool and outdoor area; no main roads nearby, so it's quiet; Egyptian and Nubian art is a nice touch. **Cons:** rooms showing some wear and tear; Wi-Fi doesn't work in rooms; uphill walk from town. ⑤ *Rooms from: $74* ✉ *1 Al Fanadek St., Aswan South* ☎ *97/248–4001* ⊕ *www.basmahotel.com* ⇌ *208 rooms* ❑ *Free Breakfast.*

Go Inn Backpackers

$ | B&B/INN | Set back in a quiet residential area this lively hostel-B&B is run by owner Gandhi, a former tour leader whose invaluable advice is guaranteed to improve your time in Aswan. **Pros:** great breakfast that includes fresh fruit; helpful on-site owner is a wealth of information; excellent value. **Cons:** facilities are basic but improving; dusty neighborhood walk required to get into town; hard beds. ⑤ *Rooms from: $23* ✉ *3VHM+WH, Aswan South* ☎ *12/2795–2197* ❑ *Free Breakfast.*

Obelisk Nile Hotel

$$ | HOTEL | The Obelisk sits in the center of it all—smack-dab on the waterfront and a quick walk to many restaurants and shops. **Pros:** attentive staff; location has the best of both worlds: on the Nile and at the heart of Downtown; pool. **Cons:** no in-room Wi-Fi; rooms near street can be noisy; riverside location invites swarms of mosquitoes. ⑤ *Rooms from: $81* ✉ *1 Corniche Al Nile, Corniche* ☎ *97/245–4100* ⊕ *obeliskhotels.com* ⇌ *100 rooms* ❑ *Free Breakfast.*

★ Sofitel Legend Old Cataract Aswan

$$$$ | HOTEL | Opened in 1899, the Old Cataract is one of Egypt's grandest hotels, well known for its scene-setting role in Agatha Christie's *Death on the Nile* (you can even stay in her suite for a whopping US$8,000 a night). **Pros:** historic cred; swimming in the pool as feluccas sail by; terrace is a top spot for sundowners. **Cons:** rooms can be eye-wateringly expensive, even for a luxury hotel; alcoholic drinks are overpriced; restaurants get mixed reviews. ⑤ *Rooms from: $341 ⊠ Abtal el-Tahrir St., Aswan South* ☎ *10/2222–9071* ⊕ *all.accor.com* ⇨ *138 rooms* ❍❙ *Free Breakfast.*

Tolip Hotel Aswan

$$ | HOTEL | FAMILY | The high-ceilinged reception area, complete with olive and maroon columns and carvings of Abu Simbel and Philae, makes the Tolip look like a neo-pharaonic temple on the northern reaches of the Corniche. **Pros:** all rooms have river views; more entertainment amenities than other hotels; lovely Nile-side pool. **Cons:** taxi required to sightsee; pool reachable only by a tunnel under the street from main building; overpriced compared with similar hotels. ⑤ *Rooms from: $95 ⊠ Corniche Al Nile, Corniche* ☎ *97/232–8828* ⊕ *www.tolipaswan.com* ⇨ *195 rooms* ❍❙ *Free Breakfast.*

Aswan's Nile Islands

Unlike the stretch of the river that passes through Luxor, the section of the Nile that cuts through Aswan has several islands. Elephantine Island is the easiest to reach: an inexpensive public ferry (LE5 one way) makes the short journey from the East Bank. The central part of the island contains two Nubian villages, which feel somewhat rural despite their proximity to Downtown Aswan. The Aswan Museum and the ruins of an ancient temple complex cover the island's southern end, while the sprawling Mövenpick Resort takes over the northern section.

You'll need to hire a boat to reach Kitchener's Island, named after Lord Horatio Kitchener, a 19th-century British commander of the Egyptian army who loved beautiful trees and plants. The entire 17-acre land mass showcases his imported collection. You can visit Seheil Island, one of the Nile's largest and once the site of a major granite quarry, independently, by hiring a felucca or motorboat, or on one of the tours offered by the Nubian guesthouses in Gharb Soheil on Aswan's West Bank.

Sights

Aswan Botanical Garden

GARDEN | This botanical garden occupies all 17 acres of Kitchener's Island, named after Lord Horatio Kitchener, a 19th-century British commander of the Egyptian army who was fascinated by botany. Some of the nearly 750 species planted here don't exist anywhere else in Egypt, hailing from tropical Africa as well as from as far away as India and Brazil. The grounds make for a mildly pleasant stroll, but unfortunately too much of the space has been taken over by market stalls selling the same sort of stuff that you'll find at every tourist site in the country.

To reach Kitchener's Island, you have two choices. The easiest way is to arrange a full- or half-day felucca tour to all the sights on the West Bank and Nile islands through a company like Aswan Individual or your accommodations. Alternatively, you can hire a boat captain along the Corniche on the East Bank. ⊠ *Kitchener's Island* ☎ *LE35.*

Aswan Museum and Temple of Khnum

HISTORY MUSEUM | In a more modern side building off the historic museum (itself built in 1898 to house the British engineer of the Aswan Dam, but seemingly indefinitely closed for renovations), a few glass cases display archaeological finds

What's In a Name?

The origin of Elephantine Island's name is a mystery. Some say it comes from the island's shape, which resembles an elephant's tusk. Others say it's a reference to the island having been an active trading hub for ivory in ancient times. Still others note that the ancient Egyptians believed the island was home to the Elephantine Triad: Khnum (ram-headed creator god), Satet (goddess of war, hunting, and fertility), and Anuket (daughter of Khnum and Satet, goddess of the Nile cataracts and Lower Nubia). The trio is said to have guarded a sacred spring on the island that fed the Nile, and Khnum controlled the flow of its water and, therefore, the fate of the Egyptians.

from Elephantine Island, including pottery, jewelry, grave goods, and a marriage contract written on papyrus.

The archaeological area sprawls across most of the southern part of Elephantine Island, but the ruins are minimal and uninspiring compared with sites elsewhere in Egypt. Temples with quite a bit of modern restoration are dedicated to two of the three gods of the Elephantine Triad: Khnum and his consort, Satet. Northwest of the Temple of Khnum is a flight of metal stairs and a platform that offers a panoramic view of the small nearby islands and southern Aswan. Near the boat dock is the Nilometer, used to gauge the annual Nile floods and therefore the taxes due.

For the site's high ticket price, the museum is disappointingly small, and the ruins are barely labeled. ⊠ *Elephantine Island* 🖃 *LE100.*

Seheil Island

ISLAND | Seheil is one of the largest islands in the Nile, and the tall hill on its southeastern flank was a quarry for granite. It was also used as a resting spot for those trading with the Nubians and by the pharaoh's army, who etched hundreds of inscriptions and cartouches on the rocks—the oldest dates from the Middle Kingdom (2130–1649 BC). A climb up the slopes reveals the Famine Stela,

a hieroglyph-covered slab. Although it was carved during the Ptolemaic Dynasty (305–30 BC), it recounts an episode from the reign of King Djoser 2,500 years prior. The story goes that Egypt had been suffering from drought and famine for seven years when an adviser to the king suggested that he make an offering to Khnum, the god that controls the Nile flood. Khnum appeared to the pharaoh in a dream and brought back the flood, and Djoser honored him by constructing a temple in his honor on Elephantine Island, the ruins of which you can still visit.

You can reach Seheil Island independently by hiring a felucca or motorboat, or as part of a tour organized by a Nubian guesthouse in Gharb Soheil. In addition to climbing the hill to the stela, the tour might also take you into a Nubian house in the nearby village for tea and cakes. ⊠ *Aswan* 🖃 *LE40.*

🛏 Hotels

★ Mövenpick Resort Aswan

$$$$ | HOTEL | FAMILY | Sprawling across the northern portion of Elephantine Island, the Mövenpick offers uber-comfortable rooms decorated in bold geometric patterns and rusty desert tones. **Pros:** secluded island location; postcard-worthy views from the restaurant; on-site

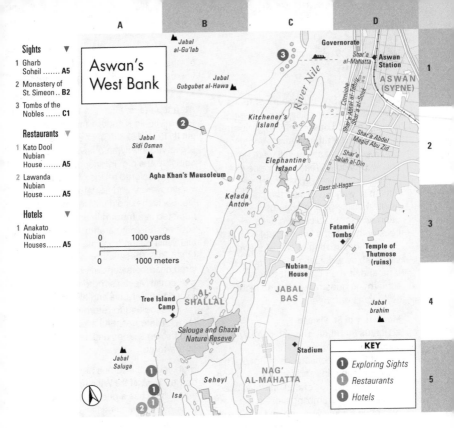

Aswan's
West Bank

KEY

1 Exploring Sights

1 Restaurants

1 Hotels

organic garden and fish farm supply the restaurant. **Cons:** slow Wi-Fi; huge resort can mean long walk to amenities; location adds to travel time. $ *Rooms from: $276* ⊠ *Elephantine Island* ☎ *97/245–4455* ⊕ *www.movenpick.com* ⇥ *404 rooms* ⦿ *Free Breakfast.*

Pyramisa Isis Island Aswan

$$ | **RESORT** | **FAMILY** | Set on 28 lush acres of beautifully landscaped grounds, the Pyramisa is a veritable oasis with an enviable location. **Pros:** idyllic setting on a secluded island; terraces for both sunrise and sunset; hotel ferry to the East Bank goes through beautiful Nile cataracts. **Cons:** hotel's tour agency gets poor reviews; required ferry adds to travel time; rooms could use renovation. $ *Rooms from: $84* ⊠ *Aswan Island, Isis Island* ☎ *97/248–0100* ⊕ *www.*

pyramisahotels.com ⇥ *450 rooms* ⦿ *Free Breakfast.*

The West Bank

The West Bank's eclectic collection of sites include Gharb Soheil, a brightly painted Nubian village across the river and through the cataracts from Aswan proper; the Coptic St. Simeon's Monastery; and the ancient Tombs of the Nobles.

The best way to see these sights is on a full- or half-day felucca trip. If you want to break it up with an overland trek, you can take a camel from the Tombs of the Nobles to St. Simeon's Monastery (about 40 minutes) or a shorter ride (about 10 minutes) from the dock close to the monastery.

⊙ Sights

Gharb Soheil

TOWN | Gharb Soheil is the most touristy of Aswan's Nubian villages, but seeing it is still a good opportunity to get better acquainted with the culture. Vendors on the main market street sell wares that you've probably already seen elsewhere, but photographers, in particular, will delight in wandering past the colorfully painted buildings and huge bowls of brightly colored spices and dyes. Kick back with a *shisha* (water pipe) on traditional floor seating at one of the many cafés, enjoy a Nubian meal at a restaurant, and, if you don't want to leave, book a charming guesthouse for the night. ⊠ *Aswan West Bank.*

Monastery of St. Simeon

RELIGIOUS BUILDING | This 7th-century sand-colored structure is one of the largest Coptic monasteries in Egypt. The complex is in ruins and feels like an abandoned fortress, full of dark barrel-vaulted passages and crumbling arches, but it was once a lively way station for monks preaching Christianity in Nubia and later for Muslim pilgrims on their way to Mecca—you can see their graffiti in some of the sleeping quarters. A few poorly preserved Christian frescos remain in the basilica and one of the rooms on the lower level. The vistas over the golden sands of the Western Desert will make you feel a million miles away from the Nile.

To reach the monastery, take a camel through the desert from the Tombs of the Nobles or from the nearby boat dock. From the dock, you can also make the uphill walk yourself, which takes about 15 minutes. It's partially paved, but wear sturdy shoes. ⊠ *Aswan West Bank* ⌑ *LE40.*

Tombs of the Nobles

TOMB | Aswan's West Bank is the final resting place of the important regional leaders and senior officials of ancient Elephantine. A long, steep staircase climbs up to the rock-carved tombs, or you can take a camel from near the ticket office.

Atop the stairs, a path to the south leads to the Middle Kingdom **Tomb of Sirenput II** (1971–1928 BC), one of the best preserved in Aswan. Allow your eyes to adjust to the dim interior and watch the brilliantly colored reliefs of the deceased local governor and his family come to life. Six niches hold statues of Sirenput depicted in a mummified form. Farther south on the path are the **Tombs of Mekhu and Sabni** dating from the Old Kingdom (2345 BC). These impressive rock-pillared chambers contain original frescoes that detail Mekhu's murder while on an expedition in Nubia and his son's quest for revenge and to return the body of his father. More peaceful everyday hunting and fishing scenes decorate Sabni's side of the tomb.

High above the tombs atop the hill is the domed **Tomb of the Wind** (Qubbet el-Hawa), which has a phenomenal panoramic view of Elephantine Island and greater Aswan.

Only a handful of these tombs are ever open to the public, and it's an active archaeological site, so even some of those are likely to be closed or undergoing excavation on your visit. If you've already seen tombs in Luxor, these might feel a tad disappointing, but they will likely be much more peaceful and less crowded. ⊠ *Aswan West Bank* ⌑ *LE60.*

🍴 Restaurants

Kato Dool Nubian House

$$$$ | AFRICAN | Dig your toes into the sand at this gorgeous restaurant that's painted in bright colors and dishes up Nubian delights. It specializes in tagine dishes, which are slow-cooked in large clay pots. **Known for:** cheery decor; riverside location; open-air dining. ⑤ *Average main: LE175* ⊠ *Gharb Soheil* ☎ *106/755-7225* ⊕ *www.katodool.com.*

The Temple of Kom Ombo is actually a complex of two temples, one for the crocodile-headed god Sobek and the other for the falcon-headed Haroeris, a manifestation of the god Horus.

Lawanda Nubian House

$$ | AFRICAN | Overlooking a bend on Gharb Soheil's busy market street, this rooftop restaurant offers a bird's-eye view of the action while you enjoy your lunch. The friendly staff will help you translate the menu, or you can just opt for the juicy chicken that comes with plenty of sides. **Known for:** great views; Arabic-only menu; lively setting. $ *Average main: LE120* ⊠ *Gharb Soheil* ⊕ *www.facebook.com/ lawandanubainhouse* ⊟ *No credit cards.*

 ## Hotels

★ Anakato Nubian Houses

$$ | B&B/INN | Get a taste of village life and Nubian hospitality at Anakato, a world away from Aswan city across the river. **Pros:** eye-catching traditional Nubian architecture; interesting range of activities, including mud baths and kayaking; huge, delicious breakfast spread. **Cons:** online questions from potential guests often go unanswered; slightly overpriced; rooms are in multiple locations around the village. $ *Rooms from: $70* ⊠ *Gharb Soheil, El-Noba* ☎ *10/2120–1201* ⊕ *www. anakato.com* ⇆ *19 rooms* ⦿l *Free Breakfast.*

 ## Activities

Take a break from the temples to experience the nature side of Aswan because the West Bank is one of the best places to swim in the Nile. Gharb Soheil has a couple of sandy beaches, or you can ask locally for recommendations.

Tree Island Camp

KAYAKING | FAMILY | This supremely relaxing West Bank beach café has everything you need for an active day followed by a sublime waterside chill-out session. They can arrange a Nile kayaking adventure—one of the most incredible and up-close ways to experience the river—as well as mud masks, sand baths, sandboarding on the high nearby escarpment, and camping. ⊠ *Gharb Soheil, Aswan West Bank* ☎ *10/6222–9106* ⊕ *www.facebook. com/shagracamp.nubia.*

Temple of Kom Ombo Touring Tips

■ **Don't miss the detail.** Some of ancient Egypt's best carvers worked their magic at Kom Ombo, and their skills can be seen in the impressively lifelike features on the bodies of the gods and pharaohs.

■ **Walk the outer wall.** Kom Ombo has a different layout than other temples, and some of the most fascinating reliefs are carved along the outer walkway.

■ **The museum is a relief.** If you're visiting on a hot day, the Crocodile Museum near the exit is dark, quiet, and air-conditioned.

■ **See the scene from your ship.** Kom Ombo is the last sightseeing stop on a Nile cruise from Luxor to Aswan. If you're feeling temple fatigue, you can still see some of the structure from your boat. That said, Kom Ombo really is worth disembarking for.

Kom Ombo

40 km (25 miles) north of Aswan, 65 km (40 miles) south of Edfu.

Set in a fertile area, Kom Ombo has long been an important town strategically because it was one of the places where the trade routes to the Nile Valley, the Red Sea, and Nubia converged. It is also the site of a very unusual double temple dedicated to two gods: Sobek, depicted as a crocodile or a crocodile-headed man, and Haroeris, a manifestation of Horus represented as a falcon or a falcon-headed man.

Today, the town is home to a large Nubian community, which was resettled here after the construction of the Aswan High Dam and the flooding of Lower Nubia.

GETTING HERE AND AROUND
Kom Ombo is always included on the itinerary of Nile cruises and *dahabiya* (traditional vessel) sailings. You can also visit on a day trip from Aswan using a local tour company or on your own by taxi.

◉ Sights

Temple of Kom Ombo
RUINS | Set on a curve in the Nile, Kom Ombo is a unique "double temple" dedicated equally to two deities: the crocodile-headed god Sobek and the falcon-headed Haroeris, a manifestation of the god Horus. Virtually all the structure visible today dates from the late Ptolemaic Dynasty (ca. 205 BC), but earlier structures and artifacts continue to be unearthed, including the January 2021 discovery of pharaohs' seals from the 5th Dynasty (2495–2345 BC).

A large open courtyard leads to the 10-column **outer hypostyle hall** with exquisite relief carvings that show gods and pharaoh coronations in fine detail, all the way down to their sculpted knees and clear-cut toenails. The reliefs continue through the **inner hypostyle hall,** a series of **offering halls,** and twin **sanctuaries.** The latter contain a set of crypts and secret passageways from which priests provided advice and the "voice" of god.

As in many other ancient Egyptian temples, much of Kom Ombo's decoration depicts scenes of pharaohs making offerings to the gods and the gods blessing

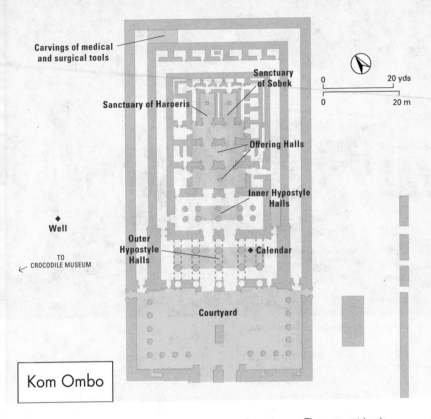

Carvings of medical and surgical tools

Sanctuary of Sobek

Sanctuary of Haroeris

Offering Halls

Inner Hypostyle Halls

Well

TO CROCODILE MUSEUM

Outer Hypostyle Halls

Calendar

Courtyard

0   20 yds
0   20 m

Kom Ombo

pharaohs. But this temple also has some unusual carvings. On the back (northeast) wall along the outer stone enclosure, surgical and medical instruments such as forceps, scales, a stethoscope, and even a sponge are depicted on a table, possibly indicating that Kom Ombo was a center of healing. The goddess Isis is also shown on a birthing chair. Also, look for a calendar on the southwest wall of the offering hall, the only carving of its kind that shows the date of the Nile's flooding season.

On the north side of the temple, a large **well** at least 15 meters (50 feet) deep is connected to a series of basins that the cult of Sobek might have used to house newborn crocodiles. Fragments of a *mammisi* (chapel depicting divine birth) stand at the temple's western corner

near the entrance. The way out leads through a dimly lit **Crocodile Museum** that houses 20 mummified crocs, the largest of which is a whopping 4 meters (14 feet) long. Those who prayed at Kom Ombo would leave behind offerings of mummified crocodiles and stelae, stone slabs decorated with the name of the pilgrim and a prayer to the god. ▧ *LE140*

Daraw Camel Market

40 km (25 miles) north of Aswan.

One of the largest in Egypt, Daraw's camel market is a spectacle that's little visited by outsiders and makes for a fascinating side trip if you're tired out by temples and tombs

Camels for sale at the Daraw Camel Market.

GETTING HERE AND AROUND

The camel market is a traditional, male-dominated space, and it's best to go with a local tour company such as Aswan Individual, which has helpful guides who can translate conversations for you. Men and women should dress modestly, covering to elbows and knees, and wear closed-toe shoes. Allow at least two to three hours, including travel time, for a visit here.

Sights

Daraw Camel Market

MARKET | Hundreds of camels await their fate in a dusty lot while men dressed in traditional *galabeyas* (long, flowing tunics) barter and bicker over the animals, which often have their front left leg bound to prevent them from walking far or fast.

Many of the camels are brought up from Sudan on the 40 Days Road, one of North Africa's ancient caravan routes. From the other direction, buyers make the journey all the way from Cairo to take their pick of the lot. Most of these animals are destined for slaughter. Sellers show off their goods by giving the camels' fur a close shave so that their bodies can be better inspected.

The main market days are Saturday and Sunday, but keep in mind that some of the market happenings and the treatmént of the camels might upset animal lovers. Trading usually ends by early afternoon. This camel market is not at all a display for tourists, so be respectful of the traders and don't get in the way of their business. ⊠ *Daraw.*

Continued on page 286

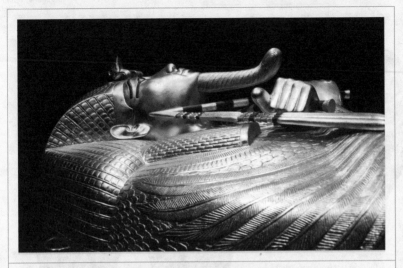

THE KINGDOMS OF EGYPT

Even while standing in the sand before the Pyramids of Giza—physical, awe-inspiring evidence of Egypt's longevity—it's hard to fully fathom a history that's measured in millennia rather than just mere centuries. Comprehension doesn't get any easier when you consider that these pyramids were already 2,000 years old by the time of Antony and Cleopatra.

The Nile Valley was, indeed, a cradle of civilization, but even after the last of the pharaohs, Egypt captivated outsiders and influenced culture. The fertile agricultural lands created by the Nile's waters intrigued the Assyrians, Persians, Macedonians, and Romans. Egypt also played formative roles in early Christianity and Islam, later drawing the attention of both the Crusaders and the Ottomans. Napoléon was here, too, and though his stay was short, it ignited an interest in ancient Egypt that spread across Europe and beyond, attracting archaeologists and some of the first modern-age tourists.

The 20th century saw the rise of a once-again fully independent Egypt. Although the nation was initially a champion of Arab unity, today's Egyptians have a strong sense of their unique national identity. Such duality seems perfectly natural in a place where ancient monuments sit on the edges of ever-expanding modern cities, and everyday life is a vibrant mix of traditional and contemporary culture.

Sarcophagus of Tutankhamun

(top right) Saqqara pyramid; (left) Cosmetic Palette from the Predynastic period, 3000 BC; (bottom right) Narmer Palette

Predynastic Egypt

ca. 4500–3100 BC

Humans have inhabited Egypt since the Paleolithic era, when much of North Africa was fertile, green, and wooded. As the Sahara expanded after 10,000 BC, sedentary communities developed closer to the Nile Valley. Much of the culture we know as ancient Egyptian began taking shape between 4500 and 3100 BC, when Egyptians developed large-scale irrigation and complex social organizations. Local kingdoms emerged, including one that ruled Upper Egypt from the capital of Abydos.

■ National Museum of Egyptian Civilization, Cairo

The Early Dynasties and the Old Kingdom

3100–2055 BC

Around 3100 BC, the pharaoh Narmer united Upper and Lower Egypt and established a new capital at Memphis. (The famous Narmer Palette depicts Narmer defeating his enemies.) According to scholarly chronologies, this union marks the beginning of the 1st Dynasty and the pharaonic era. Narmer's successors developed hieroglyphic writing, perfected the art of mummification, and built mud-brick tombs known as *mastabas*. The 3rd-Dynasty pharaoh Djoser (ca. 2687 BC) constructed the Step Pyramid of Saqqara—Egypt's first

pyramid and the world's oldest large stone structure. His reign marked the beginning the Old Kingdom during which many pyramids, including those at Giza, were built. Old Kingdom Egypt featured a strong central government, with a scribal bureaucracy and a sophisticated taxation system, headed by a god-pharaoh, who was tasked with ensuring *maat* (divine justice and order) on Earth.

■ Step Pyramid of Saqqara
■ Pyramids of Giza
■ Bent Pyramid of Dahshur

(top) Karnak Temples, Luxor;
(left) Great Temple at Abu Simbel

First Intermediate Period and the Middle Kingdom

2055–1550 BC

By the end of the Old Kingdom, regional governors grew more powerful, and the country fragmented during the First Intermediate Period. Local kings from Thebes eventually re-exerted their authority, and the Middle Kingdom witnessed a flourishing of literature and more lifelike statuary. Fortunes waned, however, and, during this period, Egypt succumbed to west Asia's Hyksos people, whose superior technology included weapons of war such as chariots.

■ Karnak Temples, Luxor

The New Kingdom

1550–1069 BC

After 90 years of Hyksos domination, a unified Egyptian kingdom arose with the 18th Dynasty, marking the start of the New Kingdom. Egypt extended its domain into Nubia to the Fourth Cataract of the Nile and as far as the Euphrates in Syria. The pharaohs venerated the new combined god of Amun-Ra, made Thebes (modern-day Luxor) their capital, added impressive features to the already imposing Karnak and Luxor temples, and began conducting royal burials in the Valley of Kings. Some of Egypt's most significant rulers are from this period. Queen Hatshepsut (1479–1458 BC) became a powerful pharaoh,

sending a trade expedition to distant lands. Akhenaten (1352–1336 BC) launched his short-lived religious reformation—replacing polytheistic worship with monotheistic devotion to Aten. When he died, his practices were reversed, and his name was stricken from history. In a twist of fate, his son and successor, Tutankhamun (1321–1334 BC), is today the best-known ancient pharaoh. Ramses II (1279–1213 BC), also known as Ramses the Great, ruled for 66 years and left massive monuments to and statues of himself across Egypt.

■ Great Temple at Abu Simbel
■ Valley of the Kings, Luxor

TIMELINE

747–656 BC Rule of
25th-Dynasty Nubian pharaohs

331 BC Alexandria
founded

1000 BC   750 BC   500 BC   250 BC

(above) Greco-Roman
Museum, Alexandria; (right)
Temple of Horus, Edfu

The Late Period

1069–332 BC

The end of the 20th Dynasty marked the end of the unified New Kingdom. For the first time since the Hyksos, outsiders ruled Egypt, starting with a Libyan dynasty in the Delta and followed by the powerful Nubian pharaohs of the 25th Dynasty (ca. 747–656 BC), who saw themselves as heirs to the New Kingdom. The powerful Assyrian Empire played kingmaker in Egyptian dynastic struggles, and twice the world-conquering Persians occupied the country, generating much resentment.

■ Nubia Museum, Aswan

The Ptolemies

332–30 BC

The return of Persian rule in 343 BC was so unpopular that the arrival of Alexander the Great in 332 BC was welcomed by many. The Macedonian conqueror shrewdly visited the desert oracle in Siwa, where the priests declared him the son of Amun. Before leaving Egypt for good, Alexander founded the city of Alexandria, creating Egypt's first substantial link to the Mediterranean. After Alexander's death in 323 BC, his general, Ptolemy, claimed Egypt, eventually declaring himself pharaoh. Under Ptolemy and his heirs, Alexandria flourished, becoming a Greek-speaking capital of learning and

culture. The Ptolemies built the Lighthouse, one of the wonders of the ancient world, as well as the fabled Library and the Mouseion, a kind of ancient university. Many of the later Ptolemies, however, were irresponsible rulers, and Egypt's declining fortunes (and growing debts) soon brought it into the orbit of Rome. Cleopatra VII, daughter of Ptolemy XII, famously attempted to preserve her dynasty by forging relationships with first Julius Caesar and then Marc Antony, but with her suicide in 30 BC, all of Egypt became an imperial province of Rome.

■ Temple of Horus, Edfu
■ Greco-Roman Museum, Alexandria

30 BC Suicide of Cleopatra VII (end of Ptolemy period)	AD 391 Theophilus burns last remnants of the Library of Alexandria	AD 639–646 Muslims invade Egypt

| 0 | AD 250 | 500 | 750 |

(left) Kom al-Dikka (Roman Theater), Alexandria; (right) Temple of Isis, Philae

Roman Egypt

30 BC–AD 330

With the Ptolemies, Egypt had ceased to be ruled by native Egyptians, but the country was at least independent. With the triumph of Octavian, Egypt became part of the Roman Empire. Alexandria continued to flourish under the Romans as a center for medicine, astronomy, and Neoplatonic philosophy. Rome also established lucrative mines in the Red Sea desert. According to Coptic tradition, Christianity arrived in Alexandria with St. Mark after AD 60, culminating in the horrific persecutions ordered by the emperor Diocletian (AD 284–305).

■ Kom al-Dikka (Roman Theater), Alexandria
■ Temple of Isis, Philae

Byzantium and the Copts

AD 330–642

The era of martyrs and Roman persecution ended when the emperor Constantine granted imperial support for Christians with the Edict of Milan in 313. Egypt played a formative role in the growth of Christianity from the beginning. Christian monasticism was born in Egypt: desert hermits such as St. Anthony (251–356) attracted numerous devotees and imitators. With the backing of the empire behind them, Christian leaders soon turned against local pagans. In 391, the bishop of Alexandria, Theophilus, led a mob against the city's remaining pagans, burning down the Serapeum temple and the last remnants of the Library of Alexandria. Egyptian Christians, however, were increasingly at odds with the Greek-speaking hierarchy, now based in Constantinople, over whether Jesus had one nature (the "Monophysite" position) or two natures, human and divine (the "Melkite" position). Nearly two centuries of resistance to Melkite orthodoxy meant that by the time Islam arrived, Egypt had little reason to rue the departure of the Byzantines.

■ Coptic Museum, Cairo
■ Church of St. Sergius, Cairo

TIMELINE

868 Ahmad Ibn Tulun
appointed governor
of Egypt

969 Cairo founded
by the Fatimids

800   900   1000   1100

(top) Mosque of Amr Ibn al-As; (far right) Mosque of Ibn Tulun; (near right) View from inside Al-Azhar Mosque

The Early Islamic Period

642–969

In 641, the Arab general Amr Ibn al-As led a Muslim army across the Sinai into mainland Egypt, where he overtook the fortress the Romans called Babylon, now Coptic Cairo. For most Egyptians, Byzantine rule had long been associated with an oppressive religious orthodoxy, so the arrival of Islam met little resistance. Muslims, in turn, considered Christians and Jews "people of the Book," allowing them to practice their religions provided they paid tax to the Muslim army. For several centuries, Egypt's primarily Christian populace was ruled by a Muslim minority. Outside the walls of the Babylon fort, al-As built the camp-city of Fustat and his mosque, the first in Africa. In 868, a Turkic soldier named Ahmad Ibn Tulun was appointed governor by the Abbasid caliph in Baghdad. But Ibn Tulun soon shored up his position, declared Egypt independent from the Abbasids, and ordered the construction of al-Qata'i, a new city of legendary splendor. However, his successors were not as capable. When the Abbasids reassumed control of Egypt in 905, they razed the city, sparing only Ibn Tulun's magnificent mosque.

- Mosque of Amr Ibn al-As, Cairo
- Mosque of Ibn Tulun, Cairo

The Fatimids

969–1171

The city of Cairo was only founded in 969, when a Shia dynasty known as the Fatimids conquered Egypt from their base in Tunisia. The Fatimids built the walled city of Al-Qahira (The Victorious), which supplanted nearby settlements such as Fustat as the country's primary city. From Egypt, the Fatimids controlled an empire stretching from North Africa to Syria and part of the Arabian Peninsula, and they controlled trade between the Mediterranean and the Red Sea. Many of Cairo's most recognizable historic monuments were constructed by the Fatimids, who, as patrons of science

1174 Salah al-Din (Saladin)
becomes sultan

1382 Khan el-Khalili
bazaar established

1200   1300   1400   1500

In Focus | THE KINGDOMS OF EGYPT

(far left) Mosque of Sultan
Hassan; (top) The Citadel;
(near left) Bab Zuweila

and learning, founded
Al-Azhar University and
Mosque. The early Fatimid
rulers Al-Mu'izz (953–975)
and Al-Aziz (975–996)
were tolerant and quick to
establish good relations with
local Jews, Christians, and
Sunni Muslims—a necessary
ingredient to economic
stability. Subsequent
caliphs, however, were less
open-minded. Al-Hakim
(996–1021) was especially
known for his harsh edicts
against non-Shiites. Internal
power struggles weakened
the Fatimid state, and the
Crusaders began eyeing
Egypt.

- Al-Azhar Mosque and
  University, Cairo
- Bab Zuweila, Cairo
- Museum of Islamic Art,
  Cairo

1171–1517 Saladin and the Mamluks

When the Crusaders
attacked Egypt in 1168,
the Fatimids requested
assistance from the Seljuk
Turks, who sent their effective
military vassal Salah al-Din
al-Ayyubi (1137–1193), known
to Europeans as Saladin. He
assumed the post of vizier,
and two years later, when
the last Fatimid caliph died,
declared himself sultan. Salah
al-Din founded a citadel
fortress above Cairo and
began the tradition of building
madrasas (religious schools)
to reorient the populace to
Sunni Islam after 200 years
of Shia rule. His relatives,
known as the Ayyubids, ruled
Egypt in his stead when he
left to battle the Crusaders

in Syria, but, by 1250,
their slaves had usurped
power and ushered in the
era of Mamluk rule. The
Mamluks, a term that means
"owned," were a caste of
professional slave-soldiers
of Circassian or Turkic
origin who were bought as
children, converted to Islam,
and educated in the houses
of the rich and powerful.
They eventually acquired
positions of considerable
influence. Despite power
struggles among the Mamluk
leaders, Egypt enjoyed
great economic prosperity
during this period, and art
and architecture were well
funded.

- The Citadel, Cairo
- Khan el-Khalili, Cairo
- Mosque and Madrasa of
  Sultan Hassan, Cairo

(left) Opening the Suez Canal 1869; (right) Muhammad Ali Mosque

The Ottoman Era

1517–1798

In 1517, the rapidly expanding Ottoman Empire defeated the last Mamluk sultan, and Egypt began three centuries as a dominion of the Ottomans, who declared themselves caliphs. They appointed *walis* (guardians) to run the country. This period also corresponded with the European age of discovery when new trade routes in the Atlantic eclipsed those in the vicinity of Egypt. Thus, Egypt entered a period of decline and increasingly came to resemble a feudal backwater.

■ Bayt al-Suhaymi, Cairo

An Egyptian Awakening

1798–1882

To disrupt British access to India, Napoléon Bonaparte invaded Egypt in 1798. Although his conquest was short-lived, it served as Egypt's jarring introduction to European technology. (Conversely, Napoléon's decision to bring along hundreds of scholars on his campaign also ushered in a European fascination with ancient Egyptian civilization.) When the dust settled, Egypt's new Ottoman viceroy, an Albanian mercenary named Muhammad Ali Pasha, understood that it was time to modernize. He brought in European advisors, reformed the military, and transformed

agriculture by introducing cotton as a cash crop. Under Muhammad Ali and his *khedive* (viceroy) successors, Egypt became quasi-independent from the Ottoman Empire. The rush to modernize, however, had its costs, including the expense of constructing the vital Suez Canal in 1869. As holders of most of Egypt's debts, England and France began taking ever greater control of Egypt's finances. In 1882, the British occupied the country, having faced down a nationalist revolt headed by an army officer, Ahmed Urabi.

■ Muhammad Ali Mosque

(right) Bibliotheca Alexandrina; (top) Begin, Carter, and Sadat at Camp David 1978

1882–1978

Revolution and Republic

Egypt chafed under British control. Nationalist feelings spilled over in 1919 during a series of demonstrations against the British. A formal independence came in 1923, but continued British meddling in Egyptian politics—and a foot-dragging royal family—hindered Egypt's political aspirations. Decades of frustrated nationalist hopes, followed by a military debacle in the 1948 war with Israel, set the stage for a surprise coup led by a group of young military men, calling themselves the "Free Officers," in 1952. The bloodless coup sent Egypt's sybaritic King Farouk into exile, and the Arab Republic of Egypt was born. Gamal Abdel Nasser, Egypt's second president, nationalized the Suez Canal in 1956, facing down a triple invasion from Britain, France, and Israel and winning major credibility among newly independent countries in the region. Though Nasser was a champion of Arab nationalism who preached socialist ideals in public, he cultivated a growing police state to stifle opposition at home. His efforts foundered after the debacle of the Six-Day War with Israel in 1967. He died three years later, only to have his successor, Anwar Sadat, make peace with Egypt's longtime adversary through the 1978 Camp David Accords.

■ Cavafy Museum, Alexandria
■ Aswan High Dam

1978–Present

Contemporary Egypt

After Sadat's 1981 assassination, Hosni Mubarak took over the presidency in a term that lasted nearly 30 years until the 2011 Arab Spring protests forced his resignation. In 2012, Egypt had its first-ever democratic elections, and Mohammed Morsi of the Muslim Brotherhood won the presidency. However, protestors returned to Tahrir Square within the year, and the army, led by Abdel Fattah el-Sisi, overthrew Morsi. El-Sisi became president and remains in power, ruling Egypt with a tightening grip.

■ Biblioteca Alexandrina

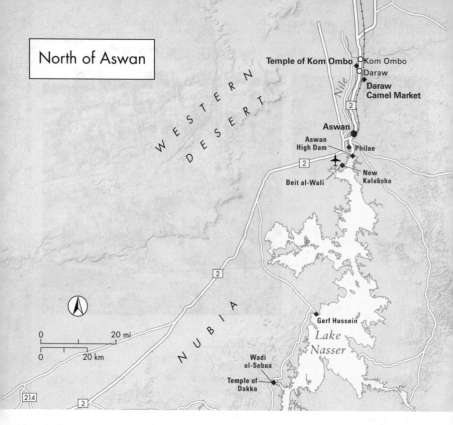

WESTERN DESERT

Nile

Temple of Kom Ombo ○ Kom Ombo
○ Daraw
● **Daraw Camel Market**

● **Aswan**

Aswan
High Dam ◆ ● Philae
✈
● New
Kalabsha

Beit al-Wali

Gerf Hussein ◆

Lake Nasser

N U B I A

Wadi al-Sebua
Temple of Dakka ◆

0 20 mi
0 20 km

214
2

Philae

Philae (Agilkia Island), 8 km (5 miles) south of Aswan.

If you've come from Luxor on a Nile cruise, then you've racked up quite a number of temple visits. But it's worth brushing off the temple fatigue to visit Philae. Seeing the columns and pylons of the temple dedicated to the goddess Isis—the life giver and nourisher—reflected in the Nile is something you will never forget. You might even want to visit twice: on an organized tour by day and for the sound-and-light show at night.

GETTING HERE AND AROUND

Philae's Temple of Isis sits on an island between the Aswan Dam and the Aswan High Dam, meaning you'll need to board a boat to reach it. The temple is a popular destination for tour groups, and joining one is the easiest way to visit.

Traveling here independently is possible but complicated because you'll have to bargain with the boatmen for a ride (expect to pay LE200 to LE300) or ask to join a group for the journey (the tour leader might tell you an amount, but count on paying at least LE50). The boatmen might argue with you and try to prevent you from joining a group because they are losing out on business—stand your ground. Also, remember to buy your ticket for the temple before you board the boat.

If you'd like to experience the **Philae Sound-and-Light Show** (⊕ *soundandlight. show/en*), generally held nightly at 7 and 8 pm, buy tickets online in advance. Not all shows are narrated in English so check before booking. The cost is about LE310.

The Cult of Isis

Isis was a central figure in the ancient Egyptian belief system. She was the sister-wife of Osiris, whom she brought back to life after he was killed by their jealous brother Set. After his reincarnation, Osiris impregnated Isis, who gave birth to Horus. Ancient Egyptians associated Isis with protection, seeing her as a life giver and nourisher, which is why she's often carved on temple walls holding the *ankh* (the key of life, symbolizing the life force). Isis's role in resurrecting her husband also imbued her with power over magic, healing, and miracles.

In the Hellenic and Roman eras, worship of Isis spread far beyond the boundaries of Egypt. Temples to the goddess were built in Delos and Delphi in Greece, Pompeii and Rome in Italy, and also in Spain, Germany, and along the Black Sea coast. The cult of Isis was even an early rival to Christianity. Worship of the goddess died out when Roman emperor Constantine outlawed pagan cults throughout the empire in the 4th century AD, but the Temple of Isis at Philae remained active into the 6th century AD because its remote location put it well beyond the reach of Rome.

◉ Sights

★ Temple of Isis

RUINS | Dedicated to one of ancient Egypt's most important goddesses, the Temple of Isis rises majestically above the calm Nile waters on small Agilkia Island. Some stone blocks found on-site date from 690 BC, but the main part of the complex standing today is from the reign of Ptolemy II Philadelphus (285–246 BC) and the Roman emperor Diocletian (284–305 AD). The devoted worshipped Isis here until the 6th century AD, long after Christianity took hold elsewhere. This building was the final temple constructed in this style, and it's where the last hieroglyph was carved.

The striking, 18-meter (59-foot) **First Pylon** is one of the temple's oldest structures, built by Nectanebo I (379–361 BC) but showing reliefs from Ptolemy XII (80–58 BC). To reach it, pass the **Kiosk of Nectanebo**—a roofless structure with offering scenes on its walls and about half of its original Hathor-head columns intact—and go through the **First Court**, lined with the Roman-built **West Colonnade** and unfinished **East Colonnade**.

On the left (west) side of the **Second Court** is the small **mammisi** (chapel depicting divine birth), showing the birth of Horus, son of Isis and Osiris. The grand **Second Pylon**, carved with gods and Ptolemaic-era pharaohs, reveals the entrance to the temple itself. Inside, the **Hypostyle Hall** consists of 10 columns that are mainly the work of Ptolemy VIII. The generous offering scenes continue, showing the pharaoh by himself or accompanied by his wife giving incense, vases, and wine to the gods. Christians repurposed the temple as a church, as evidenced by the defaced figures and Coptic crosses on the walls. Beyond this area lies the **sanctuary**, with an altar on the right. A side door leads out to the **Gateway of Hadrian**, and reliefs show the Roman emperor making offerings to the Egyptian gods.

East of the temple, close to the riverbank, the **Kiosk of Trajan** is a small open temple with supporting columns. Despite it being unfinished, it's one of Philae's most iconic structures and was often the subject of Victorian-era painters.

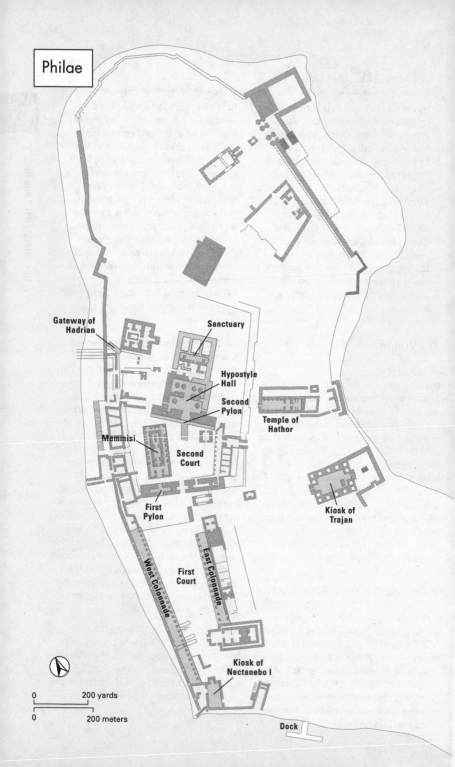

Philae

Gateway of
Hadrian

Sanctuary

Hypostyle
Hall

Second
Pylon

Temple of
Hathor

Mammisi

Second
Court

Kiosk of
Trajan

First
Pylon

West Colonnade

East Colonnade

First
Court

Kiosk of
Nectanebo I

Dock

0   200 yards

0   200 meters

Like other ancient structures in Lower Nubia, the Temple of Isis was rescued by UNESCO in the 1970s. After the completion of the Aswan Dam in 1902, water partially submerged the temple during the Nile's flood season, and archaeologists feared that the damp would soften the monument's foundations and cause its collapse. It was moved to what was then known as Agilkia Island but was renamed for the island where the Temple of Isis originally stood.

This temple is one of four ancient monuments in Egypt that has nighttime **sound-and-light shows** (⊕ *soundandlight.show/en, LE310*)—the others are Abu Simbel, Karnak in Luxor, and the Pyramids of Giza. Some say that the Philae show is the least cheesy of the bunch. The first part involves walking through the atmospheric, partly illuminated temple, and the second delivers a brief history. Book show tickets online in advance, checking to be sure that the show you select is narrated in English. ✉ *LE180*

Lake Nasser

Aswan High Dam: 23 km (14 miles) south of Aswan.

The construction of the Aswan High Dam, inaugurated in 1971, created Lake Nasser, one of the world's largest man-made bodies of water. The massive lake, which covers an area bigger than the U.S. states of Rhode Island or Delaware, came at a huge expense, both financial and cultural.

Lower Nubia, the area between the First and Second Cataracts of the Nile, was once much like the Nile valley north of Aswan, a thin ribbon of green fed by the river and hemmed in by desert. Nubians, the indigenous people of southern Egypt and northern Sudan, cultivated fields here for thousands of years, and massive ancient Egyptian monuments once lined the riverbanks.

Construction of both the Aswan Dam (completed in 1902) and the subsequent Aswan High Dam flooded much of the area, forcing the Nubians to give up their homes and land and relocate to Aswan and Kom Ombo. The ancient monuments had to be relocated, too. UNESCO launched a campaign to rally international support, and 40 archaeological missions from five continents painstakingly transferred many monuments to higher ground, block by block.

A few temples, however, couldn't be moved and rest forever at the bottom of the lake. Others, such as the Temple of Dendur in New York City's Metropolitan Museum of Art, were gifted by the Egyptian government to countries that helped with the UNESCO project.

GETTING HERE AND AROUND

The old Aswan Dam is five minutes south of town, on the way in from the airport. The Aswan High Dam is 15 minutes south of town. You can visit by taxi or on a guided tour that might stop at the Unfinished Obelisk as well. Allow 1 to 1½ hours.

New Kalabsha, set on its own island just south of the Aswan High Dam, is a stop on Lake Nasser cruises, but you can also visit it independently by hiring a taxi (about LE300 round-trip, including waiting time) from downtown Aswan and then a boat (about LE300 for the whole vessel, not per person). The dock is near the Aswan High Dam.

Multi-day cruises are the only way to see Lake Nasser's more remote temples and tombs apart from New Kalabsha, and, far to the south, Abu Simbel. Entry tickets are included in the cruise price. For more information, see Chapter 8 Cruising the Nile and Lake Nasser.

Boats float in the reservoir near the Old Aswan Dam, with the Philae temple complex in the background.

Sights

Aswan High Dam

DAM | One of the world's largest embankment dams, the Aswan High Dam gave the Egyptians control over the annual Nile floods for the first time in history. With financing from the Soviet Union, construction of the dam, a keystone project of then-president Gamal Abdel Nasser, started in 1960 and was completed in 10 years, thanks to the sweat of 30,000 Egyptians working around the clock.

The Aswan High Dam created Lake Nasser, one of the world's largest artificial lakes, which has a storage capacity of 5.97 trillion cubic feet. The dam's 12 turbines generate 10 billion kilowatt-hours of electricity yearly.

Ironically, damming the Nile has actually made Egypt's land less fertile because the silt gets caught in the lake, and farmers must now apply chemical fertilizers. An incalculable loss is the homeland of the Lower Nubians, one of Africa's oldest civilizations. The dam displaced 100,000 Nubians, who were forced to relocate and only started to receive government compensation for their lost homes and villages in 2019.

Display panels at the dam tell the story of its construction, and a stylized lotus monument commemorates the Soviet–Egyptian partnership. ■**TIP→ If you're short on time, this sight is one to skip. Most visitors spend only 15 minutes here en route to elsewhere.** ✉ *LE100*

New Kalabsha

RUINS | The largest freestanding temple in Nubia, the little-visited **Temple of Kalabsha** was built by Roman emperor Augustus, who reigned from 27 BC to AD 14. It's dedicated to Osiris, Isis, and Mandulis, an ancient Nubian sun god adopted by Ptolemies and Romans. He's often shown with an elaborate headdress of ram's horns topped with sun discs, cobras, and plumed feathers. The building was never finished, and only three inner rooms, as well as portions of the exterior, are completely decorated with reliefs.

Gamal Abdel Nasser

Lake Nasser is named after Gamal Abdel Nasser (1918–70), a military-man-turned-politician who led the 1952 overthrow of Egypt's monarchy. Nasser later became the country's second president and was an important figure in the pan-Arab movement to unify countries across the region.

Nasser tried to tread a neutral middle path between the Communist bloc and the West, but Egypt couldn't avoid making choices between the capitalists and the Soviets. After the United States and the United Kingdom pulled out of a deal to finance construction of the Aswan High Dam in 1956, Nasser nationalized the Suez Canal to pay for the project. This move prompted military action by the British and the French (the largest shareholders in the Suez Canal Company), as well as the Israelis. The Suez Crisis petered out after pressure from the United Nations and the United States, and Arabs saw this as a victory for Nasser, who became a regional hero for unshackling Egypt from its colonialist chains.

The same year that Egypt nationalized the Suez Canal, the country became a socialist state, with Nasser's government nationalizing other assets and industries, taking land, and instituting strict requirements for living in the country, thus driving out British, French, and Egyptian Jewish residents. The Soviets agreed to fund the Aswan High Dam, and construction started in 1960.

Since Israel's creation in 1948, Egypt had testy relations with its neighbor, and pressure was building for Nasser to make a military move. In 1967, Nasser closed the Straits of Tiran to Israeli shipping, cutting off the port of Eilat, and mobilized troops in Sinai near the border. Israel struck with a surprise attack, destroying nearly all of Egypt's air force, in the conflict that became known as the Six-Day War. Less than a week later, Israel had taken over the Sinai Peninsula and Gaza from Egypt, as well as the West Bank and East Jerusalem from Jordan, and the Golan Heights from Syria.

The war was a huge defeat for Egypt and an embarrassment for Nasser, who offered his resignation as president. In a swell of popular support, people took to the streets to call on him to reconsider. He reversed his decision the next day, but just a couple years later, he died of a heart attack at age 52.

Nasser was a force in Middle Eastern politics, seen as a champion of ordinary people and pan-Arab causes. Though he is still revered by some Egyptians, he was never universally popular at home. After an assassination attempt in 1954, he clamped down on domestic opposition and put his main rival, Mohammed Naguib, under house arrest. Freedom and civil liberties were traded off in the name of progress, as he controlled the media, was the only candidate on the ballot for multiple elections, and effectively had full control over the government's power and decision making.

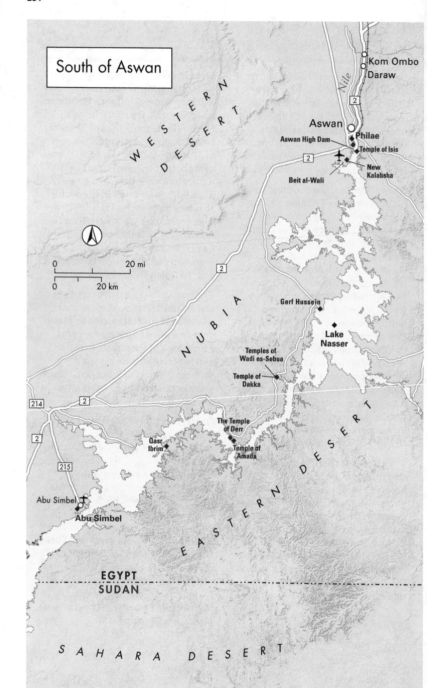

Kalabsha's temple complex includes a *mammisi* (chapel depicting divine birth), a column-surrounded court and a hypostyle hall. Stairs from one of the sanctuaries go up to the roof, where you can soak up spectacular views of the temple, Lake Nasser, and the Aswan High Dam. In the 1960s, a German team moved the temple, saving it from the lake waters, and the Egyptian government thanked Germany with one of the original gates, now in Berlin.

Northwest of the Temple of Kalabsha, a walkway leads to the small rock-cut temple of **Beit al-Wali**. Ramses II commissioned this diminutive but colorful monument, probably for show instead of worship, and the walls depict scenes of the pharaoh clutching his enemies by the hair. Other reliefs demonstrate the riches of Nubia—including gold, ebony, ivory, leopard skins, monkeys, giraffes, lions, and gazelles—being awarded to Ramses II for his conquest. ⌨ LE60

Qasr Ibrim

RUINS | Once strategically placed on a headland high above the Nile, this ancient fortress is now at water level, trapped on an island by rising lake waters that are the result of the Aswan High Dam. Thanks to its once lofty position, Qasr Ibrim is the area's only ancient monument still in its original location, and archaeological work is ongoing.

Thought to have been constructed during the Middle Kingdom (2130–1649 BC), the structure had religious as well as military significance. Shrines were built to Horus, Hathor, and local gods of the First Cataract, and the worship of traditional Egyptian deities held on here well into the era of Christianity. Eventually, some of the temples were dismantled or converted into churches, and pilgrims recorded their journey by carving footprints into the rock. Note that the site is closed to visitors except for those taking Lake Nasser cruises, which stop here for a 15-minute photo op.

Temple of Amada

RUINS | The oldest in Nubia, the Temple of Amada was started under the orders of Thutmose III (1479–1425 BC), and subsequent pharaohs continued its construction. Important inscriptions highlight ancient Egypt's military prowess against rebellious Syrians and a failed Libyan invasion. Between 1964 and 1975, the temple was moved to its current spot, about 2.5 km (1.5 miles) away from its original location. Unlike other temples in Nubia that had to be rescued from Lake Nasser, Amada could not be sawed into blocks for transport because that method would destroy its painted reliefs. Instead, a team of French architects devised a way to move the entire temple in one piece by placing it on rails and using a hydraulic system to haul it to higher ground.

Temple of Dakka

RUINS | This Ptolemaic Dynasty–era (305–30 BC) temple was dedicated to Thoth, the ibis-headed god of wisdom. When the structure was relocated from some 50 km (31 miles) away in the 1960s, archaeologists found a number of New Kingdom (1550–1077 BC) blocks had been reused in the later building.

Temple of Derr

RUINS | Constructed by the great builder, Ramses II, the rock-cut Temple of Derr was dedicated to Amun, Ptah, and Ra-Horakhty, as well as, of course the egotistical pharaoh himself. Despite its desecration by early Christians and use as a church, the temple still retains some brightly painted wall reliefs. It was dismantled and moved here along with Amada in 1964 to save it from being drowned by Lake Nasser.

Temples of Wadi es-Sebua

RUINS | Two New Kingdom (1550–1077 BC) temples were relocated to safety on this shoreline, about 4 km (2.5 miles) from their original sites. Amenhotep III constructed the smaller, **earlier temple,** using both freestanding and rock-cut

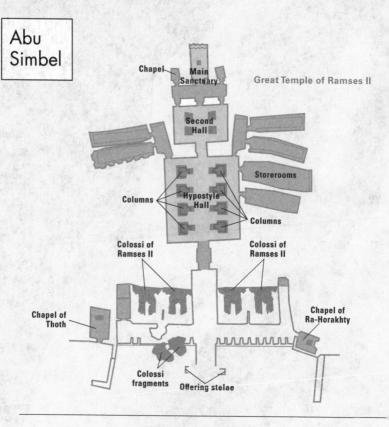

Abu Simbel

Great Temple of Ramses II

Chapel

Main Sanctuary

Second Hall

Storerooms

Columns

Hypostyle Hall

Columns

Colossi of Ramses II

Colossi of Ramses II

Chapel of Thoth

Chapel of Ra-Horakhty

Colossi fragments

Offering stelae

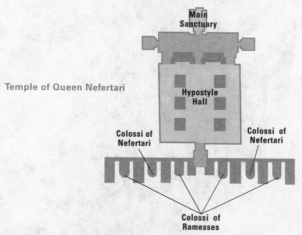

Temple of Queen Nefertari

Main Sanctuary

Hypostyle Hall

Colossi of Nefertari

Colossi of Nefertari

Colossi of Ramesses

Temples of Abu Simbel Touring Tips

■ **Don't skip these temples.** It can make for a long day, heading out very early from Aswan, but the Temples of Abu Simbel are worth the trek.

■ **Short but sweet.** Don't feel dismayed by what might feel like a short amount of time at the temples. They occupy a relatively small footprint, meaning they don't demand the time or stamina required to tackle

Karnak, Edfu, or the Valley of the Kings. A couple of hours is enough for most visitors.

■ **Stay over.** If you want to enjoy more time at the temples, see the sound and light show (soundandlight.show/en LE310)—generally held nightly at 7 pm—or just overnight somewhere quieter than Aswan, spend a night in Abu Simbel village.

---

elements, which Ramses II later added to. The temple, consisting of a sanctuary, court, hall, and pylons, was dedicated to a Nubian form of Horus and later rededicated to Amun. In Arabic, Wadi es-Sebua means Valley of the Lions, so named for the Avenue of Sphinxes leading to the larger and more dramatic **Temple of Ramses II.** As in Ramses II's other temples, towering statues of the pharaoh demand attention. Early Christians plastered over the reliefs, ironically keeping them in a well-preserved state when the plaster eventually fell off. Look out for the odd scene of Ramses II offering flowers to St. Peter.

Abu Simbel

289 km (180 miles) southwest of Aswan.

Ramses II's two striking temples at Abu Simbel are among the most awe-inspiring monuments of ancient Egypt. The pharaoh had his artisans carve the temples out of a rock face to display his might as god-king and to strike dread into the Nubians. The temples, now well above the water and back from the lake shore, originally stood at the bottom of the cliff that they now crown.

GETTING HERE AND AROUND
Most visitors come to Abu Simbel on a tour from Aswan with pre-arranged transport. Book at least 24 hours in advance because you'll need to give the tour company your passport information. Less expensive tours come on an early-morning bus or minibus, while pricier options opt for a flight. EgyptAir flies to Abu Simbel from Aswan (45 minutes) three times a day. Cruises on Lake Nasser start or end in Abu Simbel.

◉ Sights

★ Temples of Abu Simbel
RUINS | The **Great Temple of Ramses II** is fronted by four 65-foot-tall colossi of the sitting pharaoh wearing the double crown of Upper and Lower Egypt. One of the four heads fell to the ground in antiquity and was kept in that position when the temple was moved. Around the legs of the statues stand smaller figures of Ramses II's mother, his favorite wife Nefertari, and some of his children (he allegedly fathered more than 100). A row of baboons praising the rising sun tops the temple facade. A carved figure of Ra-Horakhty stands over the door to the temple between the two pairs of statues.

Inside, the **hypostyle hall** is lined with eight columns of Ramses II in the crossed-arms position of Osiris, god of the afterlife. The walls are carved with reliefs showing military conquests and other events from Ramses II's reign, including his self-proclaimed victory at the Battle of Kadesh (1274 BC) in modern-day Syria. It has some fine scenes showing Ramses on a chariot, and it also depicts the besieged city, the attack, and the counting of body parts of the defeated enemies. Protective vultures with outstretched wings decorate the ceiling. Several side chambers are accessible from this hall and were probably used as storerooms for the furniture, vessels, linen, and priestly costumes.

The **second hall** contains four square columns and is decorated with scenes of Ramses II and Queen Nefertari making offerings to the gods, including the deified Ramses himself. This hall leads into a narrow room where the pharaoh likely made in-person offerings to the gods of the temple. Beyond lie two undecorated side chapels and the **main sanctuary**, which has four rock-carved statues of temple gods: Ptah, Amun-Ra, deified Ramses II, and Ra-Horakhty. Twice a year, the first rays of the rising sun pierce the dark interior of the temple and shine on three of the four statues—Ptah, connected with the realm of the dead, remains in the dark. When the temple was moved, this solar phenomenon was taken into consideration and still happens, albeit one day later, on February 22 and October 22. Thousands visit on these dates, and ticket prices more than double.

The smaller temple at Abu Simbel is the **Temple of Queen Nefertari**, dedicated to the goddess Hathor. Six 10-meter (33-foot) standing rock-cut statues of Queen Nefertari and Ramses II front the temple, and note that it's unusual to see the pharaoh's consort shown in the same size.

The layout of this temple is a simplified version of the Great Temple. The doorway opens into a **hypostyle hall** that contains six Hathor-headed columns. The ceiling offers a dedicatory inscription from Ramses II to Queen Nefertari. The hall is decorated with scenes of the royal couple making offerings to or worshiping the gods. A narrow vestibule follows the pillared hall, and the **main sanctuary** leads off this vestibule. The sanctuary contains a niche with a statue of Hathor as a cow, protecting Ramses. ⊠ *Abu Simbel* �️ *LE240*.

Hotels

The town has a handful of Nubian-style guesthouses and small hotels, and if you want to eat outside your accommodations, basic cafés offer grilled meats, rice, and soup.

Eskaleh Nubian Ecolodge

$$ | B&B/INN | Owner Fikry Kachif can remember what Nubia was like before it was swallowed up by Lake Nasser, and he keeps that memory alive through this B&B. **Pros:** Nubian-owned and run; can arrange boat tours to the temples and dam; top-notch service. **Cons:** no in-room Wi-Fi; bathrooms could use an upgrade; the mosquito netting isn't just for show. ⑤ *Rooms from: $80* ⊠ *Abu Simbel* ☎ *97/340–1288* ⊕ *www.facebook.com/ Eskaleh* ⇱ *5 rooms* ⑪ *Free Breakfast.*

Seti Abu Simbel Lake Resort

$$$$ | HOTEL | Nubian-style bungalows are scattered around a verdant garden replete with waterfalls and a swimming pool right at the edge of Lake Nasser. **Pros:** lovely lakeside location; walking distance to Temples of Abu Simbel; panoramic views from the pool and terrace. **Cons:** overpriced, dated rooms; food offering is subpar; Wi-Fi, when it works, is available in common areas only. ⑤ *Rooms from: $220* ⊠ *Abu Simbel* ☎ *97/340–0720* ⇱ *152 rooms* ⑪ *Free Breakfast.*

Chapter 7

SHARM EL-SHEIKH AND THE RED SEA COAST

Updated by
Cassandra Brooklyn

◉ Sights	🍴 Restaurants	🛏 Hotels	🛍 Shopping	🍸 Nightlife
★★☆☆☆	★★★★☆	★★★★★	★★★☆☆	★★★★★

WELCOME TO SHARM EL-SHEIKH AND THE RED SEA COAST

TOP REASONS TO GO

★ **Scuba diving:** Some of the best diving in the world can be found in the Red Sea, particularly around Sharm el-Sheikh, where you can dive to the *Thistlegorm* wreck in the protected waters near Ras Mohammed National Park.

★ **Kitesurfing:** The tides and winds are perfect along the Red Sea Coast, especially near Hurghada. Catch some air while kitesurfing off Mangroovy Beach at El Gouna.

★ **Dancing the night away:** Coastal resorts are magnets for young club goers from all over Europe; strut your stuff on the dance floor in one of the top spots in Sharm el-Sheikh, Hurghada, or El Gouna.

Sharm el-Sheikh, at the very southern tip of the Sinai Peninsula, is both an air-transit hub and a resort hot spot. The Red Sea—with the Sinai to the north, the Eastern Sahara to the west, and the Arabian Peninsula to the east—is one of the few seas on earth that is virtually surrounded by land. Its depths reach 10,000 feet, and its underwater ecology is unique owing to minimal tidal changes, currents, and wind, as well as sunshine almost year-round.

1 Sharm el-Sheikh. Resorts here offer rest-and-relaxation opportunities on some of Egypt's best beaches. The diving is good, too.

2 Ain Sukhna. Some Cairenes make day trips to this coastal community; others have vacation homes here.

3 Monasteries of St. Anthony and St. Paul. Egypt's oldest monasteries stand at the forefront of Christian monastic history.

4 Hurghada. What was a sleepy fishing town popular with divers is now a Red Sea hub and hot spot popular with divers—as well as European resort vacationers.

5 El Gouna. Abundant activities, nightspots, and resorts attract a more mature (and more moneyed) crowd to this planned community north of Hurghada.

6 Bur Safaga (Port Safaga). Cruise ships offering land excursions to Luxor and the Valley of the Kings often make this beach resort a port of call.

7 El-Quseir. What was once a major port is slowly becoming a resort destination, thanks, in part, to its dive sites.

8 Marsa Alam. Several top dive sites and all-inclusive resorts geared to Europeans are among the highlights here.

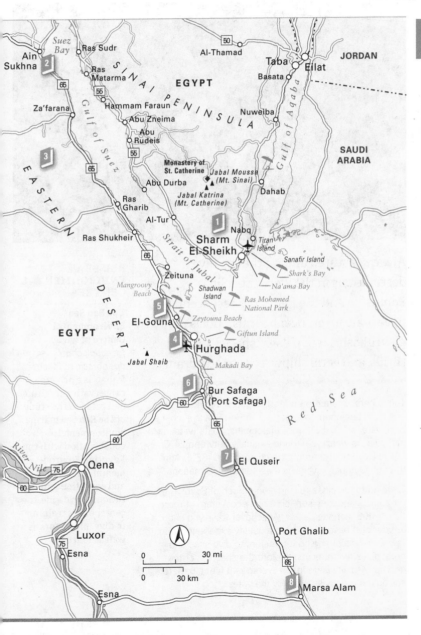

DIVING IN EGYPT

Colorful Red Sea marine life

Always featured among the top dive destinations in the world, the Sinai Peninsula and the Red Sea Coast seem to have it all: magnificent corals, shoals of playful fish, large pelagic species to add thrills, and eerie shipwrecks to add drama.

The waters here are premier diving locations for everyone from beginners to experts. The Red Sea is almost a backwater and cut off from the oceans, so its water, in particular, is warm year-round—usually between 24°C (75°F) November through March and 28°C (82°F) April through October—which is ideal for coral formation.

Coral reefs run close to land along much of Egypt's coastlines, and they support a rich ecosystem of more than 1,000 marine species. Whichever town you choose as your dive base, you'll have a quality experience with few time-consuming boat transfers to dive sites and great dives, whether you explore the shallows or the depths. Visibility is good, on average 49 feet (15 meters), so you get great views below the waves, too.

RED SEA ENVIRONMENTAL CENTRE

The Red Sea Environmental Centre (⊕ www.facebook.com/dahabrsec) in Masbat, Dahab, is a private conservation institute dedicated to the study of the Red Sea marine environment. In collaboration with the Egyptian Environmental Affairs Agency and educational institutions worldwide, the center offers training to dive instructors as well as tourists.

Egypt's Best Dive Sites

HURGHADA

Access to Hurghada sites will more likely be determined by the wind, which is especially strong in spring, than by your wish list. Wherever you end up, though, you're in for a treat.

Abu Hashish. Coral bommies (individual towers of coral) erupt from the sea floor amid the swaying fronds of seagrass that give the site its name. Expect glimpses of more secretive creatures like octopus, seahorses, and cuttlefish.

The Giftun Islands. Off Small Giftun Island, drifting ergs (underwater sand dunes) and chimney caves characterize this site. Soft and fan corals, glass fish, lionfish, and groupers are colorful inhabitants, and Erg Somaya has a deep drop where hammerheads and barracuda gather. Giftun Island, particularly well known for its beaches, also has great marine life off its shores.

MARSA ALAM

Elphinstone. A short but spectacular section of reef has precipitous walls, natural arches, and pinnacles. Sea life includes soft corals, groupers, and morays, as well as hammerhead sharks and manta rays.

The wreck of the *Thistlegorm* is a top dive site

Giftun Island from above

SAFAGA

***Salem* Express.** Some consider this a controversial site as it surrounds a ship that was carrying religious pilgrims to Mecca when it sunk in 1991. For others, the wreck's backstory makes the site intriguing, even though the sea life is like that at other nearby dives.

SHARM EL-SHEIKH

As along the Red Sea, access to Sharm el-Sheikh sites is determined by the wind. Note, too, that when conferences and summits are held in the city, boats might not be allowed to traverse the waters leading to certain sites. Regardless, the diving is guaranteed to be dazzling pretty much everywhere.

Jackson Reef, Tiran Strait. Favored by dolphins, turtles, and humphead wrasse (aka Napoleons), this reef has impressive gardens of soft and hard corals and varieties of brightly hued fish. Many consider it the Tiran Strait's most colorful and beautiful site.

SS *Thistlegorm*, Ras Muhammed National Park. A German bomb sunk this 400-foot cargo steamer in 1941. The explosion ripped the superstructure apart, scattering war supplies across the seabed and making it a spectacular wreck dive.

EGYPT'S BEST BEACHES

Sharks Bay in Sharm el-Sheikh

A long coral reef along Egypt's Red Sea Coast has resulted in superb beaches. Over thousands of years, dead coral has been eroded into fine golden sand that is fairly stable owing to the lack of tides and strong currents—or even extreme weather events, such as hurricanes.

Until the latter part of the 20th century, the sandy shores along the Sinai Peninsula and the Red Sea were almost untouched by human development. Still, despite this having changed in recent decades, making Sharm el-Sheikh and resorts towns on the so-called Red Sea Riviera increasingly popular, it's still possible to find a beach where you can escape the crowds.

Note that some of the best sandy stretches are reserved for guests of the hotels or resorts that back them. Hence, in this region, you want to select your accommodation as much for its beach as for its other amenities. Also, some beaches, either public or private, close at sunset. As this is when the mosquitos emerge, though, most beachgoers have already left by then, anyway.

TURTLES IN THE SINAI

Green, hawksbill, leatherhead, and loggerhead turtles nest in the region, coming ashore on beaches in early summer to lay their eggs. Immediately after hatching, the young make their way to the water and out into the open sea. The males never come ashore again, but the females will return to their birthplace at around the age of 20, to lay their own eggs and begin another life cycle.

Egypt's Best Beaches

EL GOUNA
Hotel beaches in El Gouna are private, reserved solely for the guests of the resorts. The region does, however, have a couple of public beaches.

Mangroovy Beach. The sand is plentiful and golden, but the main draw here is the kitesurfing in the seemingly endless offshore shallows. As the name suggests, the groove here is cool throughout the day and wild at night, when the beach parties kick off.

Zeytouna Beach. El Gouna's main and only public-access beach edges an offshore island with gently lapping waters and a whole raft of amenities and offerings, from salsa lessons to dives in coral reefs just offshore.

HURGHADA
On the whole, Hurghada's beaches aren't as good as those on the Sinai coast. Since there are no decent public options, here it's especially important to pick a resort with one of the better stretches of sand.

Makadi Bay. A house reef just a few feet offshore mirrors this long, sinuous golden beach. A series of luxury resorts have sprung up here since the late

Beach resort on Makadi Bay

1990s, each looking to cater to your every whim.

Giftun Island. Great swaths of pale sand surround this small island 45 minutes offshore, leading into iridescent shallows that are perfect for snorkeling. Not only is the marine life amazing here, but the beach is picture perfect.

SHARM EL-SHEIKH
Sharm has some of Egypt's best beaches and most lavish resorts.

Main Beach, Ras Muhammed National Park. This relatively short strand at the heart of a protected area offers options for sunning, as well as for snorkeling and diving around the corals just offshore. The sea life is incredible, even in the shallows.

Na'ama Bay. What could be better than a beautiful arc of fine golden sand fronted by azure shallows and backed by excellent restaurants, bars, and water sports shops? The catch is that this beach draws crowds.

Shark's Bay. This public beach is a bit removed from the always bustling Na'ama Bay boardwalk so it's good for those looking for a smaller, quieter option. Admission is about LE120, and there is good diving off the shore reef.

Beach at Na'ama Bay, Sharm el-Sheikh

For centuries, European traders and Arab merchants had to sail around the Cape of Good Hope to travel east to Asia from Europe and the Mediterranean. However, 2,000 years earlier, ancient Egyptians had that problem licked. The records of the Greek historian Herodotus speak of a canal begun around 600 BC that connected the Nile to the Gulf of Suez.

The canal was used during the time of Alexander the Great, left to ruin, then reopened during the Arab domination that began around AD 645. It was the primary route between the Nile Valley and the Arab world's trading center in Mecca, on the west coast of Saudi Arabia. Then the ancient canal was once again abandoned, and traders returned to desert treks that put their goods and camels at risk. Aside from the accounts of historians, all traces of that canal have vanished. The Suez Canal—an effort on the parts of thousands of Egyptian men who manually shoveled tons of sand between 1859 and 1869 to create a 110-km (66-mile) trench through the desert—follows a different course.

Since the dawn of human culture in Africa and the Middle East, the Sinai and Red Sea region have been important crossroads—then a land bridge, now a sea bridge—connecting East and West, North and South. Enormous container ships and fancy ocean liners line up to pass through the Suez Canal.

In Sharm el-Sheikh and along the Red Sea Coast, relaxing on the beach and diving amidst a wealth of marine life are probably the opposite of what you'd expect from a trip to Egypt. The desert itself, inland Sinai, has changed little since the times when Bedouins moved from one watering hole to the next. It remains awe-inspiring, especially if you get up for sunrise and catch the mountains changing from purple to red, then orange to yellow.

The Red Sea continues to be an underwater haven, a living aquarium, in spite of the impact that the rush of divers has had on the reefs. Since the mid-1990s this coastline has undergone a multimillion-dollar makeover and has been transformed into the so-called Red Sea Riviera and marketed successfully to vacationers across northern Europe and countries of the old Soviet bloc. If you want resort amenities and the option of escaping to virgin desert spotted with shady acacia trees and lazy camels, this is the place for you.

Although Egypt is conservative when it comes to everyday attire, guests in the resort areas of Sharm el-Sheikh and the Red Sea often walk around in shorts and tank tops. Some people choose to dress up for dinner, although it is not mandatory. If you plan to visit any of the monasteries, dress modestly. If you will be driving through smaller towns or traveling aboard buses, wear long pants and shirts with sleeves (nothing sleeveless).

Planning

When to Go

From April through October temperatures climb as high as 45°C (113°F). It's a great time to come for diving, though, because the visibility is at its best. From November through March temperatures can be as low as 8°C (46°F), and nighttime temperatures in the desert might even drop below freezing, so bring warm layers in winter.

Sharm el-Sheikh's high season is during the hotter months, but July and August are considered low season, as the heat is oppressive during this time. The Red Sea, on the other hand, is great in winter, which is its most popular time. With the exception the *khamaseen* (sandstorm) season in March, the sun shines here almost every day of the year.

Planning Your Time

It's best to fly directly from Cairo or Luxor to either Sharm el-Sheikh at the southern tip of the Sinai Peninsula or Hurghada on the Red Sea Coast. Both resort communities offer abundant seaside activities and vibrant nightlife, so you need pick only one. That said, if you want to relax on a beach and do some diving, opt for Sharm el-Sheikh. If you're more interested in just diving and experiencing the glitz and glam of nearby El Gouna, head for Hurghada, which also makes a good base for visits to the monasteries of St. Anthony and St. Paul.

Getting Here and Around

AIR

Multiple daily flights on EgyptAir connect both Sharm el-Sheikh and Hurghada to Cairo. Less-frequent direct flights (one to three days per week, depending on demand) connect Sharm el-Sheikh and Hurghada to each other and to Luxor and Aswan, but there is daily service between all cities if you connect through Cairo. Both Sharm and Hurghada have frequent service from many different European destinations on low-cost European airlines as well as on EgyptAir; some of this service is seasonal.

A taxi from the airport in Sharm El-Sheikh to Na'ama Bay costs LE300; add LE100 to this fare if you're heading to downtown Sharm. Hurghada International Airport is in the desert, 4 km (2½ miles) west of the Sheraton at the southern end of town. Most hotels offer airport transfers, but these will need to be pre-booked; the taxi fare from the airport to the Sheraton Road, Sakalla, is around LE100. Farther to the south on the Red Sea coast, Marsa Alam also has an airport; it's about 20 km (12 miles) to the north of the town and just 2½ km (1 mile) west of Port Ghalib.

AIRLINE CONTACTS EgyptAir. ☎ *2/2267–7101 in Cairo, 69/360–3710 in Sharm el-Sheikh, 65/364–3034 in Hurghada* ⊕ *www.egyptair.com.*

AIRPORT CONTACTS Hurghada International Airport. ⊠ *Sheraton Rd., Hurghada* ✛ *4 km (2½ miles) west of the Sheraton* ☎ *65/446–772* ⊕ *hurghada-airport. co.uk.* **Marsa Alam Airport.** ⊠ *Marsa Alam* ☎ *65/370–0021* ⊕ *www.marsa-alam-airport.com.* **Sharm el-Sheikh Airport.** ⊠ *Airport Rd., Sharm el-Sheikh* ☎ *69/360–1140* ⊕ *www.civilaviation.gov.eg/airports/3.*

BUS

Although there is long-distance bus service to Sharm el-Sheikh and places along the Red Sea coast, land travel to several destinations from other parts of Egypt is not recommended for security reasons. Taxi and bus travel between places along the Red Sea Coast is typically safe, however.

Go Bus offers the most frequent and reliable service to cities all across Egypt. It accepts (usually) credit cards, and its website is accurate, reliable, and displays schedule information in English. It offers daily buses between all major cities, and its vehicles tend to be cleaner and more reliable than those of other companies.

"Deluxe" buses don't cost much more than economy buses, and you'll find them to be more spacious and less crowded. Be sure to get to the station ahead of time (or go the day before) to book your ticket. Be aware that ticket salespeople are not always helpful and they may only speak Arabic. Since bus companies change schedules based on demand and alter pick-up/drop-off locations depending on road construction, it's best to ask your hotel which companies are currently operating which routes and how/where to buy a ticket.

CONTACTS Go Bus Company. ⊠ *Qesm Sharm Ash Sheikh* ⊕ *go-bus. com/?lang=en.*

CAR

Renting a car is mostly unnecessary in Sharm el-Sheikh because taxis and buses can easily get you anywhere you want to go. In addition, if you're staying in Na'ama Bay, you can walk to most places.

For security reasons, foreign travelers in vehicles who don't have a resident's permit will be expected to join a convoy for travel to places elsewhere on the Sinai Peninsula. The times for these can vary, so if your hotel has a concierge, ask them to confirm times and the meeting place. If you employ a driver, he will organize your departure time to take into account convoy times, so you don't need to worry.

Roads in the Sinai are mostly single lane, though a two-lane highway is partly built along the west coast. Though the main roads are in fine condition, it's easier to take a taxi instead. Getting to remote sights requires some skill, and negotiating winding roads through the mountains requires extreme caution because local drivers usually don't stay in their own lanes.

The advantage of renting a car and driving to the Red Sea Coast is flexibility, but that might not outweigh the dangers posed by other drivers, including many trucks, and the hairpin turns before Ain Sukhna. If you don't have nerves of steel, fly to Hurghada and hire a taxi (or arrange a tour) to visit the inland monasteries and other destinations along the coast. You definitely won't need a car within Hurghada or El Gouna.

CAR RENTAL CONTACTS Europcar. ☎ *16/554–4313 Sharm el-Sheikh International Airport, 16/661–1025 Hurghada International Airport* ⊕ *www.europcar. com.*

FERRY

The easiest way to get to Sharm el-Sheikh from the Red Sea Coast is by ferry but, unfortunately, ferry operation is largely dependent on tourism, so, if there's little demand, it will not operate. It's best to check with your hotel to determine if the ferry is running and how to book tickets.

When demand is high, the Sharm el-Sheikh–Hurghada ferries generally run daily with alternating slow (5 to 6 hours) and fast (2½ to 3 hours) ferry service. Note that during poor weather conditions, the ferry may take an additional hour or two to cross. Paying in U.S. dollars has traditionally been the norm, but if you pay with a credit card, you might be charged the equivalent in Egyptian pounds. Expect to pay at least $60 for slower ferries and $70 for faster ferries.

Giftun Island has alluring beaches as well as beautiful waters with great snorkeling and diving opportunities.

TAXI

Within Sharm el-Sheikh, a taxi ride will cost about LE70–LE100 and a ride to Dahab will cost about LE500. A cheaper, easier way to get around Sharm is to take the microbus (known as the Blue Bus), which runs up and down the main drag, Peace Road, and costs only LE5. You can flag it down with your hand, though drivers probably beep and slow down for you even if you don't have your hand out. The ride between Na'ama Bay and the Old Market is quick and straightforward, but if you plan to go farther, a taxi would be best.

In Hurghada, taxis are available on the street and will cost at least LE30 to LE50 for short rides around town. To travel between El Gouna and Hurghada, a taxi will cost around LE200. Within El Gouna, taxis are unnecessary since microbuses and boats stop at all key hotels and hot spots, and the Downtown area is very walkable.

Uber works in Hurghada, but sometimes the government doesn't allow the cars to take passengers all the way to the airport so it's best to take a regular taxi there to avoid being dropped off at the security booth and having to walk a long stretch with your luggage.

Emergencies

If you have any security concerns, the Tourist Police will be able to assist. They patrol resort and town centers. For minor health problems, if you are staying at a four- or five-star hotel, there should be a doctor on call. For more serious medical issues, the hospitals at Sharm el-Sheikh, Hurghada, and El Gouna have decent facilities and English-speaking staff. There are also hyperbaric chambers in Sharm el-Sheik and Hurghada, and El Gouna, as well as in El-Quseir, Safaga, and Marsa Alam.

Hotels

Around Sharm el-Sheikh and the Red Sea you'll find everything from luxury resorts to basic motels. Prices are considerably higher in peak seasons (September through November and April through June). European tour operators generally buy rooms in bulk and sell them only as part of holiday packages; therefore, independent travelers may find it difficult to book upscale resort rooms during peak periods. Bear in mind that, as elsewhere in Egypt, there is a precipitous drop in quality between high- and low-end hotels, with very few options in the middle.

■TIP→ **Many hotels cite prices in U.S. dollars or euros, but if you pay with a credit card, your payment might be charged in the equivalent of Egyptian pounds.**

Hotel reviews have been shortened. For full information, visit Fodors.com. Hotel prices are the lowest cost of a standard double room in high season, excluding taxes and service fees.

What it Costs in U.S. Dollars			
$	$$	$$$	$$$$
HOTELS			
under $50	$50–$125	$126–$150	over $150

Restaurants

Resorts in Sharm el-Sheikh and along the Red Sea Coast cater primarily to European tastes, so resort food tends to be Continental and Italian fare and buffet breakfasts. Fresh seafood can be very good. Though it's sometimes incorporated into hotel dinner buffets, typical Egyptian food is most readily available in less-touristed areas.

A few words of caution: Water is not always potable, so bring a good water filter so you don't have to purchase bottled water every day, which is not only environmentally unfriendly but can also get expensive. Likewise, vegetables are not always washed properly, so stay away from uncooked greens, especially lettuce and cucumbers. Oil, ghee, butter, and fat, in general, is very popular, so a dish that you would expect to be light, like sautéed vegetables, may come dripping with oil.

Restaurant reviews have been shortened. For full information, visit Fodors. com. Restaurant prices are the average cost of a main course at dinner or, if dinner is not served, at lunch, excluding taxes and service charges.

What it Costs in Egyptian Pounds			
$	$$	$$$	$$$$
RESTAURANTS			
under LE100	LE100–LE125	LE126–LE150	over LE150

Sharm el-Sheikh

510 km (320 miles) southeast of Cairo.

In the mid-1980s, Sharm el-Sheikh, at the Sinai Peninsula's southern tip, had one hotel, two dive centers, and a snack bar. Today, it has more than 150 hotels; myriad restaurants, dive centers, malls, and casinos; and more Europeans than Egyptians. It's now Egypt's key resort town in an area that marketers call the Red Sea Riviera.

Aside from the National Museum and its ancient artifacts, there are no sights to see here. But if you want to dive, snorkel, windsurf, waterski, parasail, and/or sunbathe before hitting a few bars or clubs, this is the place. Indeed, when it comes to beach resort vacations, Sharm, as it is fondly called, is the firm favorite of singles, couples, and families, too.

With increasing frequency, however, this small corner of the Sinai has been serving more serious purposes, taking the world stage when political leaders gather for Middle East summits or peace talks. In 2017, Sharm also began hosting the annual World Youth Summit, and, in 2022, it was the site of the World Climate Summit.

Sharm has four main areas. Popular Na'ama Bay is home to most of the hotels, as well as restaurants of various culinary merit, souvenir-filled shops, key nightspots, and excellent dive centers. Note that nearly every hotel along the waterfront in Na'ama Bay also operates a second hotel that's directly across the town's busy main drag, Peace Road (aka El Salam Road) on the "mountain side." If you opt to stay in the latter, you'll be allowed to use the beach at the waterfront sister property, and your room will be cheaper.

North of Na'ama Bay is the new district of Nabq and its handful of large resort hotels. South of Na'ama Bay is Hadaba, where an increasing number of hotels have popped up in recent years and where the main highlight is the view of the surrounding area.

South of Hadaba, Sharm al-Maya is often called downtown Sharm el-Sheikh. It's set on the more down-to-earth Sharm el-Sheikh Harbor, where the dive boats dock at night. Here you'll find a few hotels amid Egyptian *ahwas* (cafés) where men smoke *shisha* (water pipes) and play backgammon.

GETTING HERE AND AROUND

At the very tip of the Sinai Peninsula, Sharm receives multiple daily direct flights from Cairo. Daily flights are also available to Sharm from Luxor, Hurghada, and Aswan but most have layovers in Cairo.

Taxis are the best way to get to and from the airport and around the town and its environs. Just be sure to agree

Did You Know?

There are two theories regarding the origin of the name *Sinai*. The ancient inhabitants of this desert worshipped Sin, a moon goddess, therefore naming the land in her honor—perhaps. Or it could be that the Semitic word *sin* (tooth) gets the credit; the peninsula indeed has the shape of a tooth.

on a fare with the driver before you set off. The ferry service linking Sharm with Hurghada on the mainland Red Sea Coast is handy—when it's actually running. Its ability to function relies heavily on tourism, so when there are few visitors, it doesn't operate.

◉ Sights

Sharm el-Sheikh Museum

HISTORY MUSEUM | As part of a grand plan to showcase Egyptian history across the country, the state-of-the-art Sharm el-Sheikh Museum opened in 2017 with major ancient pharaonic artifacts. Notable items include the heads of statues of Hatshepsut and Ramses II; the inner and outer coffins of Isetemheb; and the ornate, 21st-Dynasty sarcophagus of the nobleman, Imesy, which was repatriated to Egypt by U.S. authorities in 2010. There's also a small collection of Coptic art. ✉ *Sharm el-Sheikh* ☎ *10/2550–8188 WhatsApp* ⊕ *egymonuments.gov.eg* 🎟 *LE200.*

✿ Beaches

El Fanar Beach

BEACH | In addition to offering Sharm's best shore diving and snorkeling, this public beach—at the southeastern tip of town and surrounded by cafés, bars, restaurants, and lounges—is a great place to relax before or after spending time in the

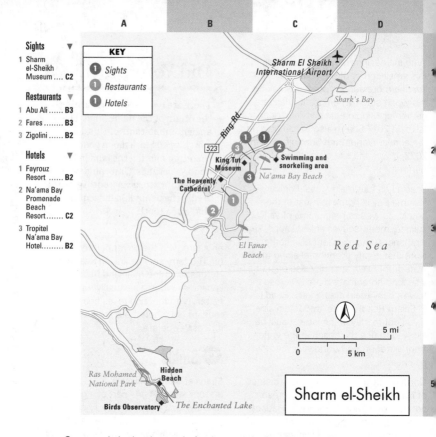

KEY

① Sights

① Restaurants

① Hotels

Sharm El Sheikh
International Airport

Shark's Bay

Ring Rd.

523

King Tut
Museum

The Heavenly
Cathedral

Swimming and
snorkeling area

Na'ama Bay Beach

El Fanar
Beach

Red Sea

0   5 mi

0   5 km

Ras Mohamed
National Park

Hidden
Beach

Birds Observatory   The Enchanted Lake

Sharm el-Sheikh

water. Come early in the day to sip fresh juice on a waterfront swing or to curl up with a book on a cushy lounge chair. At lunch, enjoy pizza, pasta, or fresh seafood. In the evening, smoke a shisha and unwind while enjoying sunset views that are the best in the city. Things hop here till about 2 am; on weekends, a lot of places have live music. **Amenities:** food and drink; water sports. **Best for:** partiers; sunset. ⊠ *Sharm el-Sheikh.*

Na'ama Bay Beach

BEACH | FAMILY | This long strip of sand has many private stretches overseen by the hotels that line the beach. Some sections are calm and quiet, while others are busy, with loud music and resort-led exercise and dance classes. Some areas also attract a lot of families with extensive playgrounds, though these are typically only accessible to hotel guests. Note, too, that the entire beach area closes at sunset. Even if you don't plan to get in the water, you can enjoy the view from one of many boardwalk restaurants that are open to everyone. Many dive shops and tour companies also have offices along the boardwalk, so it's a good place to find out about tours and water-based activities. **Amenities:** food and drink; water sports. **Best for:** swimming, walking. ⊠ *Na'ama Bay, Sharm el-Sheikh.*

🍴 Restaurants

The Na'ama Bay boardwalk is restaurant central: just stroll along the promenade and have your pick from Italian, Middle Eastern, Southeast Asian, and American-style food. Grilled sea bass marinated in lemon juice, pepper, onions, and fresh garlic and served with french fries, is a local favorite. For the best food in town, however, you'll have to leave the hotel district and head to the Old Market area.

★ Abu Ali

$$ | **MIDDLE EASTERN** | Although this is a great place to sample *ful* (a hearty, flavorful stew of mashed fava beans) and *ta'amiya* (Egyptian-style felafel), save room for baba ghanoush (stewed eggplant with tomatoes and tahini) and the *mashi* (stuffed grape leaves, zucchini, and baby eggplant). **Known for:** local favorite; near the Old Market;. Egyptian staple dishes. ⑤ *Average main: LE100* ⊠ *Sharm el-Sheikh* ⊟ *No credit cards.*

Fares

$$$ | **SEAFOOD** | Though you'll find decent fish dishes in nearly every Sharm restaurant, Fares is one of the town's best seafood restaurants, with grouper and snapper that's fresh from the Red Sea. This branch is near the Old Market shopping district; there's also a branch in Na'ama Bay. **Known for:** fantastic shrimp, calamari, and clams; you can bring your own alcohol; set in a great walking district. ⑤ *Average main: LE150* ⊠ *Old Market, Sharm el-Sheikh* ☎ *69/366–3076* ⊟ *No credit cards.*

Zigolini

$$$$ | **ITALIAN** | Inside the Maritim Jolie Ville Hotel, this Italian restaurant has been serving some of the best food—the lamb chops and the spaghetti with fried garlic and shrimp are especially good—in town since 1998. Grab a table by the window for a nice view of the shopping promenade. **Known for:** one of few hotel restaurants where locals also dine; well-trained chef from Italy; can arrange a romantic dinner on the beach. ⑤ *Average main: LE400* ⊠ *Qesm Sharm Ash Sheikh, Sharm el-Sheikh* ☎ *69/360–0100.*

 ## Hotels

Fayrouz Resort

$$$ | **HOTEL** | **FAMILY** | Across the boardwalk from the largest stretch of beachfront on Na'ama Bay, this hotel's whitewashed, low-rise bungalows sit amid mature gardens. **Pros:** within walking distance of Na'ama Bay attractions; a good range of on-site activities; family rooms mean kids aren't hidden behind a connecting door. **Cons:** some rooms are in need of attention; family atmosphere may not appeal to singles; front rooms look out over the boardwalk and lack privacy. ⑤ *Rooms from: $130* ⊠ *Na'ama Bay* ☎ *69/360–1043* ⊕ *www.jazhotels.com* ⇱ *210 rooms* ⑩ *Free Breakfast.*

Na'ama Bay Promenade Beach Resort

$ | **HOTEL** | **FAMILY** | On the waterfront side of Peace Road, this hotel offers comfortable, no-frills accommodations and good facilities. **Pros:** excellent service; great location right on the beach and boardwalk; reliable on-site restaurant. **Cons:** family atmosphere might bother couples or solo travelers; rooms are outdated; thin walls mean you'll hear kids if they're staying in the next room. ⑤ *Rooms from: $80* ⊠ *El Salam Rd., Na'ama Bay* ☎ *69/360–0190* ⊕ *all.accor.com* ⇱ *216 rooms* ⑩ *Free Breakfast.*

Tropitel Na'ama Bay Hotel

$$$ | **HOTEL** | **FAMILY** | The Downtown location suits young singles, couples, and anyone else who wants to be one step from shops, restaurants, and nightspots. **Pros:** nice pool; upper-floor rooms have private balconies; different meal plans available. **Cons:** not directly on the beach; not a lot of room around the pool if the hotel is full; can be noise from Na'ama Bay's clubs, which remain open until 3 or 4 am. ⑤ *Rooms from: $140* ⊠ *Corner of Sultan Qabous St. and King of Bahrain St., Old Market Area, Na'ama Bay* ☎ *69/360–0570* ⊕ *www.tropitelhotels.com* ⇱ *390 rooms* ⑩ *All-Inclusive.*

Nightlife

Sharm el-Sheikh may be hot, but its nightlife is super cool. The resort area is one of the must-play gigs on the international celebrity DJ circuit, and the young and beautiful from across Europe fill the clubs. Surrounded by cafés, bars, restaurants, and lounges, El Fanar Beach is a hot spot, especially on weekends, when a lot of places have live music. Elsewhere, the town also buzzes into the early hours of the morning; after a night of dancing, you can head to one of the many *shisha* (water-pipe) cafés, sink into a lounger, and reflect on life. If you feel lucky, head to a casino for slots or the gaming tables.

BARS

Camel Bar

BARS | Regulars love the relaxed atmosphere (and the air-conditioning) at Sharm's original "anything goes" dive bar. You can also head to the rooftop bar, where you'll find a comfortable area with plump cushions and rugs—as well as ringside seats for the Na'ama Bay evening bustle. ⊠ *Camel Hotel, King of Bahrain St., Na'ama Bay* ☎ *69/360–0700.*

Little Buddha

BARS | A sibling of the ultra-sophisticated Buddha Bar in Paris, this cool, laid-back lounge offers great music from the resident DJ (or the occasional special guest). The lounge is also known for its excellent sushi bar and restaurant. The atmosphere suits couples and singles over 25. ⊠ *Tropitel Na'ama Bay Hotel, Corner of Sultan Qabous St. and King of Bahrain St., Old Market Area, Na'ama Bay* ☎ *69/360–0570 WhatsApp, 069/360–1030* ⊕ *www.buddhabar.com/en/little-buddha/little-buddha-sharm-el-sheikh/.*

CASINOS

Casino Royale

THEMED ENTERTAINMENT | This casino offers American roulette, blackjack, poker, and also has 77 slot machines. It's all set in a hall designed in Ancient Egyptian–style.

⊠ *Maritim Jolie Ville Resort & Casino, El-Salam, Na'ama Bay* ☎ *69/360–1731 WhatsApp* ⊕ *www.casinoroyale.com.eg/home.*

Sinai Grand Casino

THEMED ENTERTAINMENT | The Middle East's largest casino is a veritable palace of slot machines and gaming tables, including blackjack and several styles of poker. Vegas-style shows and a restaurant put the icing on the cake. ⊠ *El-Salam Rd., Na'ama Bay* ☎ *69/360–1052 WhatsApp, 069/360–1050* ⊕ *sinaigrand-casino.com.*

CLUBS

Marquee

DANCE CLUBS | It's possible to turn day into night at this beach club, where an Italian restaurant becomes a buzzing, open-air dance club. The setting is dramatic thanks to fantastic coastal vistas. Chill out away from the beat in various private, carpeted corners or on rocks that are stunningly lit by the varying hues of the disco lights. If your taxi driver doesn't recognize the name, direct him to "El Fanar," the venue's previous moniker. ⊠ *El Fanar St., Hadaba* ☎ *10/1155–5516 WhatsApp* ⊕ *www.facebook.com/marqueesharm.*

Pacha

DANCE CLUBS | The queen of Sharm clubs—favored by an under-30 European crowd—is an open-air venue with a top-notch sound system. DJs punctuate the musical rotation of funk, house, and trance with occasional chill-out sessions. ⊠ *Sanafir Hotel, King of Bahrein St., Na'ama Bay* ☎ *12/8215–1010 WhatsApp* ⊕ *pacha-sharm.com.*

🛍 Shopping

Sharm brims with shops selling mass-produced goods. Aside from Sinai- or Red Sea–themed T-shirts, there's a dearth of good-quality, Egyptian souvenirs. Most hotels have shopping arcades, but prices will be at least double what you would pay in Cairo, so if you plan to spend time in the capital, save your shopping budget for that part of your itinerary.

Aladin

CRAFTS | This is one of the best boutiques in Na'ama Bay, and the place to find genuine Egyptian handicrafts that range from terracotta and other decorative items to hand-woven cotton or linen scarves. ✉ Front Royal Mall, Na'ama Bay ☎ 10/9941–8756 WhatsApp, 69/360–0305 ⊕ www.facebook.com/aladinSharm.

Na'ama Bay Marketplace

MARKET | This shopping center across from the Pacha nightclub has more than 20 stores selling everything from high-quality carpets and expensive jewelry to water pipes and T-shirts. When things in town are busy, many shops stay open until late, so you can stroll and shop when it's cooler. ✉ Naama Bay Hotel, Kahramana, Hussein Salem St., Na'ama Bay.

★ Sharm Old Market

MARKET | FAMILY | In addition to the usual souvenir kitsch, the region's largest traditional shopping district sells genuine Bedouin carpets and leather goods, some of which are handmade in small, family-owned workshops. You could easily spend a few hours browsing, perhaps stopping for a bite at one of the many good restaurants in the area. ✉ Sharm el Maya.

🏃 Activities

There are plenty of water sports to choose from here—waterskiing (you can take lessons or barefoot ski), windsurfing, parasailing, and paddleboarding. Another favorite, banana boating, is great fun: five or six people straddle a yellow, banana-shaped boat and hold on for dear life as a speedboat pulls them around the bay. The driver will try to throw you off by taking sharp turns; just hope you don't fall onto any fire coral.

Ask your hotel what activities it offers, or head to the beach at Na'ama Bay where several water-sports companies operate right from the beach, serving hotel guests and non-guests alike.

DIVING AND SNORKELING

Almost every hotel rents space to independent dive shops, most of which provide the same services for the same prices: PADI, SSI, and CMAS courses from beginner to instructor levels; three- to seven-day safaris; and daily trips to Ras Muhammad, Tiran, and other top local sites. What sets the dive centers apart is their degree of professionalism, quality of their guides and boats, and their level of hospitality.

Supervised introductory dives, local boat dives, and shore dives cost about $90 for two dives, weights included. The price typically goes down if you schedule more than two dives. Daily equipment rental costs about $40. A four-day, open-water certificate course costs about $375.

When business is slow, dive shops might not send boats to all the top open-water sites. If you're interested in a specific dive, you might have to check with more than one operator to see if its being offered. Remember, though, that there is also excellent shore diving.

All dive centers rent snorkeling equipment, and some run specific snorkeling trips, though there's also good snorkeling from the shore at most resorts. The best shore snorkeling is found off El Fanar beach, a 15-minute drive south of Na'ama Bay. As it's popular with both divers and snorkelers, it's best to arrive early to avoid the crowds.

■ TIP➜ Wherever you snorkel, wear a T-shirt or even a wet suit to protect your back from the sun. Sunscreen alone does not provide enough protection.

A diver surveys the *Thistlegorm,* a WW II–era wreck in the waters off Ras Muhammad National Park near Sharm el-Sheikh.

DIVE SITES
Jackfish Alley

SCUBA DIVING | This is a great drift dive, with glass fish and basking stingrays, a coral garden, and a gully where you will probably see large jackfish. ⊠ *Beach Albatros Resort, Sharm el-Sheikh.*

★ Ras Muhammad National Park

SCUBA DIVING | At the southernmost tip of the Sinai Peninsula, Ras Muhammad National Park is considered one of the world's top places for both open-water and shore diving, with great beaches and more than 10 reefs. The yellow starkness of the desert contrasts wonderfully with the explosion of life and color under the water. The most popular boat-dive plan includes Shark's Reef and Jolanda Reef, where you can see hordes of great fish, beautiful coral, and some toilets and sinks deposited by the Cypriot freight-er *Jolanda,* which sank here in 1980. Although it's a phenomenal dive, it's not the best choice for inexperienced divers. ⊠ *Sharm el-Sheikh* ✛ *30 km (15 miles) south of Sharm el-Sheikh.*

Ras Nasrani

SCUBA DIVING | Ras Nasrani is a favorite shore dive that can also done by boat. If you enter from the shore, you might be lucky enough to get a private tour of the reef with the resident Napoleon fish (large species of wrasse), which will take you around and bring you right back to your point of entry. Remember *not* to feed it—or any other fish. ⊠ *18 km (11 miles) northeast of Na'ama Bay, Sharm el-Sheikh.*

Thistlegorm

SCUBA DIVING | The *Thistlegorm* wreck, in open waters protected by and just north-west of Ras Muhammad National Park, is a diving-safari favorite. Some companies in Sharm will organize trips that begin at 4 am and return you to Sharm, exhaust-ed, at 5 pm. Strong currents and low visibility make this a hard dive, but it's a fantastic site. ⊠ *Sharm el-Sheikh.*

Tiran Straits Reefs

SCUBA DIVING | Some of Sharm's most-visited sites are situated between the peninsula's east coast and Tiran Island. Trips across the Straits of Tiran take up to an hour and can be rough, but the diving opportunities make the journey worthwhile. On a daylong outing, you cover two of the area's four reefs. North to south they are Jackson, Woodhouse, Thomas, and Gordon. The waters here are popular for their strong fly currents, sunken oil drums, and rich coral walls. You might also spot some big fish like the local Napoleon wrasse. ✉ *Sharm el-Sheikh*.

OPERATORS
Sinai Blues

SCUBA DIVING | This dive center is the cream of the crop, but, then again, what else would you expect from an operator based in a Four Seasons resort? You'll pay more for dives here, but the center not only has fantastic guides and gear but also some of the fastest speed boats around. Divers must be certified and at least 15 years of age but there is programming for children as young as 6. A minimum of four divers is required to book. ✉ *Four Seasons Resort, 1 Four Seasons Blvd., Sharm el-Sheikh* ☎ *12/7222–7379 WhatsApp, 69/360–3555* ⊕ *www.sinaiblues.com.*

★ SUBEX

SCUBA DIVING | This Swiss-run company has an international reputation for being well-equipped, with clean and modern facilities, top-notch gear, and highly trained staff. Guided dives go out with a maximum of four people, and everyone in the group must do an orientation dive to determine experience levels. Given the very small group sizes (a rarity in Sharm) and strong emphasis on safety and skill-building, SUBEX is an especially good option for divers who are just getting their feet wet. It's also popular with very experienced divers who don't want to be grouped with seven beginner divers or who may just need help renting gear or choosing where they can dive alone. The dive shop is conveniently located on the Na'ama Bay boardwalk so you can easily pop in to chat with staff. Note, too, that SUBEX offers snorkeling day trips. ✉ *Maritim Jolie Ville Hotel, Na'ama Bay* ☎ *69/366–0122, 69/360–0122* ⊕ *www.subex.org.*

GOLF
★ Jolie Ville Golf & Resort

GOLF | What do California fan palms, Jerusalem thorns, Hong Kong orchids, and sand dunes have in common? They can all be found at Egypt's top golf course. Set along the Red Sea between Sharm El-Sheikh International Airport and the center of Na'ama Bay, this Sanford Associates–designed expanse is a well-watered oasis. The 18-hole course has 17 lakes, and PGA-qualified professionals are on hand to give lessons. Call ahead for tee times and to schedule lessons. ✉ *Um Marikha Bay, Na'ama Bay* ☎ *69/360–3200 for the hotel* ⊕ *jolievillegolf.com/en* 🏌 *Greens fees: $85–$100* ⛳ *18 holes, par 72, 6585 yards.*

GUIDED TOURS
Sun 'n Fun

GUIDED TOURS | Although just about every hotel in Sharm has a travel agency desk that can book camel, jeep, trekking, and water-sport outings, if you want to chat or visit with a stand-alone, full-service agency that organizes such activities, Sun 'n Fun is the best all-around bet. Conveniently situated on the beach in front of the Fayrouz Resort, Sun 'n Fun can arrange everything from car-buggy desert adventures to snorkeling trips (from one hour to a full day), glass-bottom boat sails, banana-boat outings, and pirate-boat dinner cruises. ✉ *Fayrouz Resort, Beach Boardwalk, Sharm el-Sheikh* ☎ *10/1515–7444 WhatsApp* ⊕ *www.sunnfunegypt.com.*

Did You Know?

Coral reefs close to
Egypt's shore support
a rich—and colorful—
ecosystem with more
than 1,000 marine species.

Ain Sukhna

45 km (29 miles) south of Suez, 120 km (75 miles) southeast of Cairo, 362 km (225 miles) northwest of Hurghada.

The warm, turquoise waters off Ain Sukhna (the name means "hot spring") originate at Jabal Ataka, a mountain on the Red Sea Coast. There is little to do here in the way of sightseeing, but it's a convenient day trip from Cairo if, like picnicking Cairenes, you want a sunny day on the shore. The coastline here has been greatly developed in the last decades, with villas and apartments bought up by wealthy capital residents.

GETTING HERE AND AROUND
Although it's just a two-hour drive from Cairo to Ain Sukhna, and the roads through the town of Suez are good, you should consider taking a bus. There is regular, inexpensive service in both directions. Taxis are the best way to get around the town.

 Hotels

Palmera Resort
$ | RESORT | FAMILY | On the sea with a beautiful private beach, the Palmera sprawls amid lush gardens and attracts families and expat workers from Cairo. **Pros:** wide, sandy beach; large main pool; good choice of resort facilities for the price point. **Cons:** no activities or shows at night; some fixtures and fittings are a little worn; mosquitoes can be a problem. ⑤ *Rooms from: $70* ✉ *QC57+P3W Erban Atekah and Al Manayef, Ain Sukhna* ✛ *30 km (20 miles) south of Suez, on the way to Ain Sukhna* ☎ *22/736–0303 WhatsApp* ⊕ *palmerabeachresort.com* ⇨ *282 rooms* ⦿❘ *Free Breakfast.*

Monasteries of St. Anthony and St. Paul

Monastery of St. Anthony: 118 km (73 miles) south of Ain Sukhna, 225 km (140 miles) southeast of Cairo, 290 km (180 miles) northwest of Hurghada. Monastery of St. Paul: 146 km (87 miles) south of Ain Sukhna, 246 km (153 miles southeast of Cairo), 242 km (150 miles) northeast of Hurghada.

Isolated in the mountains near the Red Sea, both of these monasteries have spectacular settings and views. Getting to them isn't exactly a picnic, but their remoteness was the reason the saints chose these caves as their hermitages. The saints' endurance in the desert— against Bedouin raids, changing religious tides, and physical privation—make these sites alluring, and paintings and icons add color to their otherwise stark interiors.

GETTING HERE AND AROUND
To get to the monasteries you will need to rent a car or, preferably (because driving in Egypt is such a harrowing experience), hire a private taxi from Cairo or Hurghada (about LE2,000 roundtrip from either city). Note that Copts fast for 43 days in advance of Christmas, during which time most monasteries are closed to visitors. Call before you set out to confirm that the gates will be open.

Alternatively, SJP tours offers private excursions to both monasteries from Cairo or Hurghada.

CONTACT SJP Tours. ☎ *12/0163–3890* ⊕ *sjptours.com.*

 Sights

The Monastery of St. Anthony
CHURCH | FAMILY | Saint Anthony is a prominent figure in Coptic Christianity because of his influence on the monastic movement. And even though his contemporary, Paul, was the first hermit,

St. Anthony actually lived (to the age of 104) in a cave. It was only after his death in the 4th century that admirers began building his monastery.

Anthony was the more popular of the two. He was born in the middle of the 3rd century AD to wealthy parents who left him with a hefty inheritance upon their death, when he was 18. Instead of reveling in his riches, he sold all his possessions, distributed the proceeds to the poor, sent his sister to a convent, and fled to dedicate his life to God as a hermit in the mountains overlooking the Red Sea.

Disciples flocked to Anthony, hoping to hear his preaching and to be healed. But the monk sought absolute solitude and retreated to a cave in the mountain range of South Qabala. After his death in the 4th century—the hermit lived to age 104—admirers built a chapel and refectory in his memory. Saint Anthony's grew. In the 7th, 8th, and 11th centuries, periodic Bedouin predations severely damaged the structure. It was restored in the 12th century.

Saint Anthony's is deep in the mountains. Its walls reach some 40 feet in height.

Several watchtowers, as well as the bulky walls' catwalk, served as sentry posts. The **Church of Saint Anthony** was built over his grave, and it is renowned for its exquisite 13th-century wall paintings of Saint George on horseback and the three Desert Fathers, restored in the 1990s.

Four other churches were built on the grounds of the monastery over the years. The most important of them is the 1766 **Church of Saint Mark,** which is adorned with 12 domes and contains significant relics.

A 2-km (1-mile) trek—be sure to bring plenty of drinking water along—leads you to **Saint Anthony's Cave,** 2,230 feet above sea level, where he spent his last days. Views of the Red Sea and the surrounding mountains are superb, and you're likely to encounter interesting local bird life on the hike. Inside the cave, among the rocks, pilgrims have left pieces of paper asking the saint for intervention.

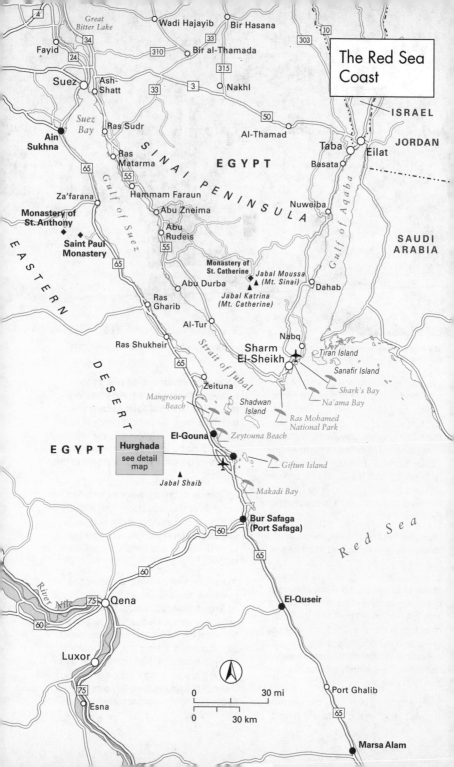

☏ 12/2332–6999 WhatsApp of Father Markos ⊗ Closed Sun.

The Monastery of St. Paul

CHURCH | **FAMILY** | Saint Paul of Thebes (also known as Saint Paul the Anchorite) made his way into the desert to live as a hermit in the 4th century AD, after a wealthy upbringing in Alexandria. The monastery was built in the 5th century, after the saint's death. Following several raids about a thousand years later, the monastery was abandoned. Monks from the Monastery of Saint Anthony eventually reopened Saint Paul's.

A 7-km (4-mile) drive west from the Red Sea Coast highway twists through the rugged mountains and deposits you near the entrance of Saint Paul's Monastery. The high walls of the monastery are surrounded by a village, which has a bakery, mills, and a few surrounding fields. The buildings of the monastery are believed to encompass the cave in which Saint Paul lived for nearly 80 years. In the **Church of Saint Paul**, paintings of the Holy Virgin cover the walls.

To experience the ascetic life of the monastery, you can overnight in guesthouses here; women lodge outside the walls, men inside. For permission to lodge here, and for information on open days and hours, contact the monastery residence in Cairo. ☏ 12/0661–3572 WhatsApp of a monk ⊗ Closed Sat.–Mon.

Hurghada

410 km (255 miles) south of Ain Suhkna; 530 km (331 miles) south of Cairo.

Hurghada is an old fishing town that became a popular base for diving in the 1960s. As a result of the 1967 war between Egypt and Israel, Hurghada was closed to tourism and did not reopen until 1976. By this time, Sharm el-Sheikh, which was under Israeli occupation, was flourishing as a diving town. Hurghada had a lot of catching up to do.

And catch up it did. The town has grown inexorably in the last decade, and most of the development is tourism-related. Now, with a population of about 250,000 and hundreds of hotels in and around it, Hurghada is definitely a Red Sea hot spot.

The first hotels took the town beach-front, which explains the name of the main boulevard (it has 15 speed bumps and runs through the Sakalla district): Shar'a Sheraton. Newer development stretches north along the road to Cairo and south through the Old Vic Village district and another 20 km (12 miles) to Sahl Hasheesh Bay, where vast all-inclusive resort hotels are set on expansive grounds.

Hurghada is known for its strong north-northwesterly winds, so if you plan to lounge about, find a spot with a protective windbreak. From April to October, the hotter months, be prepared to battle the bugs: mosquitoes, light-brown desert flies, and other flying insects that have nasty bites. July and August bring the most bugs so be sure to bring bug repellent and spend your time in the sea.

If it's sun, sand, and sea that you're after, other areas along Egypt's Red Sea Coast have more appealing beaches and desert diversions. Come to Hurghada, however, if you're into scuba diving and/or want to be based in a resort town (as opposed to being merely ensconced at a beach resort).

GETTING HERE AND AROUND

Hurghada Airport receives daily direct flights from Cairo, as well as less frequent direct flights from Sharm. There's also regular air service from/to Sharm, Luxor, and Aswan with a connection in Cairo. Road connections are good along the north coast to Cairo, west to Luxor, and south to Marsa Alam.

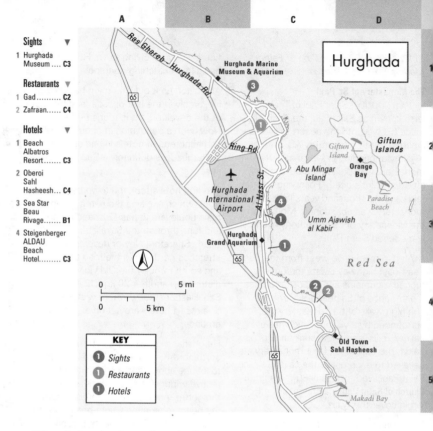

Hurghada

KEY

 Sights

 Restaurants

 Hotels

Although there has been disruption in ferry service to Hurghada from Sharm el-Sheikh, frequent Go Bus service connects the entire Red Sea coast with the rest of Egypt. There are minibuses in Hurghada town, but they tend to be crowded, lack air-conditioning, and experience frequent fare changes. Taxis, which are numerous, are the most practical way to get around.

◉ Sights

Hurghada Museum

HISTORY MUSEUM | FAMILY | Opened in 2021, the first antiquities museum in the Red Sea Governorate is state of the art. Its collection is much smaller than those at museums and archaeological sites in Cairo and Luxor, but its exhibits, nevertheless, include hundreds of artifacts that highlight 5,000 years of Egyptian history.

✉ *Airport Rd., Mubarak 6, Hurghada*
☎ *11/1111–8894 WhatsApp, 11/1111–8893 WhatsApp* ⊕ *hurghadamuseum.com*
🎫 *LE455* ⊗ *Closed Fri.*

🍴 Restaurants

Downtown Hurghada caters primarily to European and Russian package-tour visitors, who are drawn to its abundance of Italian and fast-food eateries featuring kitsch decor. The town's newer hotels are often all-inclusive featuring international buffets of varying levels of quality. There are, however, a couple notable restaurants are worth seeking out.

Gad

$ | MIDDLE EASTERN | For the city's best traditional Egyptian food, head out of your resort and to this unassuming branch of a national restaurant chain. For something special, order the stuffed pigeon, though this is also a good place to enjoy *ta'amiya* (Egyptian-style felafel) and stellar sides of baba ganoush or hummus. **Known for:** efficient service; reasonable prices; simple, well-prepared Egyptian food. $ *Average main: LE70* ✉ *Hurghada 2, Hurghada* ☎ *10/1886–5522 WhatsApp.*

★ **Zafraan**

$$$$ | **INDIAN** | Candlelight and live traditional music make the dining room here romantic, and the menu highlights the varied cuisine of India. Choose from entrees such as the rich *palak paneer* (homemade cottage cheese in spinach) or the flavorful fish curry featuring sea bass; sides include several type of naan as well as fragrant *biryani* (saffron rice with chicken). **Known for:** best Indian food anywhere on the Red Sea; live traditional music; an intimate, romantic setting. $ *Average main: LE400* ✉ *Oberoi Sahl Hasheesh, Sahl Hasheesh Bay, Hurghada* ☎ *65/346–1111, 65/346–1040* ⊕ *www.oberoihotels.com* ☽ *No lunch.*

 Hotels

Beach Albatros Resort

$$ | **ALL-INCLUSIVE** | **FAMILY** | Families love this resort's water-park-like selection of outdoor pools, couples and singles are drawn to it for its location near all the action, and everyone appreciates its clean beach and rates that are more affordable than other properties in the same category. **Pros:** 11 outdoor pools (6 of them heated); near all the nightlife; spacious rooms, some with waterfront balconies. **Cons:** buffet food can be bland; family atmosphere may not appeal to everyone; traffic on the main thoroughfare can be noisy day and night. $ *Rooms from: $120* ✉ *Safaga Rd., Hurghada* ☎ *65/346–4001* ⊕ *www.beachalbatrosresort.com* ☛ *45 rooms* ◎ *Free Breakfast.*

★ **Oberoi Sahl Hasheesh**

$$$$ | **HOTEL** | **FAMILY** | The first boutique, all-suites property along the Red Sea Coast is still the tops, featuring Moorish-style bungalows, each with a living room area, private courtyard, and luxurious bathrooms that have a sunken tub and glass-sided shower opening onto a second, smaller courtyard. **Pros:** a true luxury resort, not a package-tour hotel; 24-hour butler service; plenty of privacy. **Cons:** no evening entertainment; water shoes are required on the rocky, coral-rich beach; it's a 17-km (10-mi) journey to Downtown Hurghada. $ *Rooms from: $300* ✉ *Sahl Hasheesh Bay, Hurghada* ☎ *065/344–0777* ⊕ *www.oberoisahl-hasheesh.com* ☛ *102 suites* ◎ *Free Breakfast.*

Sea Star Beau Rivage

$$ | **ALL-INCLUSIVE** | **FAMILY** | Rooms here are spacious, with water-view balconies, and the beach has a water-sports facility. **Pros:** lots of on-site amenities; staff is friendly and helpful; clean beach. **Cons:** rooms are a bit outdated; there isn't much to see or do outside the hotel; buffet food is bland and uninspiring. $ *Rooms from: $109* ✉ *Al Hilal Military Hospital St., Hurghada* ☎ *10/0538–8592 WhatsApp* ⊕ *seastarbeaurivage.com* ☛ *293 rooms* ◎ *Free Breakfast.*

Steigenberger ALDAU Beach Hotel

$$$ | **HOTEL** | The relaxed luxury of the cathedral-like reception-area atrium—off which are restaurants and the Thalasso Spa—continues in the rooms, which are large and have expansive balconies. **Pros:** amenities include a spa, dive center, and golf course; close to in-town nightlife; fantastic pool area. **Cons:** rooms are somewhat dated; atrium design could lead to possible noise if reception area is busy; rooms are in one vast building rather than being scattered around the resort. $ *Rooms from: $150* ✉ *Yussif Afifi Rd., Old Vic Village, Hurghada* ☎ *65/346–5400* ⊕ *steigenbergeraldauresort.com* ☛ *380 rooms* ◎ *Free Breakfast.*

Nightlife

Hurghada is one of the clubbing hot spots for much younger European party goers (teens to early twenties). Numerous nightspots keep things rocking into the early hours.

BARS

Papa's Bar

BARS | By day, Papa's has a pub atmosphere; things pick up after about 10 pm, though. Whether you're stopping by for a quick cocktail or a draft beer, or you're committed to singing karaoke or dancing salsa until last call, Papa's offers a good time seven nights per week. ⊠ *Hurghada 1, Hurghada* ☎ *10/3366–3316.*

The Tavern

BARS | Part bar, part nightclub, part restaurant, The Tavern wears many hats but always delivers a good time. Depending on the night of the week, you might find live salsa music, DJs spinning electronic music, karaoke, or soccer matches on the big screen. ⊠ *Hurghada 1, Hurghada* ☎ *10/3366–3316 WhatsApp* ⊕ *www. facebook.com/thetvern.hrg.*

CLUBS

Elements Club & Lounge

DANCE CLUBS | Unlike most nightclubs and lounges along the Red Sea, which are mostly designed to mimic European nightlife, Elements is an American-inspired nightclub. From billiards and live sports up on the big screen to hosted DJs, vocal performances, and karaoke nights, Elements offers a little bit of everything. If you get hungry, the kitchen here serves American, Asian, or fusion dishes, and although most restaurants close at 11 pm, you can order from the special late-night menu until 3 am. ⊠ *Steigenberger Aqua Magic Hotel, Hurghada* ☎ *12/7221–2299 WhatsApp.*

Little Buddha

DANCE CLUBS | A sibling of the famed Paris Buddha Bar, this cool sushi bar and lounge by day transforms into a progressive music club with resident and guest DJs after 11:30 pm. And while nightlife lovers primarily come for the music and dancing, the sushi is actually really good. ⊠ *Sinbad Resort, Old Vic Village Rd., Hurghada* ☎ *12/2000–1961 WhatsApp, 65/345–0120.*

Activities

Note that because there are few public beaches—and those that exist are not worth going to—it's best to stick with your hotel's beachfront. The newer hotel developments south of the Downtown area have much better beaches but no public access at all.

In addition to diving and snorkeling, waterskiing, windsurfing, parasailing, kayaking, and paddleboarding are among the aquatic possibilities in Hurghada. Jet skis, however, have been banned from the area. Inquire at your hotel about what activities it offers; the staff can point you in the right direction if your hotel doesn't have what you're looking for.

DIVING

As Hurghada is more prone to strong winds than other areas along the Red Sea, dives on offer are dependent upon the day's weather. You might be able to choose between a wall or plateau dive, but the wind ultimately determines everything. Also don't be fooled by the depth of dive: although some of the best dives in Hurghada are only 6–7 meters deep, you'll find truly spectacular coral.

Supervised introductory dives, local boat dives, and shore dives cost about $90 for two dives, weights included. The price typically goes down if you schedule more than two dives. Daily equipment rental costs about $40; and a four-day, open-water certificate course costs about $375.

DIVE SITES

Abu Hashish

Situated offshore between Hurghada and Sagafa, this site features tall towers of coral that are home to more reclusive marine life such as octopi and seahorses. ⊠ *Hurghada.*

Carless Reef
SCUBA DIVING | Although this dive in the waters northeast of Hurghada is relatively shallow, it features thousands of corals and coral tables. ⊠ *Hurghada.*

Giftun Drift
SCUBA DIVING | Off Small Giftun Island, itself an hour offshore southeast of Hurghada, this beautiful, deep-wall dive teems with marine life. ⊠ *Hurghada.*

Gota Abu Ramada
SCUBA DIVING | Although this site has some of the most colorful and spectacular coral in the Red Sea, it's also popular with snorkelers, so you'll likely have to share the space with many boats. ⊠ *Hurghada.*

OPERATORS
James & Mac
SCUBA DIVING | Knowledgeable, professional, and well-organized, James & Mac is a great option for both new and experienced divers. Its two- and three-day mini safaris are perfect for divers who want to reach more removed sites without having to spend an entire week on a boat. This operator also offer discounts if you book and pay for your dive in advance. ⊠ *Hurghada* ☎ *12/2311–8923 WhatsApp* ⊕ *james-mac.com.*

★ SUBEX
SCUBA DIVING | Top-notch gear, highly trained staff (there's a good chance the instructor will have 25+ years of experience), and small, guided group dives (no more than four people) are among the hallmarks of this internationally recognized, Swiss-run company. Safety is also key. For instance, you must go out with a guide if you have fewer than 30 dives, and all divers must do a skills-assessment dive prior to any trips. Although SUBEX is a great option for divers who are just getting their feet wet, experienced divers appreciate the small-group offerings, as it means they won't have to head out with a lot of beginners. In addition to its office in Hurghada, SUBEX has a shop in Sahl Hasheesh, where there's an excellent 6,000-square-foot house reef. ⊠ *Hurghada 2, Hurghada* ☎ *65/354–3261, 65/354–7593* ⊕ *www. subex.org.*

KITESURFING
Kitesurfing is a growing sport in the Red Sea region, where the wind and water conditions are almost perfect year round, offering tranquil shallows just offshore. You must take a tutorial in order to head out. Prices for an introductory lesson start at about $50 for one hour ($85 for a private lesson) and become increasingly cheaper the more time you book. Although it's a very different sport, it does help to have some windsurfing experience.

In general, the kitesurfing is better in El Gouna and there are more options there, but it can also be done in Hurghada. Should you not want to make the 30-minute drive up to El Gouna (recommended), speak with your hotel to arrange kitesurfing nearby.

El Gouna

20 km (12 miles) north of Hurghada; 510 km (319 miles) south of Cairo.

El Gouna is the dream of an Egyptian businessman who, in only about 10 years, transformed virgin seacoast into a resort town and settlement for more than 20,000 full-time residents. It has its own wells in the mountains, a hospital with a hyperbaric chamber for dealing with divers' decompression issues, four power plants, a school, a department of the American University in Egypt, and an impressive array of services. It's both practically self sustaining and environmentally friendly.

Continued on page 337

THE COPTS: EGYPT'S

Stepping into a Coptic church or monastery feels like walking back into the early centuries of Christianity. Bypassed by most non-Egyptian visitors, Coptic sights have a sanctity and stillness that make them a refuge from more crowded tourist venues. Even those travelers who aren't religiously inclined will find in Egypt's rich Coptic heritage a fascinating perspective on the country's past and present.

CHRISTIANS

The Hanging Church
in Coptic Cairo

Most visitors to Egypt come to experience the splendors of the pharaohs or Islamic and Arabic culture, often overlooking the country's many Christian sites. While exact numbers are elusive, it is likely that 10% of Egypt's current population are Copts, the term for Egyptian Christians. Egypt's contributions to Christianity are many, from the key points of Christian doctrine hammered out in Alexandria, to monasticism and the first compilation of the New Testament. Today, the Coptic Church is undergoing a revival and maintains a large diaspora outside of Egypt. Visiting the ancient churches of Coptic Cairo, strolling through desert monasteries, or tracing the path of the Holy Family during their time in Egypt all offer glimpses of an unforgettable facet of Egypt's spiritual life.

DEEP ROOTS

The Coptic Orthodox Church traces the origin of Christianity in Egypt to St. Mark, who is said to have come to Alexandria around AD 60 and begun making converts. At the time, Alexandria was a thriving intellectual center, where dogma on the nature of Christ was worked out in debates. Other early Egyptian Christians turned to the mystical philosophy known as Gnosticism, as shown by the revealing Gnostic Gospels, an eye-opening cache of papyrus texts found in Nag Hammadi in Upper Egypt in 1945.

Some scholars think that Christianity took hold so firmly in Egypt because it melded easily with pagan concepts and symbols: for Egyptians familiar with the divine triads such as Osiris, Isis, and Horus, the leap to the Christian trinity was not difficult. Likewise, the common motif of Isis nursing Horus was easily transferable to the image of Virgin and Child. Others have pointed to the similar shapes of the ankh and the cross.

MONASTICISM

Roman persecutions of Christians fell hard on Egypt's growing Christian population, most notably under the emperor Diocletian. Even earlier, persecutions had often led Christians to seek refuge in desert places, far from both ecclesiastical and imperial authorities. Their experiences almost certainly contributed to the emergence of monasticism in Egypt: one early desert hermit was St. Anthony (251–356), whose anchoritic life inspired numerous followers. But it was the communal religious life, according to rules laid out by St. Pachomius (290–346) that became the model for monasteries across the Christian world. By the early 4th century, monasteries were springing up all over Egypt, including the Red Sea

St. Paul Monastery

monasteries of St. Anthony and St. Paul. Interest in Coptic monasteries has seen a revival in recent decades.

RIFTS

The nature of Jesus' divinity took on national and ethnic dimensions in the 5th century, when a debate over whether Jesus had one divine nature or two natures—both human and divine. Adherents of the one-nature belief (known as "Monophysites") tended to be Egyptian Christians, while the dual-nature advocates had the backing of Constantinople and its Greek-speaking hierarchy. Following the divisive Council of Chalcedon in 451, the resistance of Egyptian Monophysites to Constantinople's imposed orthodoxy became the basis for the separate Coptic Orthodox Church. Although Copts rarely describe themselves as Monophysites today, they remain a separate religious church, with their own Pope, known formally as the "Pope of Alexandria and the Patriarch of the See of St. Mark." The Cop-

Dome inside St. George Church, Coptic Cairo

tic language, a late derivation of ancient Egyptian, is no longer spoken today but continues to be the primary ecclesiastical language of the Coptic Church.

THE COPTS TODAY

The word "Copt" comes from an Arabic alteration of the Greek Aiguptos, which is also the source of our word "Egypt." Aiguptos was the Greek rendering of the ancient Egyptian name for the capital Memphis, known as Ha-ka-Ptah, or "The Abode of the Soul of Ptah." So while "Copt" once referred to Egyptians in general, it now refers specifically to those Egyptians who have remained Christian. Copts are well-represented in the ranks of Egypt's business elite and in public life. Boutros-Boutros Ghali, for example, served as Egypt's foreign minister before becoming the United Nations Secretary General. While they are a religious minority today, and there are occasional flare-ups of Muslim–Copt tension, Egyptians' strong sense of a shared Egyptian identity that transcends

religious affiliation has ensured Copts a place in the modern nation.

THE HOLY FAMILY IN EGYPT

The Gospel of St. Matthew relates that an angel appeared to Joseph in a dream, warning him of Herod's plans to have the infant Jesus killed: "Arise, take the young Child and His mother, flee to Egypt, and stay there until I bring you word" (Matthew, 2:13). Drawing on this brief scriptural reference, Egyptian Christians early on embraced the tradition of the Holy Family's flight to Egypt.

In the Coptic tradition, the Holy Family stayed 3½ years in Egypt, passing through various locations from the Delta all the way to Asyut in Upper Egypt and performing miracles en route. In all, the Coptic Church recognizes around two dozen sites as part of the Holy Family's route, and these are often revered by both local Copts and Muslims alike as holy places.

THE HOLY FAMILY ROUTE

Since 2000, Egypt has officially promoted Holy Family tourism encouraging religiously inclined tourists to visit Coptic sites. The Coptic Church officially celebrates the Holy Family's sojourn on June 1 each year, when these sites are likely to be crowded. Other times they are not. Except in greater Cairo, many of these places are well off the beaten path. The full Holy Family route is circuitous, with some places practically inaccessible to tourists. In addition, some of the more accessible sites experience long-term closures for restoration work and other reasons. With the right planning and/or a good guide, however, it is possible to visit many of them.

❶ FARMA: Fleeing from Herod, the Holy Family crossed northern Sinai, arriving in Pelusium (now Farma) in what is now the east side of the Suez Canal. Note that this site may be closed for security reasons. Check ahead.

❷ BUBASTIS: The first city in the Delta they came to was the cult center of the cat goddess Bastet. Although the locals were unwelcoming, the infant Jesus created a spring here that is believed to have healing properties (although as punishment for the townsfolk's ill treatment, the well has no effect on locals). The well is still in use and is located just outside the modern city of Zagazig. Check on this site before heading out as it may be closed for security reasons.

❸ SAKHA: The town is famous for a stone purporting to show the mark of Jesus' footprint. The stone, known as "Bikha Isus" (Jesus' Footprint), was buried for centuries, but unearthed during excavations

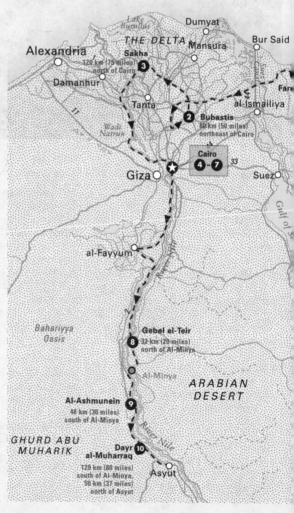

Church of St. Sergius

*Mediterranean
Sea*

al-Arish

55

5 km (47 miles) from Bur Said
by service taxi

3

of an ancient church in the 1980s. Although accessible by bus or taxi from Cairo, for security reasons, this site may be closed. Check before heading out.

4 THE VIRGIN'S TREE AT MATARIYA: This site, near the Ain Shams district of northeast Cairo, is accessible by Cairo subway (the EL MATARIYA stop). The site is a sycamore tree under which the Virgin Mary rested and where Jesus again brought forth a spring. The tree and spring are now in a sizeable walled enclosure, along with an open-air shrine. Although the site is an easy afternoon from Cairo, it might be closed owing to ongoing restoration work. Check ahead.

5 CHURCH OF OUR LADY OF EL-ZEITOUN: While this church was not on the original Holy Family route, it was the site of a yearlong apparition of the Virgin in 1968, where she appeared at the top of the church spires. Thousands came to see it (including Egyptian president Gamal Abdul Nasser), and it has since become a popular pilgrimage site. The El-Zeitoun neighborhood is just southeast of Matariya, one stop away on the Cairo Metro, at HELMIYET EL-ZEITOUN.

6 CHURCH OF ST. SERGIUS: The church in Coptic Cairo is built over a cave where the Holy Family spent the night. The cave, now a crypt below the altar, is unfortunately flooded.

7 CHURCH OF THE HOLY VIRGIN AT MA'ADI: Located on the waterfront corniche in Cairo's Ma'adi district, south of the Maadi Yacht Club, this church was built at the site where the Holy Family boarded a boat to take them to Upper Egypt. The stone stairs leading down to the water are believed to be the same ones the Holy Family used.

8 GEBEL EL-TEIR: Its name means "Bird Mountain," and fittingly enough it sits high on the east side of the Nile and is home to plenty of birds. The site itself is a 4th-century monastery called Deir al-'Adhra (Monastery of the Virgin), built on a site where the Holy Family spent the night. The church at this monastery has been greatly restored in recent years. The complex is a few miles' drive from the town of Al-Minya, which is 272 km (168 miles) south of Cairo.

9 AL-ASHMUNEIN: About 30 miles south of Al-Minya, this was a further stop on the itinerary and the site of a major ancient city called Hermopolis Magna. The extensive ruins still visible (including an early Coptic basilica) testify to its importance then as a pagan center. Taxis can be hired in Al-Minya for a round-trip visit.

10 DAYR AL-MUHARRAQ: Literally meaning "The Burnt Monastery," this working monastery is built over a cave where the Holy Family lived for six months—their longest single stay during their time in Egypt. Coptic tradition calls the church here the oldest in Egypt.

TIPS FOR THE HOLY FAMILY ROUTE

Mosaic at the Hanging Church, Coptic Cairo.

GETTING AROUND

Seeing some of Egypt's Coptic sites independently has its difficulties. Bus service is hit or miss, and renting a car and driving yourself can be stressful, with overly cautious local authorities possibly requiring that you be accompanied by a police escort to certain out-of-the-way places. In some instances, like visiting sites in the Delta on a day trip from Cairo, you might be able to use taxis. Before setting out, check that the driver knows the area, and negotiate a fixed round-trip fare, including wait time. Alternatively, you could ask the staff at your hotel to arrange a car and driver.

TOUR COMPANIES

As Holy Family tourism has grown in the last decade, a number of specialized travel companies have appeared to facilitate tours. Dr. Cornelis (Kees) Hulsman, a Dutch authority on Coptic life, runs Holy Family Egypt (⊕ www. holyfamilyegypt.com). SJP Tours (⊕ sjptours.com, ☎ 2/0163–3890) can arrange tours along the Holy Family route and also to the St. Paul and St. Anthony monasteries from either Cairo

or Hurghada. While both companies primarily focus on private tours, they can sometimes incorporate solo travelers into existing group tours.

ADVICE FOR VISITORS

All of the Holy Family sites are places of worship for Egyptian Copts, so appropriate dress is a must. That means no shorts, short skirts, or sleeveless tops, for both genders. In many monasteries and churches, you should remove your shoes and leave them outside the door before entering a chapel. Often a monk or priest will be happy to show you around the site; due to the extensive Coptic diaspora, don't be surprised to find a monk who speaks fluent English in even the most remote location. There is no cost, but donations are always welcome.

PRACTICAL TIPS

■ Note that Fridays tend to be the busiest days.

■ A number of monasteries also own farmland and sell their produce to visitors. If you're so inclined, pick up a bag of fruit for the ride back to Cairo or a bottle of olive oil.

■ A visit to the Virgin's Tree at Matariya is a surprisingly serene experience; although the city is just outside the walls, the water and the ancient tree make for a peaceful experience. Note, though, that the site is undergoing restoration and may be closed.

■ Gebel El-Teir is best visited in the morning, so the sun is behind you when you look west across the river. Also, without much shade at the top of the hill, the monastery gets quite warm in the afternoon. If you want to stay the night, there's a clifftop hotel here with fabulous views of the Nile and surrounding fields.

Designed around a series of seawater lagoons, the heart of El Gouna is al-Qafr, also known as Downtown, a modern rendition of a traditional Egyptian settlement. To the north is Abu Tig, a majestic marina that's filled with multimillion-dollar yachts and was designed to re-create the atmosphere of the French or Italian Riviera. A second, larger marina with accompanying hotels, apartments, and a golf course was added in 2010. South of al-Qafr is El Gouna's original golf course, which is surrounded with lagoon-side villas and apartments.

Compared to Hurghada, El Gouna (often referred to simply as "Gouna") looks clean, fresh, and brand new. Year round, it's full of beautiful people—a mix of wealthy and famous Egyptians, expat workers from Cairo, and foreign tourists—who come to see and be seen and who expect sophisticated hotels and a wide range of water sports activities. Bank on spending significantly more for most things than you would in Hurghada.

GETTING HERE AND AROUND

Hurghada is a 20-minute drive to the south, and its airport offers links to Aswan, Cairo, and Sharm el-Sheikh. Go Bus offers regular connection from Hurghada and on to Cairo and other cities to the north.

El Gouna's excellent public transport system connects all the hotels to the central districts. Downtown and the marina area are walkable, but if you need to go farther afield, you can hire a *tuk tuk* (motorbike taxi) for a few dollars (or Euros). Flag the drivers down on the street, or ask your hotel to call one for you. Transportation within the resorts is free, whether by microbus, *tuff-tuff* (open-air bus), tuk-tuk, or boat.

VISITOR INFORMATION

Water sports, desert excursions, and golf are available in El Gouna. If you can't arrange these at your hotel, the local information center can help. What's

Did You Know?

El Gouna recycles 97% of its waste by using gray water on the golf course, composting what's natural, and selling or up-cycling plastics and other items.

more, if you call its hotline, a staffer can connect you with any hotel or restaurant in town.

CONTACT Info Center. ✉ *El Gouna* ☎ *16650 hotline number from any phone within El Gouna* ⊕ *www.elgouna.com.*

🍴 Restaurants

El Gouna has a wide range of international eateries throughout Downtown and in the hotels, and they offer everything from snacks to silver-service dining. Although the dining options are better and more varied than those in Hurghada, prices are higher here, too.

Hydra

$$$$ | SEAFOOD | A good option in the heart of El Gouna, this restaurant serves a wide range of seafood as well as steaks in the evening. During the day, you'll find light snacks and sandwiches like their delicious *shawarma* (thin-cut meat and salad wrapped in unleavened bread—like a gyro). **Known for:** one of few restaurants that's open 24 hours; slightly less expensive than other restaurants in El Gouna; great view from the upstairs terrace. ⑤ *Average main: LE300* ✉ *Tamr Hedr Food Court, 1 Road, Downtown* ☎ *12/2795–6565 WhatsApp.*

Saigon

$$$$ | VIETNAMESE | While finding sushi and Japanese food isn't too terribly difficult around the Red Sea, finding Vietnamese food—and good Vietnamese food, at that—is a rarity. Saigon serves excellent roasted duck and noodle soups, and it has a good selection of vegetarian options. **Known for:** excellent roast duck; cash only; the only place to find Vietnamese food anywhere along the coast. ⑤ *Average main: LE300* ⊠ *next to Coffee Bean and Tea Leaf, Abu Tig Marina* ☎ *12/2116–4418* ▭ *No credit cards.*

🛏 Hotels

Dawar El Omda

$ | **HOTEL** | The name of this hotel within the Qafr means "the mayor's house," and that is its theme, with decorative touches depicting 19th-century Cairene styling. **Pros:** slightly more affordable than other Downtown hotels; in the heart of the walkable Downtown area; hourly shuttle to private beach. **Cons:** proximity to Downtown bars and restaurants means evenings can be noisy; service can be spotty; rooms and design are somewhat dated. ⑤ *Rooms from: $100* ⊠ *Hurghada 2, al-Qafr* ☎ *065/358–0064, 065/358–0063* ⊕ *www.dawarelomda-elgouna.com* ⤳ *69 rooms* ⫶⊙⫶ *Free Breakfast.*

★ Mövenpick Resort and Spa El Gouna

$$$$ | **HOTEL** | **FAMILY** | El Gouna's oldest resort—it opened in 1995—has its longest beachfront, plus such a range of amenities that it might be tempting not to leave the resort and explore the rest of the town. **Pros:** excellent selection of on-site eateries and activities; attractions of El Gouna are just a shuttle-bus ride away; all no-smoking rooms. **Cons:** far from the center of town; facilities are spread out and can require a long walk to access; poolside rooms can be noisy. ⑤ *Rooms from: $160* ⊠ *Hurghada 2, southeast of Downtown, about 10 minutes by foot, El Gouna* ☎ *065/354–4501* ⊕ *www.movenpick.com/en/africa/egypt/el-gouna/resort-el-gouna.html* ⤳ *426 rooms* ⫶⊙⫶ *Free Breakfast.*

Turtles Inn

$$ | **HOTEL** | Usually booked up by the diving and kitesurfing crowd, Turtles Inn offers unpretentious accommodation in the heart of El Gouna marina. **Pros:** right in the marina, with direct access to restaurants, bars, and shops; on-site Orca Dive Center; energetic, youthful vibe. **Cons:** prices vary dramatically between low and high seasons; not on the beach (a shuttle takes you to Zeytouna Beach); lack of on-site amenities won't suit families with young children. ⑤ *Rooms from: $120* ⊠ *Hurghada 2, Abu Tig Marina* ☎ *065/358–0170* ⊕ *turtles-inn.el-gouna-hotel.com/el* ⤳ *28 rooms* ⫶⊙⫶ *No Meals.*

Nightlife

The cream of Cairo society has second homes in El Gouna (and often a yacht in the harbor). They visit on weekends and holidays, adding a touch of glamour to the nightlife venues.

BARS

The Bartender

BARS | Arguably the coolest bar in town, The Bartender (casually referred to simply as "Bartender") is known for craft cocktails—and some of the highest prices in an already pricey area. The retro, vintage vibe combines old-school boomboxes with black-and-white photographs of musical legends like John Lennon. Although drink service starts at 4 pm, the party doesn't get going until at least 8 or 9 pm. ⊠ *El Gouna* ☎ *12/2783–6337 WhatsApp* ⊕ *www.facebook.com/thebartenderelgouna.*

★ Moods Bar

BARS | At the mouth of Abu Tig Marina and flanked by motor cruisers and yachts, this is the place to watch day turn to evening over a sunset cocktail. Everyone gathers here for aperitifs before moving on to dinner and then, perhaps, a club. Since Moods has its own small stretch of sand (admission to its beach is LE250), you could also spend the day hanging out here, and grab some seafood, pizza, or pasta before freshening up for a night on the town. No matter when you go, it's

a great location with beautiful people.
✉ *Abu Tig Marina* ☎ *12/2090–0777
WhatsApp.*

CLUBS
Aurora
COCKTAIL LOUNGES | This contemporary
spot is part cocktail lounge, part restaurant, and part nightclub. Although techno
and electronic seem the most popular,
the music changes every evening, and
weekends see big crowds. The food is
fantastic (expect grilled seafood and
mezze platters), so feel free to arrive
hungry. Unlike many of the clubs in
Gouna or Hurghada, which cater to those
in their late teens and early 20s, Aurora
tends to attract a slightly more mature
crowd, mostly in their late 20s to 40s.
✉ *Hurghada 2, El Gouna* ☎ *12/8809–6086
WhatsApp.*

DuPort Pool Club
DANCE CLUBS | By night, the classical
temple-like interior of the DuPort Lido
is transformed into a cool lounge with
views out across the marina. The venue
has a pool; specializes in commercial,
techno, and electronic music; and tends
to attract a younger crowd (mostly
ages 18 to 25). ✉ *Ocean View Hotel,
Abu Tig Marina* ☎ *065/+201227991304
WhatsApp.*

🏃 Activities

There's a wide variety of land-based and
water-sports activities here, with top-
notch facilities and outfitters to match.
Note that El Gouna is particularly known
as a good place for kitesurfing/boarding.

Hotel beaches here are reserved for the
use of guests only (and if a hotel isn't
directly on the beach, it will provide a
free shuttle to a nearby and equally private sandy shore). The two public-access
beaches are Mangroovy, a dedicated
kitesurfing and water-sports beach with
some great action, and Zeytouna, which
is an island. To get there, hop on one

Scubility

Scubility—a revolutionary program
designed to allow people with
mobility issues to try diving and
to undertake open-water certifica-
tion—is available at dive shops
throughout Hurghada and El
Gouna. The program also offers
buddy training, which helps
companion divers understand
how best to provide assistance
if it's needed. Dive instructors
can upgrade their expertise by
undertaking a Scubility Instructor
upgrade program.

of the boat buses that moor along the
canals.

DIVING
Um Gamar means "mother of the
moon." Roughly 90 minutes offshore by
speedboat, this is truly an amazing dive,
with great walls and caves. The current
here is light, making this one of the
area's easier dives.

Abu Nahas is a wreck-diver's haven, with
four large freighters sunk at reachable
depths. About 25 years ago, a ship
carrying copper (*nahas* in Arabic) hit
the reef and sank, hence the name of
the site. The Tile Wreck carried Spanish
tiles and sank in the same vicinity. The
Lentil Wreck, as you can guess, was
transporting a shipload of lentils. You will
encounter huge Napoleons, groupers,
schools of snappers, and catfish. The
Giannis D. is also known as the "Wood
Wreck" because it was carrying a load of
soft wood. It hit the reef in 1983 and is
another favorite.

Scuba World
SCUBA DIVING | El Gouna's major dive
operator is right on the beach at the
Mövenpick Hotel. The young, international staff is passionate about diving and
water sports. The impressive selection of

An aerial view of the chic El Gouna residential and resort area just north of Hurghada.

offerings includes all levels of PADI courses and technical diving, including the "Scubility" diving course. ✉ *Mövenpick Resort and Spa, Hurghada 2, southeast of Downtown, about 10 minutes by foot, El Gouna* ☎ *10/0530–1068 WhatsApp* ⊕ *www.scubaworlddivers.com.*

GOLF
El Gouna Golf Course
GOLF | Designed by professional golfer Fred Couples and course architect Gene Bates, El Gouna's championship green has a sinuous design amid the lagoons of El Gouna. Practice on the putting green or the Aqua Driving Range. Lessons and training programs are available for players of all levels. ✉ *Hurghada 2, south of Downtown, El Gouna* ☎ *12/746–4712, 12/746–4712* ⊕ *www.elgouna.com* 🎫 *Greens Fees: May 1–Sept. 20, 18 holes $50, 9 holes $30. Oct.1–Apr. 30, 18 holes $85, 9 holes $50.* ⛳ *18 holes, 6856 yards, par-72.*

GUIDED TOURS
Pro Tours
SPECIAL-INTEREST TOURS | FAMILY | This company can arrange anything from quad ATV rides, Bedouin tea experiences, and safaris in the desert to golf outings, glass-bottom boat tours, and overnight Nile cruises. ✉ *Hurghada 2, Abu Tig Marina* ☎ *12/2887–4997 WhatsApp* ⊕ *www.elgouna.com/excursions.*

KITESURFING
The wide stretches of coastal shallows of El Gouna offer ideal conditions for the sport, and several international competitions have been held here. Private lessons start at about $60 per hour ($45 for group lessons) and become increasingly less expensive the more hours you book.

★ Kiteboarding Club El Gouna
WINDSURFING | FAMILY | Excellent customer service and the ability to cater to a variety of kitesurfers/boarders are what set KBC, as it's known locally, apart from other companies along Buzzha Beach. Newbies and experienced kitesurfers

alike will appreciate the well-maintained facilities, which include a pool, and families will love the on-site playground. KBC also offers wing foiling, which requires less wind and is more appropriate for children. ✉ *Hurghada 2, El Gouna* ☎ *12/2661–0878* ⊕ *www.kiteboarding-club.com.*

Red Sea Zone
WINDSURFING | Located on Mangroovy Beach, past the New Marina, Red Sea Zone is a full-service kitesurfing school. ✉ *El Gouna* ☎ *10/1921–9072* ⊕ *redsea-zone.com.*

FOUR-WHEELING
Moto Club
FOUR-WHEELING | As the only motor-cross destination in the entire country, El Gouna's Moto Club is *the*place for dirt bike, ATV, and motor-cross enthusiasts. You can ride around on the track or book a safari trip in the desert. ✉ *Hurghada 2, El Gouna* ⚓ *near the El Gouna dog park* ☎ *32620 Hotline, 12/1227–44143 WhatsApp* ⊕ *motoclubegypt.com.*

SPAS
Angsana Spa
SPAS | The main branch of Angsana Spa has 14 treatment rooms, a sauna, steam room, and whirlpool tub. The Asian-inspired treatments are designed to ease tension or to sooth the muscles you've strained on the golf course or while kiteboarding. There are also smaller Angsana Spa outlets at El Gouna Golf Club and Steigenberger Golf Resort. ✉ *Mövenpick Resort and Spa El Gouna, southeast of downtown, about 10 minutes by foot, El Gouna* ☎ *65/354–4501* ⊕ *www.angsanaspa.com.*

WATER SPORTS
Sliders Cable Park
WATER SPORTS | Not only is this new cable park the only one in Egypt, but it's also one of the biggest in the world. Although the water park does attract observers who just want to eat, drink, and relax by the pool, adventure lovers come for the

wake boarding and water skiing. Obstacles range from rookie to expert level, and some are appropriate for children. ✉ *Hurghada 2, El Gouna* ☎ *10/2602–2226 WhatsApp* ⊕ *www.sliderscablepark.com.*

Bur Safaga (Port Safaga)

40 km (25 miles) south of Hurghada, 200 km (124 miles) northeast of Luxor.

When cruise ships offer land excursions to Luxor, they often do so through Bur Safaga (often referred to as just Safaga), which is the closest beach resort to Luxor's Valley of the Kings. Like other Red Sea communities, Safaga has great offshore dive sites, including the *Salem Express,* a passenger ship that sunk in 1991 en route to Mecca.

Development here has been slower than elsewhere. If the mass tourism in Hurghada is a turnoff, this town is a smaller, much more low-key alternative.

GETTING HERE AND AROUND
Bur Safaga is a 30-minute drive south of Hurghada, and there is regular bus service between the two towns, continuing through Suez to Cairo. There is also a good road heading west to the Nile River and Luxor, though before heading out on this route, check that there are no restrictions on foreigners using public transport before you book tickets. Once in Bur Safaga, taxis are the best way to get around town.

El-Quseir

85 km (53 miles) south of Bur Safaga.

Until the completion of the Suez Canal, El-Quseir was a crucial port, principally because of the *hajj* (pilgrimage to Mecca) and Middle East trade. With the canal in place, the port here was no longer needed as a stop for ships, laden with goods, passing from the Nile Valley across the Red Sea and beyond, and so it fell into decline. The Red Sea coast's resort development boom, however, has reached the town.

Modern construction aims to be environmentally conscious, not only in terms of the sea but also of the land, which is thought to be rich in artifacts, from bits of Roman-era glass to Mamluk archways. The region's waters are filled with coral and other marine life, so if you're interested in scuba diving, speak with your hotel to arrange a dive nearby or in Hurghada.

GETTING HERE AND AROUND

El-Quseir is approximately 70 minutes south of Hurghada by road. Regular bus service through Go Bus connects the town with Hurghada, continuing north through Suez to Cairo. There is also a good road heading west to the Nile River and Luxor, though check that there are no restrictions on foreigners using public transport on this route before you book tickets. Taxis are the best way to get around town.

Sights

Quseir Fort

MILITARY SIGHT | Quseir Fort was one of many strategically located military posts that the Ottoman Turks built along the Red Sea Coast, and it was one of the chief posts that the Napoleonic Expedition in 1799 thoroughly bombed and then rebuilt. It is estimated that the fort was commissioned in the early 16th century by the sharifs of Mecca and Medina. They wanted to protect the hajj route and to maintain control of the passage of goods against the threat posed by the Portuguese fleet. (The area around El-Quseir was a profitable granary for wheat and coffee from Yemen, and the most valuable spices of India and Persia were reloaded here.) Although the fort is a bit run down, it has a small museum containing finds uncovered during

excavation work at the site. ⊠ *El-Quseir* 🖾 *LE50*.

Hotels

Mövenpick Resort El Quseir

$$$$ | HOTEL | FAMILY | This is one of the more tranquil settings on the Red Sea Coast—even the buildings blend with the surrounding environment. **Pros:** environmentally aware; traditional styling; extensive range of on-site activities. **Cons:** can be very hard to get a room during peak season; the beach is good but somewhat small; isolated location. ⑤ *Rooms from: $180* ⊠ *Sirena Beach, al-Quadim Bay, Al Owina, El-Quseir* ⊹ *7 km (4½ miles) north of El-Quseir* 🖀 *65/335–0410* ⊕ *www.moevenpick.com* 🛏 *250 rooms* ⑩ *Free Breakfast.*

Marsa Alam

132 km (82 miles) south of El-Quseir.

The far southern enclave of the Egyptian Red Sea Coast, Marsa Alam, has flourished since the opening of an international airport in 2001. The Port Ghalib project planned a living community of nine Arabian- and Nubian-style villages, along with beach resorts and a 1,000-vessel marina, and the first villa owners took possession of their new homes in 2007.

Today, Marsa Alam's mostly all-inclusive and luxury resorts are primarily geared to European and Russian package clients who rarely leave the grounds, aside from taking a day trip to Wadi el Gemal National Park or a snorkeling or diving excursion. Indeed, the area has some top dive sites, including Elphinstone—where manta rays and morays flit amid a short reef as well as arches, pinnacles, and walls that drop precipitously—and Abu Dabbab featuring turtles and dugongs (cousins of the manatee).

Chapter 8

CRUISING THE NILE AND LAKE NASSER

Updated by
Lauren Keith

A cruise on the Nile is the most comfortable and scenic way to see the country's best ancient sites. What's more, the only way to access most of the temples on the shores of Lake Nasser south of the Aswan High Dam is by boat.

Tourists have been cruising the Nile since Victorian times, when 19th-century British businessman Thomas Cook introduced paddle steamers to the river. Today, hundreds of boats of various sizes, from traditional *dahabiyas* to huge cruisers and even one of Thomas Cook's original boats from the early 1900s, take passengers up (that's south, not north!) and down the Nile.

Choosing a Nile Cruise

Taking a cruise on the Nile is a great way to see Egypt's incredible historic monuments as well as a slice of rural life along the river. Many visitors to Egypt book a full tour of the country that includes a Nile cruise, as well as time in Cairo, Luxor, and Aswan, but it's also possible to book a river cruise separately and see the cities on your own.

Cruise Itineraries

Most river cruises travel between Luxor and Aswan in both directions, but a few, dubbed "long Nile cruises," run from Cairo to Aswan, nearly the length of the country. Prices generally include all meals, tour guides, and admission tickets to the ancient sites. Alcohol and tips are not included.

STANDARD NILE CRUISES: BETWEEN LUXOR AND ASWAN

The stretch of the Nile between Luxor and Aswan is the busiest, both in terms of boat traffic and the number of big-hit ancient monuments.

Depending on the itinerary, cruises can last from four to eight days. Longer cruises either spend the additional time sightseeing in the cities or do a round trip and drop you off in your starting location.

Large Nile cruisers let passengers off at the temples in Edfu and Kom Ombo, while smaller *dahabiyas* often make additional stops at Esna, El-Kab, and Gebel el-Silsila, which don't have docks for bigger ships.

Cruise itineraries don't leave a lot of time for sightseeing in Luxor and Aswan themselves, so consider booking extra nights at a hotel in those cities at the beginning or end of your cruise to give yourself time to see sights not included on the boat's itinerary or to revisit monuments that you want to explore more thoroughly.

LONG NILE CRUISES: BETWEEN CAIRO AND ASWAN

Not many companies operate long Nile cruises between Cairo and Aswan, but the few that do offer itineraries that stop at fascinating off-the-beaten-track sites

Continued on page 351

Kalabsha Temple, Lake Nasser

THE NILE: EGYPT'S LIFELINE

Fourth-century BC Greek historian Herodotus called Egypt the "gift of the Nile," and this evocative description still rings true. For 6,000 years, Egyptian culture has blessed the riverbanks with many of the world's most inspiring monuments.

The Nile is synonymous with Egypt, but the world's longest river actually runs 5,105 km (3,172 miles) through four countries before it reaches Egypt. The ancient Egyptians constructed their most sacred and enduring places of worship on the banks of the Nile, the bringer of life. Temples and tombs were built to last for eternity, and they dot the 1,545-km (960-mile) length of the country's fluvial landscape—from Abu Simbel near Egypt's southern border with Sudan all the way to the Mediterranean.

For millennia, the Nile has been a watery highway. Ancient Egyptian merchants, troops, and even priests parading statues of gods used the river to forge connections and unite the country. Today, sailing along this time-honored avenue is one of the best ways to visit Egypt's most fascinating ancient sites. You will find plenty of ways to get out on the river, from boarding a cruiser that's akin to a floating hotel to setting sail in a smaller traditional vessel that offers a more intimate experience.

CRUISING THE NILE

S.S. *Sphinx*, Uniworld Boutique River Cruises

Cruising the legendary Nile is a once-in-a-lifetime experience. To see the river by boat is to tap into a slower pace, one that allows you to savor scenes of rural life on lush, palm tree–lined riverbanks between stops at docks near some of the world's most significant ancient monuments. The classic Nile cruise between Luxor and Aswan takes in the temples at Edfu and Kom Ombo, while smaller vessels also stop at Esna, El-Kab, and Gebel el-Silsila. Longer Nile cruises between Cairo and Aswan pack in even more history.

Taking a cruise on Lake Nasser—one of the world's largest manmade bodies of water, created by the construction of the Aswan High Dam in the 1960s—gives you exclusive access to Egypt's lesser-visited historic sites, some of which can be reached only by boat. A monumental, UNESCO-led project rescued these temples from a watery grave. They were moved to new lakeside locations and grouped together, making it a bit easier to explore them. Lake Nasser cruise itineraries stop at Kalabsha, Wadi es-Sebua, Amada, Qasr Ibrim, and Abu Simbel.

NILE CRUISE PLANNING

- Most Nile cruises travel between Luxor and Aswan.
- Long Nile cruises go between Cairo and Aswan, taking in the full breadth of ancient sites, but they require a much larger time investment.
- You can travel north to south or south to north on the Nile, but if you're set on a particular cruise boat or company, ensure that they leave on a day that fits your schedule.
- Some companies that operate *dahabiyas*, which have double lateen sails and are pulled by tugboats in low wind, run itineraries south from Esna to Aswan and sometimes don't take passengers north.

FROM ABYDOS TO EDFU

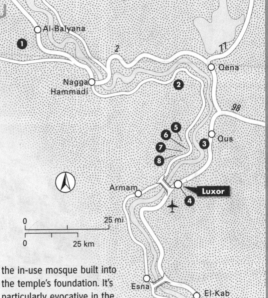

Not all vessels stop at all sites—for example, only longer cruises stop at Abydos and Dendera—and some itineraries don't include tours around Luxor or Aswan. If you're set on seeing a particular site, check that it is on the itinerary before booking your cruise.

❶ ABYDOS
Don't let the plain-Jane facade fool you. The inner halls and corridors of the Temple of Seti I in Abydos preserve a peerless combination of vibrant colors painted on gracefully detailed reliefs.

❷ DENDERA
The late-Ptolemaic Temple of Hathor is a knockout: a hypostyle hall of Hathor-headed columns, ceiling frescoes on a faience-blue background, and Cleopatra VII and Caesarion carved into the exterior walls.

❸ KARNAK TEMPLES
Pack your walking shoes: this multi-temple behemoth covers more than 200 acres. Enter along an avenue of sphinxes, gawk at the lofty hypostyle hall, and save energy to make it to the little-visited shrines, obelisks, and kiosks away from the crowds.

❹ LUXOR TEMPLE
This jewel in downtown Luxor is much smaller than Karnak but impressive in its own way. It's still an active place of worship, as evidenced by

the in-use mosque built into the temple's foundation. It's particularly evocative in the evening when floodlights bathe it in a golden glow.

❺ VALLEY OF THE KINGS
Tutankhamun might be the most famous pharaoh buried here, but several less-visited tombs in this steep-walled canyon offer a more rewarding experience.

❻ MORTUARY TEMPLE OF HATSHEPSUT
From a distance, this temple's cascade of colonnaded terraces fools the eye. It appears to be both built into and projected from the cliff face.

❼ TOMBS OF THE NOBLES
Too lowly for Valley of the Kings but too lofty for the Workmen's Village, at least a thousand of Thebes's ranking nobles were buried in a scattering of West Bank necropoli.

❽ RAMESSEUM
The colossal broken statue of the pharaoh at Ramses II's mortuary temple is said to have been the inspiration for Percy Bysshe Shelley's poem "Ozymandias."

❾ EDFU
Just because it was built by the Ptolemies during Egypt's Greco-Roman Period doesn't mean that the Temple of Horus in Edfu isn't authentic. In fact, its relative youth makes it the most intact temple around.

TOP SIGHTS

Philae

Kom Ombo
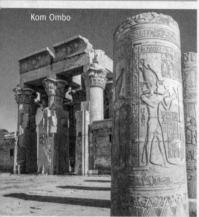

Abu Simbel

Amada

New Kalabsha

Wadi es-Sebua

Qasr Ibrim

FROM KOM OMBO TO ABU SIMBEL

Abu Simbel

Not all cruises include time in or tours of Aswan because many people arrange city visits on their own before or after a cruise. To see the ancient sites around Lake Nasser, you need to book a separate cruise.

❶ KOM OMBO
The unique "double temple" at Kom Ombo is dedicated to the gods Haroeris and Sobek. It's thought to have been a center of healing—don't miss the medical hieroglyphs that depict surgical tools and a birthing chair.

❷ PHILAE
Rescued at the eleventh hour from Lake Nasser's rising waters, the last pagan temple to close still honors the goddess Isis nightly during the Philae Sound & Light Show.

❸ NEW KALABSHA
Walk the quiet grounds of Nubia's largest freestanding temple, constructed by the Roman emperor Augustus. The temple was never finished, but some inner rooms are completely covered in decorated reliefs.

❹ WADI ES-SEBUA
An avenue of sphinxes leads to the Temple of Ramses II at Wadi es-Sebua, lending it its name of Valley of the Lions in Arabic. Early Christians plastered over the pagan reliefs with their own religious scenes, but some has fallen away, revealing scenes of ancient Egyptian gods next to Christian saints.

❺ AMADA
The painting-filled Temple of Amada is the oldest in Nubia. To save it from Lake Nasser and preserve its paintings, a team of French architects moved the entire temple in one piece on a hydraulic rail system in the 1960s.

❻ QASR IBRIM
Originally built on a head-land high above the Nile, this ancient fortress is now trapped on an island just above water level. Thanks to its once-lofty position, Qasr Ibrim is the area's only ancient monument still in its original location.

❼ ABU SIMBEL
These two temples are beloved in Egypt: partly for their mighty colossi and construction straight into the rock face and partly for the highly publicized miracle of being moved to their current location.

NILE MYTHOLOGY

Seti I worships
Osiris (seated),
Isis (middle),
and Horus (left)
at Abydos

Just as the daily life of Egyptians played out along the river, so too did that of their gods. Ancient Egyptians believed that the Nile's annual inundation arose in the vicinity of present-day Aswan from an underground source near the First Cataract. This was home to the male fertility god Hapi—depicted with blue or green skin, heavy breasts, and a full belly, and sporting a false beard.

Hapi was the god of the Nile floods and the resulting abundance the rising waters brought with them.

The Nile also was deeply associated with the god Osiris, whose dismembered body was scattered across the country and into the river by his assassin and brother, Set. A resurrected Osiris nevertheless sired a son, Horus, who avenged his father and whose temple stands at Edfu, 172 km (107 miles) from the temple of his wife, Hathor, at Dendera. The Nile brought them together for an annual reunion, and the statue of Hathor was taken from her temple at Dendera and sailed upriver with great pomp by barge to Horus's temple in Edfu. Such annual reunifications involving coupled gods took place along the Nile elsewhere in Egypt as well.

Hapi, the god of the Nile floods, ties together the symbols of Upper Egypt (the lotus, left) and Lower Egypt (the papyrus, right).

Hathor-headed column

seldom seen by visitors, including Tell el-Amarna (the capital city created by the "heretic" pharaoh Akhenaten) and the rock-cut tombs at Beni Hasan. Long Nile cruises take at least 14 days, and you can travel in either direction.

Long Nile cruises run infrequently—sometimes just once a month or even once a year depending on the company—so if you're set on this trip, book it far in advance.

LAKE NASSER CRUISES: BETWEEN ASWAN AND ABU SIMBEL

On Lake Nasser cruises, boats starting in Aswan take five days and usually depart on Monday, while boats beginning in Abu Simbel take four days and depart on Friday.

Not many tourists take lake cruises, so not many companies offer them. The body of water stretches across a sensitive international border, which brings more headache and hassle for operators and drives up the prices for travelers. But if you're interested in seeing southern Egypt's lesser-visited temples and spending more time at Abu Simbel away from the crowds and with time to catch the nighttime sound-and-light show, this journey is an excellent experience.

The Aswan High Dam prevents boats of any kind from traveling south of the city, so if you want to pair a Nile cruise with a journey around Lake Nasser, you'll have to board a different boat. Lake Nasser cruises do not include any sightseeing time in Aswan.

Types of Ships

NILE CRUISER

Nile cruisers are the largest and most common boats on the river. They look like boxy floating hotels, with three or four levels of windows stacked above the hull. The top sun deck is a communal, open-air space with a pool, bar, and sun loungers. These boats have an average of

Did You Know?

The word "dahabiya" comes from the Arabic word for gold (*dahab*), and these boats are so called because they were originally painted in a golden color. Dahabiyas have two lateen sails, and this style of boat has been used since pharaonic times.

about 60 standard cabins and a handful of suites, and the passenger capacity can be as high as 150.

Lower levels have a dining room, lounge bar, and panoramic viewing area. Some of the larger ships also have a gym, sauna, steam room, and massage services. Prices and amenities vary greatly and depend on the boat size (fewer cabins means more expensive), available amenities, and how recently the ship was renovated. But don't cut costs too far: some cheaper vessels have abysmally small rooms and substandard hygiene practices. Book only through a reputable travel agency.

DAHABIYA

Dahabiyas were once the main form of transport on the Nile, and after losing ground to larger vessels, they are making a comeback as a more intimate alternative to the big-group cruise ship experience.

These elegant wooden houseboats have two triangle-shaped sails, one at the bow and one at the stern, and six to 10 cabins, ensuring small-group outings to the monuments. Cabins are on the lower deck, and the covered upper deck has space for dining and relaxing. *Dahabiyas* are generally designed in a luxurious and traditional style, with lots of polished wood and brass, but they also have modern comforts like in-cabin air-conditioning. There's no pool, but some companies allot time in the itinerary for a swim in the Nile.

Small, traditional *felucca* vessels offer the most intimate Nile sailing experiences.

Their size allows *dahabiyas* to dock just about anywhere, so you'll stop at smaller, off-the-beaten-track sites in addition to the main temples. You'll be sailing some but not 100% of the time: when the wind is low, these motorless vessels are sometimes pulled by tugboats to keep to the schedule. Although *dahabiyas* can be significantly more expensive than a Nile cruiser, the more personalized experience and slightly more flexible itinerary is worth it.

Sails usually start in Esna, a town south of Luxor with a stunning temple, to skip having to go through the Esna Locks, and they sail only in the direction of the wind (south from Esna to Aswan). Some companies offer journeys north from Aswan to Esna, but be aware that you'll be pulled by the tug the entire time instead of sailing.

FELUCCA
Feluccas are small, single-masted sailboats that offer an up-close experience of the Nile with a maximum capacity of eight passengers. Larger *feluccas* have cushioned benches along the sides and a table at the center, while smaller craft have a cushioned sitting area on the back half of the boat.

Most visitors set sail on a *felucca* for a sunset ride in Aswan or Luxor for just a couple of hours, but it's also possible to take one on a multi-day trip.

An overnight excursion is an adventure akin to wild camping: think sleeping bags on the deck under the stars and bathroom breaks on the beach. Two captains are onboard to work the sails and cook the meals. *Felucca* sails offer slow travel at its finest, as these boats are entirely dependent on the wind. You won't find a secret motor or tugboat waiting in the wings. But that means sticking to a schedule is nearly impossible.

Multi-day journeys start in Aswan and head north with the flow of the river, zig-zagging across the river to catch the wind. You might make it downriver to Kom Ombo, about 50 km (30 miles) north of Aswan, in a day or two, but maybe not. Flexibility is essential.

You can bargain with captains along the Corniche in Aswan, but it's better to book a multi-day *felucca* trip with a reputable travel company.

The Cruise Experience

Cruising on the Nile or Lake Nasser is the perfect combination of relaxation and sightseeing. Itineraries are structured around the ancient monuments with plenty of time for reading and swimming in between.

ON-BOARD ENTERTAINMENT
Some Nile cruisers and *dahabiyas* offer evening entertainment, such as cocktails, dancing to local music, belly dancers, and fancy dress parties. Large Nile cruisers have swimming pools and sometimes hot tubs.

MEALS
Meals on Nile cruisers are usually buffet style, with a selection of Egyptian and international dishes. Some higher-end Nile cruisers offer an à la carte restaurant service at dinner.

Because of the much smaller group sizes, meals on *dahabiyas* and *feluccas* are served at communal tables.

WATER
Water onboard is safe for bathing and brushing your teeth, but it's best not to drink it from the tap on the boat or anywhere in Egypt. A few bottles of water are usually offered for free each day on the boat, but it's more environmentally friendly to bring your own water bottle with a filter, such as Lifestraw or Grayl.

WHAT TO PACK
Egypt is predominately Muslim, and tradition remains strong throughout the country but especially in Upper Egypt and rural areas. It's best for both male and female visitors to dress modestly, covering shoulders and to the knees.

Sailing Time

It's about 215 km (134 miles) between Luxor and Aswan, which isn't a huge distance to cover in a five-day cruise. Nile cruisers and *dahabiyas* typically spend about four hours a day or less on the move between stops.

On the boat, it's fine to wear sleeveless shirts, but keep swimwear to the pool area. The weather is sunny all year, but winter evenings can get cool, so bring layers.

Closed-toe shoes are best in the cities. For the ancient sites, you'll want shoes that stay on through sand. Bring a hat, sunglasses, sunscreen, and bug repellant.

WHEN TO GO
Spring and fall are the best times of year for a Nile cruise. Summers are unbearably hot and necessitate very early morning monument visits. Winter is sunny and beautiful, but the water in the pool (unless it's heated) and the Nile will be too cold for swimming.

Cruise Costs

The cost of a cruise on the Nile varies significantly, and it's worth shopping around. Rates go down drastically in summer because of the oppressive heat (and some cruises don't run at all), and prices increase around Christmas, New Year's, and the Easter holidays.

Cruises on Lake Nasser are generally more expensive than cruises on the Nile between Luxor and Aswan because more red tape is involved and only a few companies operate boats on the lake.

TIPPING
Like every activity in Egypt, a tip is expected at the end of the service. Envelopes can be found in your room to

add a gratuity for the boat crew. If you're booked on a wider tour of Egypt that includes a Nile cruise, your tour leader might pass around an envelope and suggest an amount based on the number of passengers in your group.

Nile Cruise Lines

Cruisers

Farah Nile Cruise

Its name means "happiness" in Arabic, and the *Farah* (60 cabins, two suites) is sure to delight those on board. The decor throughout the boat is mostly neutral—white, beige, and dark woods—with pops of accent purple. Thoughtful amenities include on-board cooking classes, a pillow menu, a library dedicated to Brazilian writer Paulo Coelho (who wrote *The Alchemist*), and a top-deck telescope for stargazing. ⊕ *farahnilecruise.com.*

Jaz Cruises

Jaz Cruises offers a number of more budget-friendly cruises on the Nile on older vessels that are in decent condition. It runs one of the largest boats on the river, MS *Iberotel Crown Empress* (120 cabins, eight suites), which has a steam room, sauna, and massage services. The company operates boats under the Jaz, Iberotel, and Steigenberger brands, as well as "brandless" boats that have about half the number of cabins. Many of these vessels save space in the schedule for the fascinating Temple of Khnum in Esna, an uncommon itinerary stop. ⊕ *www.jazcruises.com.*

Mayfair Cruises

This family-run operation has three boats done up in a chic modern style: think glitzy chandeliers and bold bedroom fabrics. MS *Mayfair* (72 cabins, two suites), MS *Esplanade* (71 cabins, two suites), and MS *Mayflower* (38 cabins, 18 suites) all have pools, hot tubs, and spas, as well

Top Tip

Most three- and four-day Nile cruises sail during the night, which means you miss a lot of the wonderful river landscape. If you want to enjoy the scenery along the water as well as the ancient temples and tombs, book a longer tour.

as libraries and glam lounge bars. ⊠ *Cairo* ⊕ *www.mayfaircruises.com.*

Mövenpick

Swiss-based Mövenpick runs five Nile cruisers that depart from both Aswan and Luxor. To enjoy Egypt's history, both on the water and on land, book onto the SS *Misr* (16 cabins, eight suites). Originally built in 1918 by the British Royal Navy, the vessel was later used by King Farouk, and it still maintains its regal style and atmosphere. Mövenpick's other vessels (MS *Hamees*, MS *Sun Ray*, MS *Royal Lily*, MS *Royal Lotus*) have more cabins and are furnished in a contemporary style similar to the company's hotels. ⊕ *www. movenpick.com/en/africa/egypt/nilecruisers.html.*

Oberoi

This India-based luxury hotel empire operates two boats on the Nile between Luxor and Aswan. MS *Philae* (22 cabins) has rooms decorated in a desert color palette, and some of the luxury cabins have a whirlpool on a private terrace. MS *Zahra* (27 cabins) has high-end amenities, including rain showers and a full-service spa. ⊕ *www.oberoihotels.com.*

Original Travel

This British tour operator has exclusive use of a piece of floating history: the early 1900s steamer SS *Sudan* (18 cabins, six suites), the same boat that Agatha Christie sailed on that inspired her to write the still-captivating murder mystery, *Death on the Nile*. SS *Sudan* is the last surviving vessel of its kind but has been renovated and remodeled. It still has original features including teak decking, and the cabins hark back to the golden age of Nile travel, with brass bed frames and polished wood wall paneling. ⊕ www.originaltravel.co.uk/destination/egypt-holidays.

Sanctuary Retreats

This outfit got its start in luxury safari lodges in East Africa, and its attention to detail and experience is evident in its Nile river vessels. Sanctuary Retreats has three Nile cruisers, which it calls "river yachts" because of their smaller size and intimate feel. *Sanctuary Sun Boat III* (14 cabins, four suites) has space for just 36 passengers, and the cabana-style daybeds that surround the curvy, clay-edged pool are inviting after a long day of sightseeing. The classy teak-floor cabins on *Sanctuary Sun Boat IV* (36 cabins, four suites) all have floor-to-ceiling windows and are decorated in a contemporary style with some Middle Eastern flourishes. *Sanctuary Nile Adventurer* (28 cabins, four suites) was renovated in 2019 and is done up in black-and-white Egyptian designs with a splash of cerulean river blue. Note that these boats are sometimes leased out to high-end tour operators such as Abercrombie & Kent. ⊕ www.sanctuaryretreats.com/egypt-holidays.

Sonesta

An American hotel chain started in 1937, Sonesta operates three high-end Nile cruisers. The MS *Star Goddess* (33 suites) is an all-suite ship whose rooms all have wood paneling and accents and private balconies. The MS *St. George I* (47 cabins, 10 suites) has a classic French, light-blue-and-cream color scheme and old-timey paintings in the rooms. The third vessel, the MS *Moon Goddess,* is under renovation. ⊕ www.sonesta.com/sonesta-cruise-collection-nile-river.

The Sales Pitch

Tourism revenue makes up a huge chunk of Egypt's GDP, up to 15%. Egyptian souvenir touts have long been known for the hard sell, but in times when tourist numbers are low, the pressure can be even higher. When you're on a Nile cruise, sellers will call to the boat from the shore or even motor over and tie up their small two-seater boat to the huge Nile cruiser while it's in motion to make a sale. The Nile cruiser itself will likely also have at least one souvenir shop on board.

Uniworld

California-based Uniworld has the Nile's most beautifully outfitted river cruisers. SS *Sphinx* (16 cabins, 26 suites) was launched in 2021, with custom-made and regionally sourced furnishings from local artisans. The delightfully over-the-top suites burst with color, and the dining and lounge areas showcase masterfully carved wooden latticework and ornate metal light fixtures. MS *River Tosca* (41 suites) goes for a more reserved style, with dark wood panelling in common areas balanced by crisp whites in the rooms. Both boats cruise north on the Nile to Dendera, setting them apart from the pack. These boats can only be booked as part of Uniworld tours that include time in Cairo. ⊕ www.uniworld.com/ap/river-cruise/egypt.

Viking

This Swiss-headquartered river cruise line has doubled its fleet of Nile boats, with Viking *Osiris* setting sail in 2022 and Viking *Aton* launching in 2023. Both have 33 cabins, eight suites and are equipped with the latest fittings, such as USB plugs. Each room has a private veranda and a sun lounger. The lobby area is all muted colors and clean lines, decorated in Scandinavian style with light wood and

The Royal Suite epitomizes the luxury aboard Uniworld's Nile cruiser, the SS *Sphinx*.

glass. The airy atmosphere continues to the Aquavit Terrace and Lounge, which has floor-to-ceiling glass doors for meals al fresco. The boats' itineraries deviate from most others and includes stops in Dendera and Esna. ⊕ *www.vikingriver-cruises.co.uk/cruise-destinations/egypt.*

Long Nile Cruises

Mövenpick

Mövenpick's MS *Darakum* cruises the Nile in epic fashion, with out-of-the-ordinary itineraries between Cairo and Aswan and Cairo and Luxor in both directions. Lush jungle green and black wood fill the standard and superior cabins, while crimson accents decorate the suites. Multifoil Moroccan-style arches surround the main restaurant, and the sun deck has plush daybeds and an enticing swimming pool. ⊕ *www.movenpick.com/en/africa/egypt/nilecruisers/cruise-darakum.html.*

Dahabiyas

Ashranda

In the Nubian language, "ashranda" means "the most beautiful girl in the world," and the company's four *dahabiyas* are certainly stunners. *Eyaru* is the boldest, with geometric Nubian designs, blonde wood, and earthy greens and blues that evoke the natural world outside the boat's windows. The sun deck has an air-conditioned gazebo as well as an open-air-but-sheltered lounge. ⊕ *www.ashranda.com/dahabyat.*

Mövenpick

If you don't have the numbers for a private *dahabiya* charter but still want the experience, book onto the Mövenpick's SB *Feddya*, a boutique sailboat with only four suites. Cabins have eye-catching decor, with rich reds and striking purples, and wood-beam ceilings overlook four-post beds in the two Senior Suites. The Panorama Suites offer expansive river views from large private balconies.

Thomas Cook and Mass Tourism

Born in 1808 in Derbyshire, England, Thomas Cook was a cabinetmaker, a Baptist preacher, and a member of the Temperance Society—perhaps an unlikely candidate for starting one of the world's best known travel companies. He began by organizing day trips for his fellow members to nearby towns. In 1841, he arranged for a train trip for a fixed fee that included transport and food, now considered the world's first package holiday tour.

Cook quickly expanded this travel sideline. He organized trips for thousands of people to attend the Great Exhibition in London in 1851. Four years later, he arranged his first tour to Europe, taking customers to the Universal Exposition in Paris, and soon after expanded to the United States, Egypt, and the Holy Land.

Cook went into partnership with his son, John Mason Cook, who had more business acumen than his father. John invested in the first Nile *dahabiyas* and steam ships that were said to be the most luxurious on the river since Cleopatra's royal barge. When the British took control of Egypt in the 1880s, Thomas Cook Inc. became involved in military transport and postal services, and John became one of the most powerful men in Egypt. The company even constructed grand hotels along its Nile tour route, such as Aswan's Old Cataract hotel, which is still open to guests.

Thomas Cook died in 1892 and John in 1899. The business stayed in the family until 1928, when Cook's grandsons sold it to a French company that operated the Orient Express trains. After nearly 180 years in business, Thomas Cook declared bankruptcy in 2019, but it's still remembered as one of the biggest tourism companies in Egypt.

⊕ *www.movenpick.com/en/africa/egypt/nilecruisers/cruise-feddya.html.*

Nile Dahabeya

Nile Dahabeya has seven traditional *dahabiya* boats in its fleet, three of which were newly constructed or renovated in 2021. Polished, honey-colored wood features throughout, from the exteriors to the cabin floors. The newer boats have more local touches, like metal light fixtures and wooden latticework, and you can enjoy the sun or the shade from the upper decks. Note that Overseas Adventure Travel, an American company that markets to travelers over 50, privately charters these boats for its Egypt tours. ⊕ *nile-dahabeya.com.*

Nile Dahabiya Boats

Constructed by builders in Esna, where most *dahabiya* tours begin, this company's four small craft have antique and Islamic-style furnishings, such as inlaid wooden tables and chairs, four-post brass beds, and metalwork lamps. All suites have private terraces, and for those staying in other cabins, the spacious upper decks have hammocks, traditional cushioned seating on the floor, and comfortable sofas and chairs. ⊕ *www.nile-dahabiya.com.*

Nour El Nil

Nour El Nil takes the credit for reintroducing *dahabiya* travel to the Nile, and it remains one of the best experiences on the river. Its flotilla of six vessels happily glide down the river with candy-cane-striped sails, and the small number of cabins guarantees fast friendships and a cozy atmosphere. The company launched its largest and most modern *dahabiya* in 2019—the the *Adelaide* (10 cabins, two suites)—but rooms on all the boats have gleaming white interiors, plus comfortable traditional seating lit by crystal chandeliers on the covered upper deck. While Nour El Nil's boats stick to a sailing schedule, they also leave time for more personal and rewarding encounters, such as meeting local people in rural villages, desert walks, and island swimming stops. ⊕ www.nourelnil.com.

Original Travel

Sail back in time on Original Travel's vessel, La Flaneuse du Nil (six cabins, one suite). The dahabiya has throwback furniture, including roll-top desks, old-timey swing-arm lamps, and elegant armchairs. Solar panels have been installed on the sun deck, which nearly eliminates the need for a generator, making this mode of transport quite eco-friendly. ⊕ www.originaltravel.co.uk/place/the-flaneuse-du-nil-holidays.

Sanctuary Retreats

If you're with a group of family or friends and want to sail down the Nile, you can privately charter Sanctuary Zein Nile Chateau, a custom-built dahabiya with just four cabins and two suites. The rooms are individually decorated and radiate personality, from the Baladi Cabin, with collaged portraits of Egyptian musicians, to the spacious Farouk Suite, a perfect fit for its indulgent namesake. Because it's a private excursion, you can pick from a list of sightseeing options, tailoring the itinerary to suit your interests. ⊕ www.sanctuaryretreats.com/egypt-cruises-zein-nile-chateau.

Feluccas

Aswan Individual

This local tour operator offers overnight and multi-day felucca trips from Aswan with super-friendly, knowledgeable Nubian captains. Travel is blissfully slow and entirely wind-dependent. For example, it will take a full day or more to reach Kom Ombo, 40 km (25 miles) to the north. ⊕ aswan-individual.com.

Lake Nasser Cruise Lines

Mövenpick

MS Prince Abbas (43 cabins, 22 suites) is every bit as tasteful as Mövenpick's other vessels that travel on the Nile north of Aswan's dams. All cabins have panoramic windows to watch one of the world's largest man-made bodies of water go by. The biggest treat, however, is seeing Abu Simbel's colossal statues of Ramses II from the pool on the sun deck. ⊕ www.movenpick.com/en/africa/egypt/nilecruisers/cruise-prince-abbas.html.

Saï Safari Boat

With just six cabins that can accommodate a maximum total of 12 passengers, the Saï is the most intimate and interesting way to explore Lake Nasser. The smaller size of this wooden boat, which is named after a Nile island upriver in northern Sudan, allows you to experience not just the lake region's culture but also its nature, with lakeshore walks and birdwatching sessions. The vessel is also eco-friendly, with a solar-panel-fitted upper deck. ⊕ saisafariboat.com.

Steigenberger

MS Omar El Khayam (68 cabins, 12 suites) is a huge floating hotel spread over four decks. It has nearly all the amenities you'd find in a land-based resort, such as a spacious pool area, a billiard room, two lounge bars, a gym, and a spa. Damask fabrics feature prominently in the ship's decor. ⊕ www.steigenberger.com/en/nile-cruises/steigenberger-omar-el-khayam.

360

Photo Credits

Front Cover: Art Kowalsky / Alamy Stock Photo [Description: Statue Of Ramesses II At Luxor Temple, Egypt]. **Back cover, from left to right:** Nete/Dreamstime. Antonaleksenko82/ Dreamstime. Mountains Hunter/Shutterstock. **Spine:** Ginasanders/Dreamstime. **Interior, from left to right:** Nosyrevy/Dreamstime (1). Mustang79/Dreamstime (2-3). Unterwegs/Shutterstock (5). **Chapter 1: Experience Egypt:** Alex Anton/Shutterstock (6-7). Alexander Lipko/iStockphoto (8-9). Fabio Concetta/Dreamstime (9). Paula french/Shutterstock (9). Matyas Rehak/ Shutterstock (10). Vlad61/Shutterstock (10). Leonid Andronov/Shutterstock (10). Elena Pavlovich/Shutterstock (10). Anton_Ivanov/ Shutterstock (11). Agsaz/Shutterstock (11). Danbreckwoldt/Dreamstime (12). Jon Chica/Shutterstock (12). Ebonyeg/Shutterstock (12). Antonaleksenko82/Dreamstime (12). Unai Huizi Photography/Shutterstock (13). Anton_Ivanov/ Shutterstock (13). Merydolla/Dreamstime (14). Octasy/Shutterstock (14). Martink/Dreamstime (15). Gkrphoto/Shutterstock (18). Santusya/Dreamstime (18). Viktoriyakz765/Dreamstime (18). Veliavik/Shutterstock (19). Chudo2307/Shutterstock (19). Zevana/Shutterstock (20). Parilov/ Shutterstock (21). Mohamedfathy1/Shutterstock (22). Calinstan/Dreamstime (22). Takepicsforfun/ Dreamstime (22). Merlin74/Shutterstock (22). Waj/Shutterstock (23). Airphoto/ Dreamstime (28). NatUlrich/Shutterstock (29). Asier Villafranca/iStockphoto (30). Public Domain wikimediacommons Book of the Dead (34). Angel Cristi/ Shutterstock (35). Rosetta Stone International Congress of Orientalists ILN 1874 (36). Rosetta Stone BW wikipedia.org (36). **Chapter 3: Cairo With Abu Sir, Memphis, Saqqara, Dashur, and The Fayyum:** Merydolla/ Dreamstime (63). Lshiy985/Shutterstock (66). Food Shop/Shutterstock (67). Nour Tanta/ Shutterstock (67). Efesenko/Dreamstime (72). Efesenko/Dreamstime (77). Akimov Konstantin/ Shutterstock (78). Keladawy/Dreamstime (82). Joelsuganth/Wikimedia Commons (86). Joel Carillet/iStockphoto (87). Pierdelune/Shutterstock (87). BertrandmGardel/Hemis.fr/Egyptian Tourist Authority (88). Efesenko/Dreamstime (88). Joel Carillet/iStockphoto (89). Andrew Griffith/Egypt Market (89). Amy Nichole Harris/Shutterstock (90). Nat Ulrich/Shutterstock (90). Paul Paladin/Shutterstock (90). Lui Tat Mun/Shutterstock (90). Evgeny Drobzhev/Dreamstime (90). Steven Allan/Khan El-Khalili bazaar Cairo Egypt (91). Javarman/Shutterstock (91). Chubykin Arkady/ Shutterstock (91). Jo De Vulder/Dreamstime (91). Paolo Gallo/Shutterstock (91). Bracketing Life/El Souk Hurghada (92). Pat Glover/Colorful spice bags (93). Kochneva Tetyana/Shutterstock (93). Amr Hassanein/Shutterstock (96). Sun_Shine/Shutterstock (98). AlexAnton/Shutterstock (104-105). Victor Jiang/Shutterstock (109). Doityourself13/Dreamstime (110). Anton_Ivanov/Shutterstock (114). Fairmont Nile City (117). Khaled ElAdawy/Shutterstock (122-123). Mohamedfathy1/Shutterstock (125). Efesenko/Dreamstime (127). Efesenko/ Dreamstime (130). Witr/Dreamstime (136-137). Holger Mette/iStockphoto (138). ePhotocorp/ Dreamstime (139). Tamaguramo/Shutterstock (140). Cobalt88/ Dreamstime (141). Sculpies/ Shutterstock (142-143). WitthayaP/Shutterstock (142). Ian Stewart/Shutterstock (144). Tarek Ezzat/Shutterstock (150). LindaHarms/Dreamstime (161). Daniel Fleck/iStockphoto (164). **Chapter 4: Alexandria:** Evannovostro/Shutterstock (171). Shaimailbox/Dreamstime (174). Dina Saeed/Shutterstock (175). Akin Ozcan/Shutterstock (175). Hazem Omar/Shutterstock (178). Cristian Zamfir/Shutterstock (184). LindaHarms/Dreamstime (187). Justina Atlasito/Shutterstock (188). Littlewormy/Dreamstime (190). Leshiy985/Dreamstime (195). Krechet/Shutterstock (198-199). Dahlia Mustafa/Shutterstock (200). **Chapter 5: Luxor and the Nile Valley:** Mustang79/Dreamstime (203). Matrioshka/Dreamstime (216). Whatafoto/Shutterstock (218). Moonfish8/Shutterstock (220-221). Zaruba Ondrej/Shutterstock (224). Leonid Andronov/ Shutterstock (226-227). Electropower/Dreamstime (232). Anton Belo/Shutterstock (237). Florin Cnejevici/Shutterstock (238). Zbigniew Guzowski/Shutterstock (239). Jakub Kyncl/Shutterstock (239). Nick Brundle Photography/Shutterstock (239). Merlin74/Shutterstock (239). Andradedave/ Dreamstime (239). George Stoyanov/Shutterstock (240). Heaslet/Dreamstime (240). Agsaz/Shutterstock (241). agefotostock / Alamy Stock Photo (242). Ali Fadhil/ Shutterstock (242). Abrilla/Dreamstime (243). Stigalenas/Dreamstime (244). Akimov konstanrin/Shutterstock (251). Alexandree/Shutterstock (255). **Chapter 6: Aswan and Lake Nasser:** Sompol/Shutterstock (257). JackKPhoto/Shutterstock (262-263). Sergey-73/ Shutterstock (268). CL-Medien/Shutterstock (273). Paul prescott/Shutterstock (276). Wesleyc1701/ Dreamstime (277). Alain Guilleux / Alamy Stock Photo (278). Charles J Sharp/ Wikimedia Commons (278). Captmondo/Wikimedia Commons (278). Sompol/Shutterstock (279). AlexanderLipko/Shutterstock (279). Allan Gluck_wikimediacommons (280). B.Rieger/ Hemis.fr/Egyptian Tourism Authority (280). Anei/Dreamstime (281). Bertrand Rieger/Egyptian Tourism Authority (281). Michel Benoist/Wikimedia Commons (282). Tentoila/Wikimedia Commons (282). Ahmed Aboul-Seoud/Shutterstock (282). Jeff Schultes/Shutterstock (283). Gardel Bertrand/ EGYPTIAN TOURIST AUTHORITY (283). Amr Hassanein/Shutterstock (283). Suez Canal/Wikimedia Commons (284). Alvin Empalmado/Mosque of Muhammad Ali (284). White House Staff Photographers/Wikimedia Commons (285). Gardel Bertrand/EGYPTIAN TOURIST AUTHORITY (285). Alexandree/Shutterstock (290-291). Witr/Dreamstime (292). Edwardje/Dreamstime (296-297). **Chapter 7: Sharm el-Sheikh and the Red Sea Coast:** Ovbelov/Dreamstime (301). VitalyEdush/iStockphoto (304). Boshy911/Shutterstock (305). Anna segeren/Shutterstock (305). Dmitriy Fesenko/iStockphoto (306). Vale_T/iStockphoto (307). Brytta/iStockphoto (307). SimonDannhauer/Dreamstime (311). Adam Ke/ Shutterstock (318). Cinzia Osele/Shutterstock (320-321). Bayazed/Shutterstock (323). Creativity lover/Shutterstock (330-331). Albert6712/ Shutterstock (332). Orhan Cam/Shutterstock (333). Matyas Rehak/ Shutterstock (335). Daniel Samray/Shutterstock (336). Ahmed El Araby/ Shutterstock (340). **Chapter 8: Cruising the Nile and Lake Nasser:** Paulvinten/Dreamstime (343). Unterwegs/ Shutterstock (345). Uniworld Boutique River Cruises (346). AlexAnton/Shutterstock (348). Andrzej Trutkowski/Shutterstock (348). Anton_Ivanov/Shutterstock (348). Mohamed Ramez/Shutterstock (348). Storm Is Me/Shutterstock (348). Unterwegs/Shutterstock (348). Mohamed Ramez/Shutterstock (348). CSLD/Shutterstock (349). LuVo/iStockphoto (350). Wynnter/iStockphoto (350). Jeff Dahl/Wikimedia Commons (350). commons.wikimedia.org/ wiki/S_F-E-CAMERON_EGYPT(350). Mauriehill/Dreamstime (352). Uniworld Boutique River Cruises (356). **About Our Writers:** All photos are courtesy of the writers.

*Every effort has been made to trace the copyright holders, and we apologize in advance for any accidental errors. We would be happy to apply the corrections in the following edition of this publication.

Notes

Fodor's ESSENTIAL EGYPT

Publisher: Stephen Horowitz, *General Manager*

Editorial: Douglas Stallings, *Editorial Director;* Jill Fergus, Amanda Sadlowski, *Senior Editors;* Kayla Becker, Brian Eschrich, Alexis Kelly, *Editors;* Angelique Kennedy-Chavannes, *Assistant Editor*

Design: Tina Malaney, *Director of Design and Production;* Jessica Gonzalez, *Senior Designer;* Erin Caceres, *Graphic Design Associate*

Production: Jennifer DePrima, *Editorial Production Manager;* Elyse Rozelle, *Senior Production Editor;* Monica White, *Production Editor*

Maps: Rebecca Baer, *Senior Map Editor;* Mark Stroud (Moon Street Cartography), David Lindroth, Roberta Stockwell, *Cartographers*

Photography: Viviane Teles, *Senior Photo Editor;* Namrata Aggarwal, Neha Gupta, Payal Gupta, Ashok Kumar, *Photo Editors;* Eddie Aldrete, *Photo Production Intern;* Kadeem McPherson, *Photo Production Associate Intern*

Business and Operations: Chuck Hoover, *Chief Marketing Officer;* Robert Ames, *Group General Manager;* Devin Duckworth, *Director of Print Publishing*

Public Relations and Marketing: Joe Ewaskiw, *Senior Director of Communications and Public Relations*

Fodors.com: Jeremy Tarr, *Editorial Director;* Rachael Levitt, *Managing Editor*

Technology: Jon Atkinson, *Director of Technology;* Rudresh Teotia, *Lead Developer*

Writers: Cassandra Brooklyn, Monica Gerges, Lauren Keith, Marnie Sehayek

Editors: Laura M. Kidder (lead editor), Brian Eschrich, Douglas Stallings, Caroline Trefler

Production Editor: Elyse Rozelle

1st Edition

ISBN 978-1-64097-351-0

ISSN 2833-0900

All details in this book are based on information supplied to us at press time. Always confirm information when it matters, especially if you're making a detour to visit a specific place. Fodor's expressly disclaims any liability, loss, or risk, personal or otherwise, that is incurred as a consequence of the use of any of the contents of this book.

SPECIAL SALES
This book is available at special discounts for bulk purchases for sales promotions or premiums. For more information, e-mail SpecialMarkets@fodors.com.

PRINTED IN CANADA

10 9 8 7 6 5 4 3 2 1

About Our Writers

Cassandra Brooklyn is a freelance writer and guidebook author whose work has appeared in the *New York Times,* the *Wall Street Journal, National Geographic,* Lonely Planet, and The Daily Beast, among other outlets. She specializes in sustainable, accessible, and ethical travel, as well as all things outdoors. She's the owner of the small travel company, EscapingNY, and leads tours in the Middle East and Latin America. For this edition, Cassandra updated the Alexandria and the Sharm el-Sheikh and the Red Sea Coast chapters. Find her at ⊕ *www.Escaping-NY.com* or on Instagram at @escapingny.

Adventure, people, and a healthy disregard for conventionality led **Monica Gerges,** our Cairo updater, to uproot her life in Canada and hop on a one-way flight to Egypt's capital, and she hasn't yet looked back. She works with words for a living, but what really makes Monica tick is creating content to capture the chaos of Cairo through the lens of someone who's not foreign, yet not quite a local. Go along for the ride @monicagerges or ⊕ *www.monicagerges.com.*

Lauren Keith is a freelance travel writer and guidebook author whose work has been published in Lonely Planet, *Smithsonian Magazine,* Atlas Obscura, Al Jazeera, and elsewhere. She's written and edited more than 20 books about the Middle East and London, where she lived for a decade. She previously worked as Lonely Planet's editor for the Middle East and North Africa and continues to travel the region widely. For this edition, Lauren updated the Know Before You Go and Great Itineraries sections of Travel Smart, as well as the Experience, Luxor and the Nile Valley, Aswan and Lake Nasser, and Cruising the Nile and Lake Nasser chapters. Find her on Instagram at @noplacelike_it.

Marnie Sehayek has been exploring Egypt since the 1990s, when her father first took her to the stunning Sinai Peninsula. She has worked in travel editorial with The Culture Trip and Vice Media and has extensively written about and photographed the subculture in her native Los Angeles for *LA Weekly* and other publications. With a penchant for off-the-beaten-path adventure, Semitic languages, and Oum Kalthoum, she splits her time between the U.S. and the Middle East. For this edition, Marnie provided up-to-date local intel and navigation tips for the Essentials, Getting Here and Around, and Contacts sections of the Travel Smart chapter.